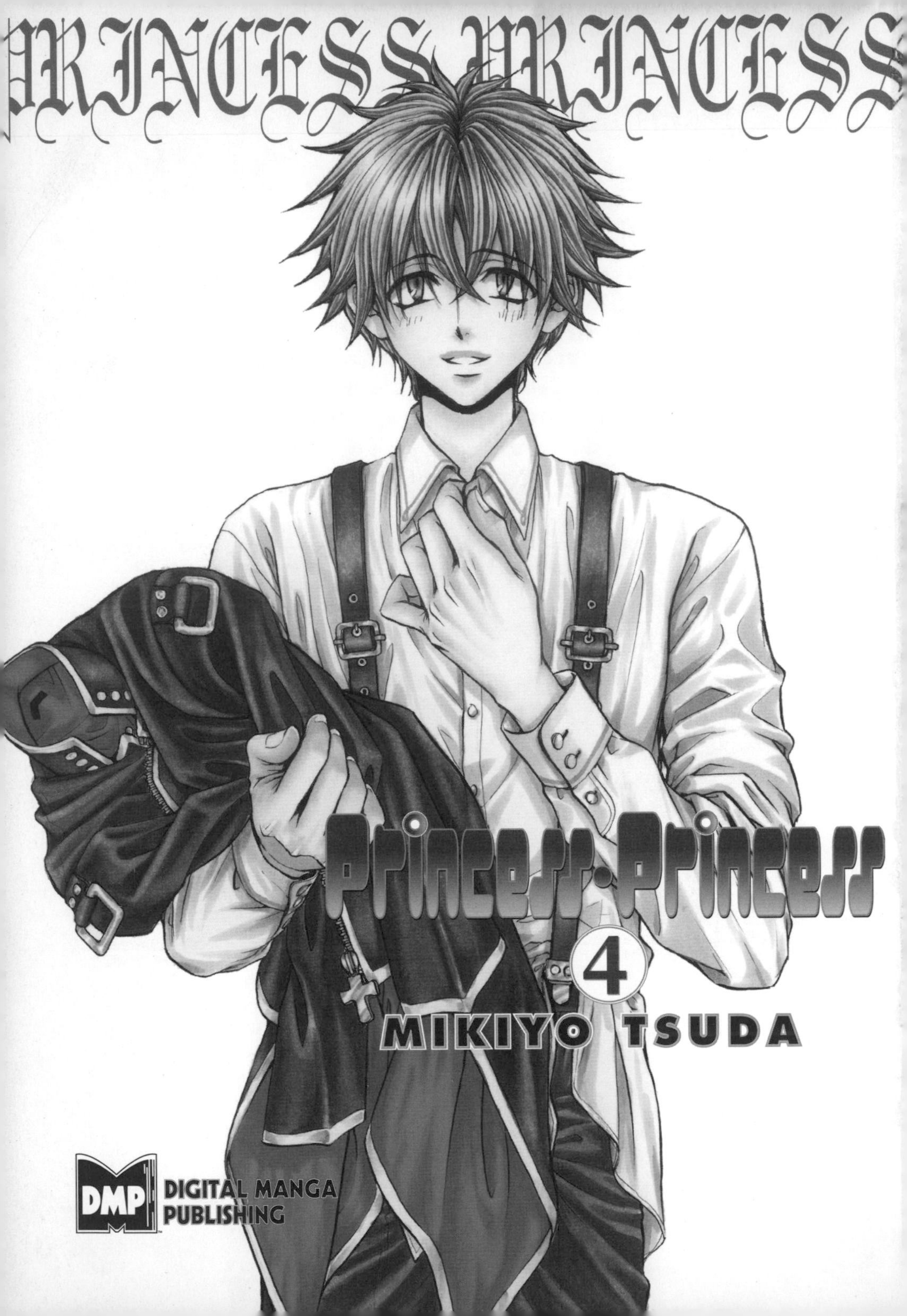
PRINCESS PRINCESS
Princess·Princess
4
MIKIYO TSUDA
DMP
DIGITAL MANGA PUBLISHING

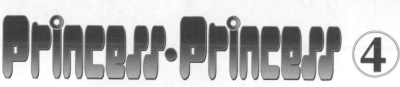

Princess·Princess ④

CONTENTS

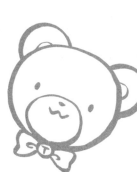

The Story So Far...

Tohru Kouno transferred to an all boys school and received a very warm welcome. He soon discovered that his new school has a "Princess System" where a select few students dress up as girls to give the rest of the guys an outlet for their frustrations. Tohru is selected, and tempted by many perks of the job, agrees to become a princess alongside Shihoudani and Mikoto...

Translation	*Earl Gertwagen*
Lettering	*Geoff Porter*
Graphic Design	*Daryl Kuxhouse*
Editing	*Daryl Kuxhouse*
Editor in Chief	*Fred Lui*
Publisher	*Hikaru Sasahara*

English Edition Published by
DIGITAL MANGA PUBLISHING
A division of DIGITAL MANGA, Inc.
1487 W 178th Street, Suite 300
Gardena, CA 90248

www.dmpbooks.com

First Edition: August 2007
ISBN-10: 1-56970-851-7
ISBN-13: 978-1-56970-851-4

1 3 5 7 9 10 8 6 4 2

Printed in China

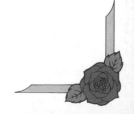

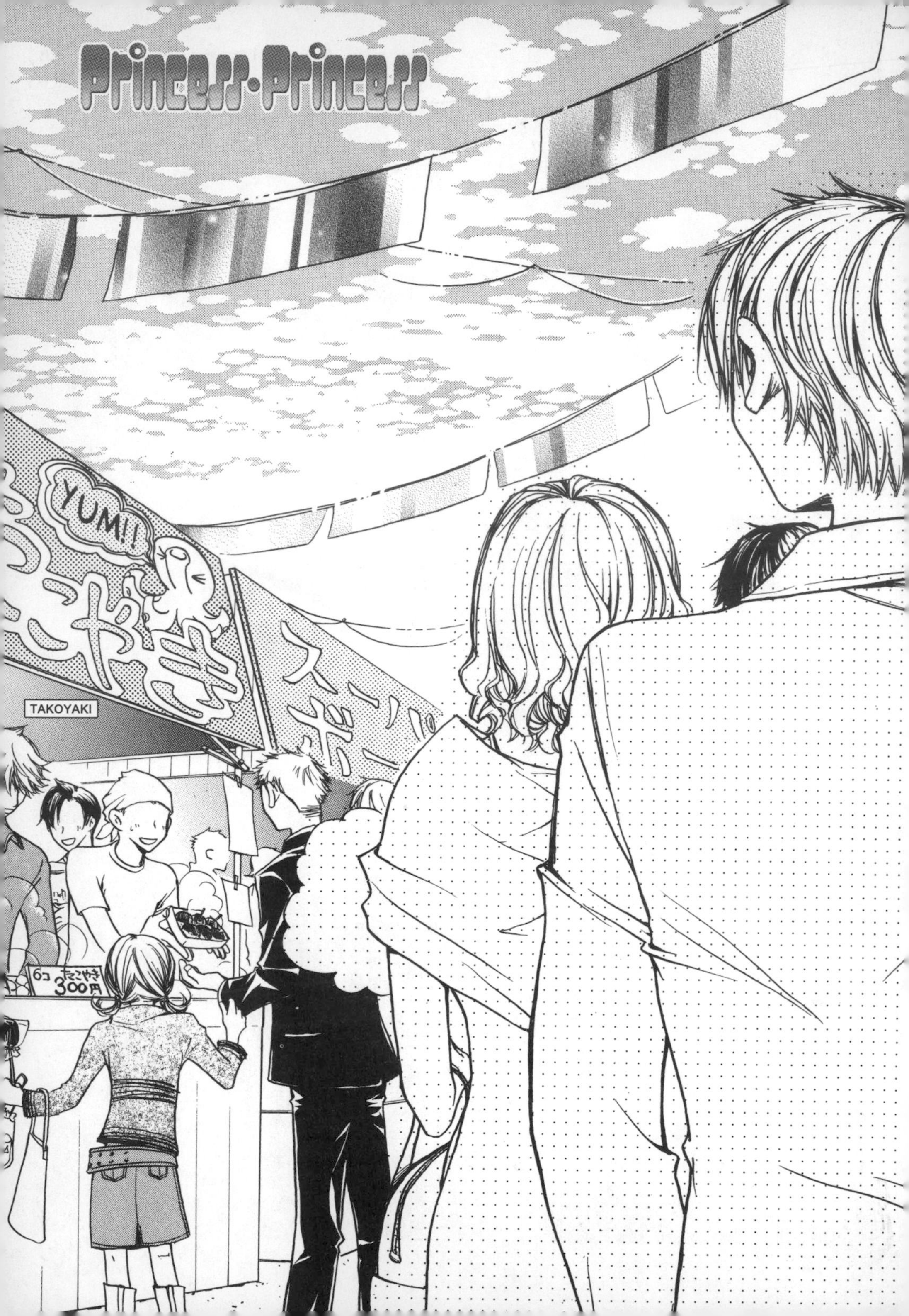
Princess·Princess
YUM!!
TAKOYAKI
6コ たこやき
300円

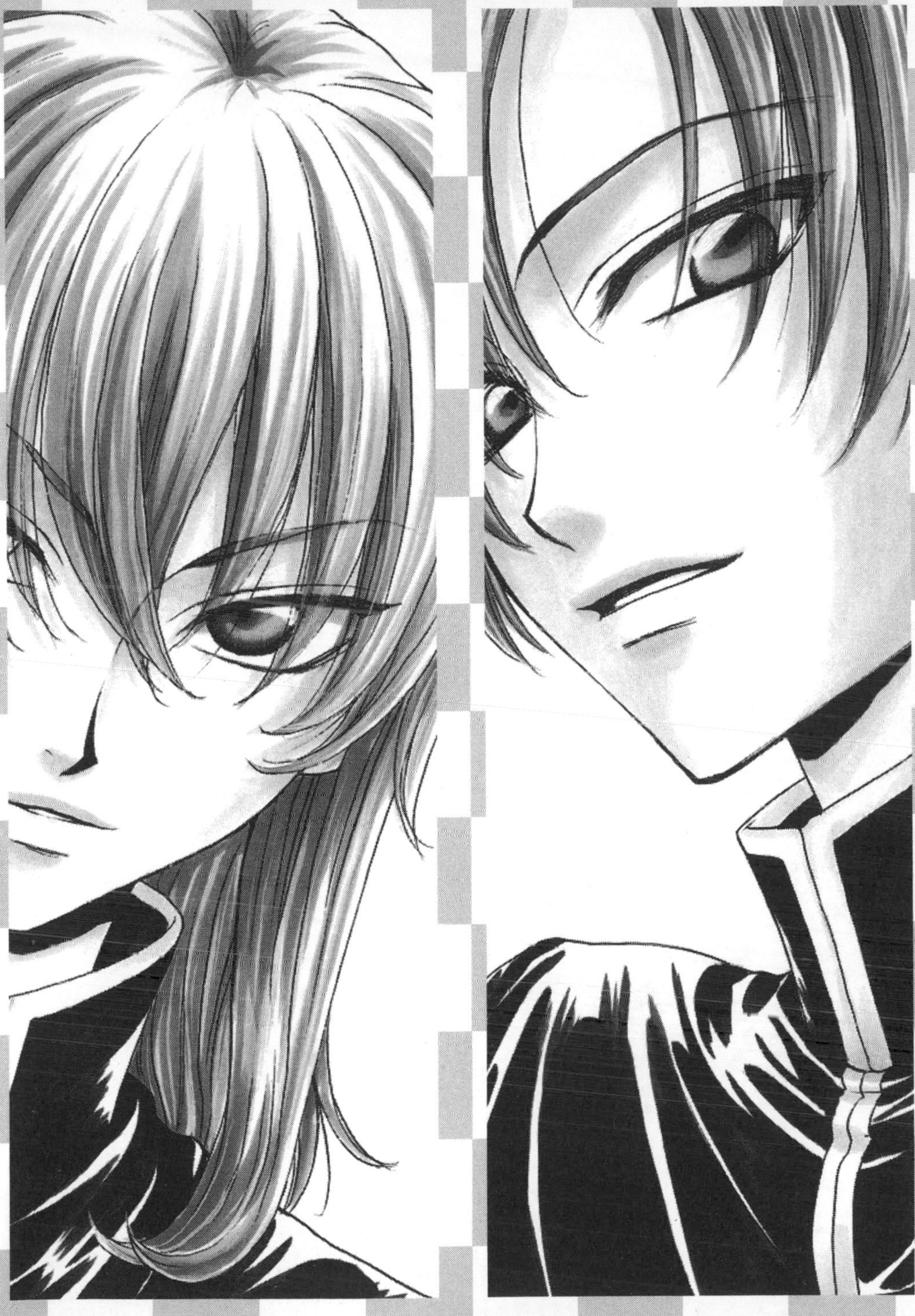

プリンセス・プリンセス

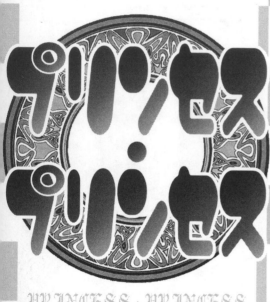

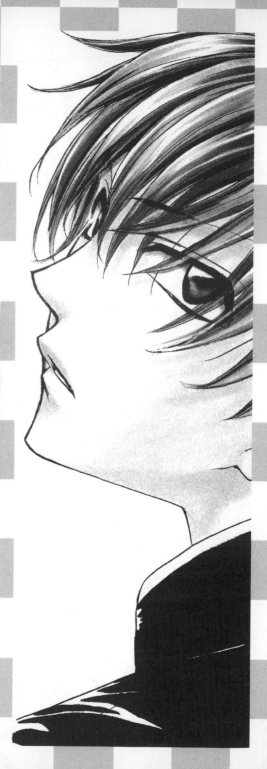

PRINCESS・PRINCESS

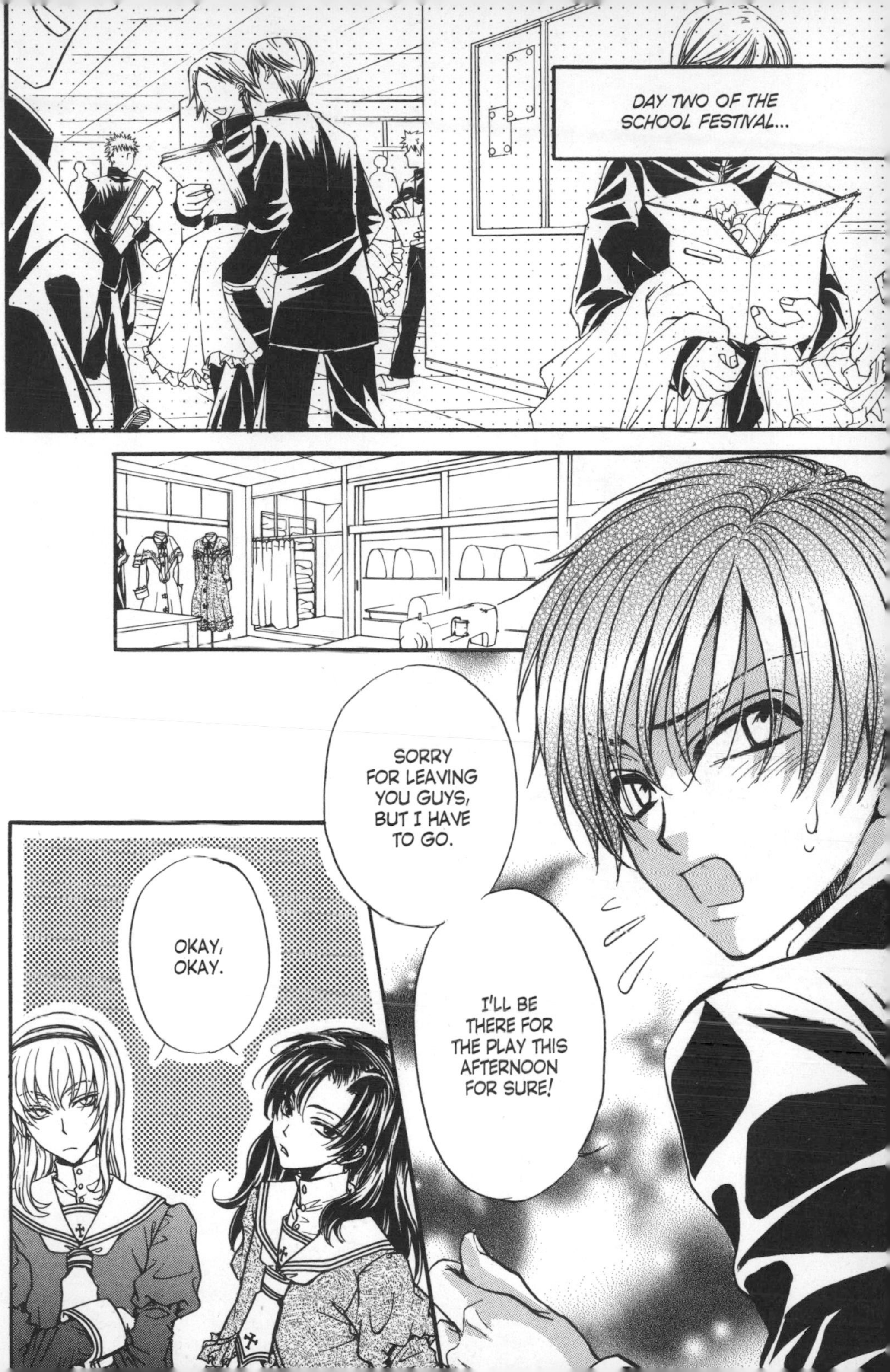
DAY TWO OF THE SCHOOL FESTIVAL...
SORRY FOR LEAVING YOU GUYS, BUT I HAVE TO GO.
I'LL BE THERE FOR THE PLAY THIS AFTERNOON FOR SURE!
OKAY, OKAY.

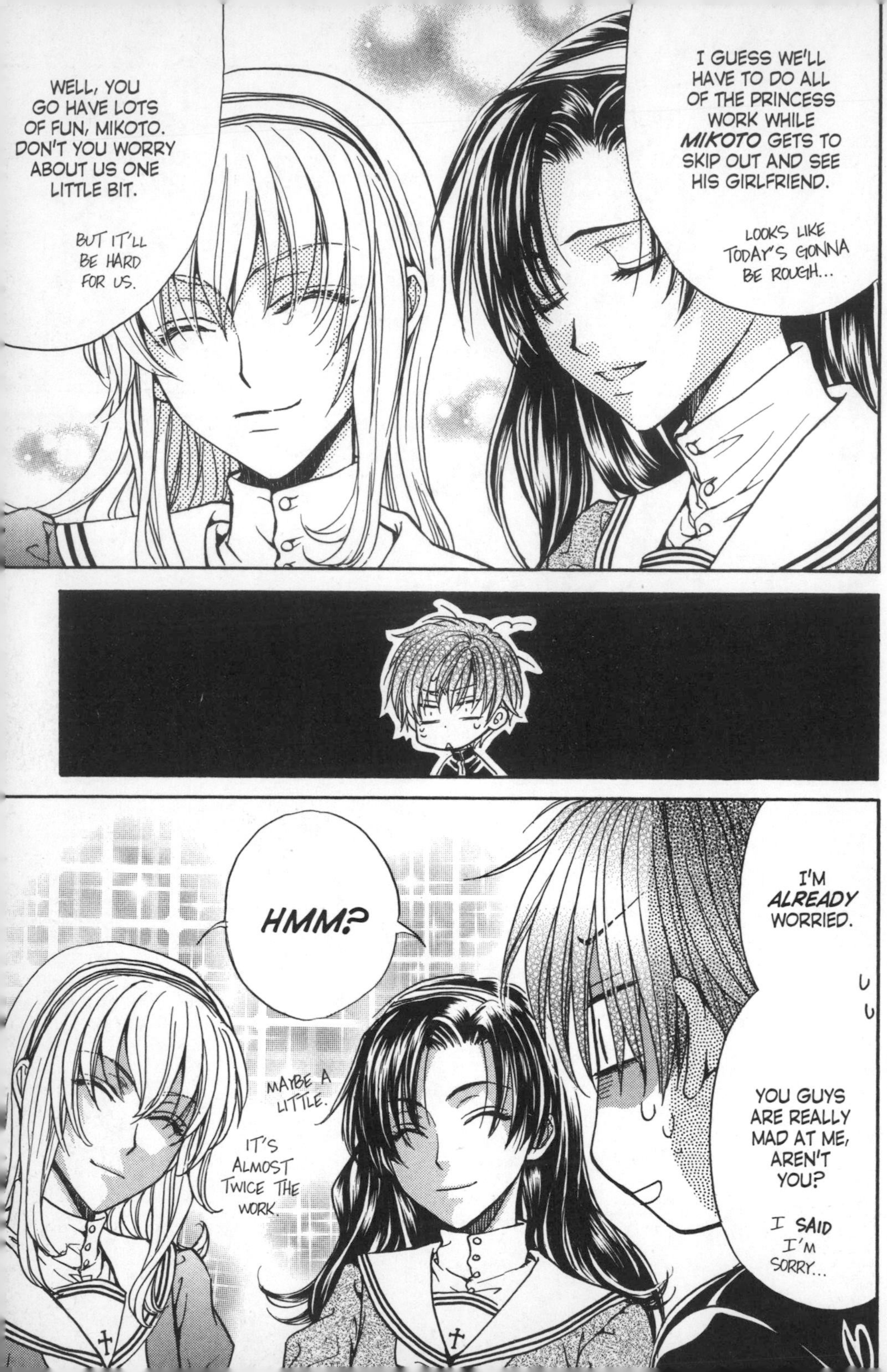
I GUESS WE'LL HAVE TO DO ALL OF THE PRINCESS WORK WHILE *MIKOTO* GETS TO SKIP OUT AND SEE HIS GIRLFRIEND.
LOOKS LIKE TODAY'S GONNA BE ROUGH...
WELL, YOU GO HAVE LOTS OF FUN, MIKOTO. DON'T YOU WORRY ABOUT US ONE LITTLE BIT.
BUT IT'LL BE HARD FOR US.
I'M *ALREADY* WORRIED.
HMM?
YOU GUYS ARE REALLY MAD AT ME, AREN'T YOU?
MAYBE A LITTLE.
IT'S ALMOST TWICE THE WORK.
I **SAID** I'M SORRY...

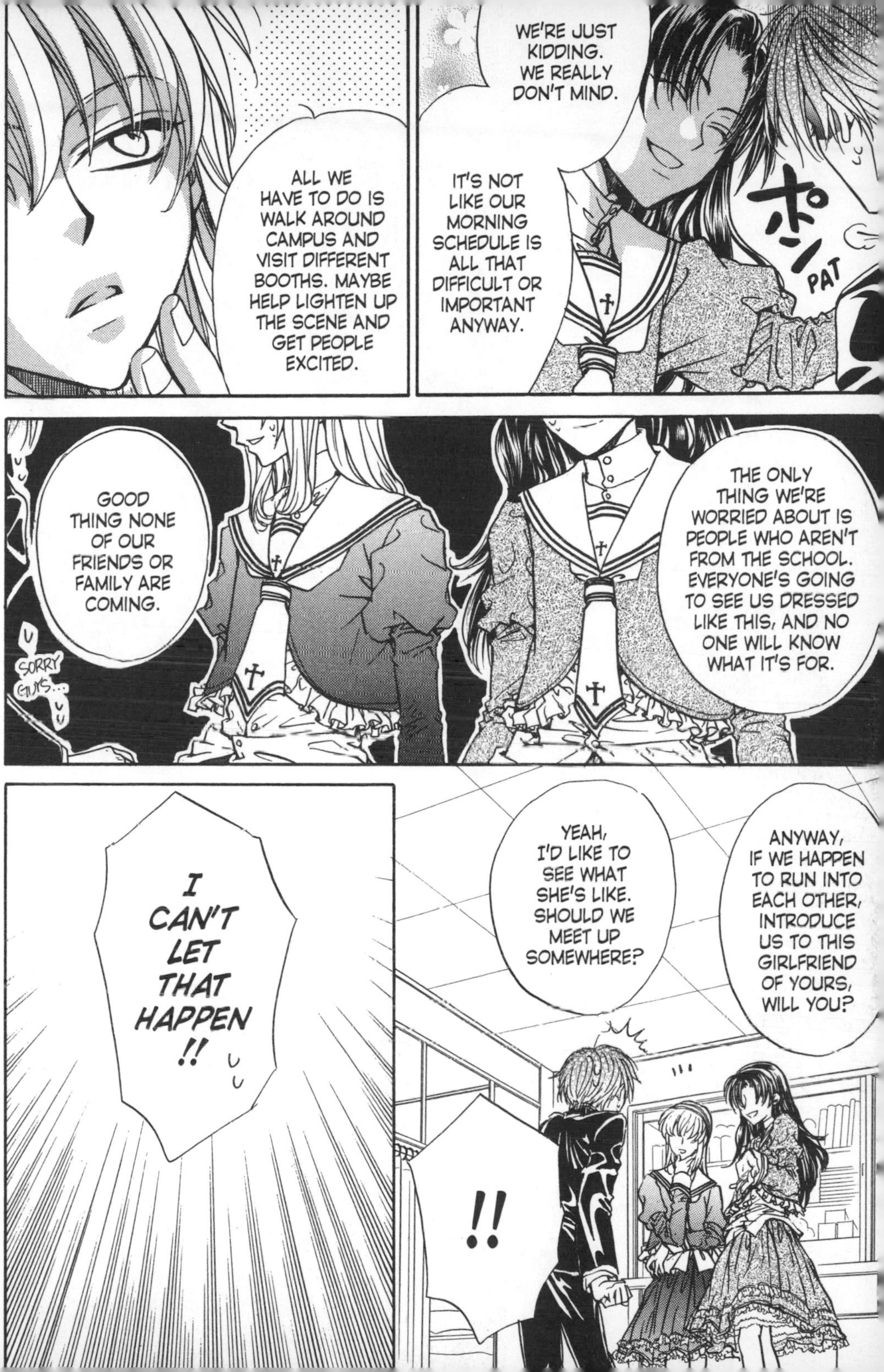
WE'RE JUST KIDDING. WE REALLY DON'T MIND.
IT'S NOT LIKE OUR MORNING SCHEDULE IS ALL THAT DIFFICULT OR IMPORTANT ANYWAY.
PAT
ALL WE HAVE TO DO IS WALK AROUND CAMPUS AND VISIT DIFFERENT BOOTHS. MAYBE HELP LIGHTEN UP THE SCENE AND GET PEOPLE EXCITED.
THE ONLY THING WE'RE WORRIED ABOUT IS PEOPLE WHO AREN'T FROM THE SCHOOL. EVERYONE'S GOING TO SEE US DRESSED LIKE THIS, AND NO ONE WILL KNOW WHAT IT'S FOR.
GOOD THING NONE OF OUR FRIENDS OR FAMILY ARE COMING.
SORRY GUYS...
ANYWAY, IF WE HAPPEN TO RUN INTO EACH OTHER, INTRODUCE US TO THIS GIRLFRIEND OF YOURS, WILL YOU?
YEAH, I'D LIKE TO SEE WHAT SHE'S LIKE. SHOULD WE MEET UP SOMEWHERE?
!!
I CAN'T LET THAT HAPPEN!!

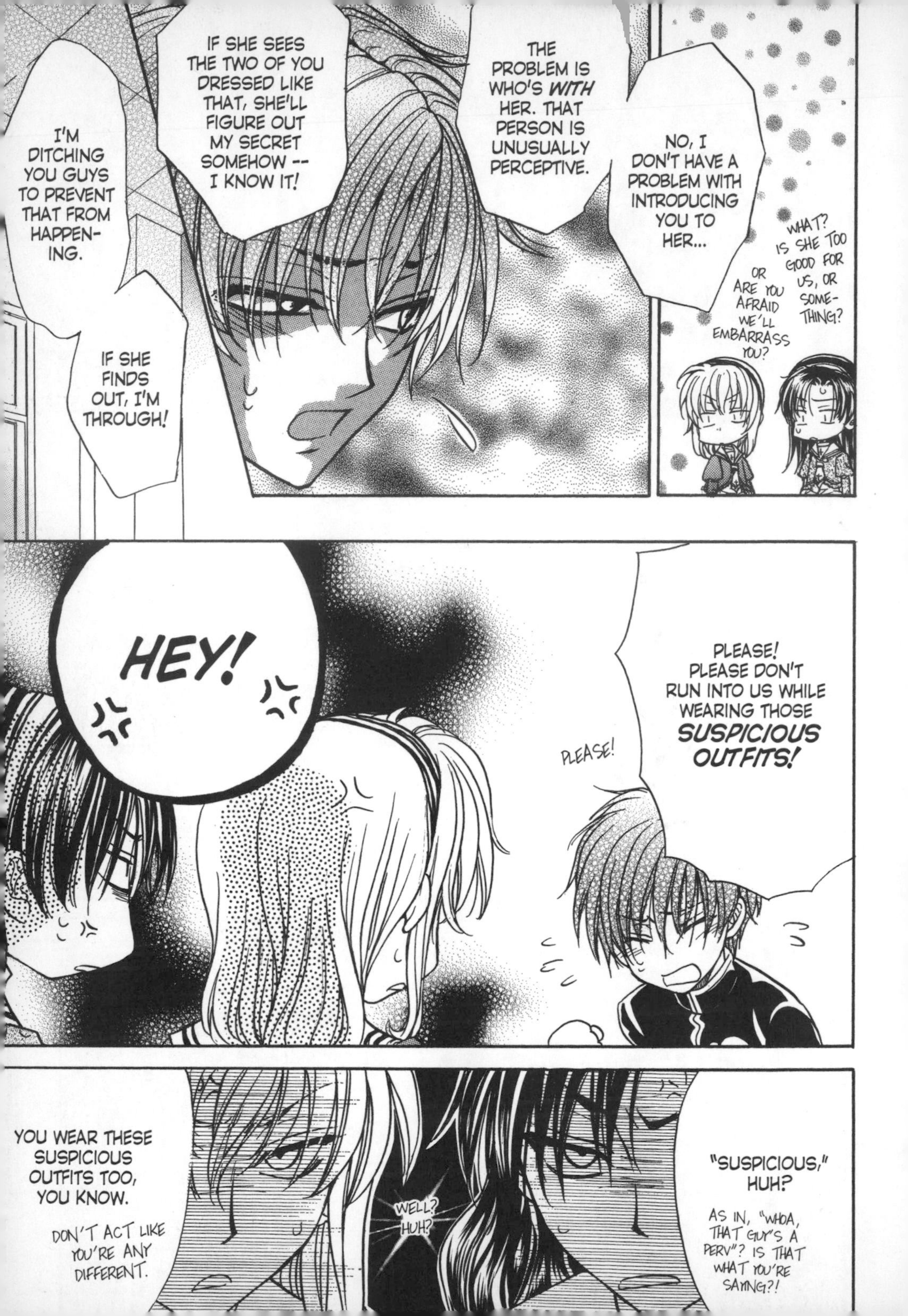
WHAT? IS SHE TOO GOOD FOR US, OR SOME-THING?
OR ARE YOU AFRAID WE'LL EMBARRASS YOU?
NO, I DON'T HAVE A PROBLEM WITH INTRODUCING YOU TO HER...
THE PROBLEM IS WHO'S *WITH* HER. THAT PERSON IS UNUSUALLY PERCEPTIVE.
IF SHE SEES THE TWO OF YOU DRESSED LIKE THAT, SHE'LL FIGURE OUT MY SECRET SOMEHOW -- I KNOW IT!
I'M DITCHING YOU GUYS TO PREVENT THAT FROM HAPPEN-ING.
IF SHE FINDS OUT, I'M THROUGH!
PLEASE! PLEASE DON'T RUN INTO US WHILE WEARING THOSE ***SUSPICIOUS OUTFITS!***
PLEASE!
HEY!
"SUSPICIOUS," HUH?
AS IN, "WHOA, THAT GUY'S A PERV"? IS THAT WHAT YOU'RE SAYING?!
WELL? HUH?
YOU WEAR THESE SUSPICIOUS OUTFITS TOO, YOU KNOW.
DON'T ACT LIKE YOU'RE ANY DIFFERENT.

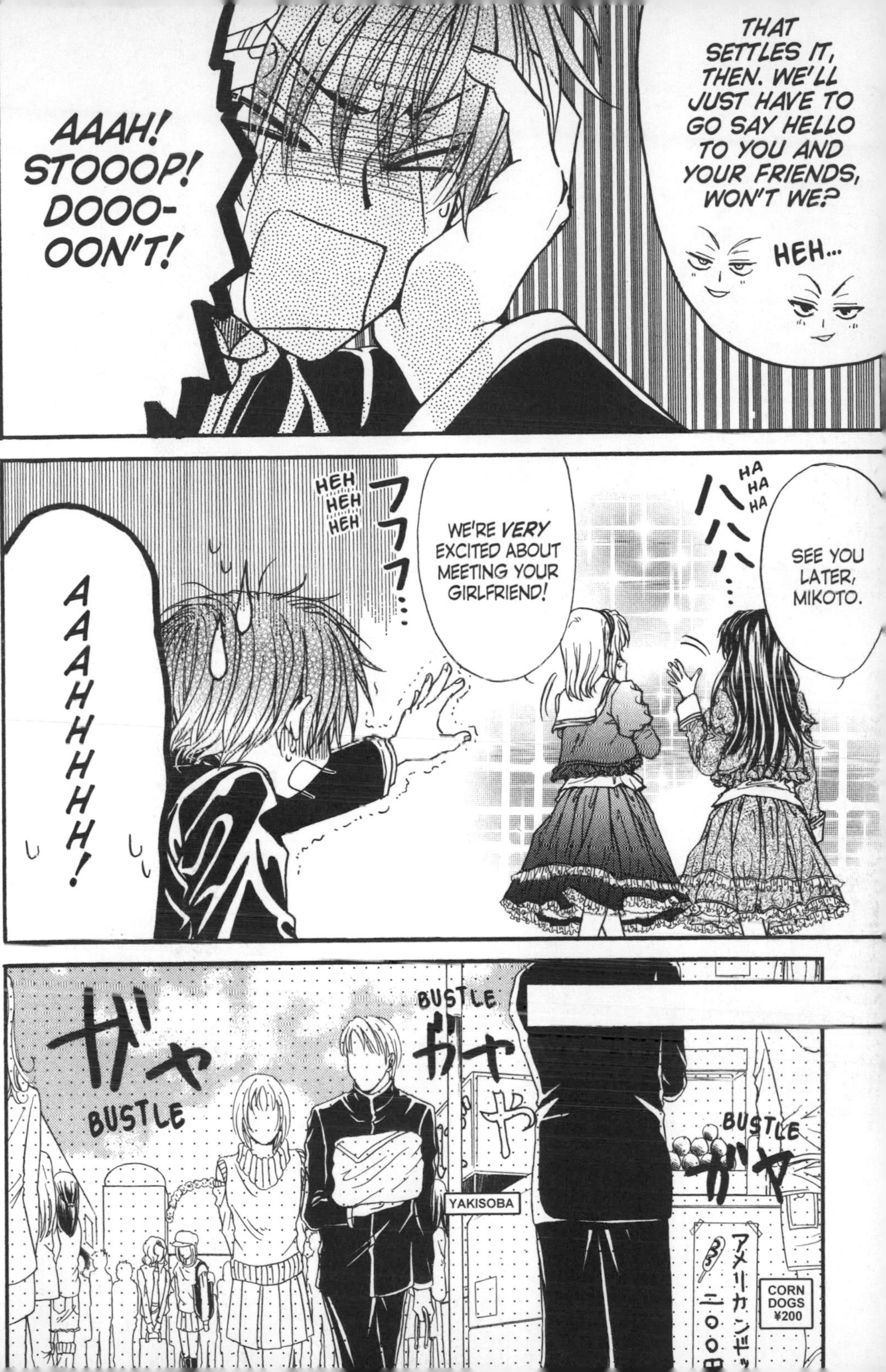
THAT SETTLES IT, THEN. WE'LL JUST HAVE TO GO SAY HELLO TO YOU AND YOUR FRIENDS, WON'T WE?
HEH...
AAAH! STOOOP! DOOOO-OON'T!
ハハハ...
HA HA HA
SEE YOU LATER, MIKOTO.
WE'RE *VERY* EXCITED ABOUT MEETING YOUR GIRLFRIEND!
フフフ...
HEH HEH HEH
AAAAHHHHHHH!
BUSTLE
BUSTLE
ガヤ
BUSTLE
YAKISOBA
アメリカンドッグ 二〇〇円
CORN DOGS ¥200

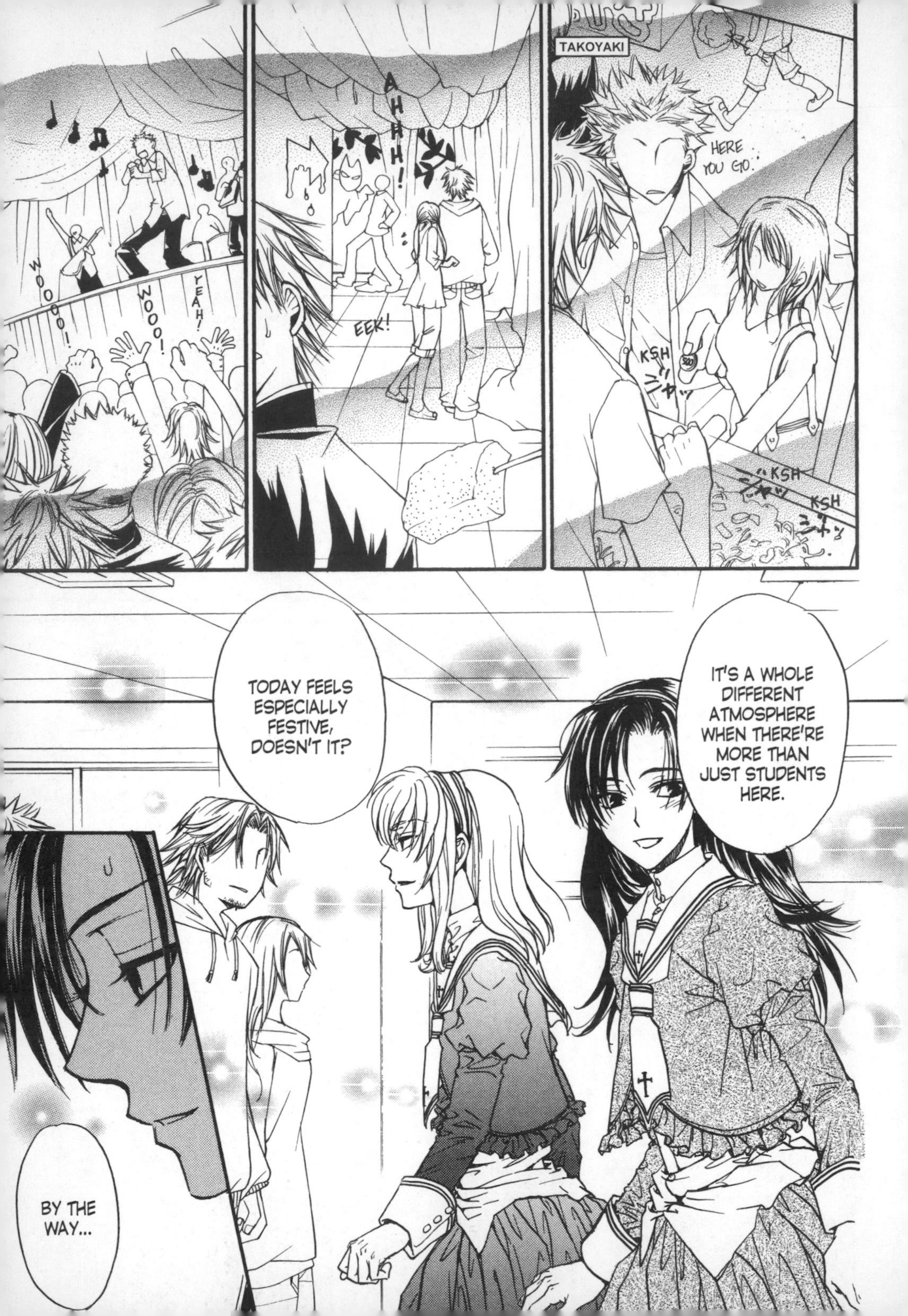
TAKOYAKI
HERE YOU GO..
KSH
KSH
KSH
AHHH!
EEK!
YEAH!
WOOOO!
WOOOO!
IT'S A WHOLE DIFFERENT ATMOSPHERE WHEN THERE'RE MORE THAN JUST STUDENTS HERE.
TODAY FEELS ESPECIALLY FESTIVE, DOESN'T IT?
BY THE WAY...

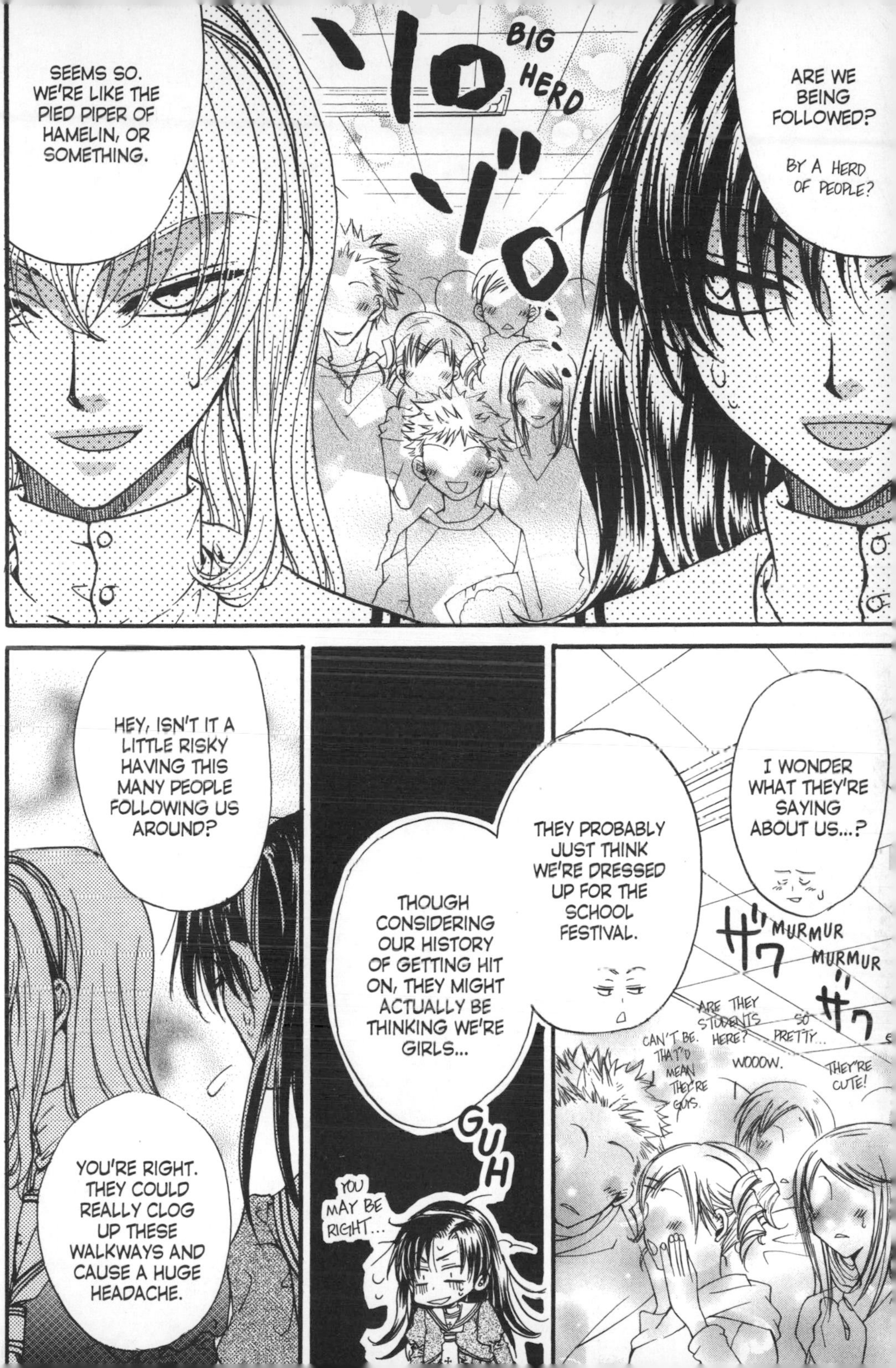
ARE WE BEING FOLLOWED?
BY A HERD OF PEOPLE?
BIG HERD
SEEMS SO. WE'RE LIKE THE PIED PIPER OF HAMELIN, OR SOMETHING.
I WONDER WHAT THEY'RE SAYING ABOUT US...?
MURMUR
MURMUR
ARE THEY STUDENTS HERE?
SO PRETTY...
CAN'T BE. THAT'D MEAN THEY'RE GUYS.
WOOOW.
THEY'RE CUTE!
THEY PROBABLY JUST THINK WE'RE DRESSED UP FOR THE SCHOOL FESTIVAL.
THOUGH CONSIDERING OUR HISTORY OF GETTING HIT ON, THEY MIGHT ACTUALLY BE THINKING WE'RE GIRLS...
GUH
YOU MAY BE RIGHT...
HEY, ISN'T IT A LITTLE RISKY HAVING THIS MANY PEOPLE FOLLOWING US AROUND?
YOU'RE RIGHT. THEY COULD REALLY CLOG UP THESE WALKWAYS AND CAUSE A HUGE HEADACHE.

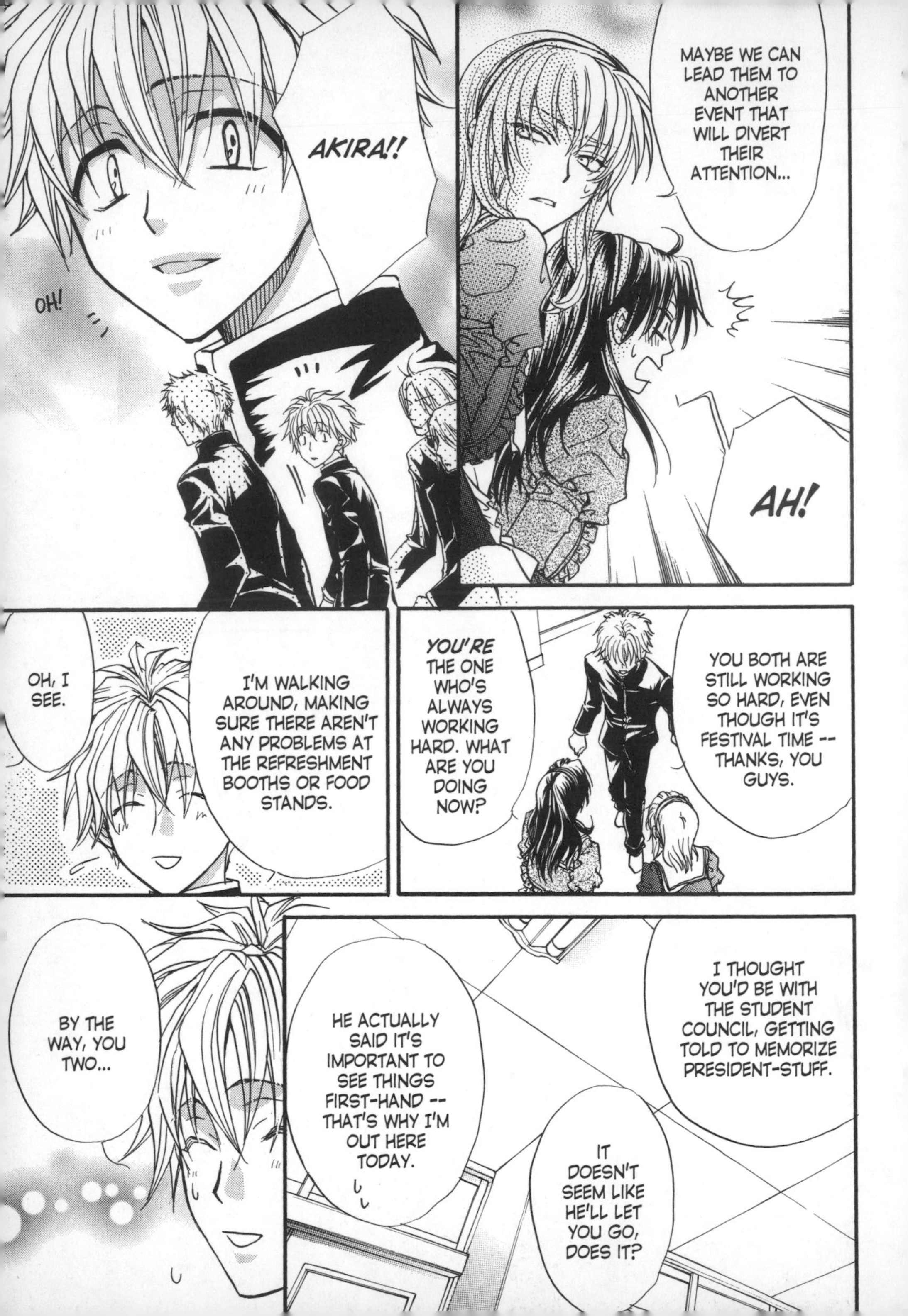
MAYBE WE CAN LEAD THEM TO ANOTHER EVENT THAT WILL DIVERT THEIR ATTENTION...
AH!
AKIRA!!
OH!
YOU BOTH ARE STILL WORKING SO HARD, EVEN THOUGH IT'S FESTIVAL TIME -- THANKS, YOU GUYS.
YOU'RE THE ONE WHO'S ALWAYS WORKING HARD. WHAT ARE YOU DOING NOW?
I'M WALKING AROUND, MAKING SURE THERE AREN'T ANY PROBLEMS AT THE REFRESHMENT BOOTHS OR FOOD STANDS.
OH, I SEE.
I THOUGHT YOU'D BE WITH THE STUDENT COUNCIL, GETTING TOLD TO MEMORIZE PRESIDENT-STUFF.
HE ACTUALLY SAID IT'S IMPORTANT TO SEE THINGS FIRST-HAND -- THAT'S WHY I'M OUT HERE TODAY.
IT DOESN'T SEEM LIKE HE'LL LET YOU GO, DOES IT?
BY THE WAY, YOU TWO...

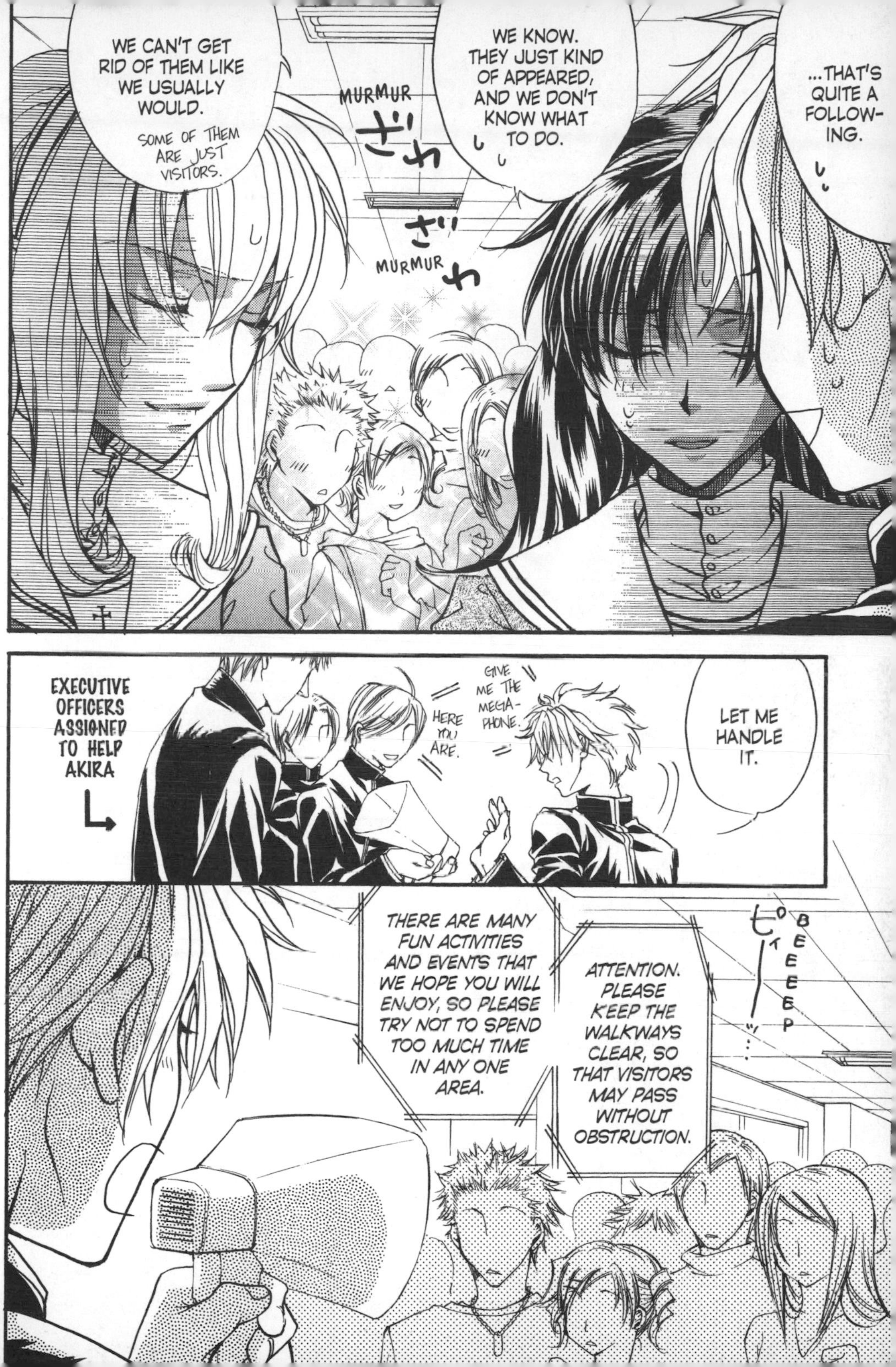
...THAT'S QUITE A FOLLOWING.
WE KNOW. THEY JUST KIND OF APPEARED, AND WE DON'T KNOW WHAT TO DO.
MURMUR
MURMUR
WE CAN'T GET RID OF THEM LIKE WE USUALLY WOULD.
SOME OF THEM ARE JUST VISITORS.
LET ME HANDLE IT.
GIVE ME THE MEGA-PHONE.
HERE YOU ARE.
EXECUTIVE OFFICERS ASSIGNED TO HELP AKIRA
BEEEEEP
ATTENTION. PLEASE KEEP THE WALKWAYS CLEAR, SO THAT VISITORS MAY PASS WITHOUT OBSTRUCTION.
THERE ARE MANY FUN ACTIVITIES AND EVENTS THAT WE HOPE YOU WILL ENJOY, SO PLEASE TRY NOT TO SPEND TOO MUCH TIME IN ANY ONE AREA.

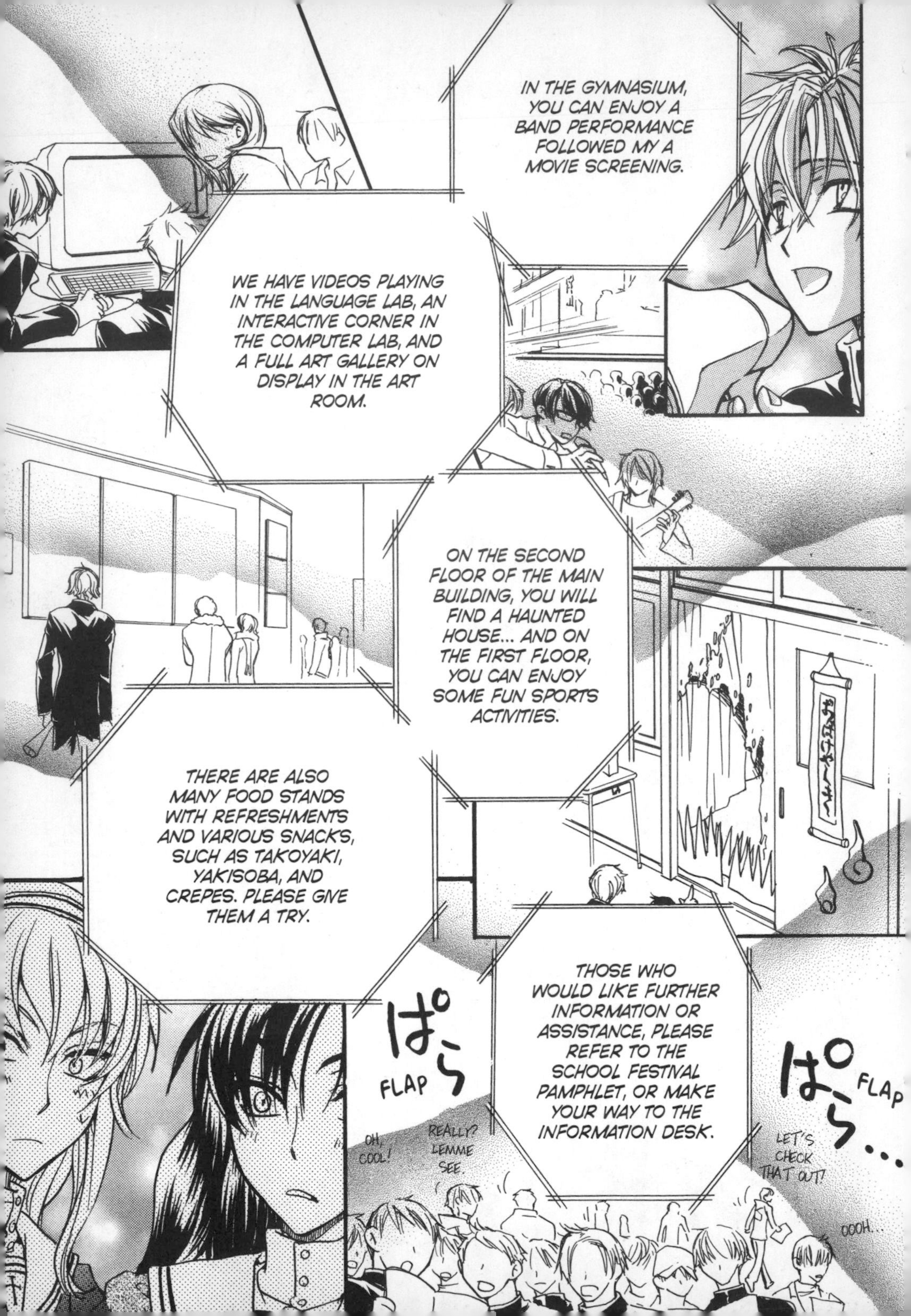
IN THE GYMNASIUM, YOU CAN ENJOY A BAND PERFORMANCE FOLLOWED MY A MOVIE SCREENING.
WE HAVE VIDEOS PLAYING IN THE LANGUAGE LAB, AN INTERACTIVE CORNER IN THE COMPUTER LAB, AND A FULL ART GALLERY ON DISPLAY IN THE ART ROOM.
ON THE SECOND FLOOR OF THE MAIN BUILDING, YOU WILL FIND A HAUNTED HOUSE... AND ON THE FIRST FLOOR, YOU CAN ENJOY SOME FUN SPORTS ACTIVITIES.
THERE ARE ALSO MANY FOOD STANDS WITH REFRESHMENTS AND VARIOUS SNACKS, SUCH AS TAKOYAKI, YAKISOBA, AND CREPES. PLEASE GIVE THEM A TRY.
THOSE WHO WOULD LIKE FURTHER INFORMATION OR ASSISTANCE, PLEASE REFER TO THE SCHOOL FESTIVAL PAMPHLET, OR MAKE YOUR WAY TO THE INFORMATION DESK.
ぱら...
FLAP
LET'S CHECK THAT OUT!
OOOH...
REALLY? LEMME SEE.
OH, COOL!
ぱら
FLAP

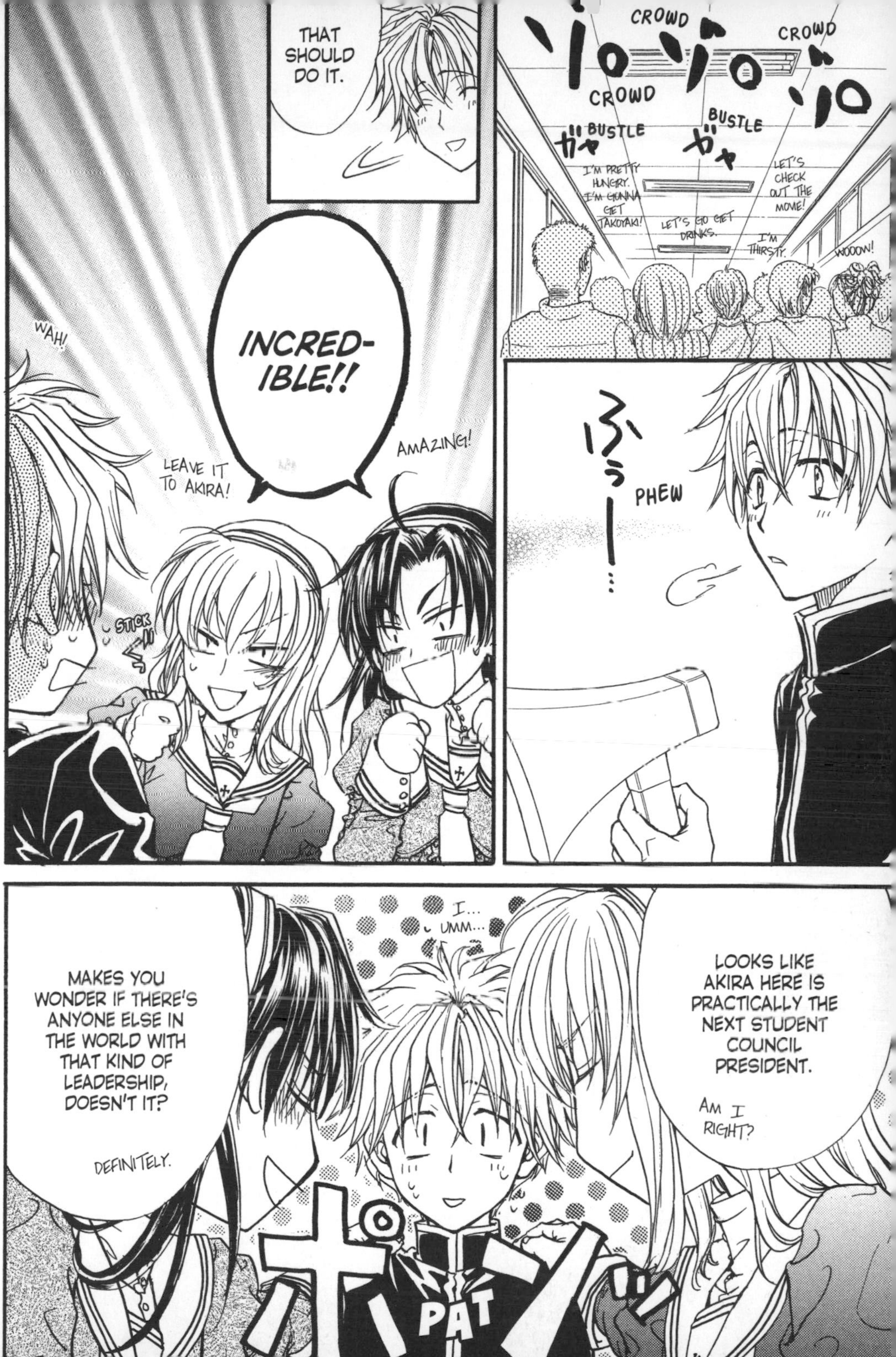
CROWD
CROWD
CROWD
ガヤ BUSTLE
ガヤ BUSTLE
LET'S CHECK OUT THE MOVIE!
I'M PRETTY HUNGRY. I'M GONNA GET TAKOYAKI!
LET'S GO GET DRINKS.
I'M THIRSTY.
WOOOW!
PHEW
THAT SHOULD DO IT.
INCREDIBLE!!
AMAZING!
LEAVE IT TO AKIRA!
WAH!
STICK
LOOKS LIKE AKIRA HERE IS PRACTICALLY THE NEXT STUDENT COUNCIL PRESIDENT.
AM I RIGHT?
I... UMM...
MAKES YOU WONDER IF THERE'S ANYONE ELSE IN THE WORLD WITH THAT KIND OF LEADERSHIP, DOESN'T IT?
DEFINITELY.
PAT

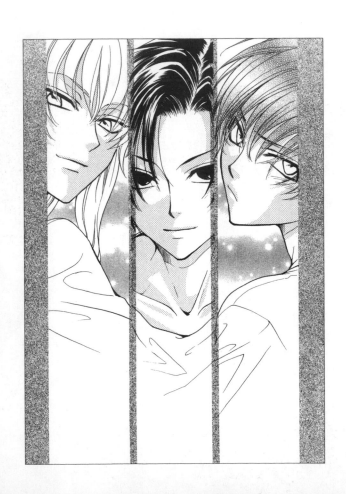

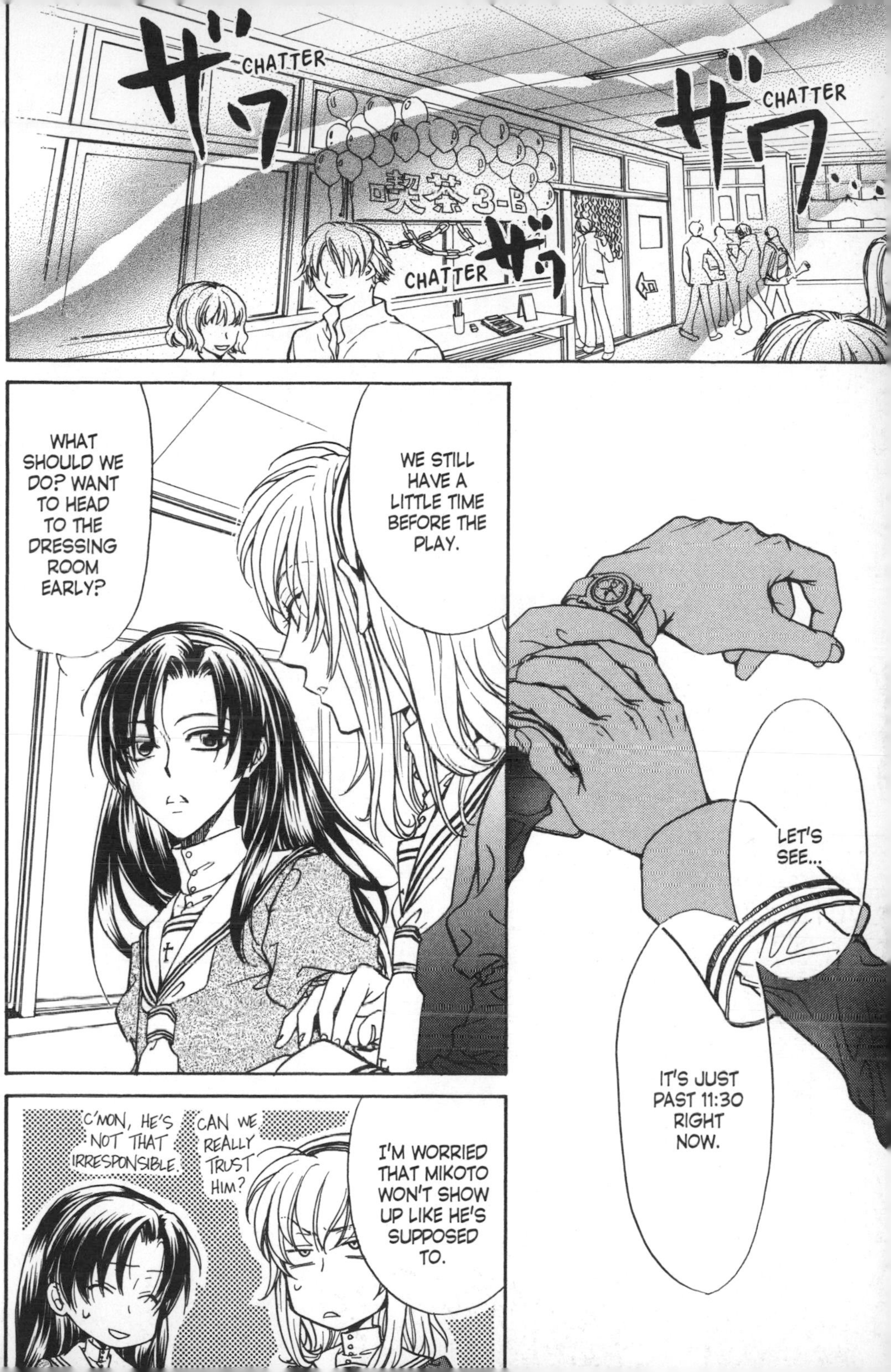
ザワ
CHATTER
ザワ
CHATTER
喫茶3-B
ザワ
CHATTER
LET'S SEE...
IT'S JUST PAST 11:30 RIGHT NOW.
WE STILL HAVE A LITTLE TIME BEFORE THE PLAY.
WHAT SHOULD WE DO? WANT TO HEAD TO THE DRESSING ROOM EARLY?
I'M WORRIED THAT MIKOTO WON'T SHOW UP LIKE HE'S SUPPOSED TO.
CAN WE REALLY TRUST HIM?
C'MON, HE'S NOT THAT IRRESPONSIBLE.

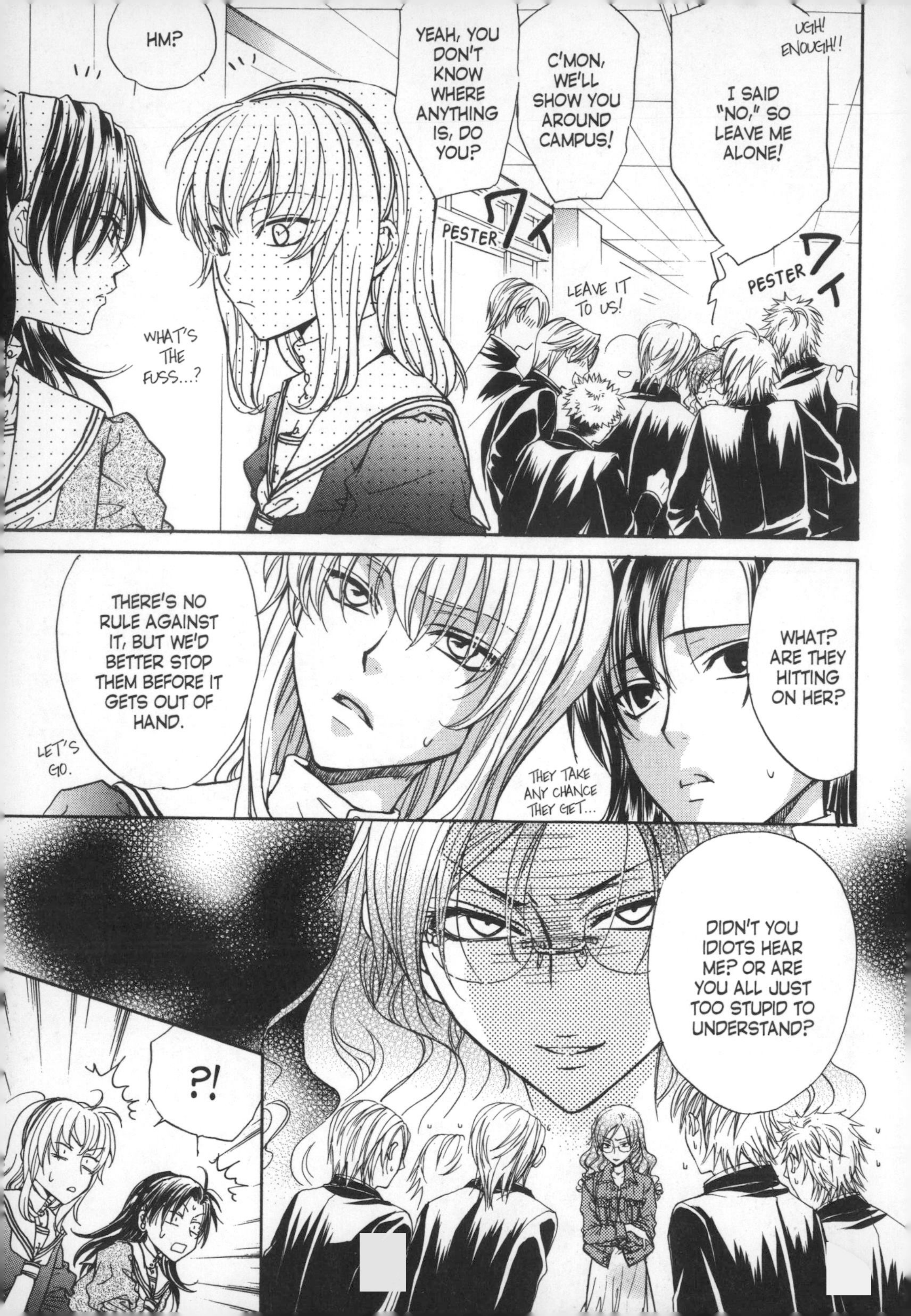
UGH! ENOUGH!!
I SAID "NO," SO LEAVE ME ALONE!
PESTER
C'MON, WE'LL SHOW YOU AROUND CAMPUS!
YEAH, YOU DON'T KNOW WHERE ANYTHING IS, DO YOU?
PESTER
LEAVE IT TO US!
HM?
WHAT'S THE FUSS...?
WHAT? ARE THEY HITTING ON HER?
THEY TAKE ANY CHANCE THEY GET...
THERE'S NO RULE AGAINST IT, BUT WE'D BETTER STOP THEM BEFORE IT GETS OUT OF HAND.
LET'S GO.
DIDN'T YOU IDIOTS HEAR ME? OR ARE YOU ALL JUST TOO STUPID TO UNDERSTAND?
?!

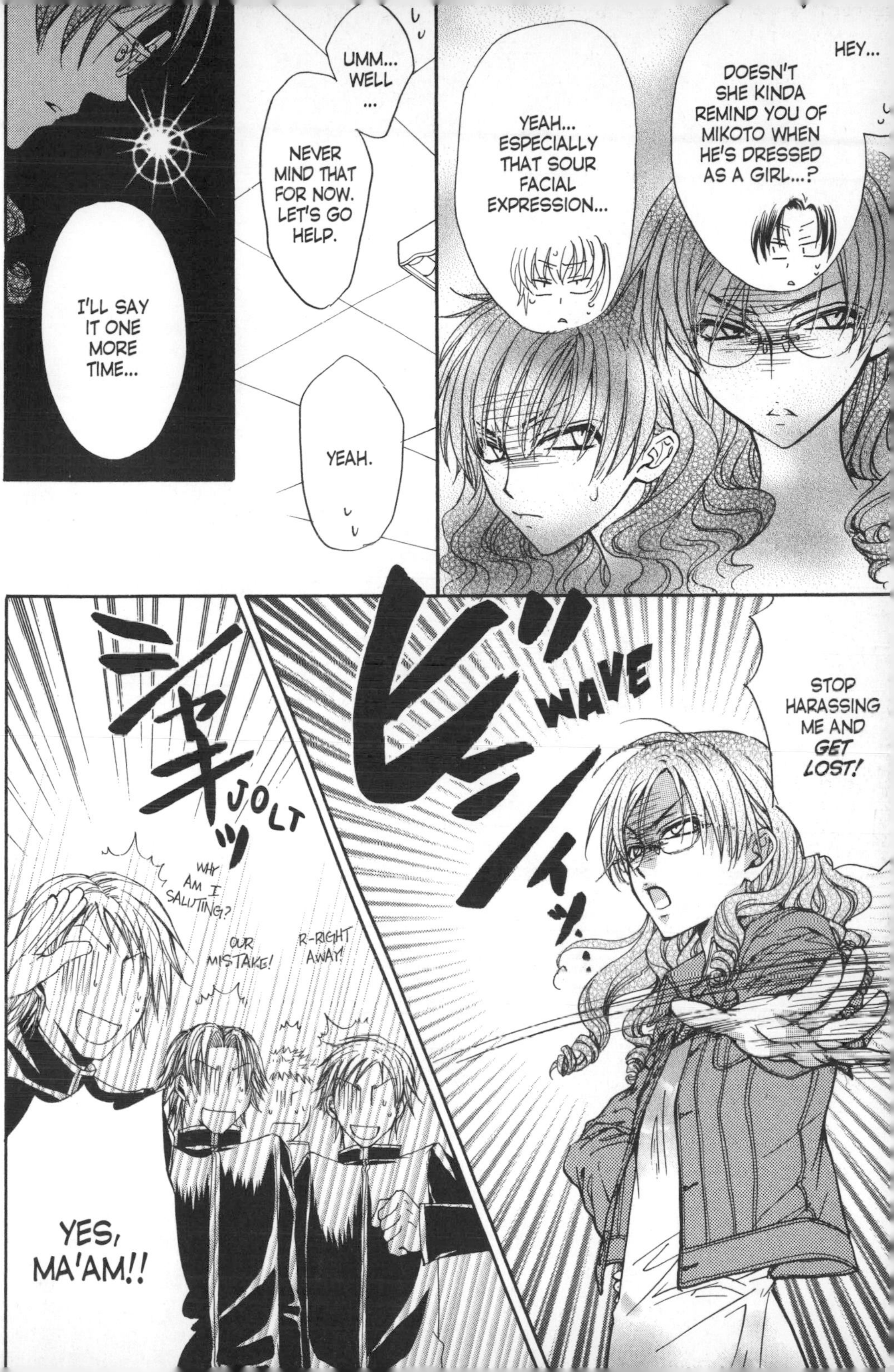
HEY...
DOESN'T SHE KINDA REMIND YOU OF MIKOTO WHEN HE'S DRESSED AS A GIRL...?
YEAH... ESPECIALLY THAT SOUR FACIAL EXPRESSION...
UMM... WELL ...
NEVER MIND THAT FOR NOW. LET'S GO HELP.
YEAH.
I'LL SAY IT ONE MORE TIME...
STOP HARASSING ME AND GET LOST!
WAVE
JOLT
WHY AM I SALUTING?
R-RIGHT AWAY!
OUR MISTAKE!
YES, MA'AM!!

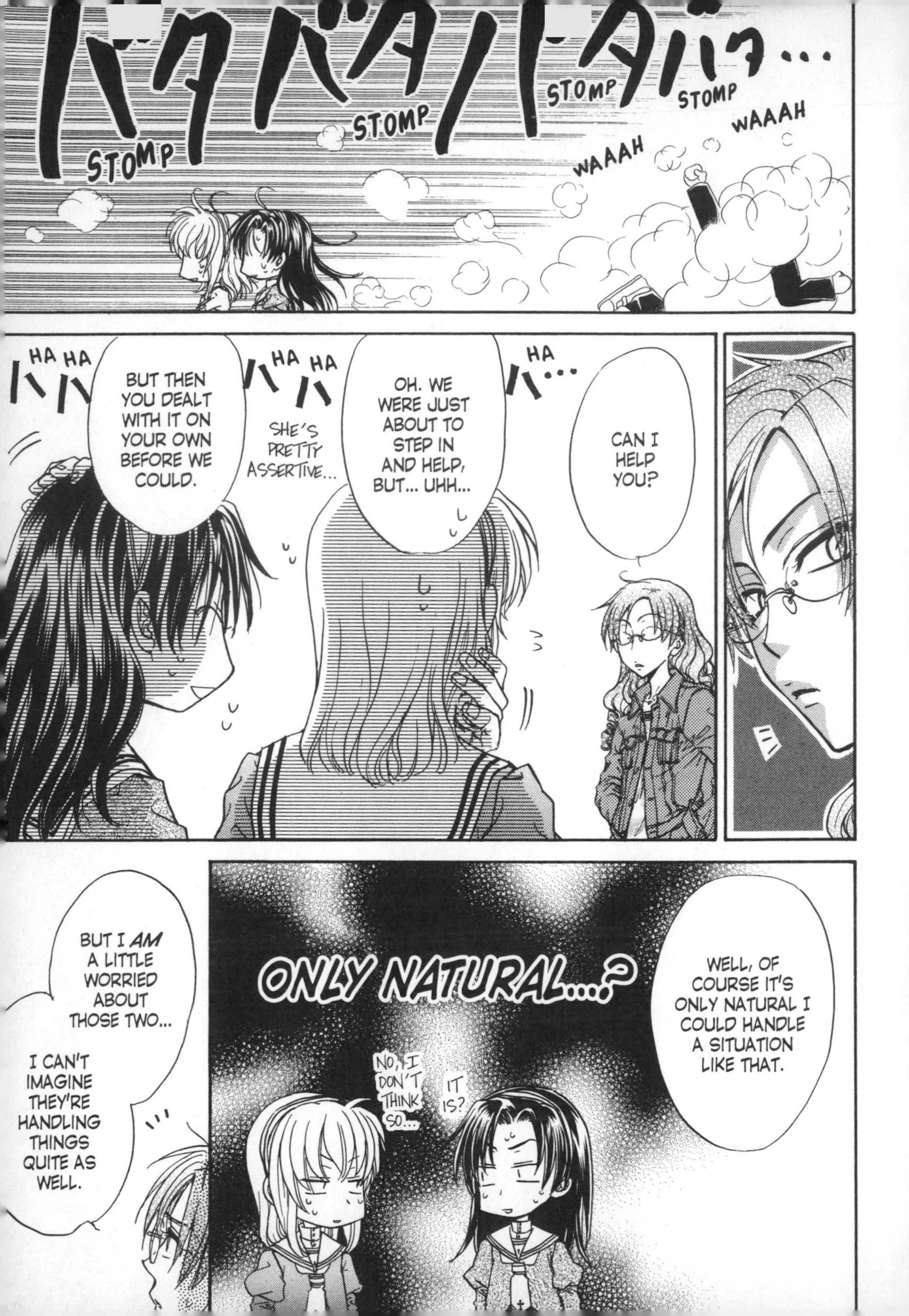
バタバタドタバタ…
STOMP
STOMP
STOMP
STOMP
WAAAH
WAAAH
HA
ハ…
CAN I HELP YOU?
OH. WE WERE JUST ABOUT TO STEP IN AND HELP, BUT... UHH...
HA HA
ハハ
SHE'S PRETTY ASSERTIVE...
BUT THEN YOU DEALT WITH IT ON YOUR OWN BEFORE WE COULD.
HA HA
ハハ
WELL, OF COURSE IT'S ONLY NATURAL I COULD HANDLE A SITUATION LIKE THAT.
ONLY NATURAL...?
IT IS?
NO, I DON'T THINK SO...
BUT I *AM* A LITTLE WORRIED ABOUT THOSE TWO...
I CAN'T IMAGINE THEY'RE HANDLING THINGS QUITE AS WELL.

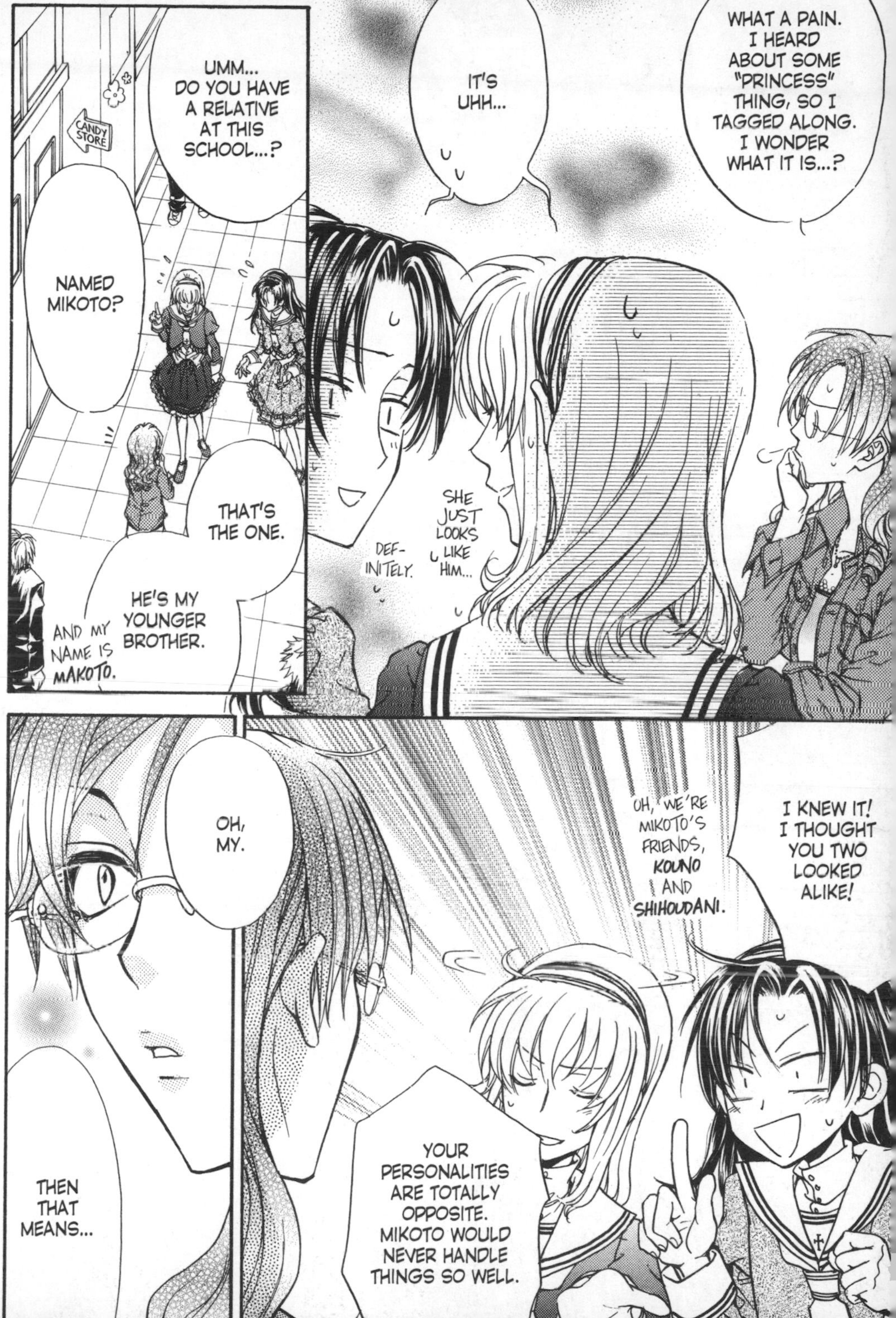
WHAT A PAIN. I HEARD ABOUT SOME "PRINCESS" THING, SO I TAGGED ALONG. I WONDER WHAT IT IS...?
IT'S UHH...
SHE JUST LOOKS LIKE HIM...
DEF-INITELY.
UMM... DO YOU HAVE A RELATIVE AT THIS SCHOOL...?
CANDY STORE
NAMED MIKOTO?
THAT'S THE ONE.
HE'S MY YOUNGER BROTHER.
AND MY NAME IS MAKOTO.
I KNEW IT! I THOUGHT YOU TWO LOOKED ALIKE!
OH, WE'RE MIKOTO'S FRIENDS, KOUNO AND SHIHOUDANI.
YOUR PERSONALITIES ARE TOTALLY OPPOSITE. MIKOTO WOULD NEVER HANDLE THINGS SO WELL.
OH, MY.
THEN THAT MEANS...

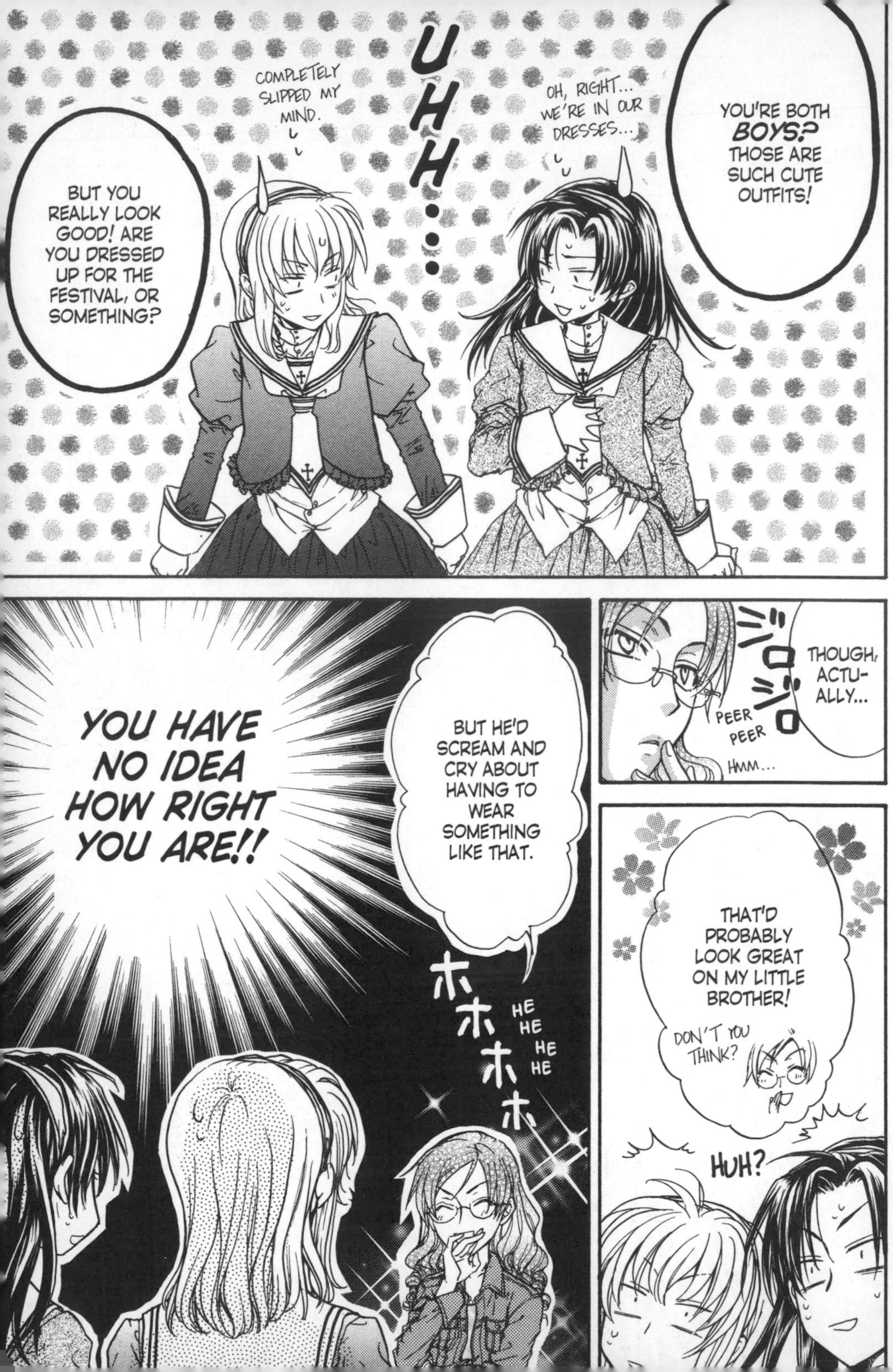
YOU'RE BOTH *BOYS?* THOSE ARE SUCH CUTE OUTFITS!
UHH...
OH, RIGHT... WE'RE IN OUR DRESSES...
COMPLETELY SLIPPED MY MIND.
BUT YOU REALLY LOOK GOOD! ARE YOU DRESSED UP FOR THE FESTIVAL, OR SOMETHING?
THOUGH, ACTU-ALLY...
ジロジロ
PEER PEER
HMM...
THAT'D PROBABLY LOOK GREAT ON MY LITTLE BROTHER!
DON'T YOU THINK?
HUH?
BUT HE'D SCREAM AND CRY ABOUT HAVING TO WEAR SOMETHING LIKE THAT.
ホホホホ
HE HE HE HE
YOU HAVE NO IDEA HOW RIGHT YOU ARE!!

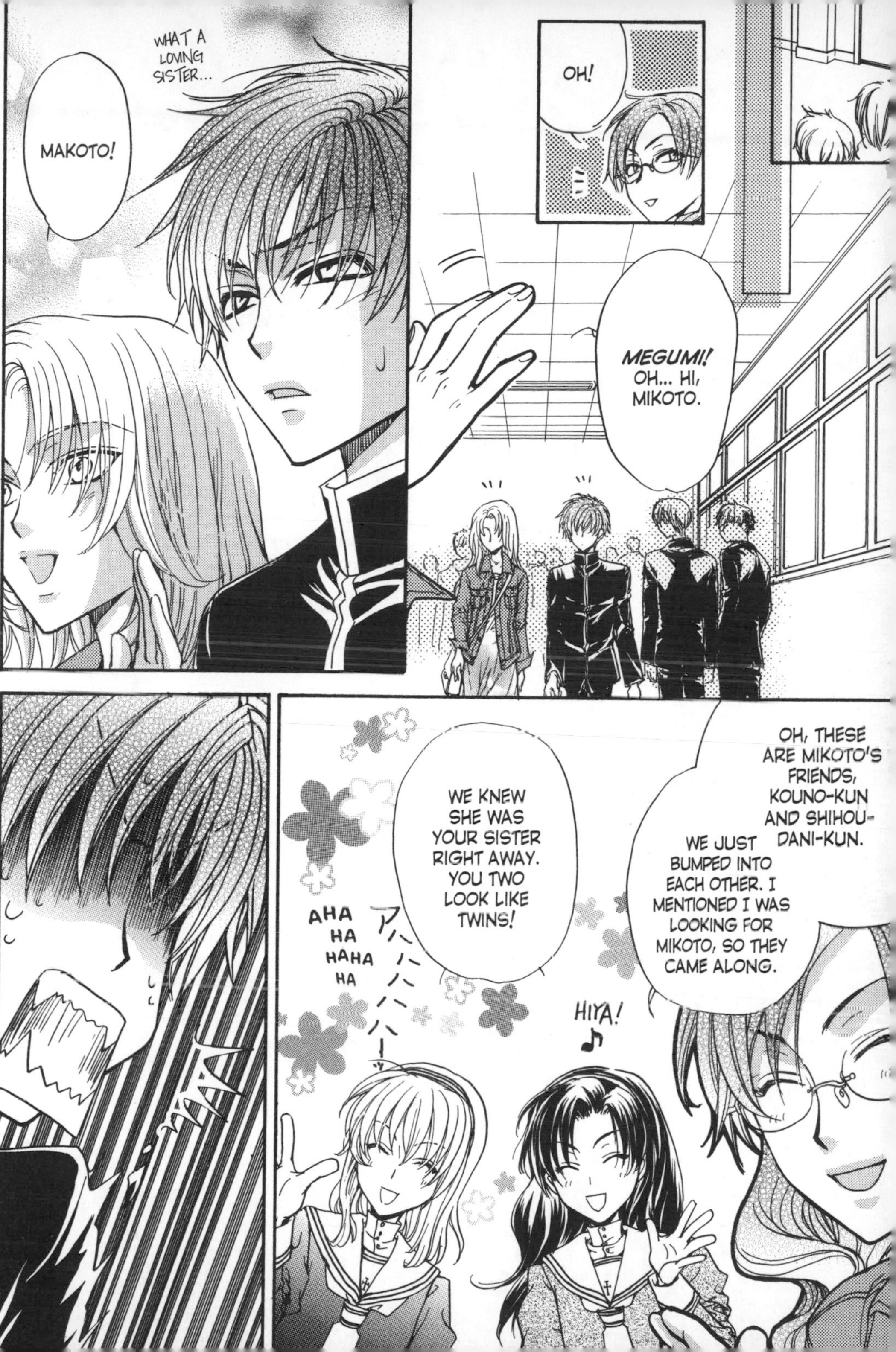
OH!
MEGUMI! OH... HI, MIKOTO.
WHAT A LOVING SISTER...
MAKOTO!
OH, THESE ARE MIKOTO'S FRIENDS, KOUNO-KUN AND SHIHOU-DANI-KUN.
WE JUST BUMPED INTO EACH OTHER. I MENTIONED I WAS LOOKING FOR MIKOTO, SO THEY CAME ALONG.
HIYA! ♪
WE KNEW SHE WAS YOUR SISTER RIGHT AWAY. YOU TWO LOOK LIKE TWINS!
AHA HA HAHA HA

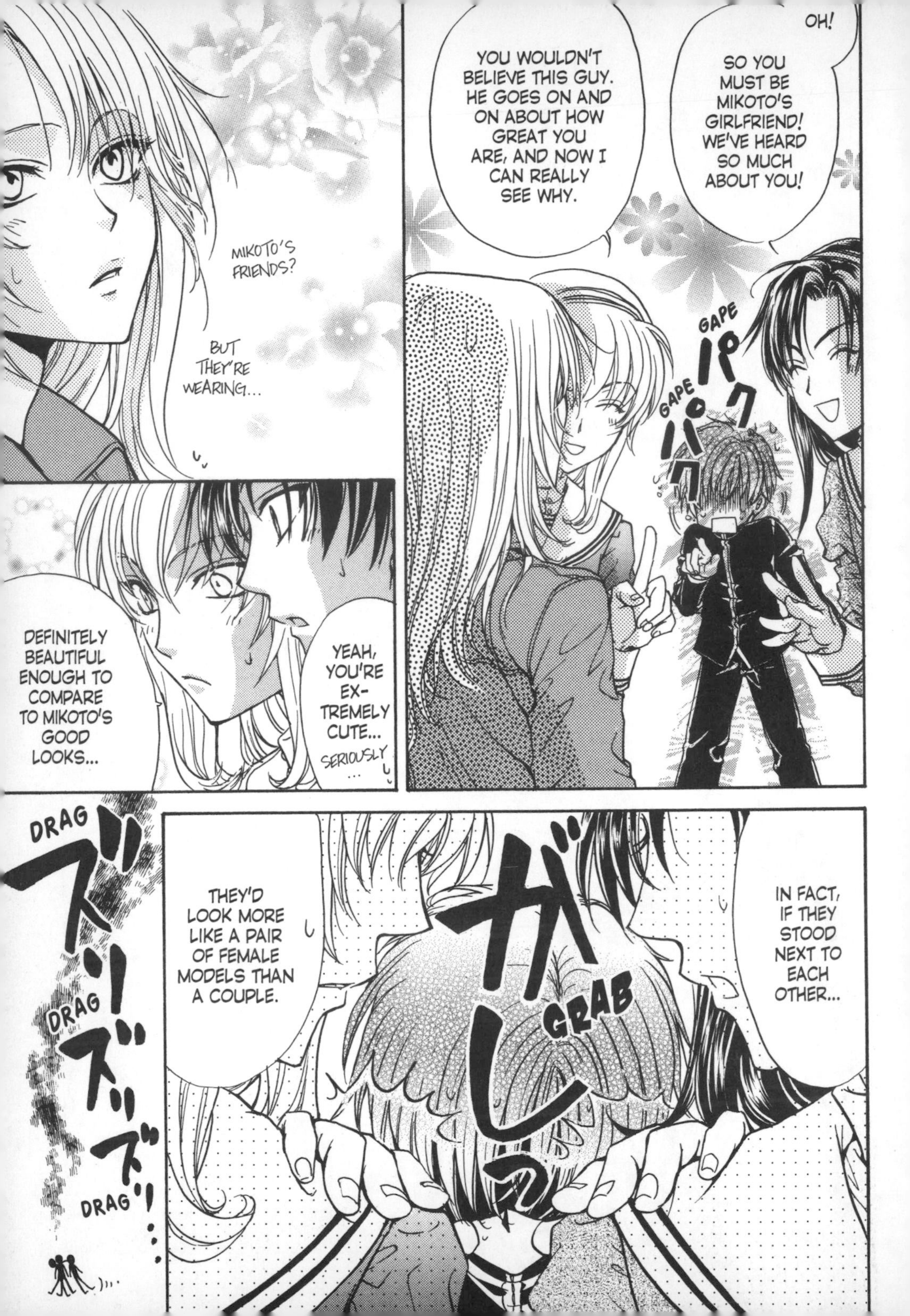
OH!
SO YOU MUST BE MIKOTO'S GIRLFRIEND! WE'VE HEARD SO MUCH ABOUT YOU!
YOU WOULDN'T BELIEVE THIS GUY. HE GOES ON AND ON ABOUT HOW GREAT YOU ARE, AND NOW I CAN REALLY SEE WHY.
GAPE
GAPE
MIKOTO'S FRIENDS?
BUT THEY'RE WEARING...
YEAH, YOU'RE EX-TREMELY CUTE...
SERIOUSLY...
DEFINITELY BEAUTIFUL ENOUGH TO COMPARE TO MIKOTO'S GOOD LOOKS...
IN FACT, IF THEY STOOD NEXT TO EACH OTHER...
GRAB
THEY'D LOOK MORE LIKE A PAIR OF FEMALE MODELS THAN A COUPLE.
DRAG
DRAG
DRAG

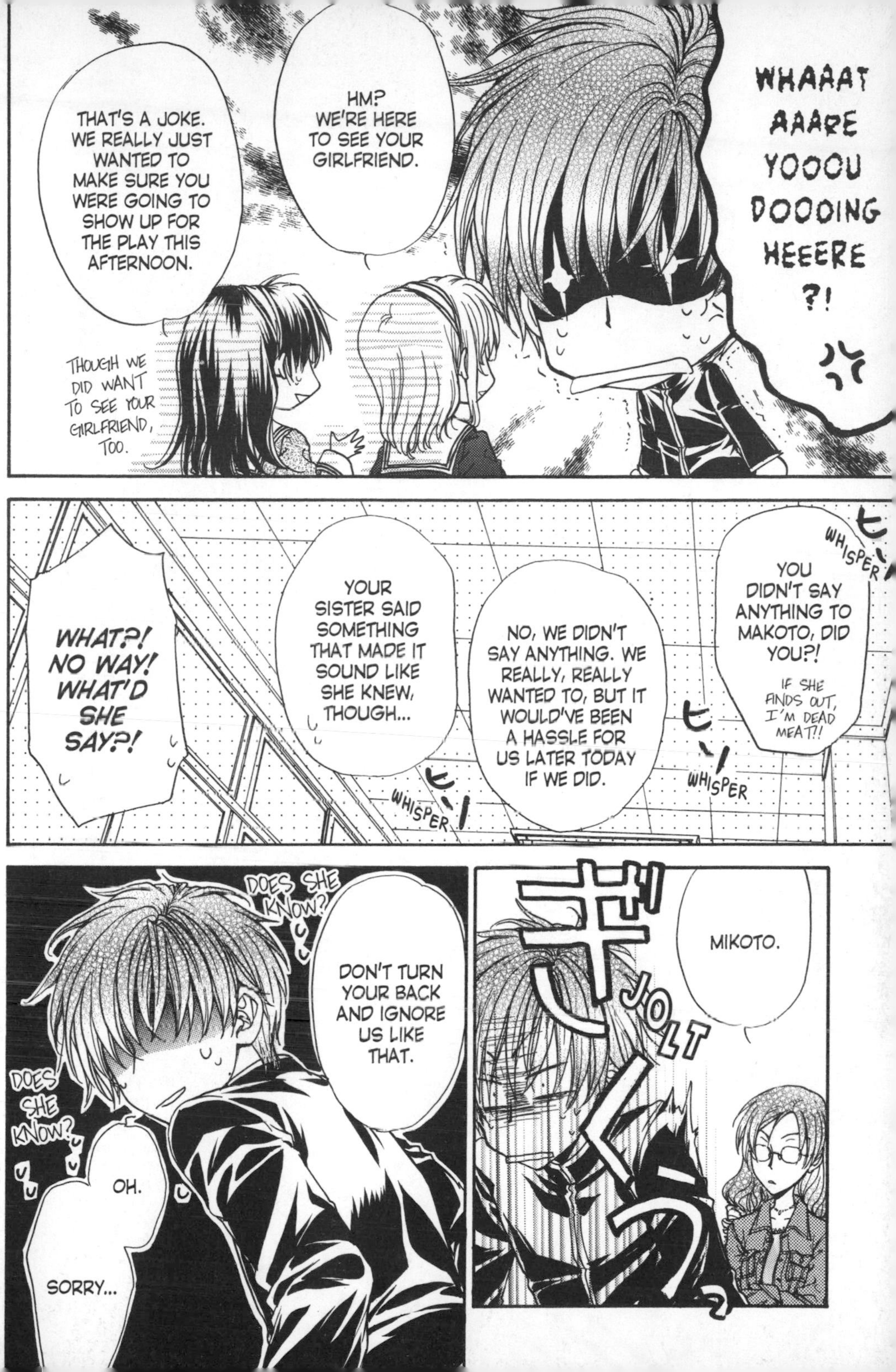
WHAAAT AAARE YOOOU DOOOING HEEERE ?!
HM? WE'RE HERE TO SEE YOUR GIRLFRIEND.
THAT'S A JOKE. WE REALLY JUST WANTED TO MAKE SURE YOU WERE GOING TO SHOW UP FOR THE PLAY THIS AFTERNOON.
THOUGH WE DID WANT TO SEE YOUR GIRLFRIEND, TOO.
WHISPER
YOU DIDN'T SAY ANYTHING TO MAKOTO, DID YOU?!
IF SHE FINDS OUT, I'M DEAD MEAT?!!
WHISPER
NO, WE DIDN'T SAY ANYTHING. WE REALLY, REALLY WANTED TO, BUT IT WOULD'VE BEEN A HASSLE FOR US LATER TODAY IF WE DID.
YOUR SISTER SAID SOMETHING THAT MADE IT SOUND LIKE SHE KNEW, THOUGH...
WHISPER
WHAT?! NO WAY! WHAT'D SHE SAY?!
MIKOTO.
JOLT
DOES SHE KNOW?
DON'T TURN YOUR BACK AND IGNORE US LIKE THAT.
DOES SHE KNOW?
OH.
SORRY...

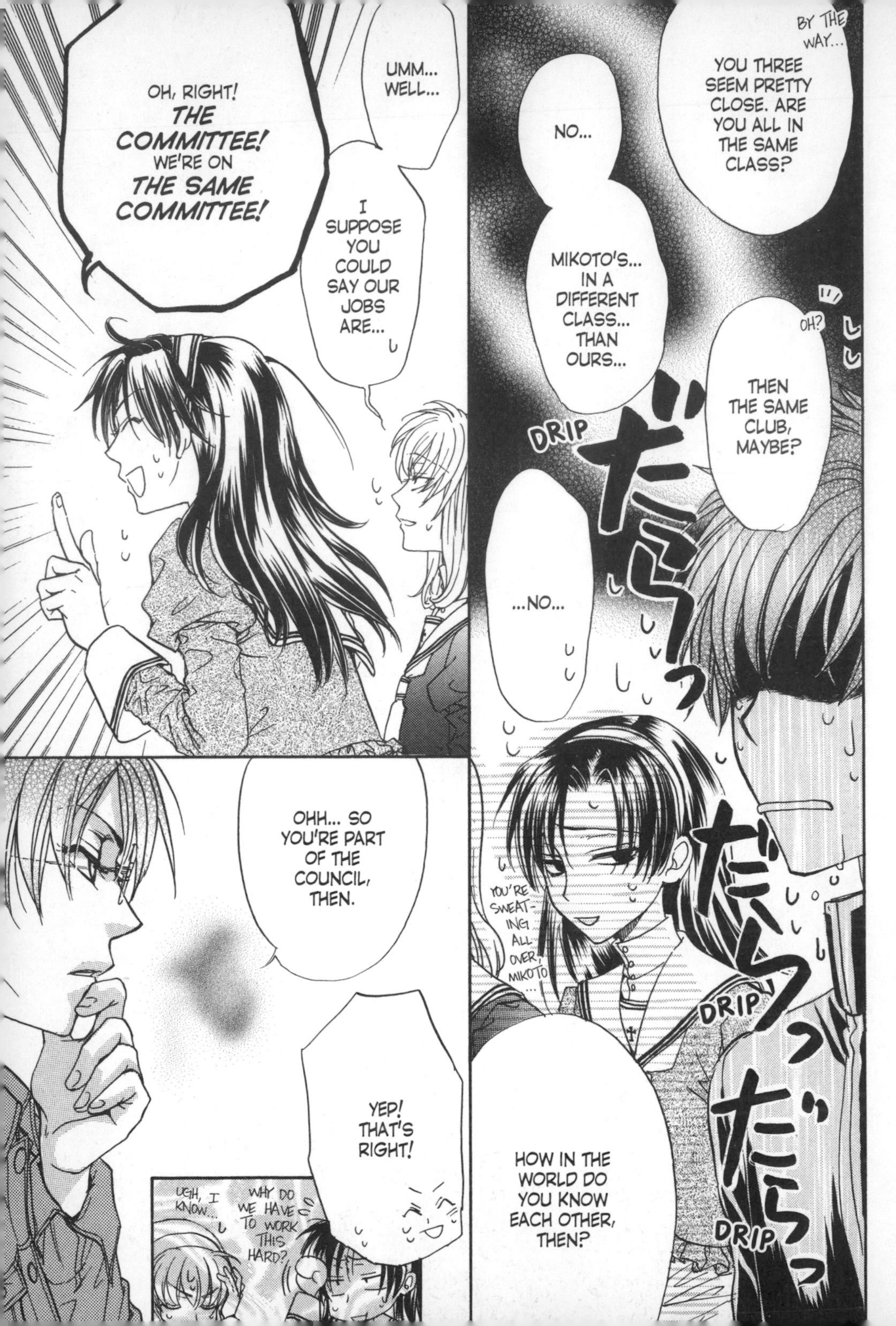
BY THE WAY...
YOU THREE SEEM PRETTY CLOSE. ARE YOU ALL IN THE SAME CLASS?
NO...
MIKOTO'S... IN A DIFFERENT CLASS... THAN OURS...
OH?
THEN THE SAME CLUB, MAYBE?
DRIP
...NO...
YOU'RE SWEATING ALL OVER, MIKOTO...
DRIP
HOW IN THE WORLD DO YOU KNOW EACH OTHER, THEN?
DRIP
UMM... WELL...
I SUPPOSE YOU COULD SAY OUR JOBS ARE...
OH, RIGHT! THE COMMITTEE! WE'RE ON THE SAME COMMITTEE!
OHH... SO YOU'RE PART OF THE COUNCIL, THEN.
YEP! THAT'S RIGHT!
WHY DO WE HAVE TO WORK THIS HARD?
UGH, I KNOW...

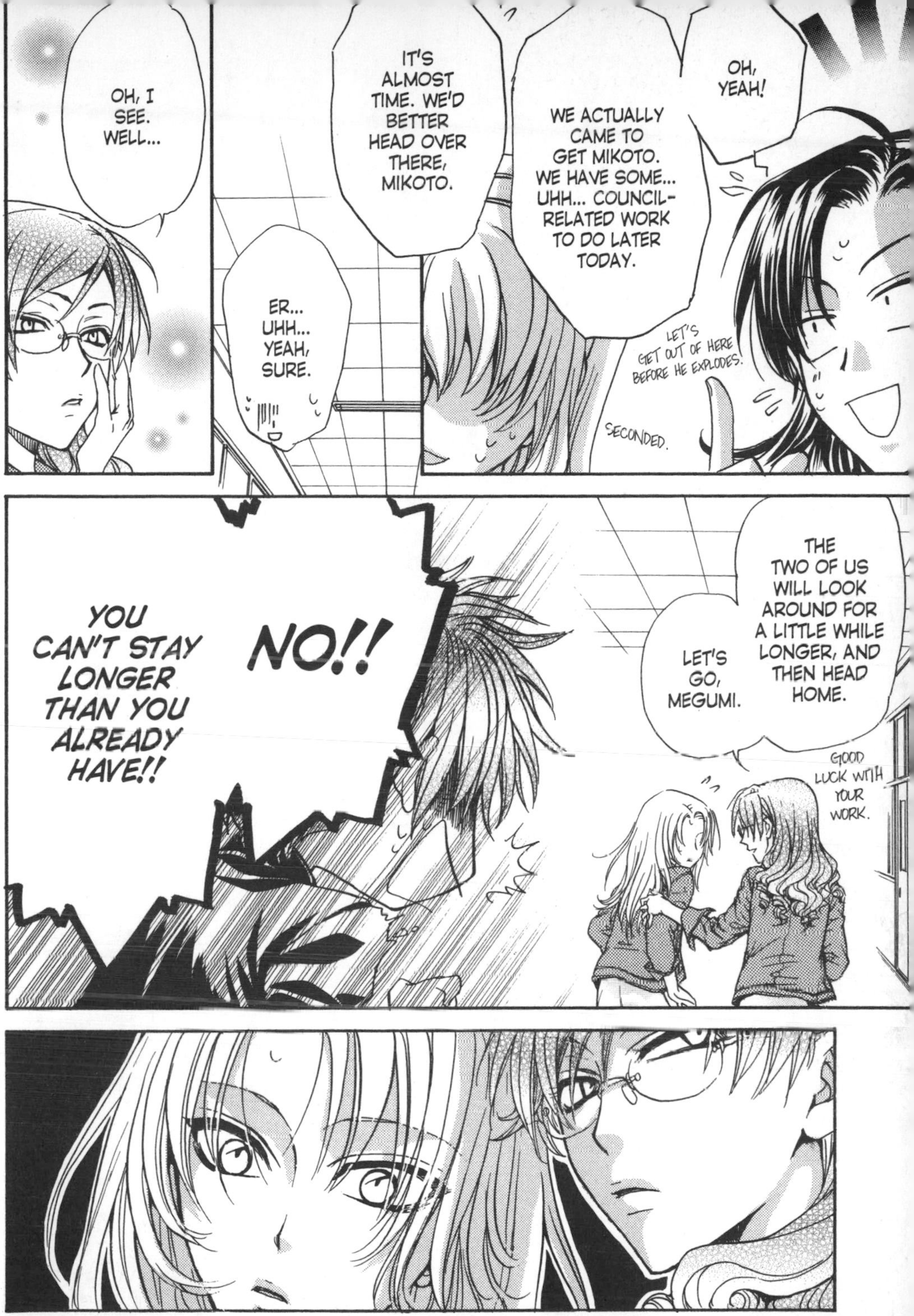
OH, YEAH!
WE ACTUALLY CAME TO GET MIKOTO. WE HAVE SOME... UHH... COUNCIL-RELATED WORK TO DO LATER TODAY.
LET'S GET OUT OF HERE BEFORE HE EXPLODES.
SECONDED.
IT'S ALMOST TIME. WE'D BETTER HEAD OVER THERE, MIKOTO.
ER... UHH... YEAH, SURE.
OH, I SEE. WELL...
THE TWO OF US WILL LOOK AROUND FOR A LITTLE WHILE LONGER, AND THEN HEAD HOME.
LET'S GO, MEGUMI.
GOOD LUCK WITH YOUR WORK.
NO!!
YOU CAN'T STAY LONGER THAN YOU ALREADY HAVE!!

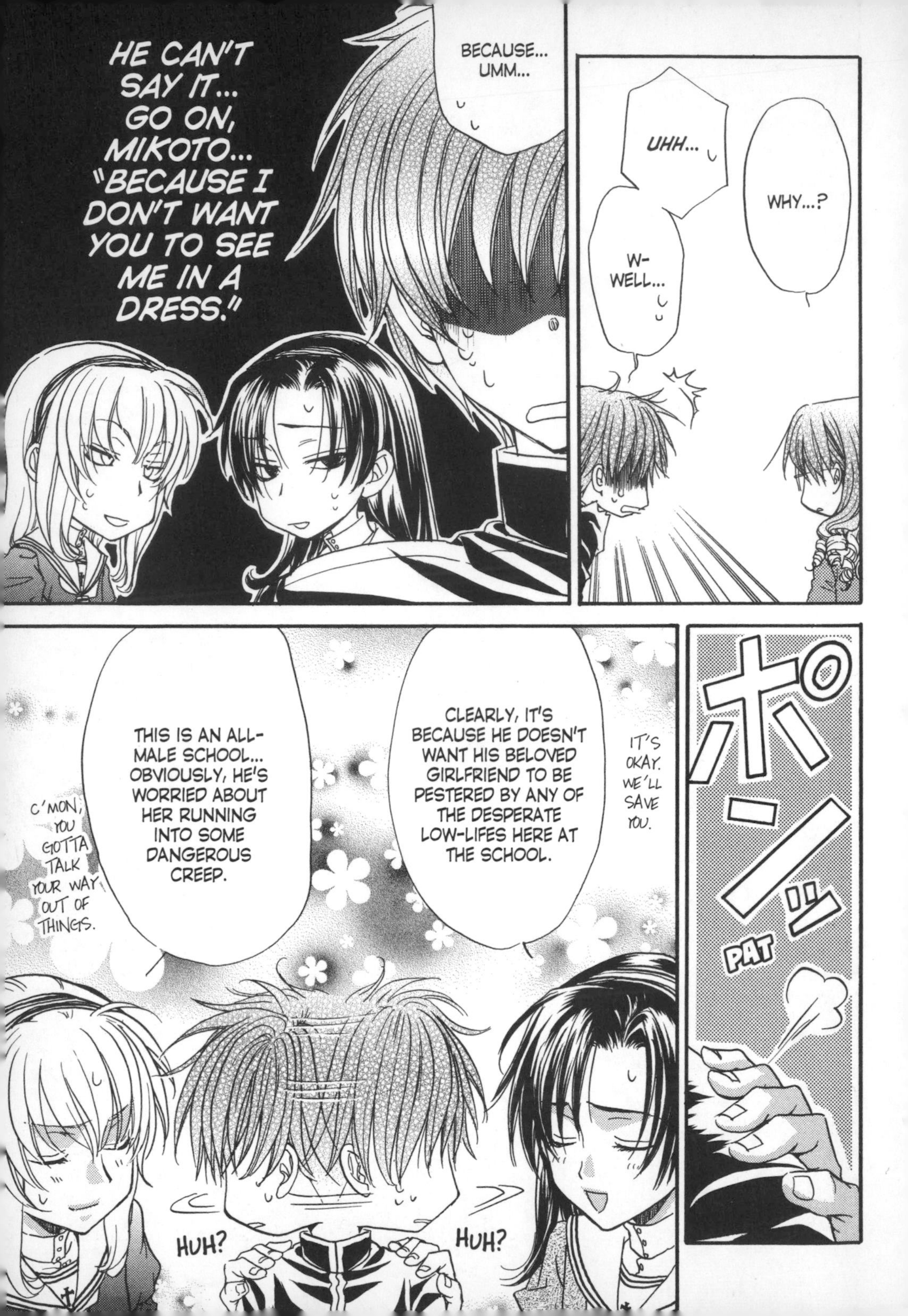
WHY...?
UHH...
W-WELL...
BECAUSE... UMM...
HE CAN'T SAY IT... GO ON, MIKOTO... "BECAUSE I DON'T WANT YOU TO SEE ME IN A DRESS."
ポーンッ
PAT
IT'S OKAY. WE'LL SAVE YOU.
CLEARLY, IT'S BECAUSE HE DOESN'T WANT HIS BELOVED GIRLFRIEND TO BE PESTERED BY ANY OF THE DESPERATE LOW-LIFES HERE AT THE SCHOOL.
THIS IS AN ALL-MALE SCHOOL... OBVIOUSLY, HE'S WORRIED ABOUT HER RUNNING INTO SOME DANGEROUS CREEP.
C'MON, YOU GOTTA TALK YOUR WAY OUT OF THINGS.
HUH?
HUH?

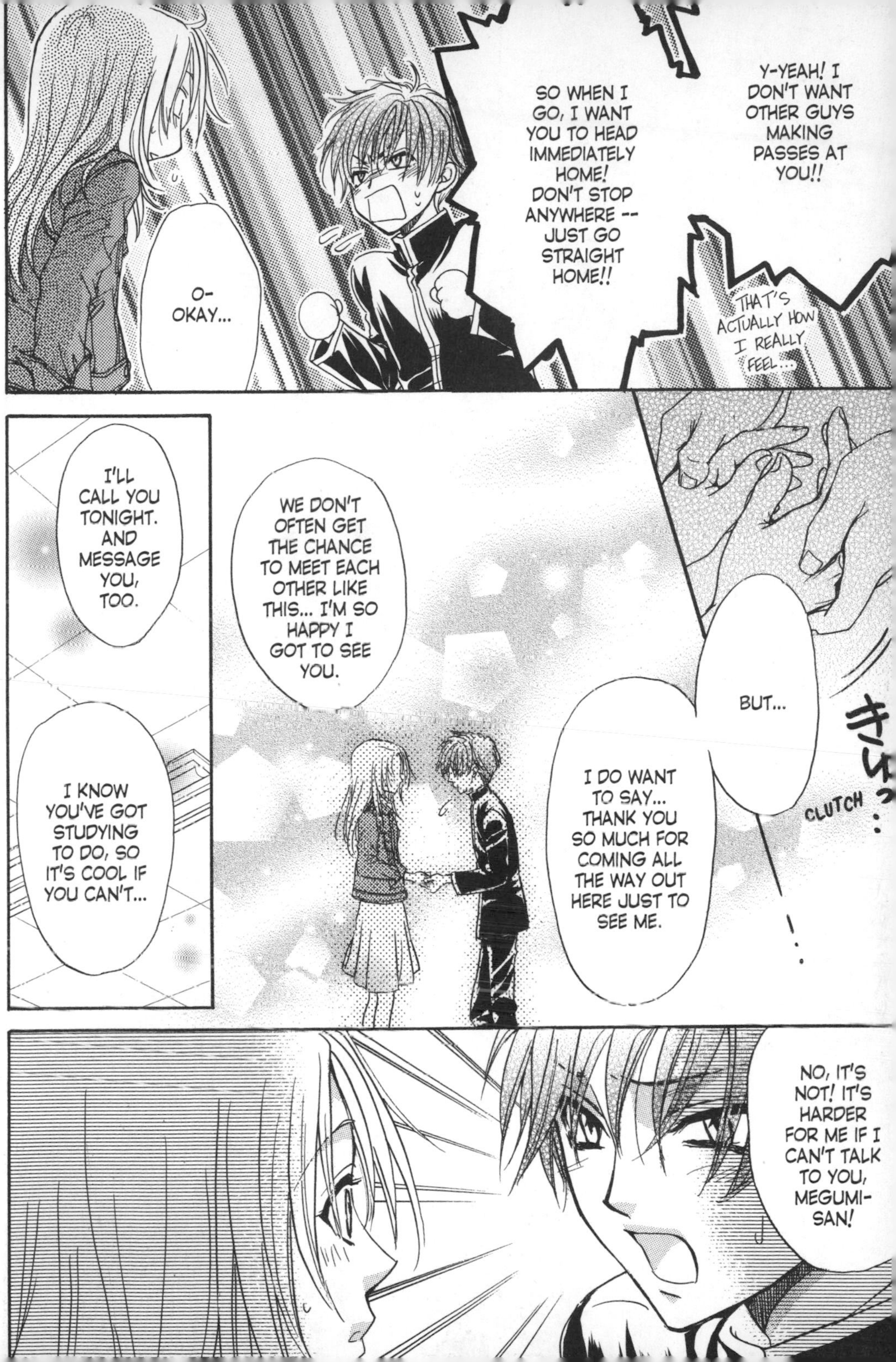
Y-YEAH! I DON'T WANT OTHER GUYS MAKING PASSES AT YOU!!
SO WHEN I GO, I WANT YOU TO HEAD IMMEDIATELY HOME! DON'T STOP ANYWHERE -- JUST GO STRAIGHT HOME!!
THAT'S ACTUALLY HOW I REALLY FEEL...
O-OKAY...
CLUTCH
BUT...
I DO WANT TO SAY... THANK YOU SO MUCH FOR COMING ALL THE WAY OUT HERE JUST TO SEE ME.
WE DON'T OFTEN GET THE CHANCE TO MEET EACH OTHER LIKE THIS... I'M SO HAPPY I GOT TO SEE YOU.
I'LL CALL YOU TONIGHT. AND MESSAGE YOU, TOO.
I KNOW YOU'VE GOT STUDYING TO DO, SO IT'S COOL IF YOU CAN'T...
NO, IT'S NOT! IT'S HARDER FOR ME IF I CAN'T TALK TO YOU, MEGUMI-SAN!

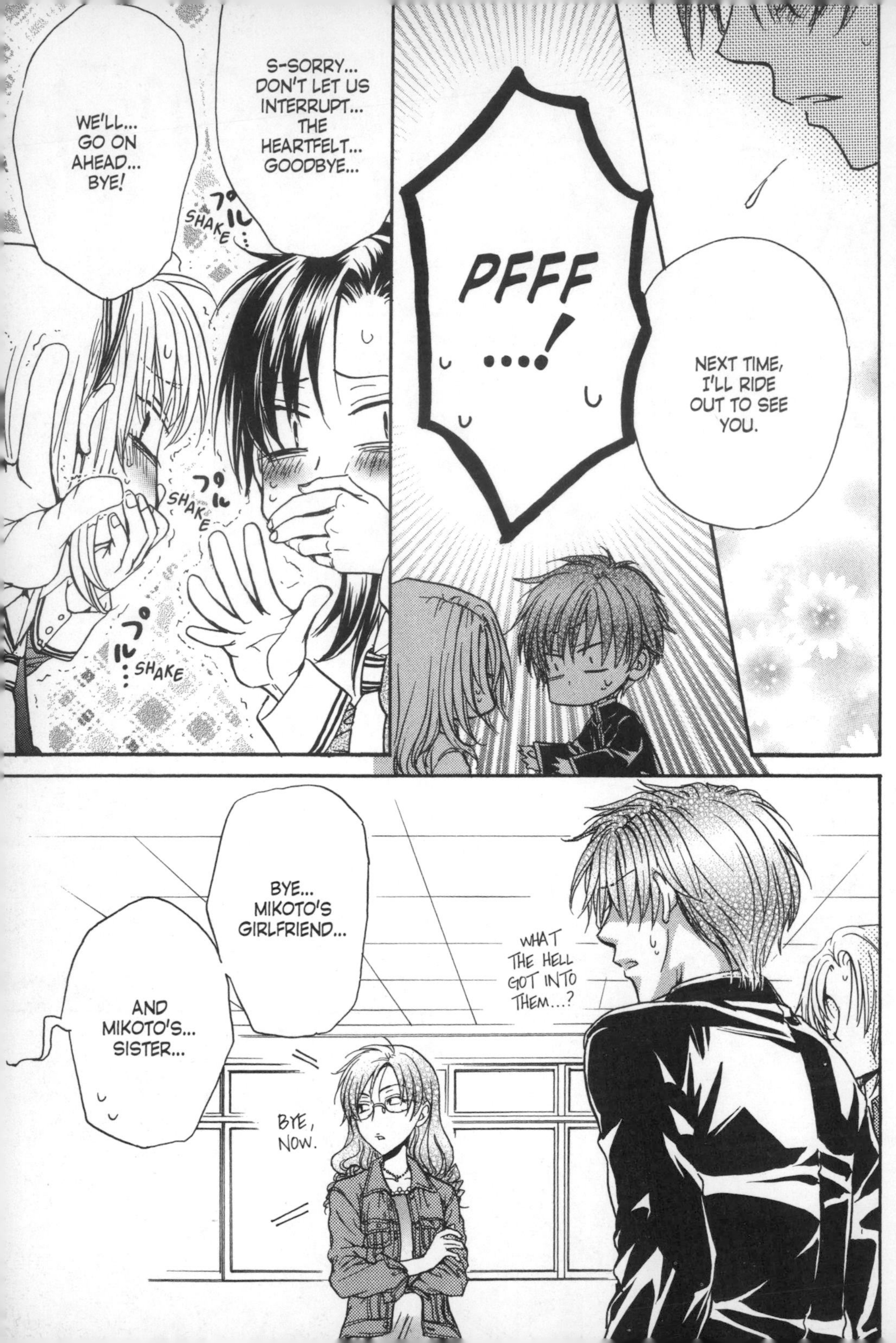
NEXT TIME, I'LL RIDE OUT TO SEE YOU.
PFFF ....!
S-SORRY... DON'T LET US INTERRUPT... THE HEARTFELT... GOODBYE...
WE'LL... GO ON AHEAD... BYE!
プル... SHAKE
プル SHAKE
プル... SHAKE
BYE... MIKOTO'S GIRLFRIEND...
AND MIKOTO'S... SISTER...
BYE, NOW.
WHAT THE HELL GOT INTO THEM...?

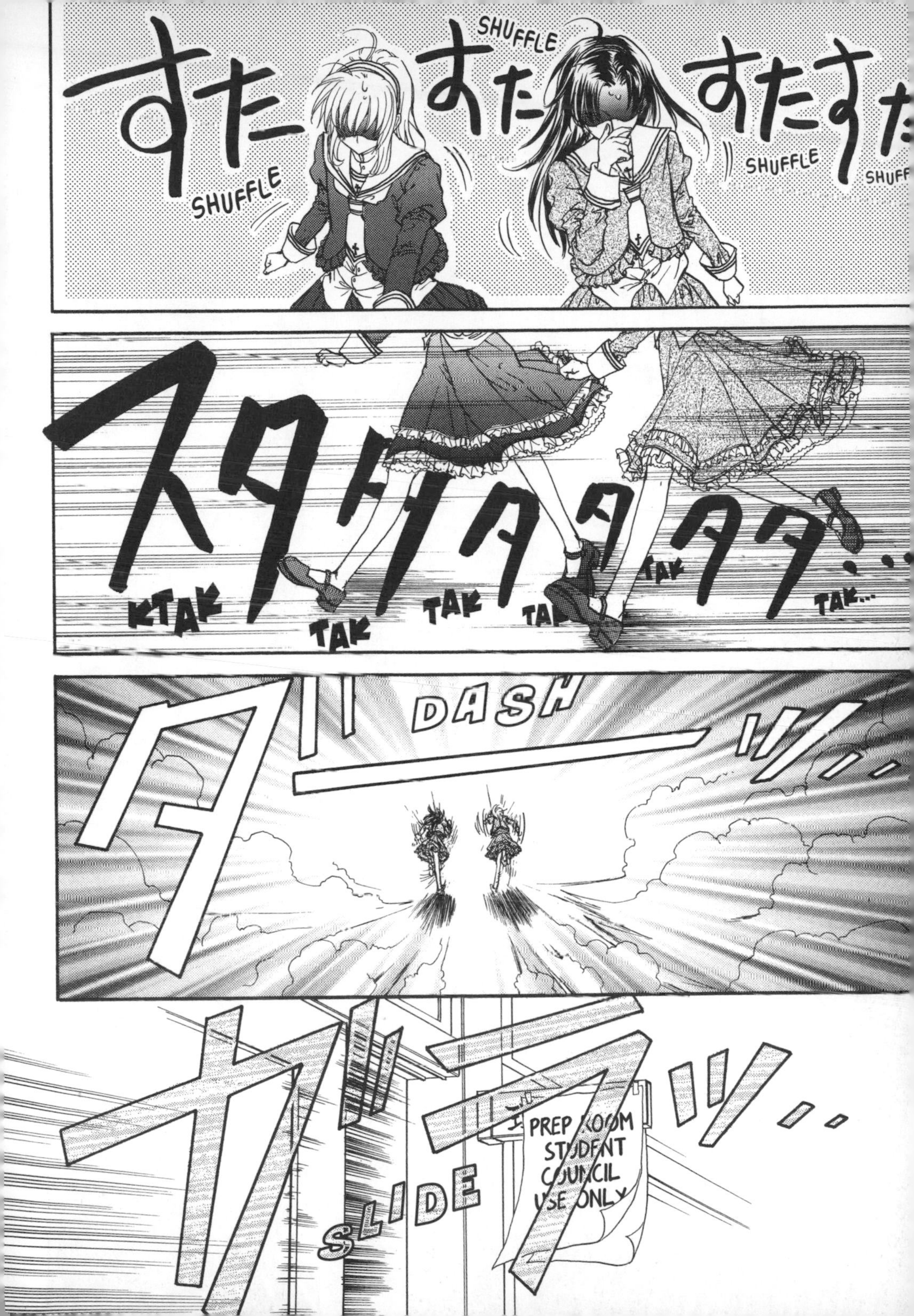
SHUFF
SHUFFLE
SHUFFLE
SHUFFLE
TAK...
TAK
TAK
TAK
TAK
KTAK
DASH
PREP ROOM
STUDENT
COUNCIL
USE ONLY
SLIDE

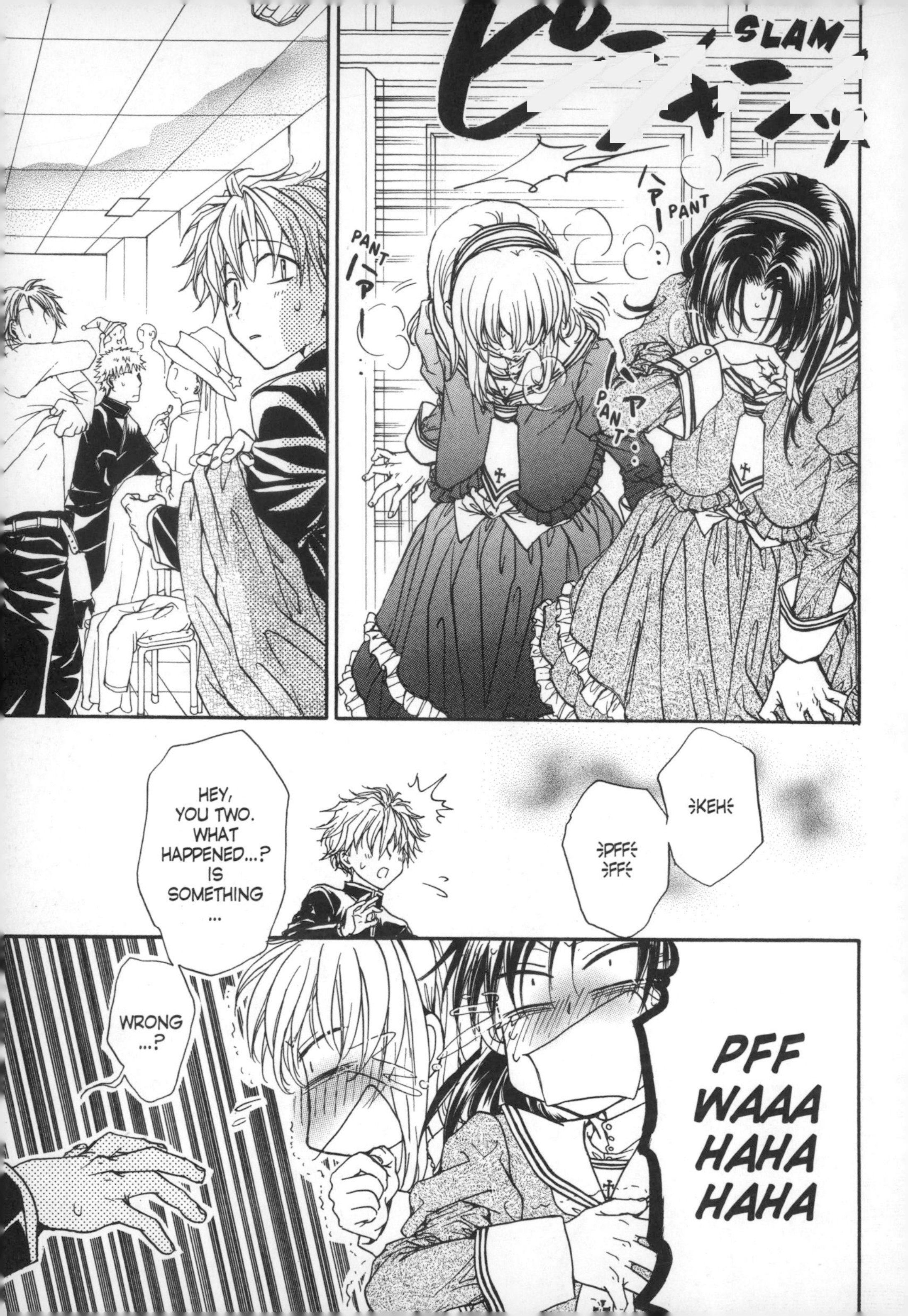
SLAM
PANT
PANT
PANT
KEH
PFF FF
HEY, YOU TWO. WHAT HAPPENED...? IS SOMETHING ...
WRONG ...?
PFF WAAA HAHA HAHA

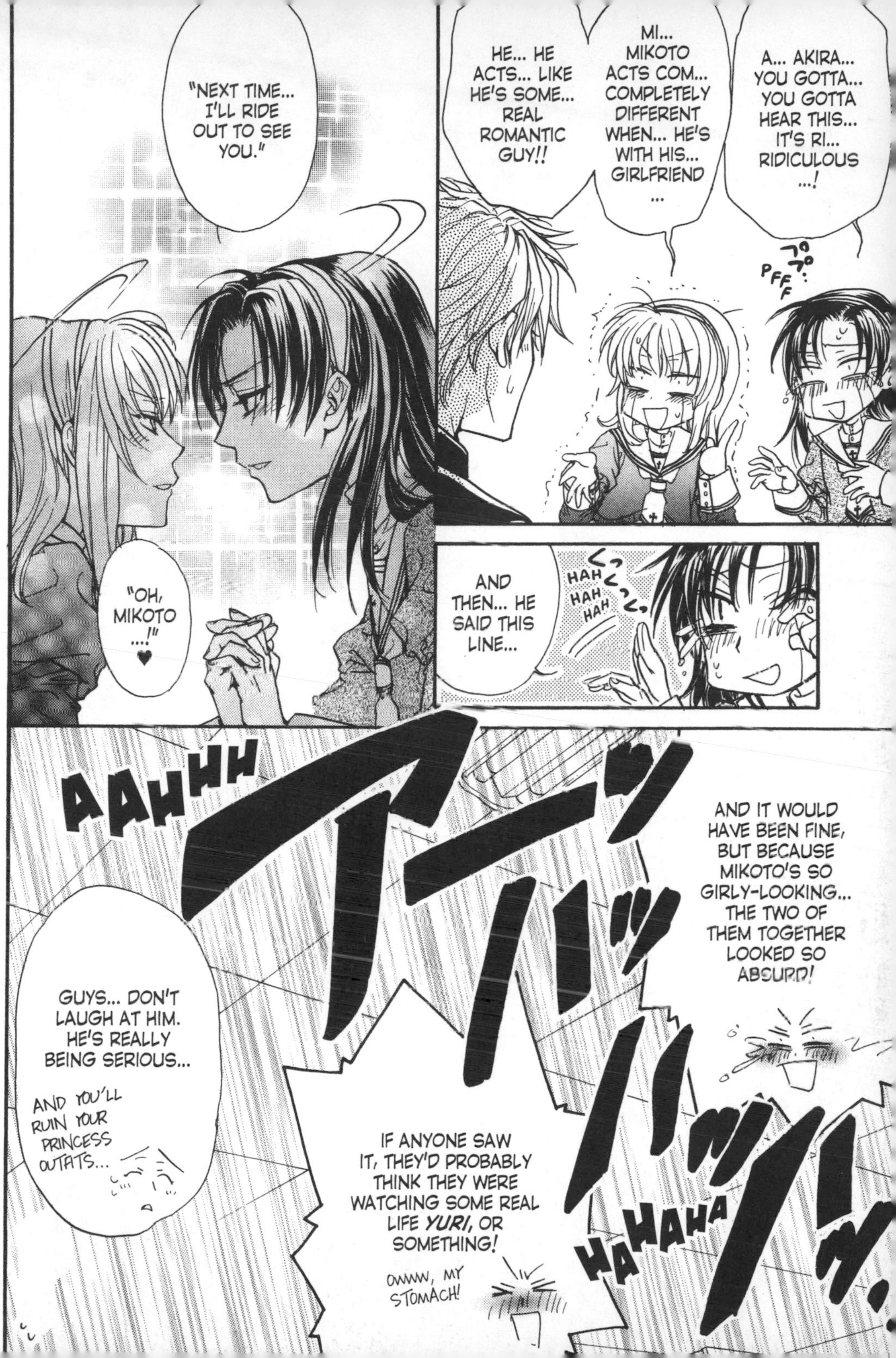
A... AKIRA... YOU GOTTA... YOU GOTTA HEAR THIS... IT'S RI... RIDICULOUS ...!
MI... MIKOTO ACTS COM... COMPLETELY DIFFERENT WHEN... HE'S WITH HIS... GIRLFRIEND ...
HE... HE ACTS... LIKE HE'S SOME... REAL ROMANTIC GUY!!
PFFF
HAH HAH HAH
AND THEN... HE SAID THIS LINE...
"NEXT TIME... I'LL RIDE OUT TO SEE YOU."
"OH, MIKOTO ...!" ♥
AND IT WOULD HAVE BEEN FINE, BUT BECAUSE MIKOTO'S SO GIRLY-LOOKING... THE TWO OF THEM TOGETHER LOOKED SO ABSURD!
AAHHH
HAHAHAHA
IF ANYONE SAW IT, THEY'D PROBABLY THINK THEY WERE WATCHING SOME REAL LIFE *YURI*, OR SOMETHING!
OWWW, MY STOMACH!
GUYS... DON'T LAUGH AT HIM. HE'S REALLY BEING SERIOUS...
AND YOU'LL RUIN YOUR PRINCESS OUTFITS...

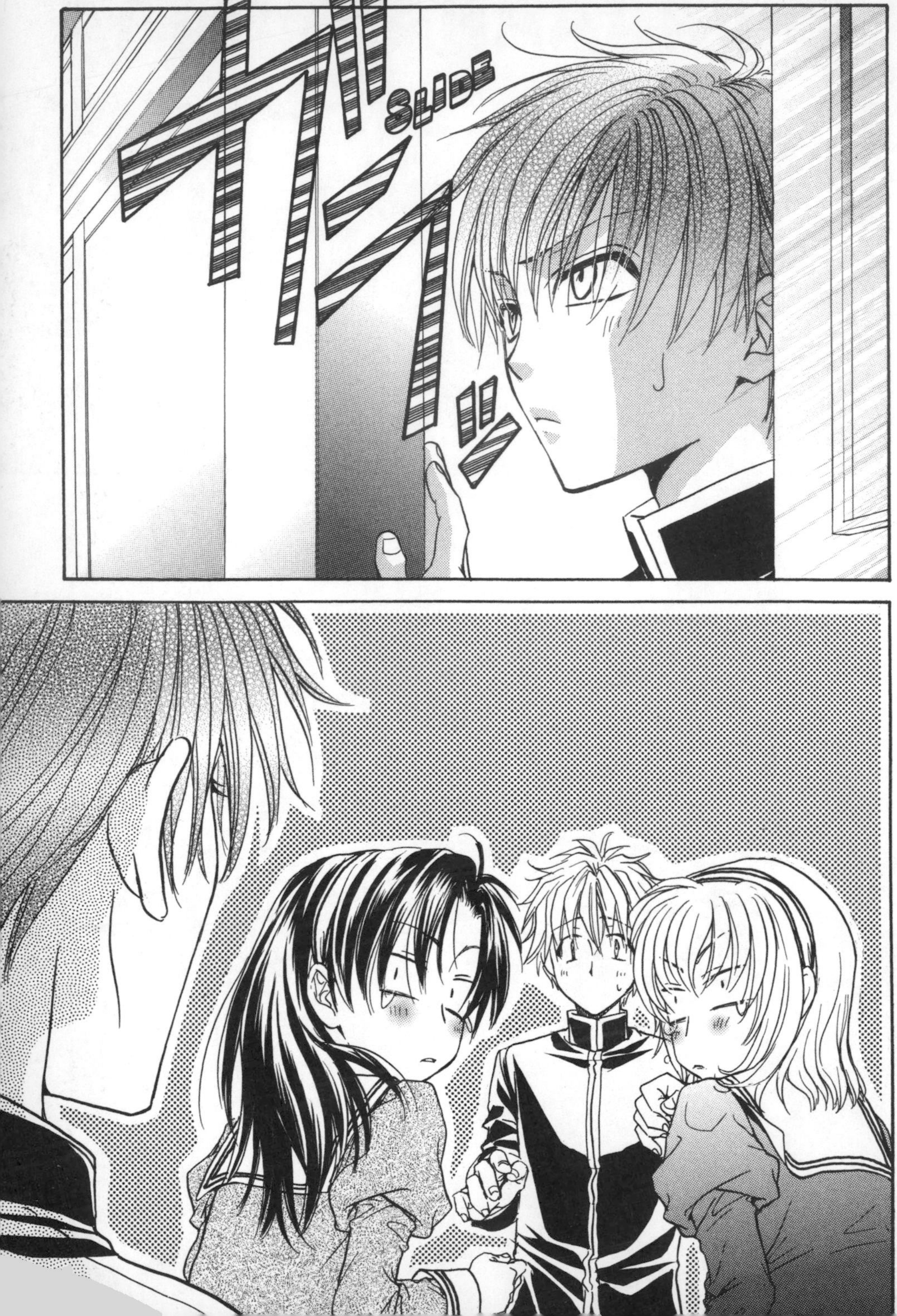
SLIDE

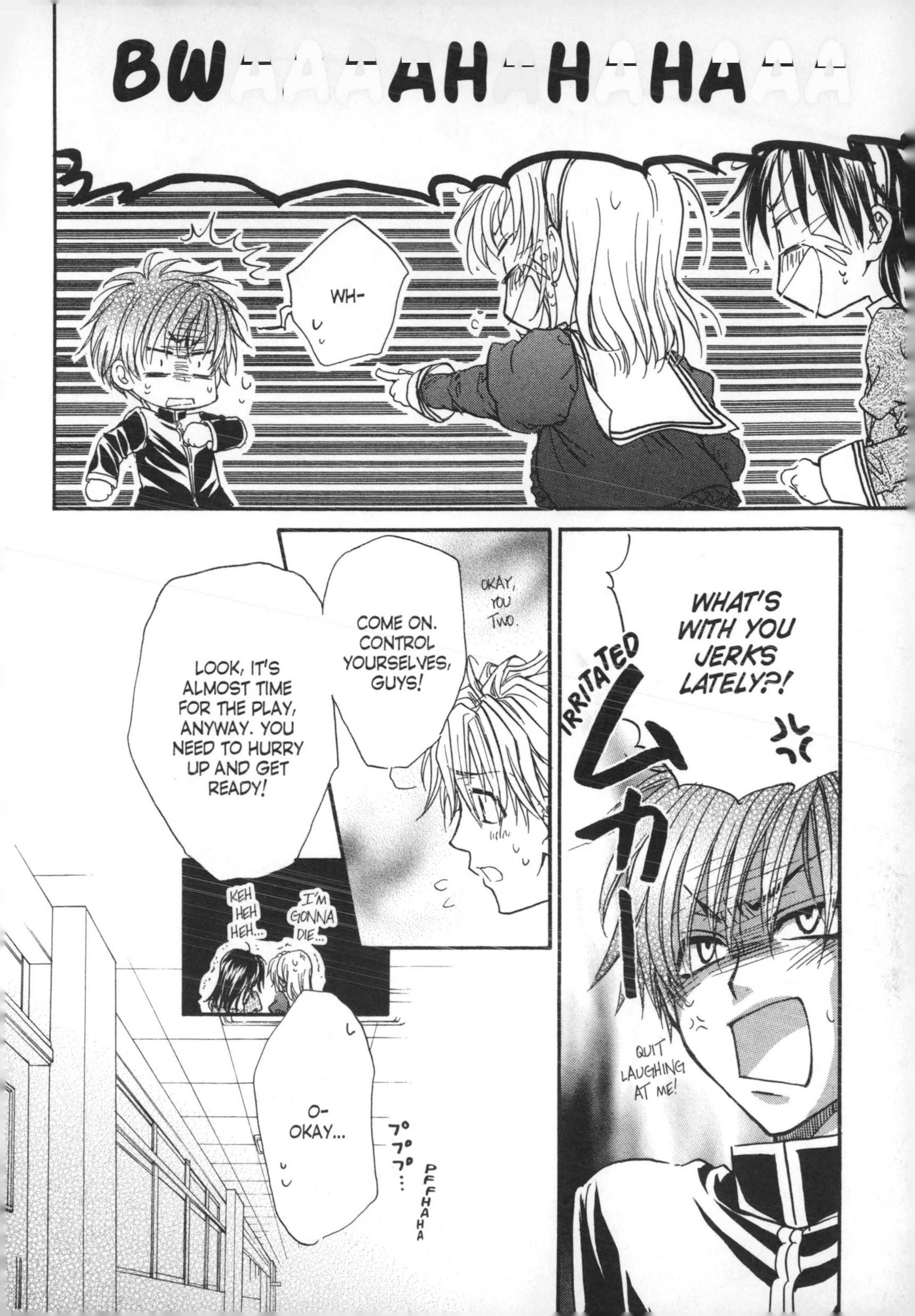
BWAAAAHAHAHAAA
WH-
IRRITATED
WHAT'S WITH YOU JERKS LATELY?!
QUIT LAUGHING AT ME!
OKAY, YOU TWO.
COME ON. CONTROL YOURSELVES, GUYS!
LOOK, IT'S ALMOST TIME FOR THE PLAY, ANYWAY. YOU NEED TO HURRY UP AND GET READY!
I'M GONNA DIE...
KEH HEH HEH...
O-OKAY...
PFFHAHA

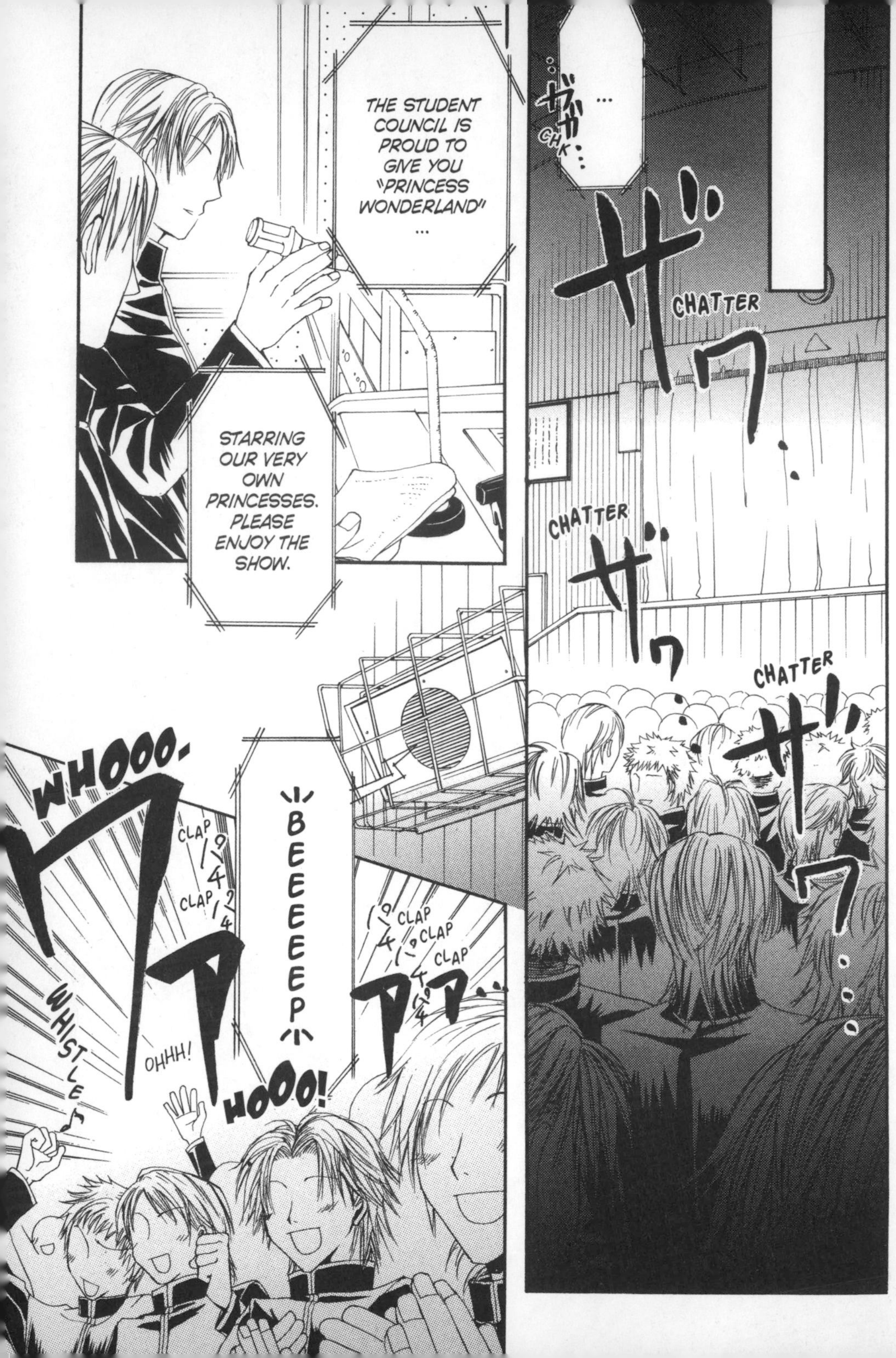
...
CHK...
CHATTER
CHATTER
CHATTER
THE STUDENT COUNCIL IS PROUD TO GIVE YOU "PRINCESS WONDERLAND" ...
STARRING OUR VERY OWN PRINCESSES. PLEASE ENJOY THE SHOW.
BEEEEEEEP
CLAP CLAP CLAP
WHOOO-
CLAP
CLAP
WHISTLE
OHHH!
HOOO!

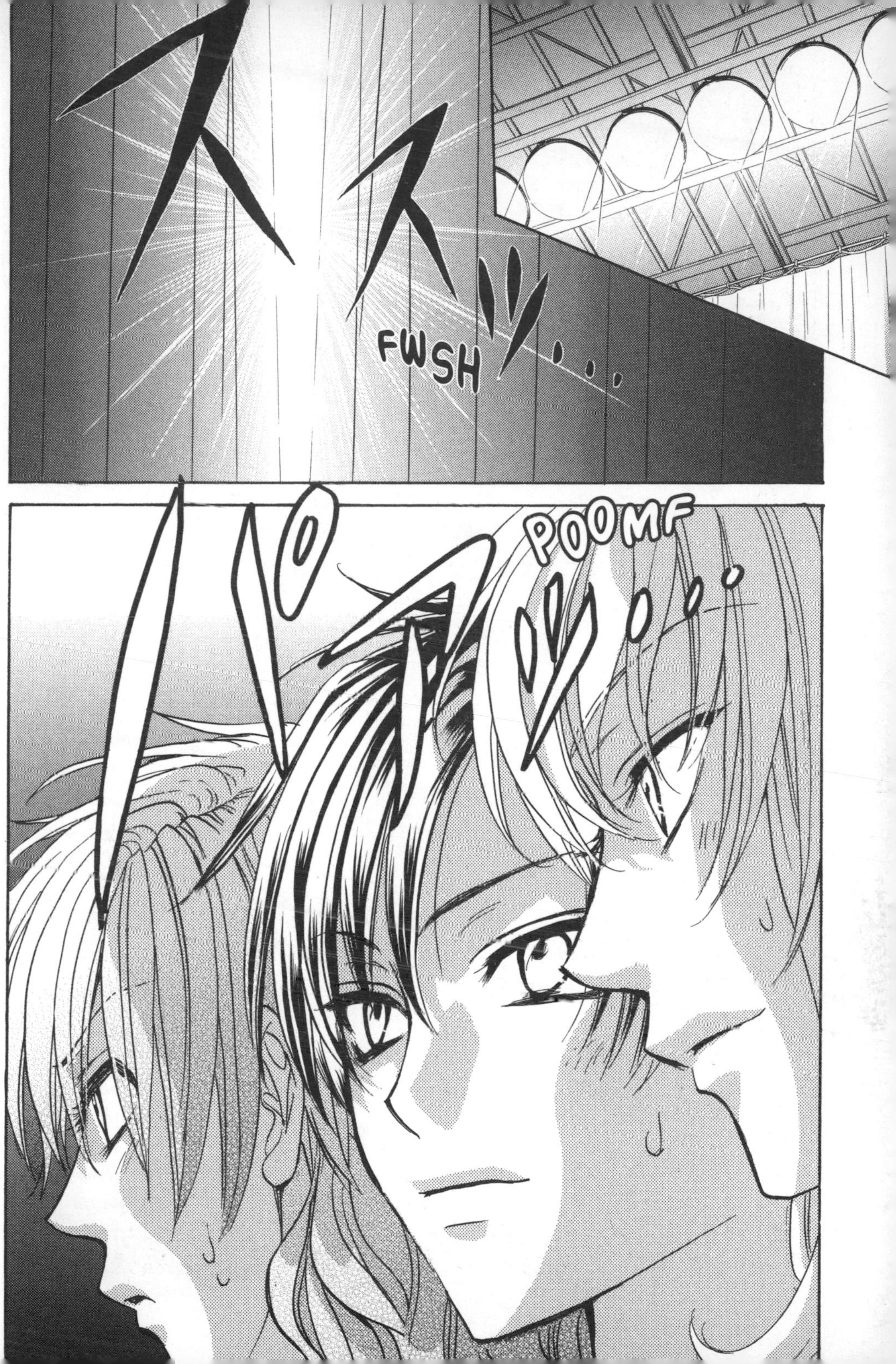
ススッ…
FWSH
パフッ…
POOMF

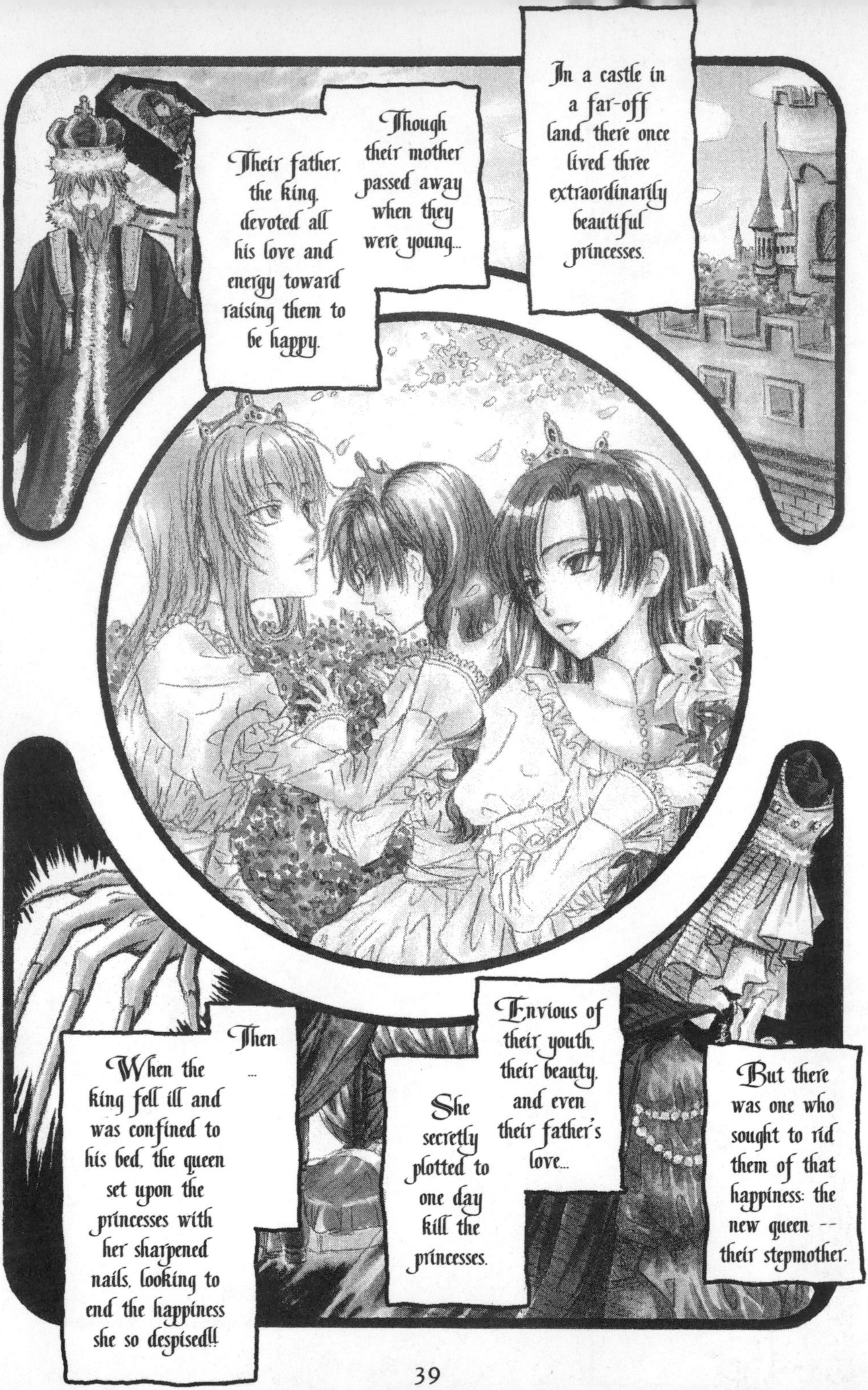
In a castle in a far-off land, there once lived three extraordinarily beautiful princesses.
Though their mother passed away when they were young...
Their father, the king, devoted all his love and energy toward raising them to be happy.
But there was one who sought to rid them of that happiness: the new queen -- their stepmother.
Envious of their youth, their beauty, and even their father's love...
She secretly plotted to one day kill the princesses.
Then ...
When the king fell ill and was confined to his bed, the queen set upon the princesses with her sharpened nails, looking to end the happiness she so despised!!

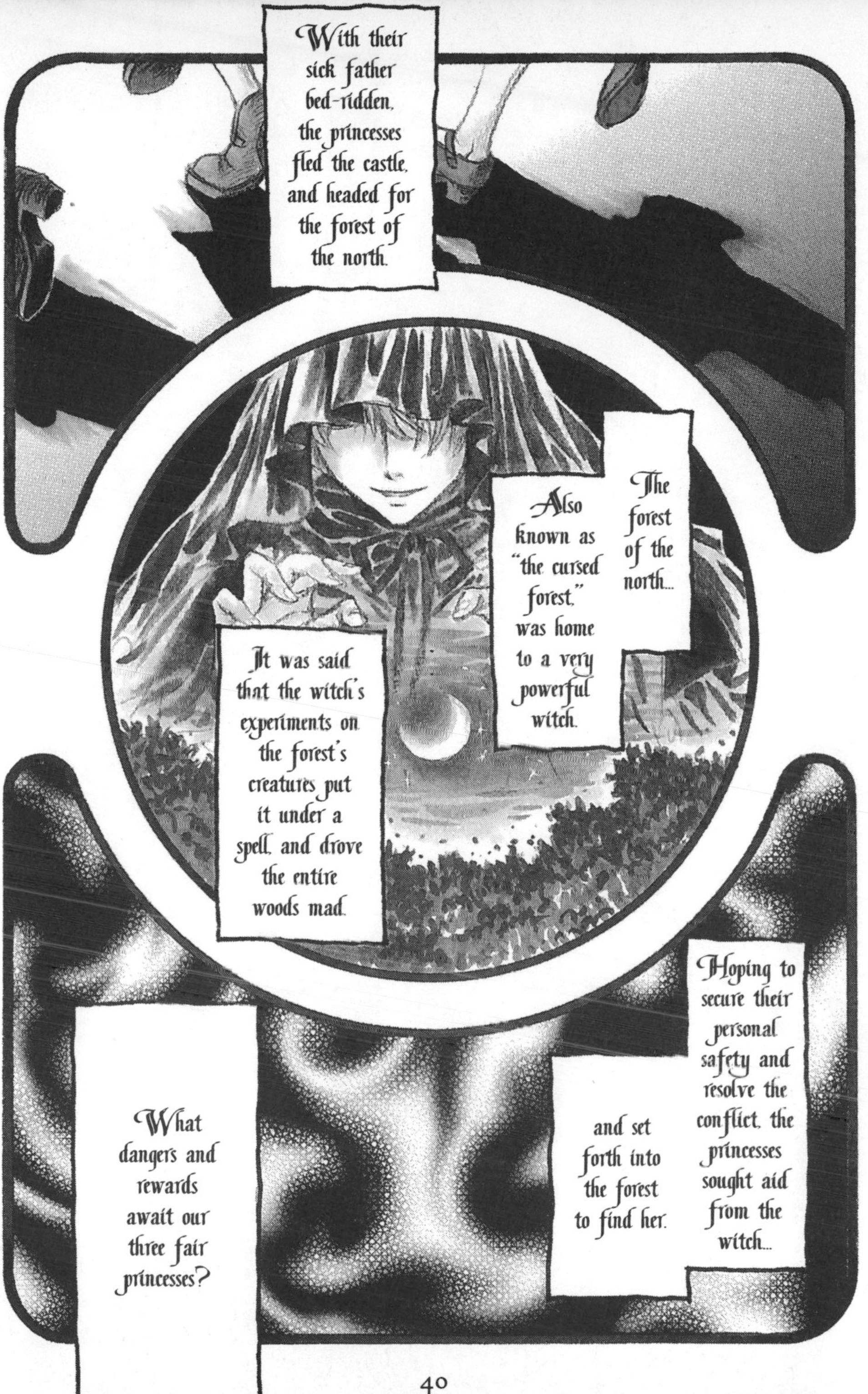
With their sick father bed-ridden, the princesses fled the castle, and headed for the forest of the north.
The forest of the north...
Also known as "the cursed forest," was home to a very powerful witch.
It was said that the witch's experiments on the forest's creatures put it under a spell, and drove the entire woods mad.
Hoping to secure their personal safety and resolve the conflict, the princesses sought aid from the witch...
and set forth into the forest to find her.
What dangers and rewards await our three fair princesses?

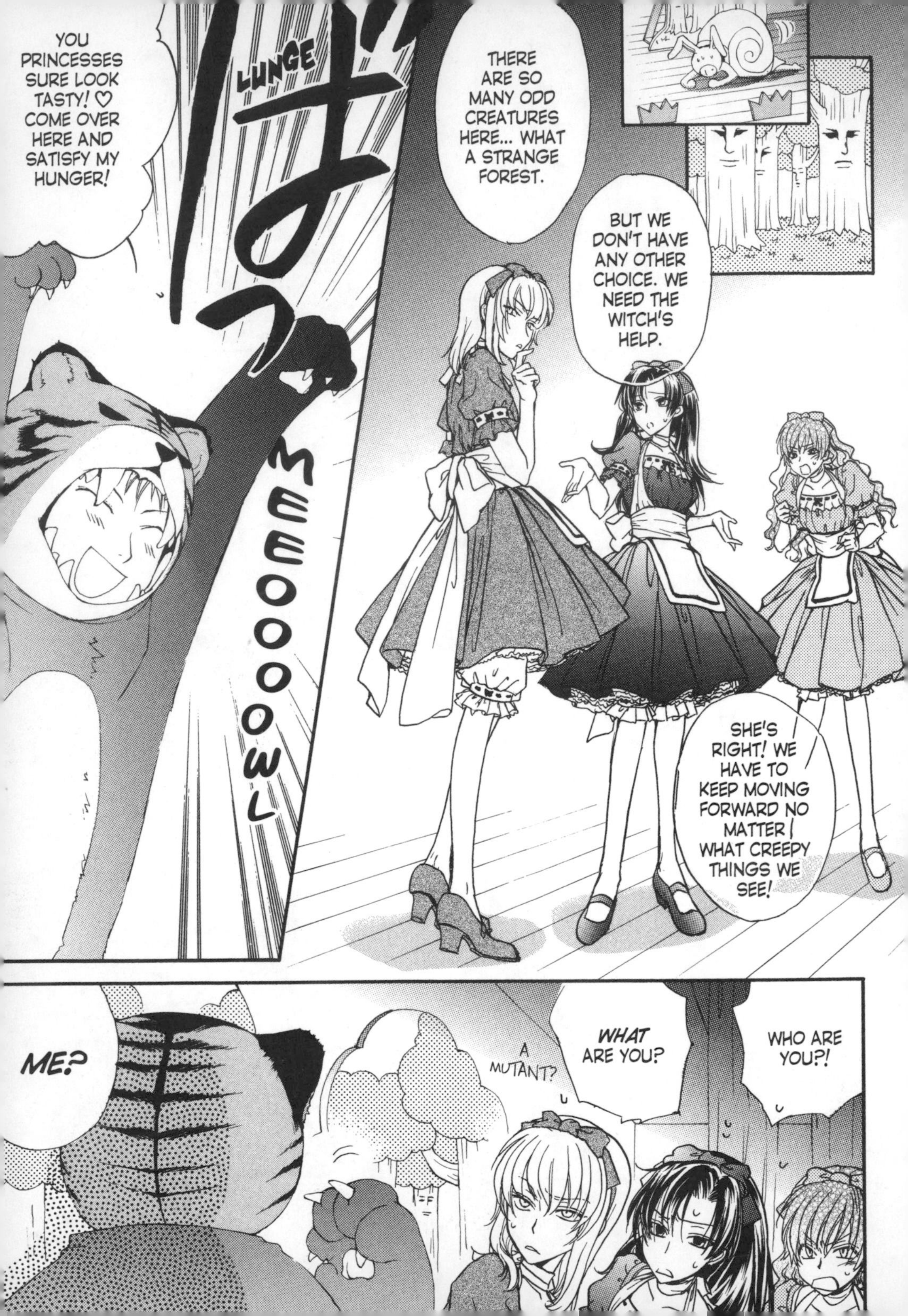
THERE ARE SO MANY ODD CREATURES HERE... WHAT A STRANGE FOREST.
BUT WE DON'T HAVE ANY OTHER CHOICE. WE NEED THE WITCH'S HELP.
SHE'S RIGHT! WE HAVE TO KEEP MOVING FORWARD NO MATTER WHAT CREEPY THINGS WE SEE!
ばっ
LUNGE
YOU PRINCESSES SURE LOOK TASTY! ♡ COME OVER HERE AND SATISFY MY HUNGER!
MEEOOOOOOWL
WHO ARE YOU?!
WHAT ARE YOU?
A MUTANT?
ME?

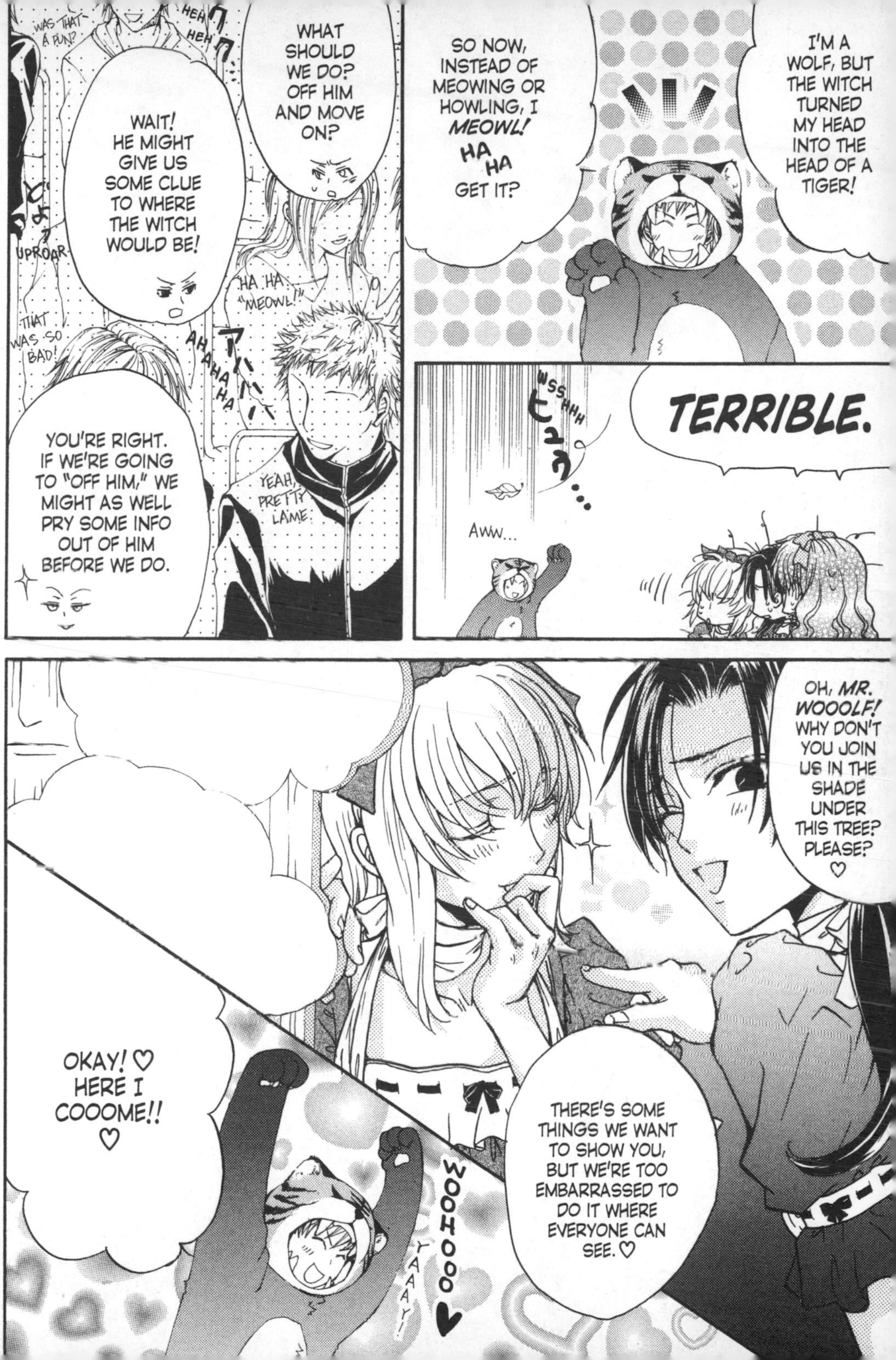

I'M A WOLF, BUT THE WITCH TURNED MY HEAD INTO THE HEAD OF A TIGER!
SO NOW, INSTEAD OF MEOWING OR HOWLING, I *MEOWL!*
HA HA
GET IT?
TERRIBLE.
WSSHHH
AWW...
WHAT SHOULD WE DO? OFF HIM AND MOVE ON?
HEH HEH
WAS THAT A PUN?
WAIT! HE MIGHT GIVE US SOME CLUE TO WHERE THE WITCH WOULD BE!
UPROAR
HA HA "MEOWL!"
THAT WAS SO BAD!
AHAHAHA
YOU'RE RIGHT. IF WE'RE GOING TO "OFF HIM," WE MIGHT AS WELL PRY SOME INFO OUT OF HIM BEFORE WE DO.
YEAH, PRETTY LAME
OH, *MR. WOOOLF!* WHY DON'T YOU JOIN US IN THE SHADE UNDER THIS TREE? PLEASE? ♡
THERE'S SOME THINGS WE WANT TO SHOW YOU, BUT WE'RE TOO EMBARRASSED TO DO IT WHERE EVERYONE CAN SEE. ♡
OKAY! ♡ HERE I COOOME!! ♡
WOOHOOO♥
YAAAY!

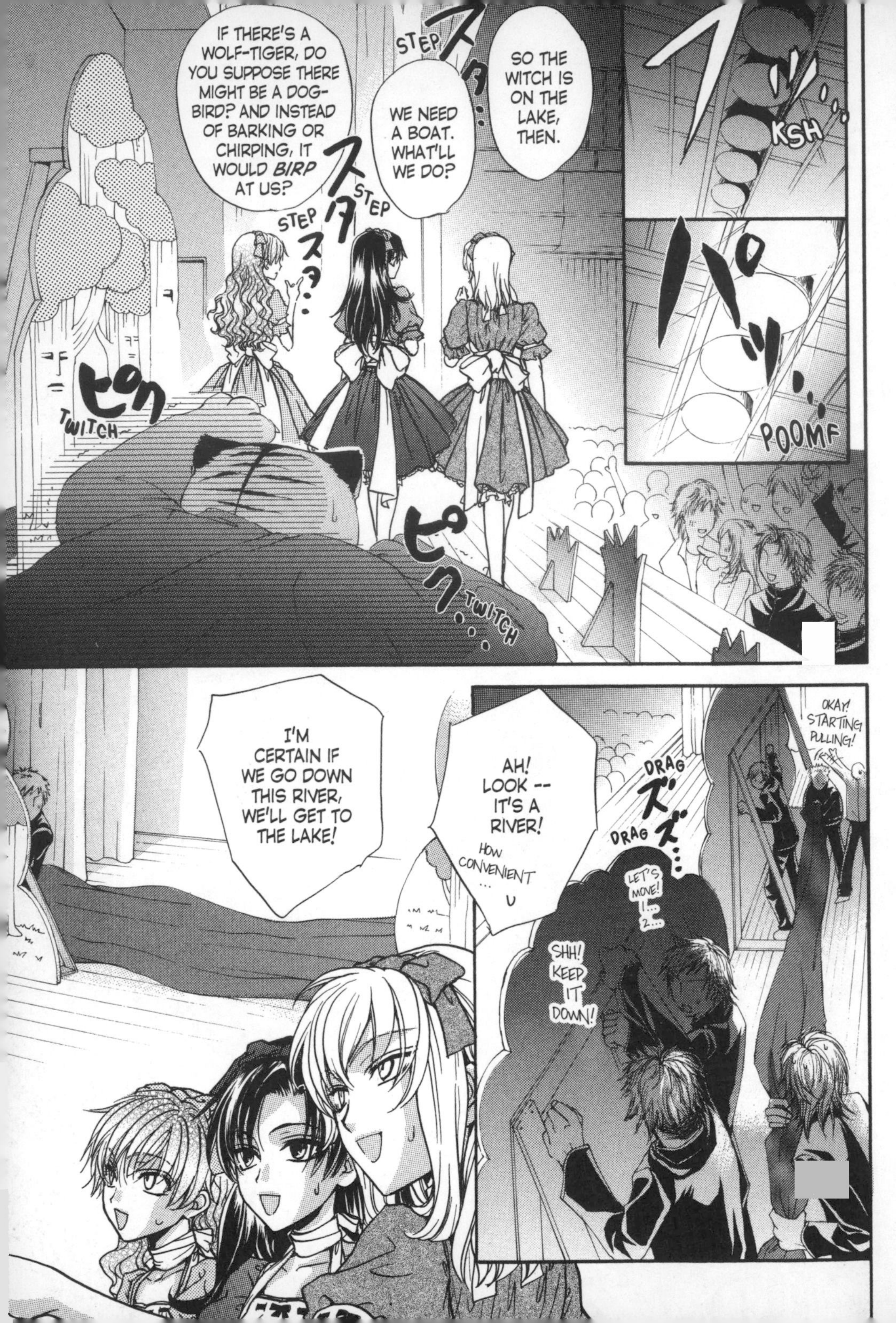
KSH
POOMF
SO THE WITCH IS ON THE LAKE, THEN.
STEP
WE NEED A BOAT. WHAT'LL WE DO?
IF THERE'S A WOLF-TIGER, DO YOU SUPPOSE THERE MIGHT BE A DOG-BIRD? AND INSTEAD OF BARKING OR CHIRPING, IT WOULD *BIRP* AT US?
STEP
STEP
TWITCH
TWITCH
OKAY! STARTING PULLING!
DRAG
DRAG
LET'S MOVE! 1... 2...
SHH! KEEP IT DOWN!
AH! LOOK -- IT'S A RIVER!
HOW CONVENIENT...
I'M CERTAIN IF WE GO DOWN THIS RIVER, WE'LL GET TO THE LAKE!

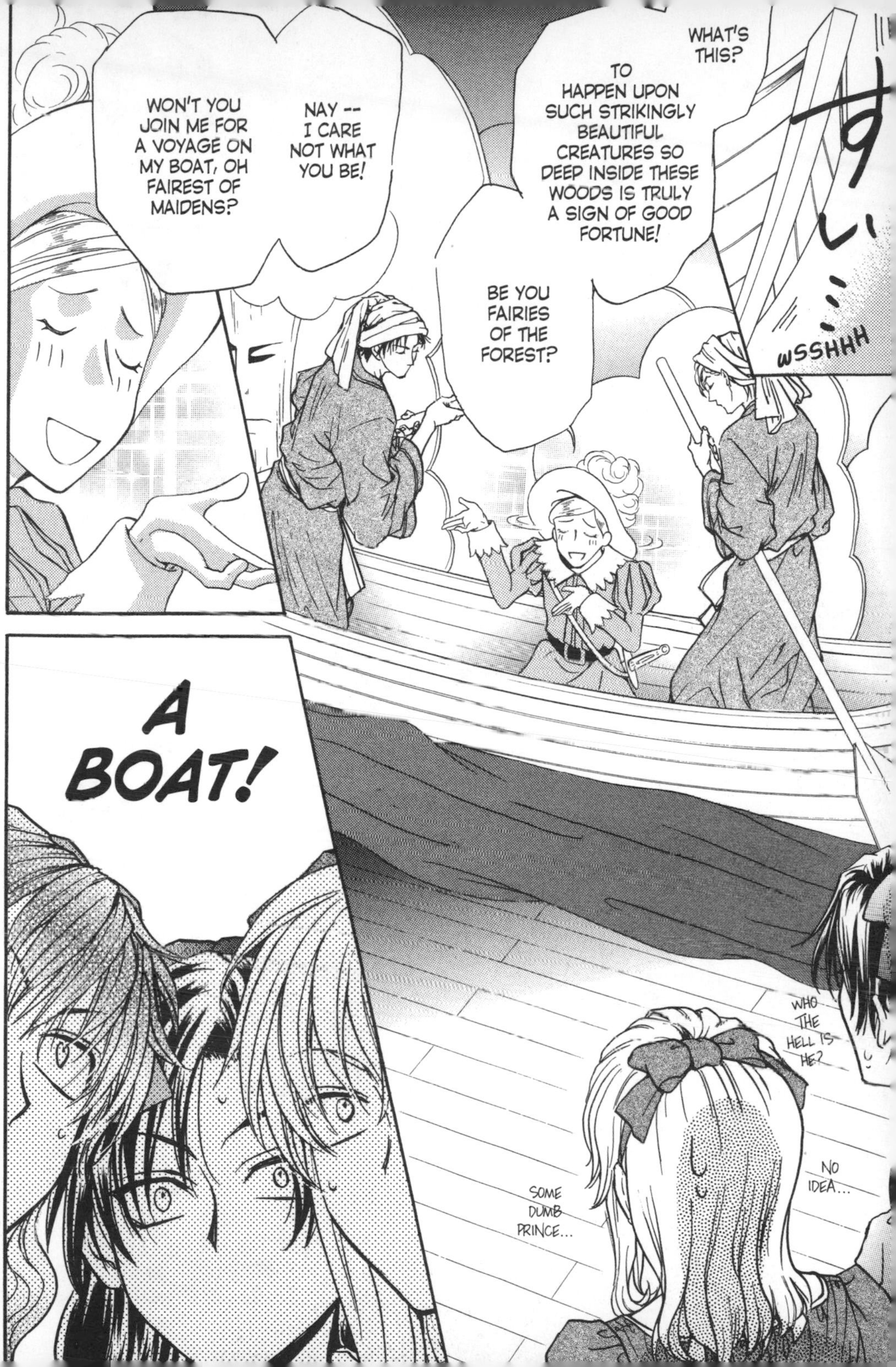
すい…
WSSHHH
WHAT'S THIS?
TO HAPPEN UPON SUCH STRIKINGLY BEAUTIFUL CREATURES SO DEEP INSIDE THESE WOODS IS TRULY A SIGN OF GOOD FORTUNE!
BE YOU FAIRIES OF THE FOREST?
NAY -- I CARE NOT WHAT YOU BE!
WON'T YOU JOIN ME FOR A VOYAGE ON MY BOAT, OH FAIREST OF MAIDENS?
WHO THE HELL IS HE?
NO IDEA...
SOME DUMB PRINCE...
A BOAT!

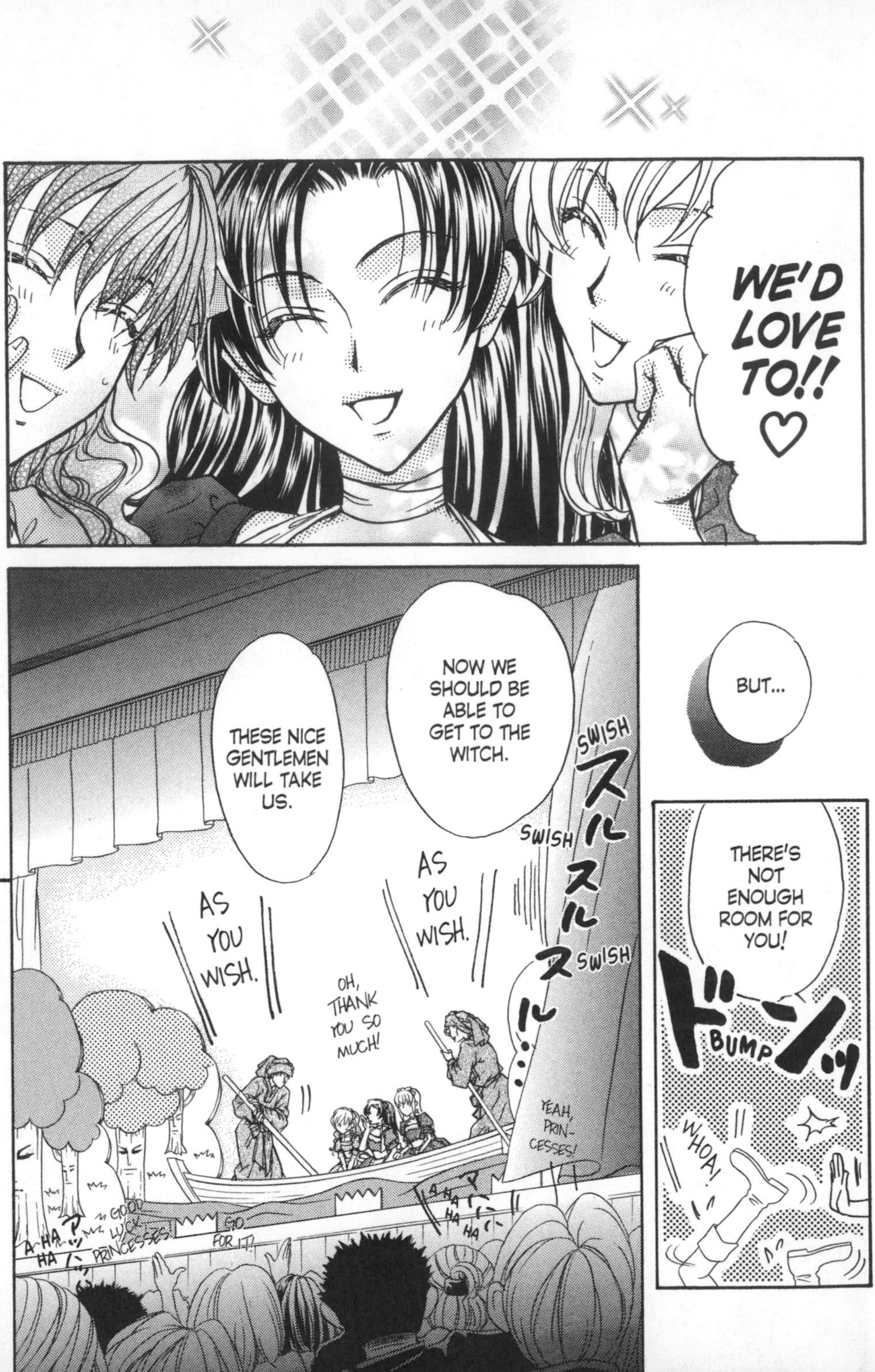
WE'D LOVE TO!! ♥
BUT...
THERE'S NOT ENOUGH ROOM FOR YOU!
BUMP
WHOA!
NOW WE SHOULD BE ABLE TO GET TO THE WITCH.
THESE NICE GENTLEMEN WILL TAKE US.
SWISH
SWISH
SWISH
AS YOU WISH.
AS YOU WISH.
OH, THANK YOU SO MUCH!
YEAH, PRINCESSES!
HA HA HA HA
GO FOR IT!
GOOD LUCK PRINCESSES!
A HA HA

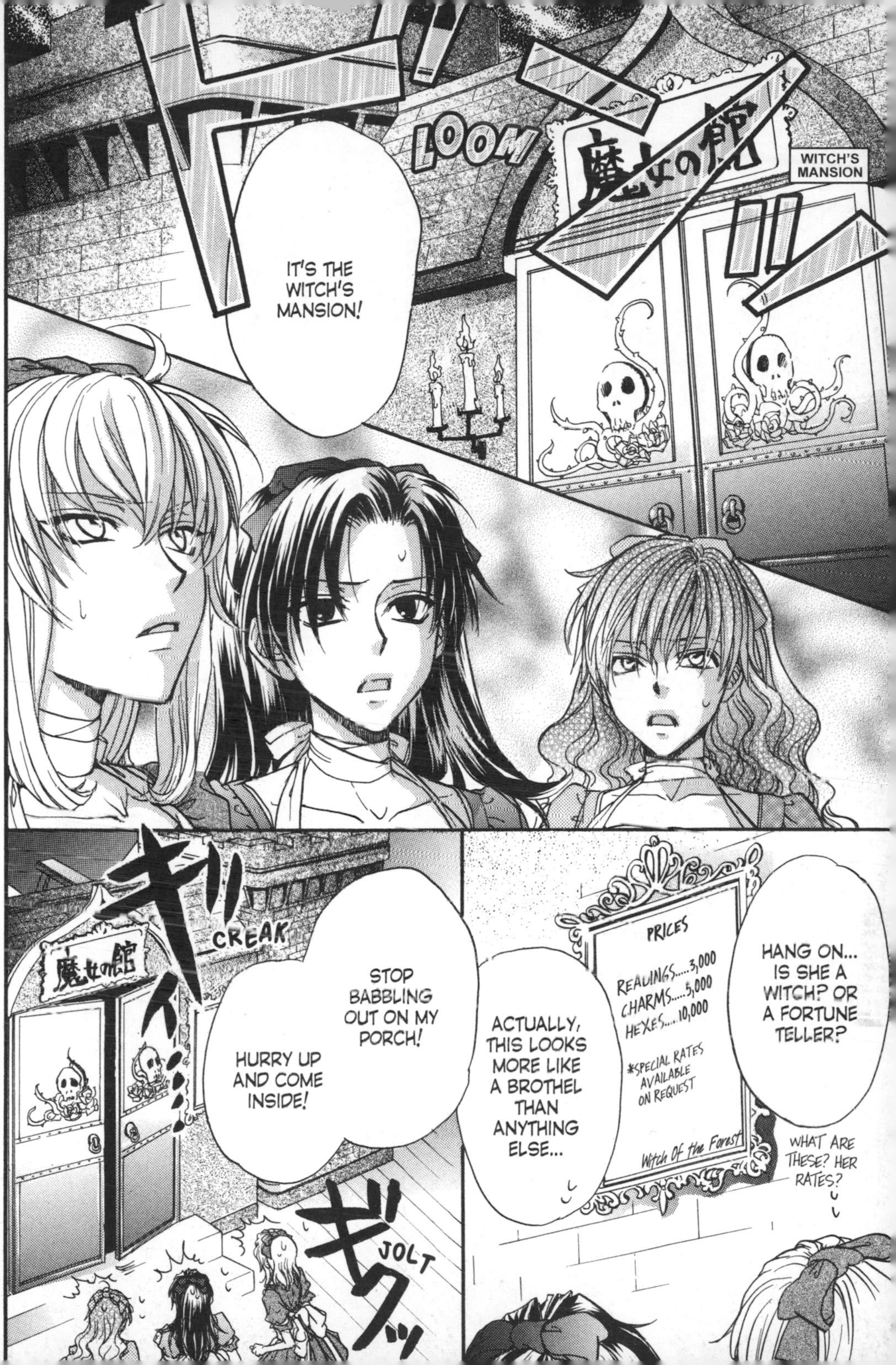
LOOM
魔女の館
WITCH'S MANSION
IT'S THE WITCH'S MANSION!
HANG ON... IS SHE A WITCH? OR A FORTUNE TELLER?
PRICES
READINGS.....3,000
CHARMS.....5,000
HEXES.....10,000
*SPECIAL RATES AVAILABLE ON REQUEST
Witch Of the Forest
WHAT ARE THESE? HER RATES?
ACTUALLY, THIS LOOKS MORE LIKE A BROTHEL THAN ANYTHING ELSE...
STOP BABBLING OUT ON MY PORCH!
HURRY UP AND COME INSIDE!
魔女の館
CREAK
JOLT

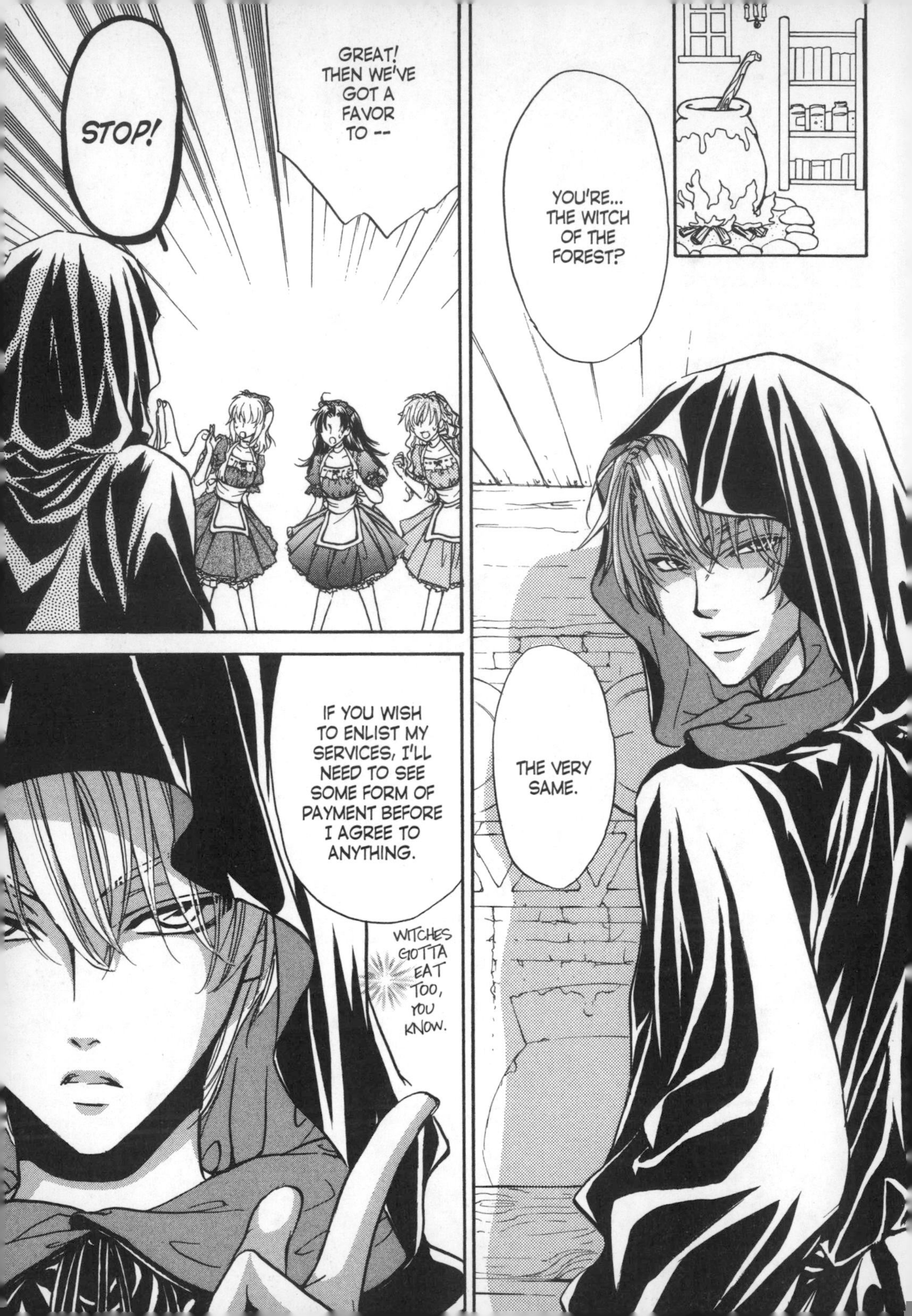
YOU'RE... THE WITCH OF THE FOREST?
THE VERY SAME.
GREAT! THEN WE'VE GOT A FAVOR TO --
STOP!
IF YOU WISH TO ENLIST MY SERVICES, I'LL NEED TO SEE SOME FORM OF PAYMENT BEFORE I AGREE TO ANYTHING.
WITCHES GOTTA EAT TOO, YOU KNOW.

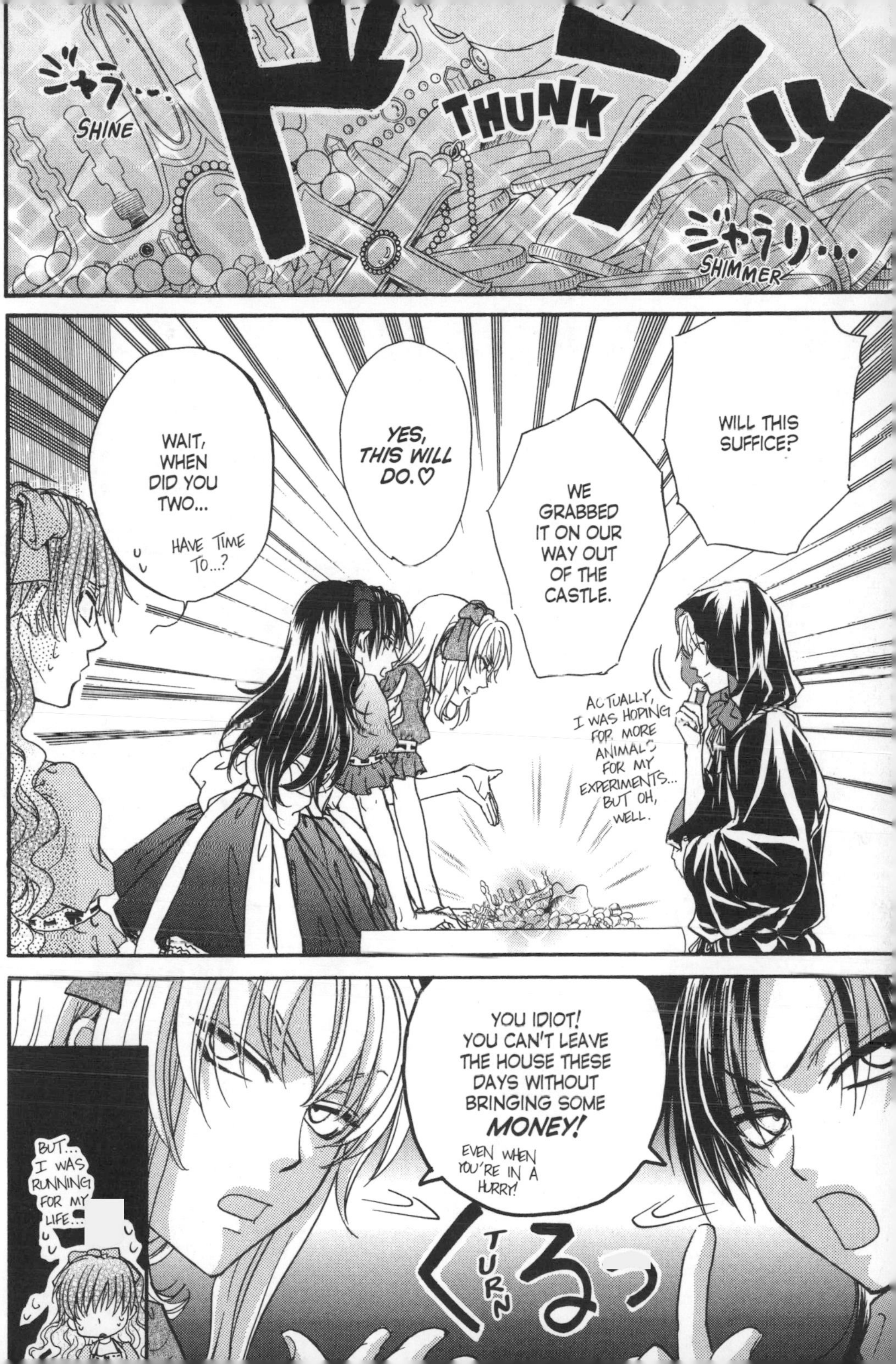
ジャラリ…
SHIMMER
ドンッ
THUNK
ジャラ…
SHINE
WILL THIS SUFFICE?
WE GRABBED IT ON OUR WAY OUT OF THE CASTLE.
ACTUALLY, I WAS HOPING FOR MORE ANIMALS FOR MY EXPERIMENTS... BUT OH, WELL.
YES, THIS WILL DO.♡
WAIT, WHEN DID YOU TWO...
HAVE TIME TO...?
YOU IDIOT! YOU CAN'T LEAVE THE HOUSE THESE DAYS WITHOUT BRINGING SOME MONEY!
EVEN WHEN YOU'RE IN A HURRY!
くるっ
TURN
BUT... I WAS RUNNING FOR MY LIFE...

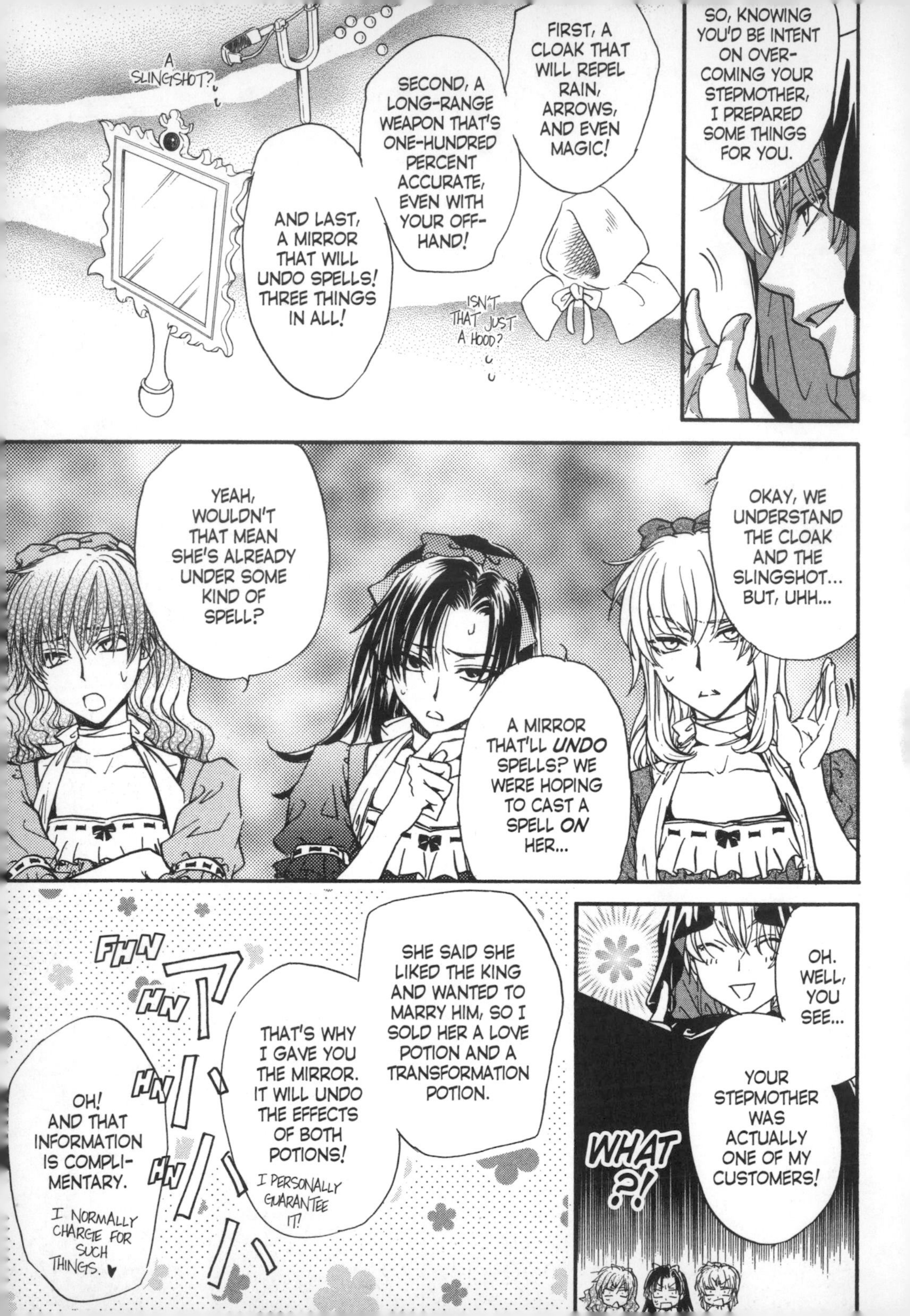
SO, KNOWING YOU'D BE INTENT ON OVER-COMING YOUR STEPMOTHER, I PREPARED SOME THINGS FOR YOU.
FIRST, A CLOAK THAT WILL REPEL RAIN, ARROWS, AND EVEN MAGIC!
SECOND, A LONG-RANGE WEAPON THAT'S ONE-HUNDRED PERCENT ACCURATE, EVEN WITH YOUR OFF-HAND!
A SLINGSHOT?
ISN'T THAT JUST A HOOD?
AND LAST, A MIRROR THAT WILL UNDO SPELLS! THREE THINGS IN ALL!
OKAY, WE UNDERSTAND THE CLOAK AND THE SLINGSHOT... BUT, UHH...
A MIRROR THAT'LL *UNDO* SPELLS? WE WERE HOPING TO CAST A SPELL *ON* HER...
YEAH, WOULDN'T THAT MEAN SHE'S ALREADY UNDER SOME KIND OF SPELL?
OH. WELL, YOU SEE...
YOUR STEPMOTHER WAS ACTUALLY ONE OF MY CUSTOMERS!
WHAT?!
SHE SAID SHE LIKED THE KING AND WANTED TO MARRY HIM, SO I SOLD HER A LOVE POTION AND A TRANSFORMATION POTION.
THAT'S WHY I GAVE YOU THE MIRROR. IT WILL UNDO THE EFFECTS OF BOTH POTIONS!
I PERSONALLY GUARANTEE IT!
OH! AND THAT INFORMATION IS COMPLI-MENTARY.
I NORMALLY CHARGE FOR SUCH THINGS. ♥
FHN
HN
HN
HN

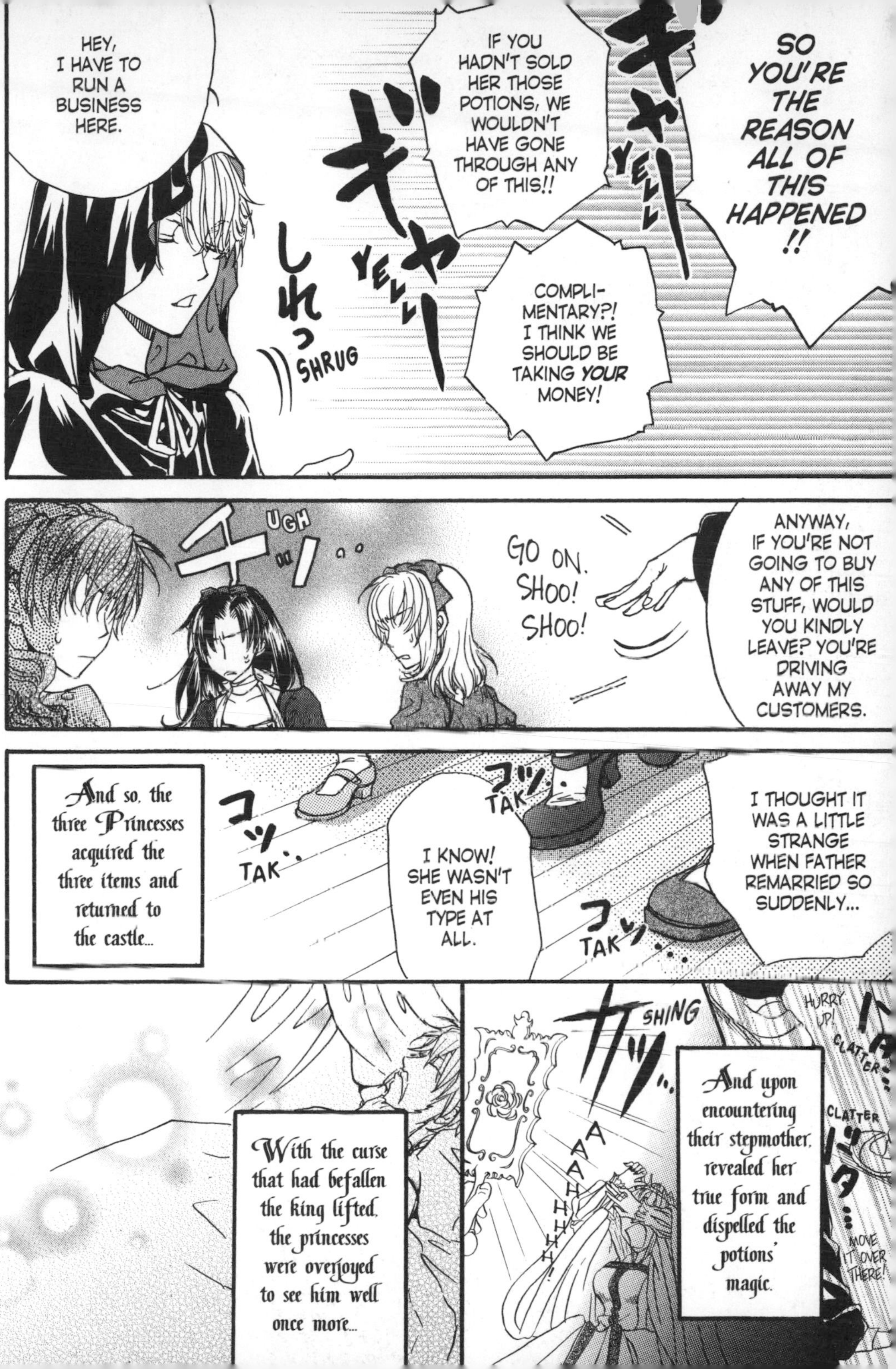
SO YOU'RE THE REASON ALL OF THIS HAPPENED!!
YELL
IF YOU HADN'T SOLD HER THOSE POTIONS, WE WOULDN'T HAVE GONE THROUGH ANY OF THIS!!
COMPLI-MENTARY?! I THINK WE SHOULD BE TAKING YOUR MONEY!
YELL
SHRUG
HEY, I HAVE TO RUN A BUSINESS HERE.
ANYWAY, IF YOU'RE NOT GOING TO BUY ANY OF THIS STUFF, WOULD YOU KINDLY LEAVE? YOU'RE DRIVING AWAY MY CUSTOMERS.
GO ON. SHOO! SHOO!
UGH
I THOUGHT IT WAS A LITTLE STRANGE WHEN FATHER REMARRIED SO SUDDENLY...
TAK
I KNOW! SHE WASN'T EVEN HIS TYPE AT ALL.
TAK
TAK
And so, the three Princesses acquired the three items and returned to the castle...
HURRY UP!
CLATTER
CLATTER
MOVE IT OVER THERE!
And upon encountering their stepmother, revealed her true form and dispelled the potions' magic.
SHING
AAAHHHHH!
With the curse that had befallen the king lifted, the princesses were overjoyed to see him well once more...

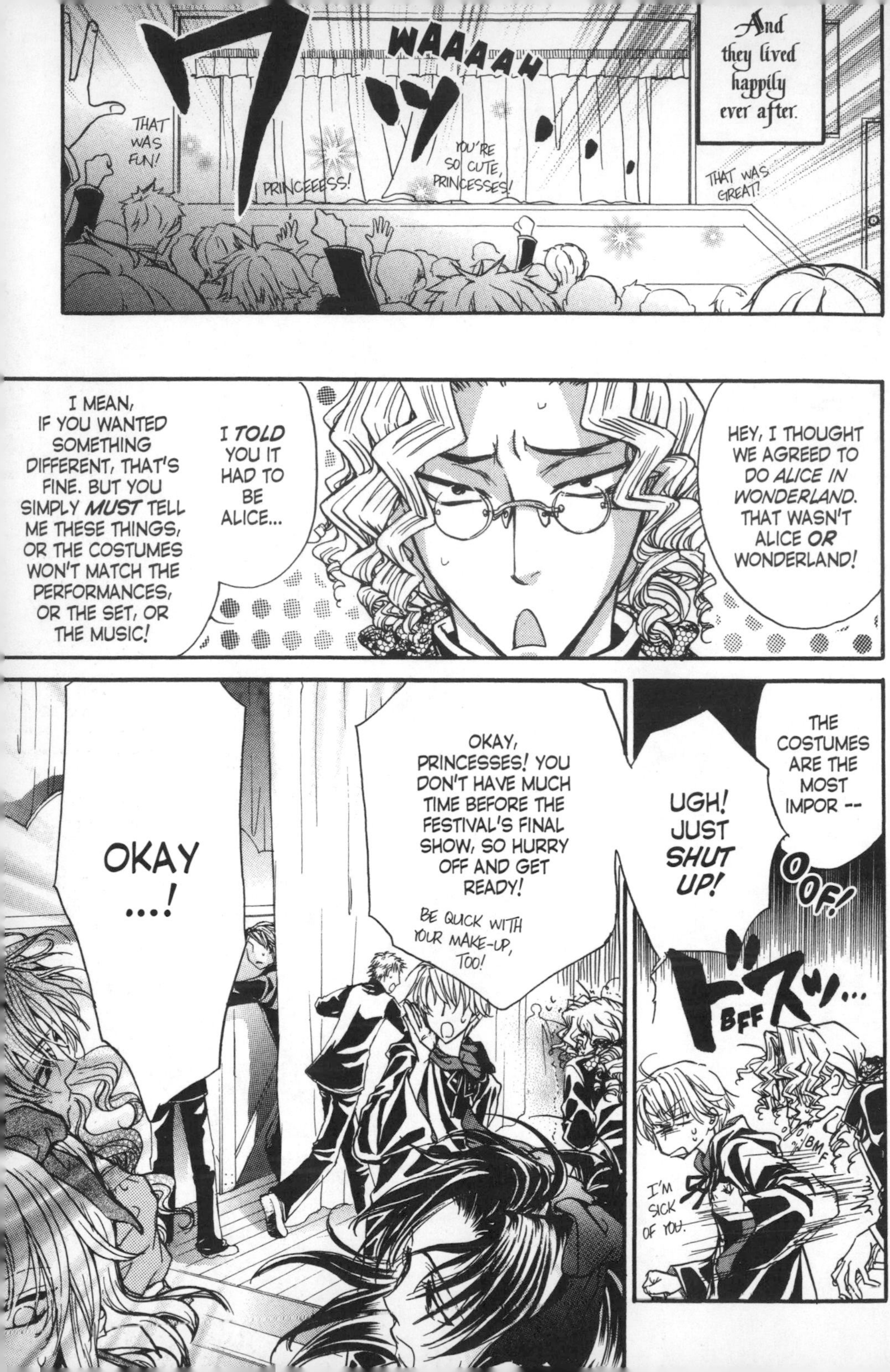

And they lived happily ever after.
WAAAAH
THAT WAS GREAT!
YOU'RE SO CUTE, PRINCESSES!
PRINCEEESS!
THAT WAS FUN!
HEY, I THOUGHT WE AGREED TO DO *ALICE IN WONDERLAND*. THAT WASN'T ALICE *OR* WONDERLAND!
I *TOLD* YOU IT HAD TO BE ALICE...
I MEAN, IF YOU WANTED SOMETHING DIFFERENT, THAT'S FINE. BUT YOU SIMPLY ***MUST*** TELL ME THESE THINGS, OR THE COSTUMES WON'T MATCH THE PERFORMANCES, OR THE SET, OR THE MUSIC!
THE COSTUMES ARE THE MOST IMPOR --
UGH! JUST *SHUT UP!*
OOF!
BFF
BMF
I'M SICK OF YOU.
OKAY, PRINCESSES! YOU DON'T HAVE MUCH TIME BEFORE THE FESTIVAL'S FINAL SHOW, SO HURRY OFF AND GET READY!
BE QUICK WITH YOUR MAKE-UP, TOO!
OKAY ...!

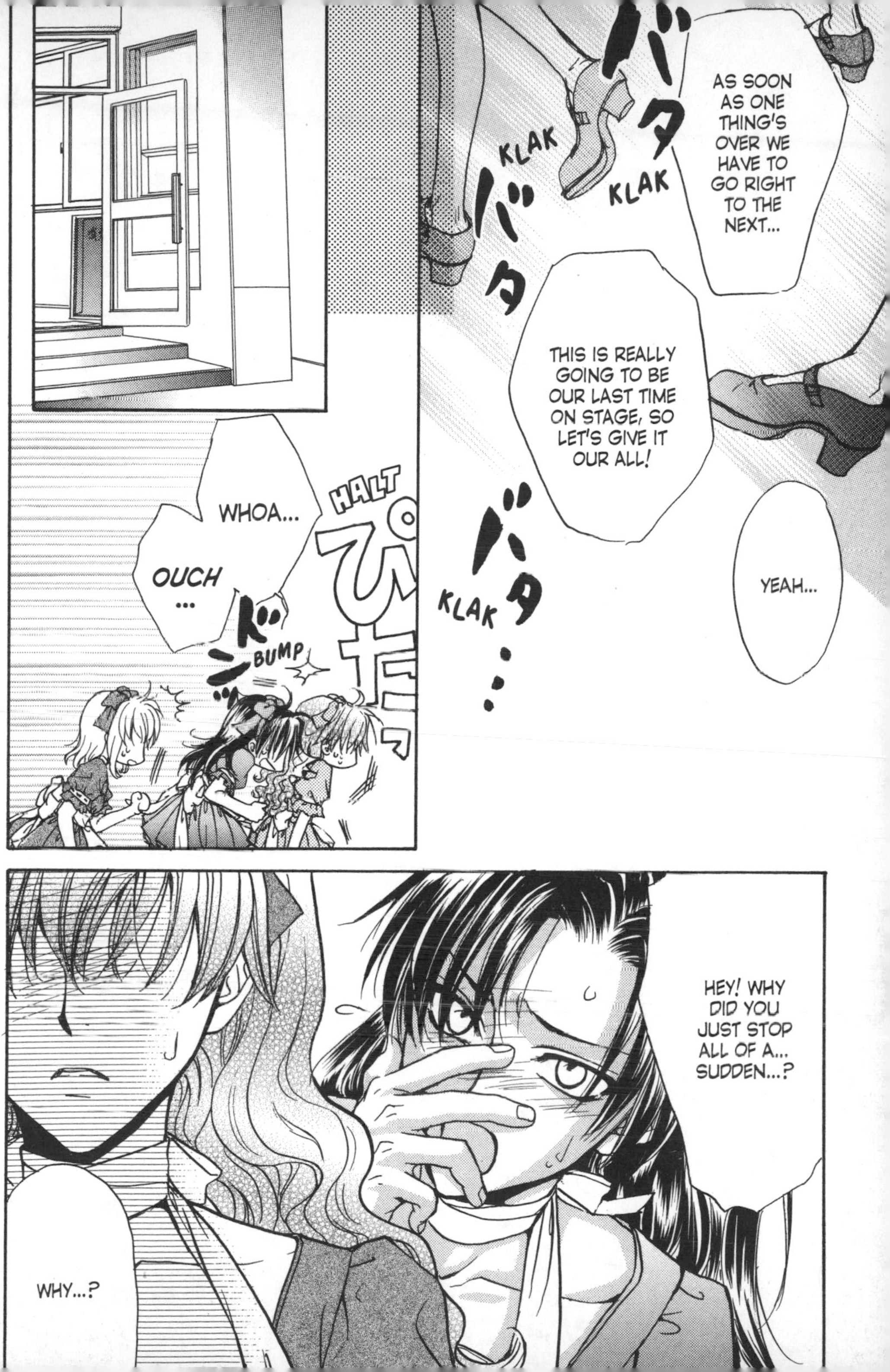
バタ
KLAK
バタ
KLAK
AS SOON AS ONE THING'S OVER WE HAVE TO GO RIGHT TO THE NEXT...
THIS IS REALLY GOING TO BE OUR LAST TIME ON STAGE, SO LET'S GIVE IT OUR ALL!
YEAH...
バタ...
KLAK
HALT
ぴたっ
WHOA...
OUCH...
ドン
BUMP
HEY! WHY DID YOU JUST STOP ALL OF A... SUDDEN...?
WHY...?

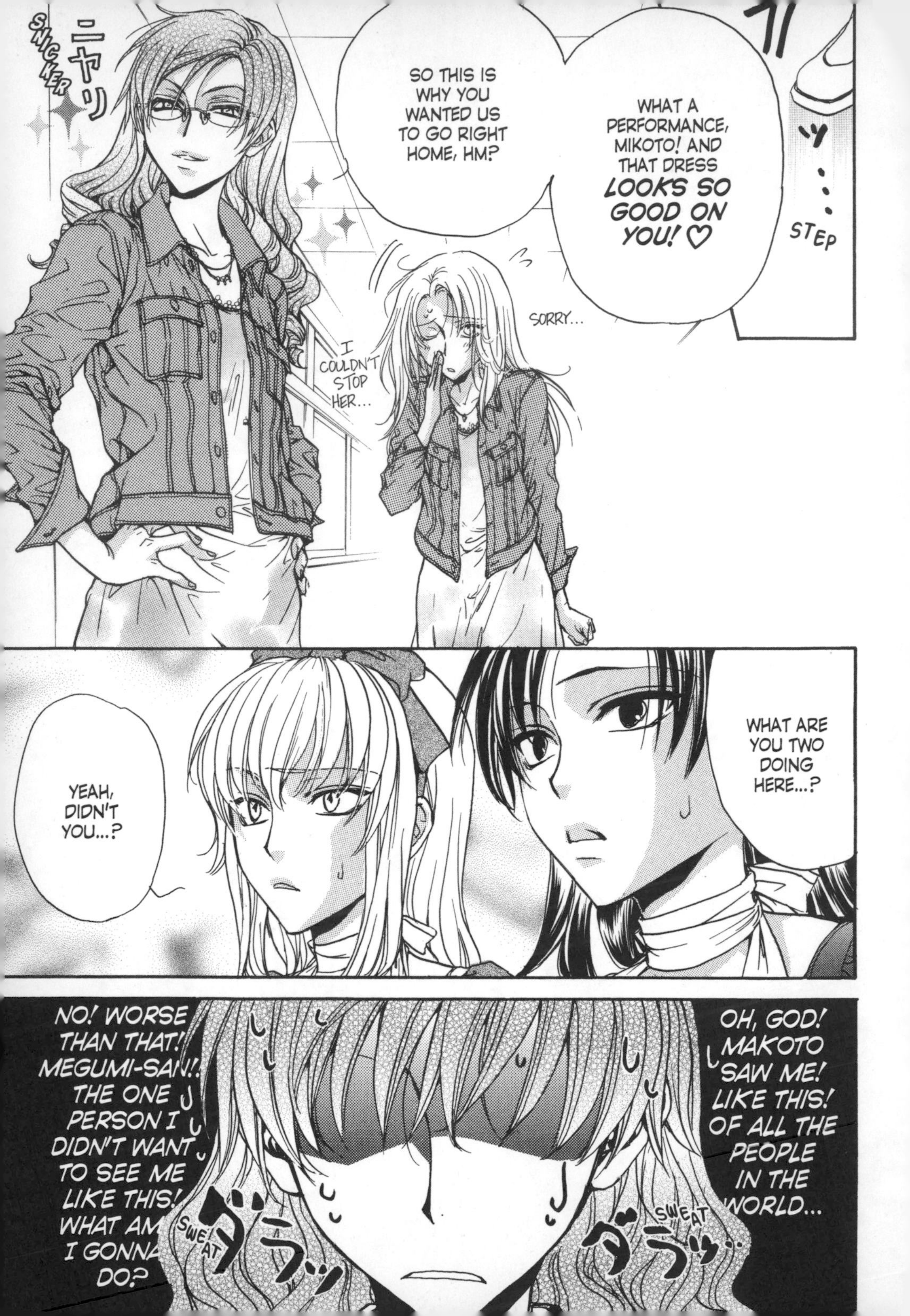

ツ...
STEP
WHAT A PERFORMANCE, MIKOTO! AND THAT DRESS LOOKS SO GOOD ON YOU! ♡
SO THIS IS WHY YOU WANTED US TO GO RIGHT HOME, HM?
ニヤリ
SNICKER
SORRY...
I COULDN'T STOP HER...
WHAT ARE YOU TWO DOING HERE...?
YEAH, DIDN'T YOU...?
OH, GOD! MAKOTO SAW ME! LIKE THIS! OF ALL THE PEOPLE IN THE WORLD...
NO! WORSE THAN THAT! MEGUMI-SAN!! THE ONE PERSON I DIDN'T WANT TO SEE ME LIKE THIS! WHAT AM I GONNA DO?
SWEAT
SWEAT

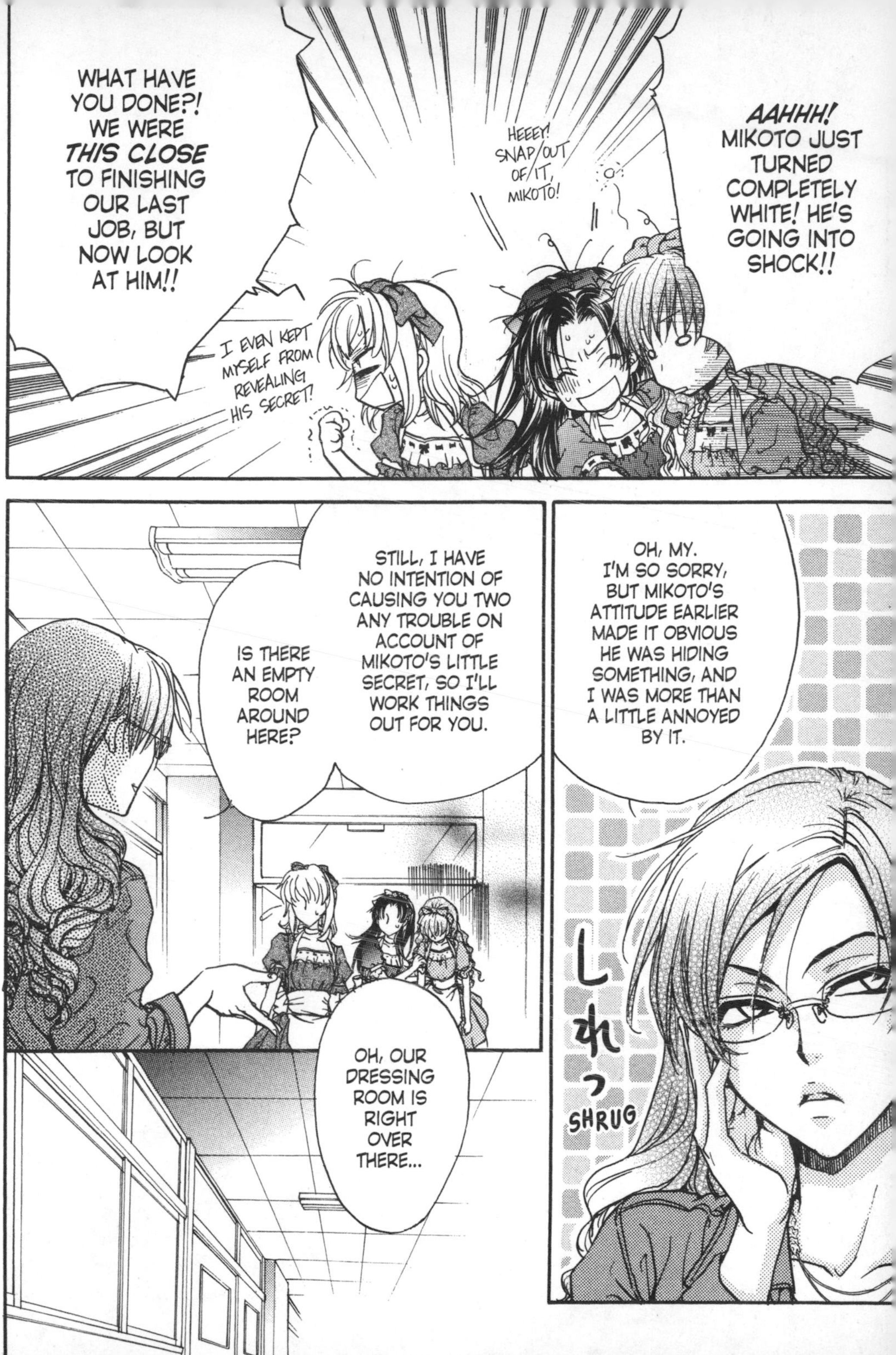
AAHHH! MIKOTO JUST TURNED COMPLETELY WHITE! HE'S GOING INTO SHOCK!!
HEEEY! SNAP OUT OF IT, MIKOTO!
WHAT HAVE YOU DONE?! WE WERE THIS CLOSE TO FINISHING OUR LAST JOB, BUT NOW LOOK AT HIM!!
I EVEN KEPT MYSELF FROM REVEALING HIS SECRET!
OH, MY. I'M SO SORRY, BUT MIKOTO'S ATTITUDE EARLIER MADE IT OBVIOUS HE WAS HIDING SOMETHING, AND I WAS MORE THAN A LITTLE ANNOYED BY IT.
しれっ
SHRUG
STILL, I HAVE NO INTENTION OF CAUSING YOU TWO ANY TROUBLE ON ACCOUNT OF MIKOTO'S LITTLE SECRET, SO I'LL WORK THINGS OUT FOR YOU.
IS THERE AN EMPTY ROOM AROUND HERE?
OH, OUR DRESSING ROOM IS RIGHT OVER THERE...

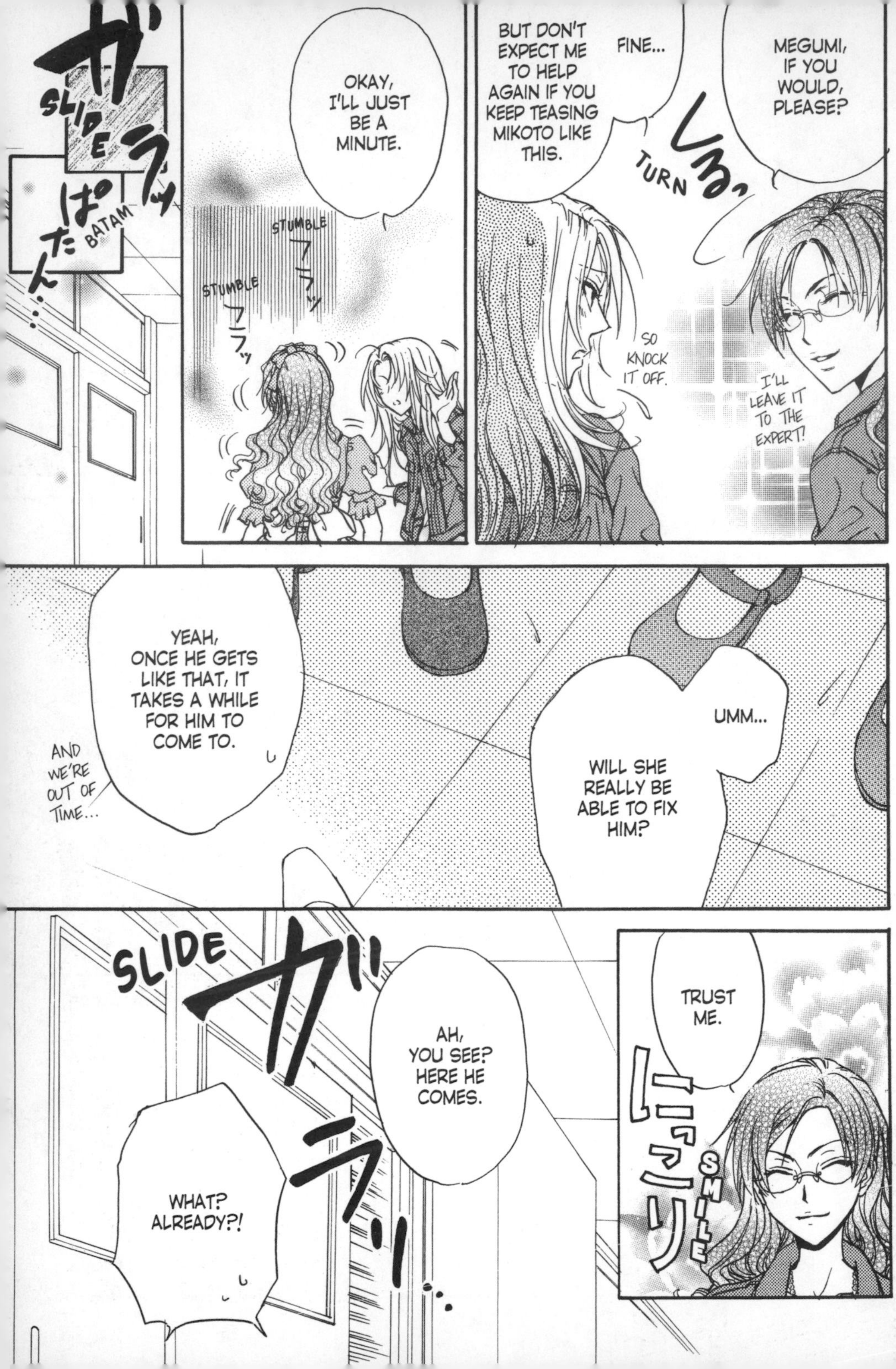
MEGUMI, IF YOU WOULD, PLEASE?
TURN
FINE...
BUT DON'T EXPECT ME TO HELP AGAIN IF YOU KEEP TEASING MIKOTO LIKE THIS.
SO KNOCK IT OFF.
I'LL LEAVE IT TO THE EXPERT!
OKAY, I'LL JUST BE A MINUTE.
STUMBLE
STUMBLE
SLIDE
BATAM
UMM...
WILL SHE REALLY BE ABLE TO FIX HIM?
YEAH, ONCE HE GETS LIKE THAT, IT TAKES A WHILE FOR HIM TO COME TO.
AND WE'RE OUT OF TIME...
TRUST ME.
SMILE
AH, YOU SEE? HERE HE COMES.
SLIDE
WHAT? ALREADY?!

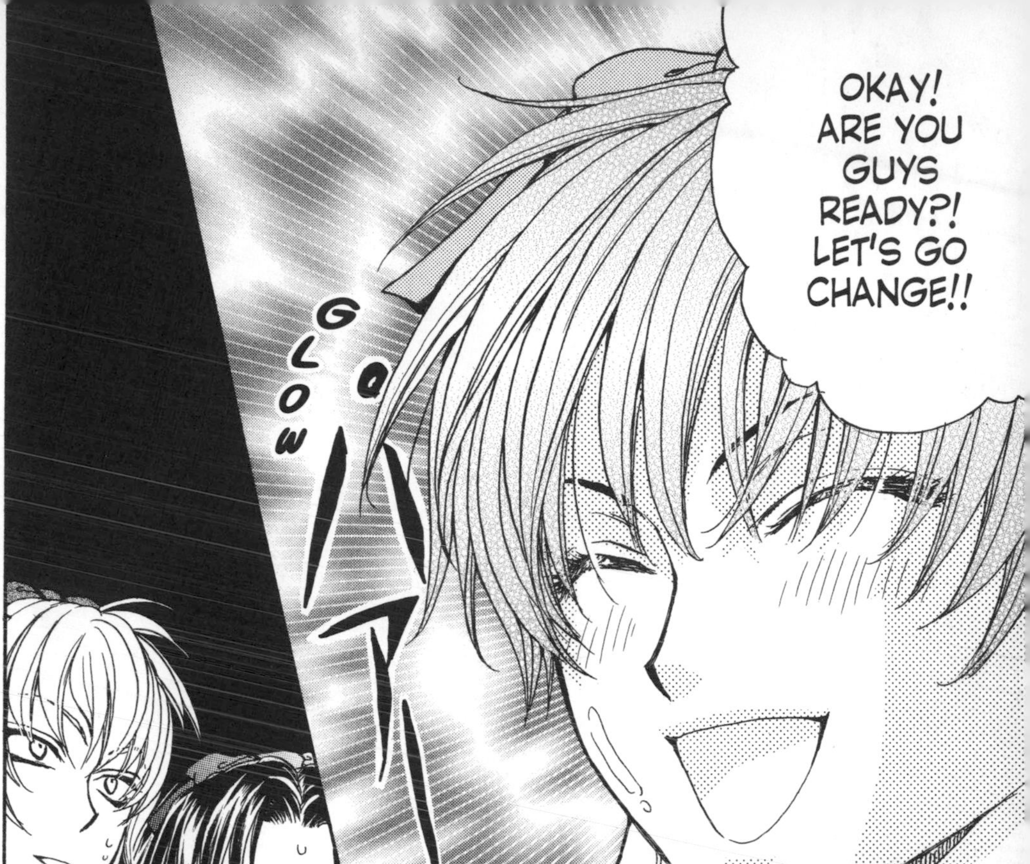
OKAY! ARE YOU GUYS READY?! LET'S GO CHANGE!!
GLOW
ELATED!!

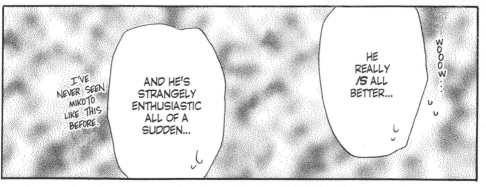

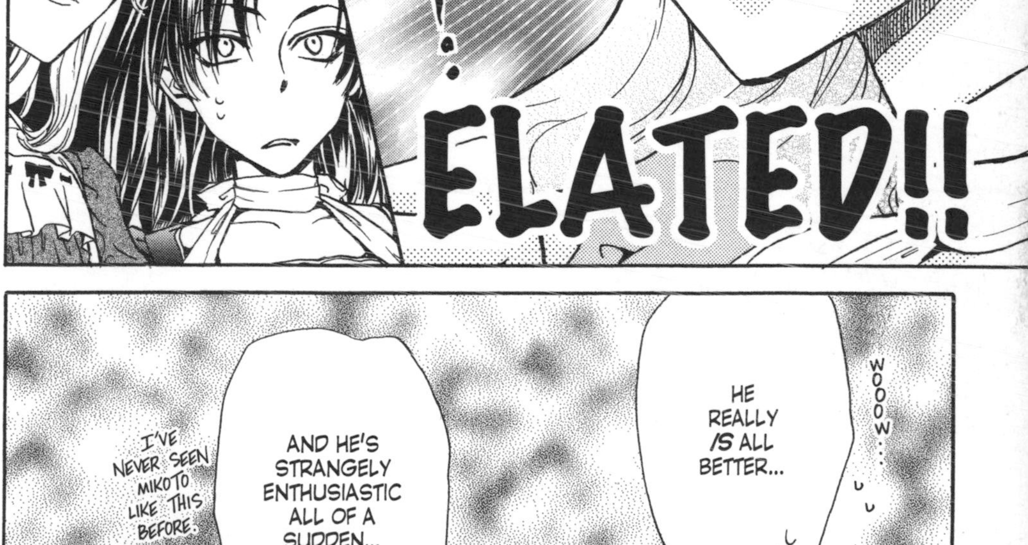
WOOOW...
HE REALLY IS ALL BETTER...
AND HE'S STRANGELY ENTHUSIASTIC ALL OF A SUDDEN...
I'VE NEVER SEEN MIKOTO LIKE THIS BEFORE.

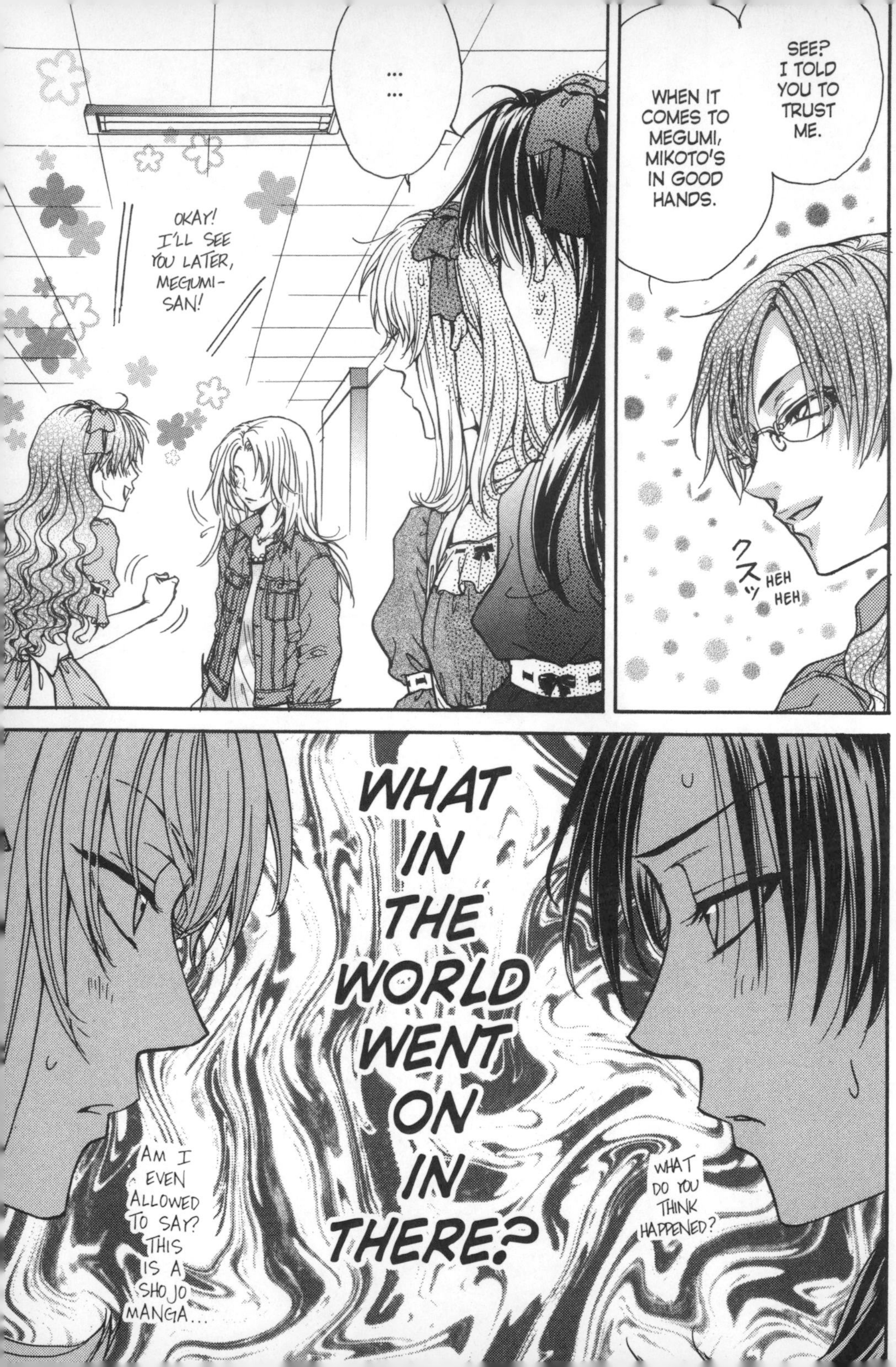
SEE? I TOLD YOU TO TRUST ME.
WHEN IT COMES TO MEGUMI, MIKOTO'S IN GOOD HANDS.
クスッ HEH HEH
...
...
OKAY! I'LL SEE YOU LATER, MEGUMI-SAN!
WHAT IN THE WORLD WENT ON IN THERE?
WHAT DO YOU THINK HAPPENED?
AM I EVEN ALLOWED TO SAY? THIS IS A SHOJO MANGA...

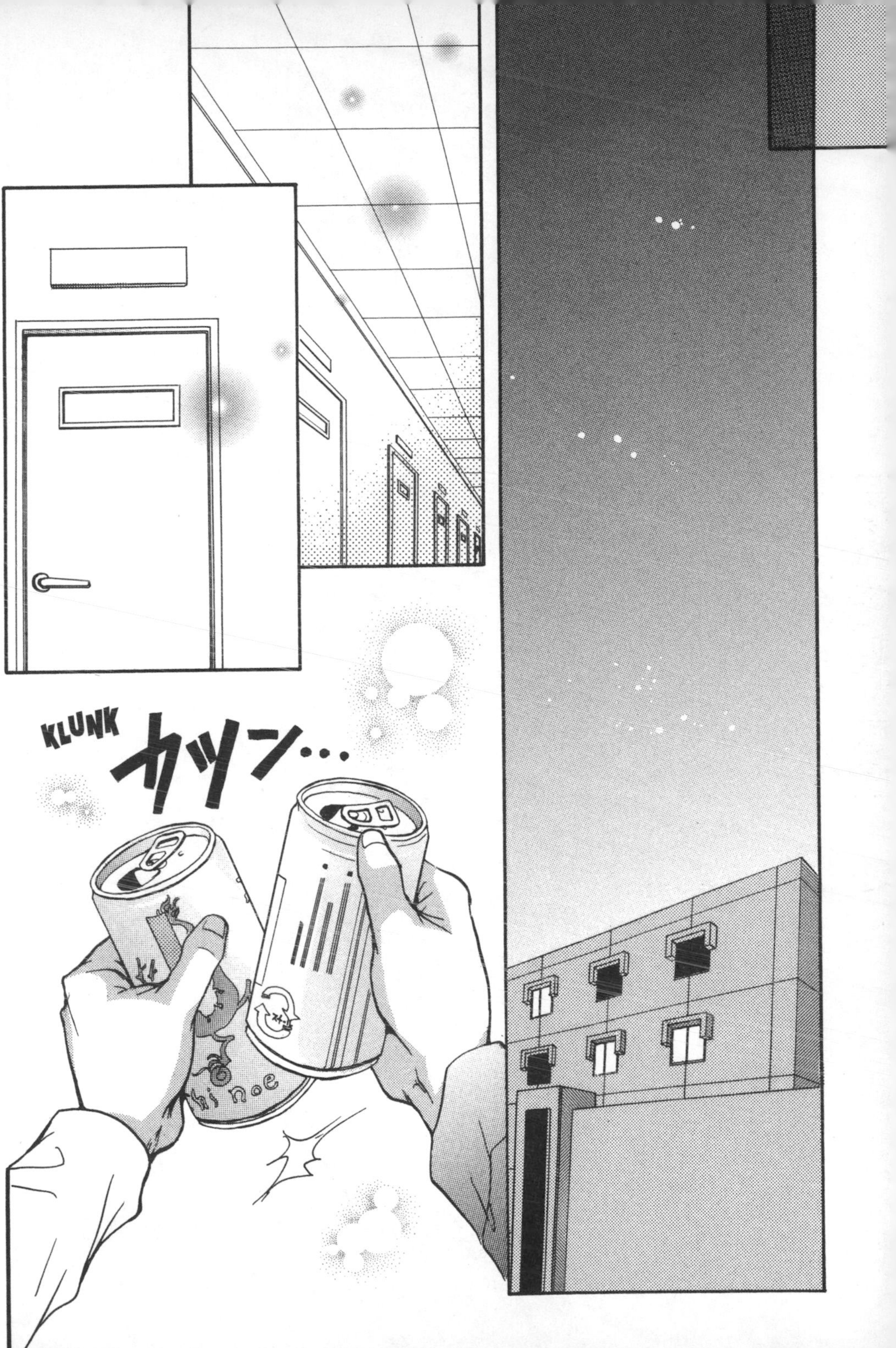
KLUNK
カツン…

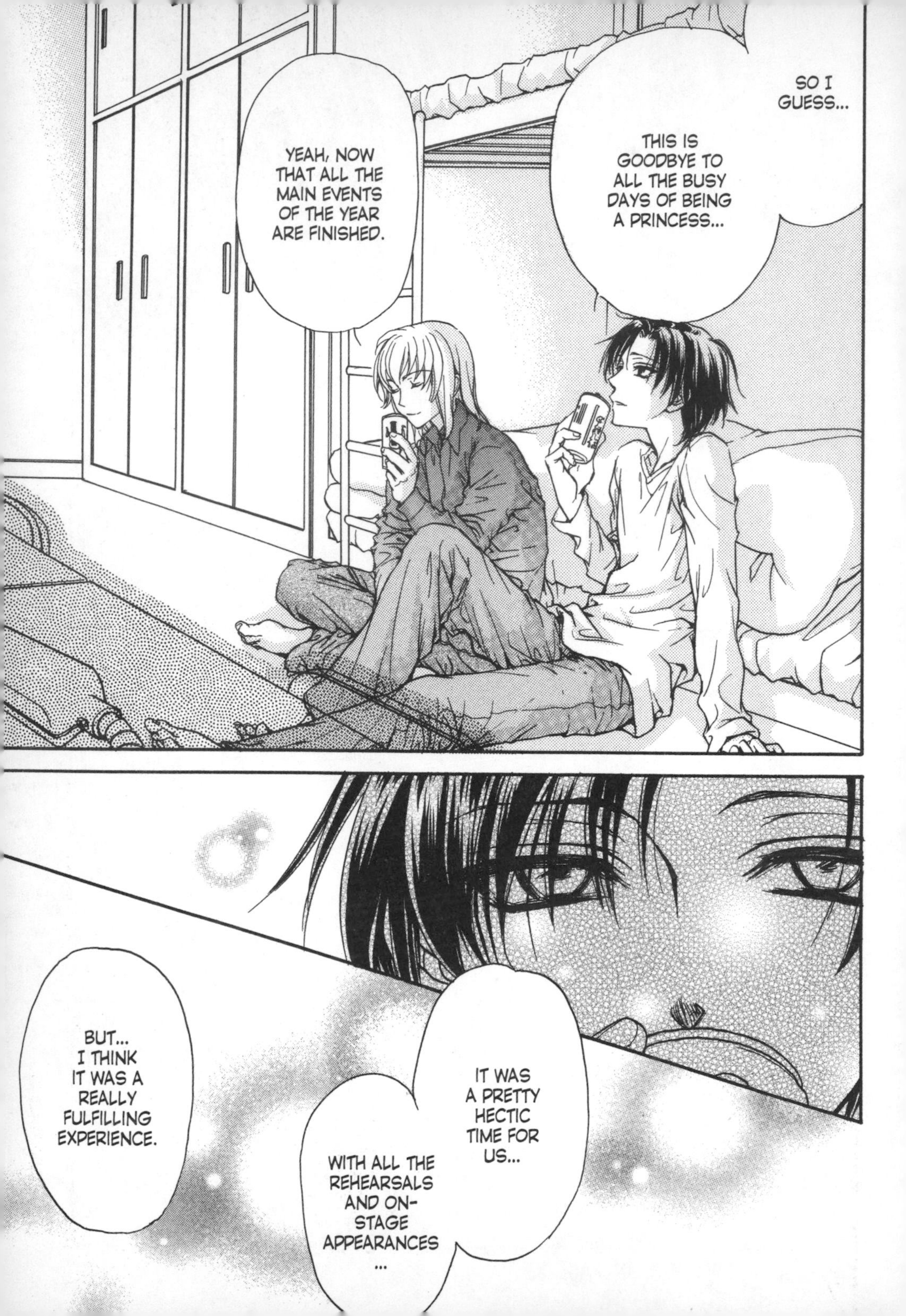
SO I GUESS...
THIS IS GOODBYE TO ALL THE BUSY DAYS OF BEING A PRINCESS...
YEAH, NOW THAT ALL THE MAIN EVENTS OF THE YEAR ARE FINISHED.
IT WAS A PRETTY HECTIC TIME FOR US...
WITH ALL THE REHEARSALS AND ON-STAGE APPEARANCES ...
BUT... I THINK IT WAS A REALLY FULFILLING EXPERIENCE.

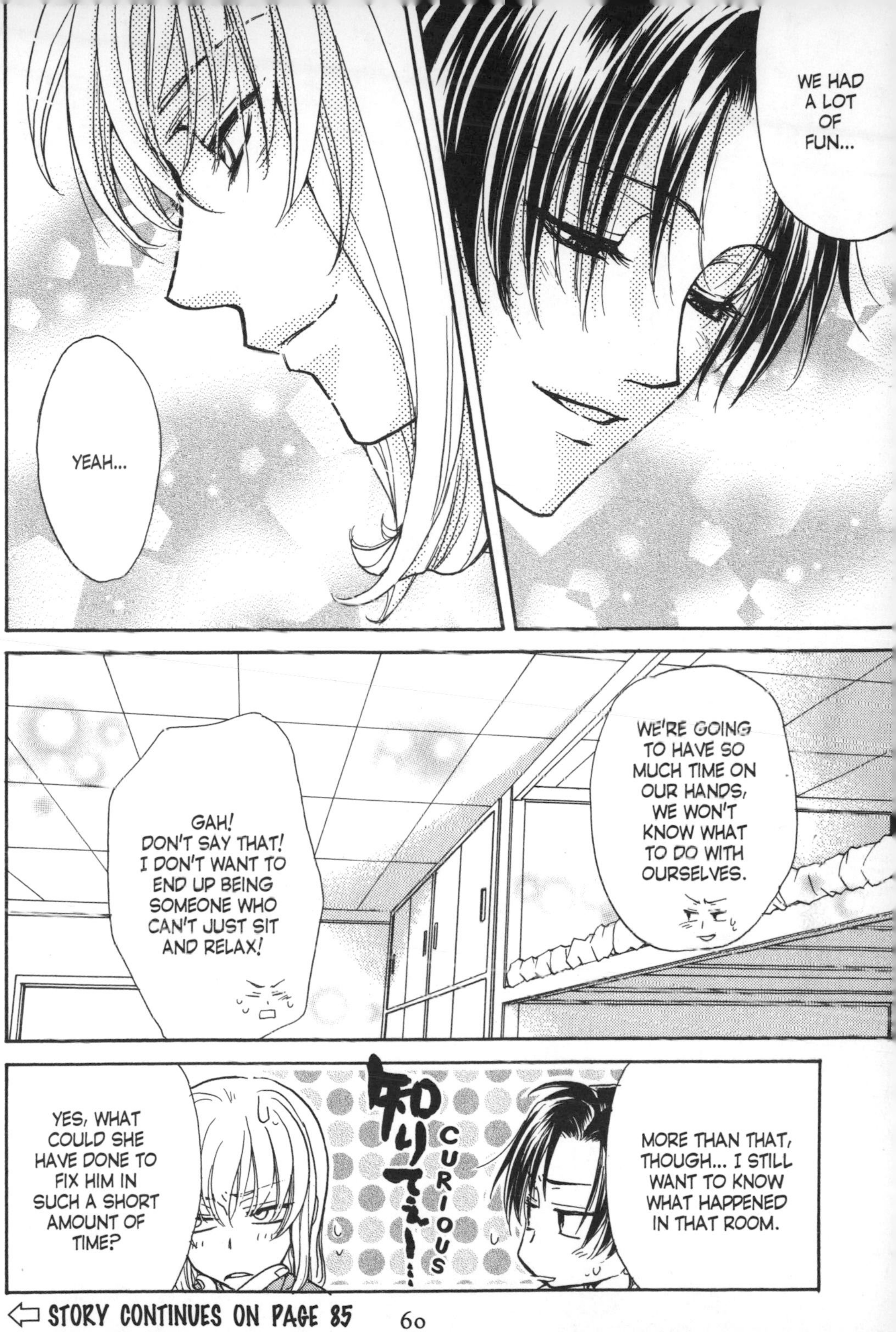
WE HAD A LOT OF FUN...
YEAH...
WE'RE GOING TO HAVE SO MUCH TIME ON OUR HANDS, WE WON'T KNOW WHAT TO DO WITH OURSELVES.
GAH! DON'T SAY THAT! I DON'T WANT TO END UP BEING SOMEONE WHO CAN'T JUST SIT AND RELAX!
MORE THAN THAT, THOUGH... I STILL WANT TO KNOW WHAT HAPPENED IN THAT ROOM.
CURIOUS
YES, WHAT COULD SHE HAVE DONE TO FIX HIM IN SUCH A SHORT AMOUNT OF TIME?

⇦ STORY CONTINUES ON PAGE 85

JUST FYI ①

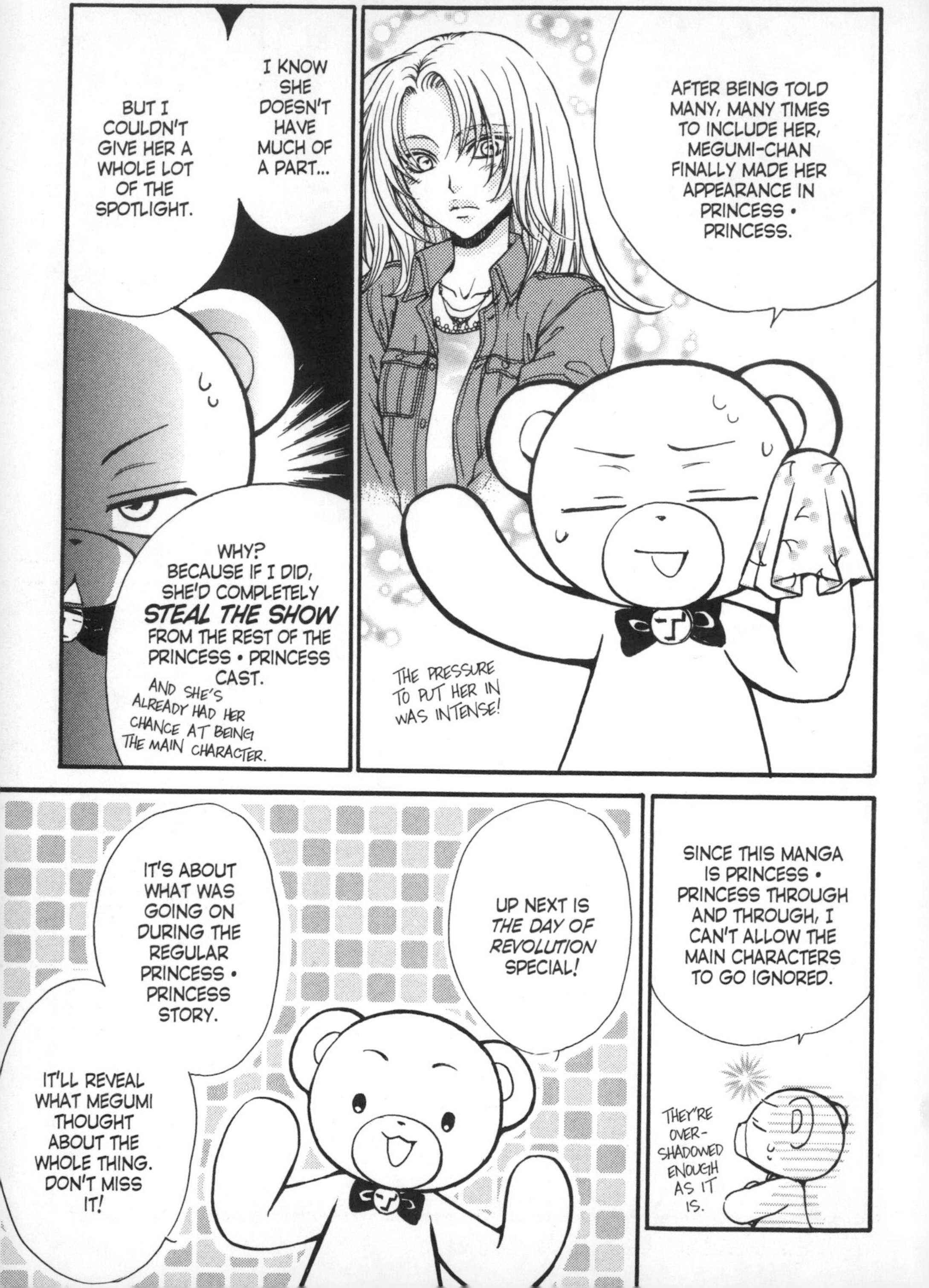
AFTER BEING TOLD MANY, MANY TIMES TO INCLUDE HER, MEGUMI-CHAN FINALLY MADE HER APPEARANCE IN PRINCESS • PRINCESS.
THE PRESSURE TO PUT HER IN WAS INTENSE!
I KNOW SHE DOESN'T HAVE MUCH OF A PART...
BUT I COULDN'T GIVE HER A WHOLE LOT OF THE SPOTLIGHT.
WHY? BECAUSE IF I DID, SHE'D COMPLETELY ***STEAL THE SHOW*** FROM THE REST OF THE PRINCESS • PRINCESS CAST.
AND SHE'S ALREADY HAD HER CHANCE AT BEING THE MAIN CHARACTER.
SINCE THIS MANGA IS PRINCESS • PRINCESS THROUGH AND THROUGH, I CAN'T ALLOW THE MAIN CHARACTERS TO GO IGNORED.
THEY'RE OVER-SHADOWED ENOUGH AS IT IS.
UP NEXT IS *THE DAY OF REVOLUTION* SPECIAL!
IT'S ABOUT WHAT WAS GOING ON DURING THE REGULAR PRINCESS • PRINCESS STORY.
IT'LL REVEAL WHAT MEGUMI THOUGHT ABOUT THE WHOLE THING. DON'T MISS IT!

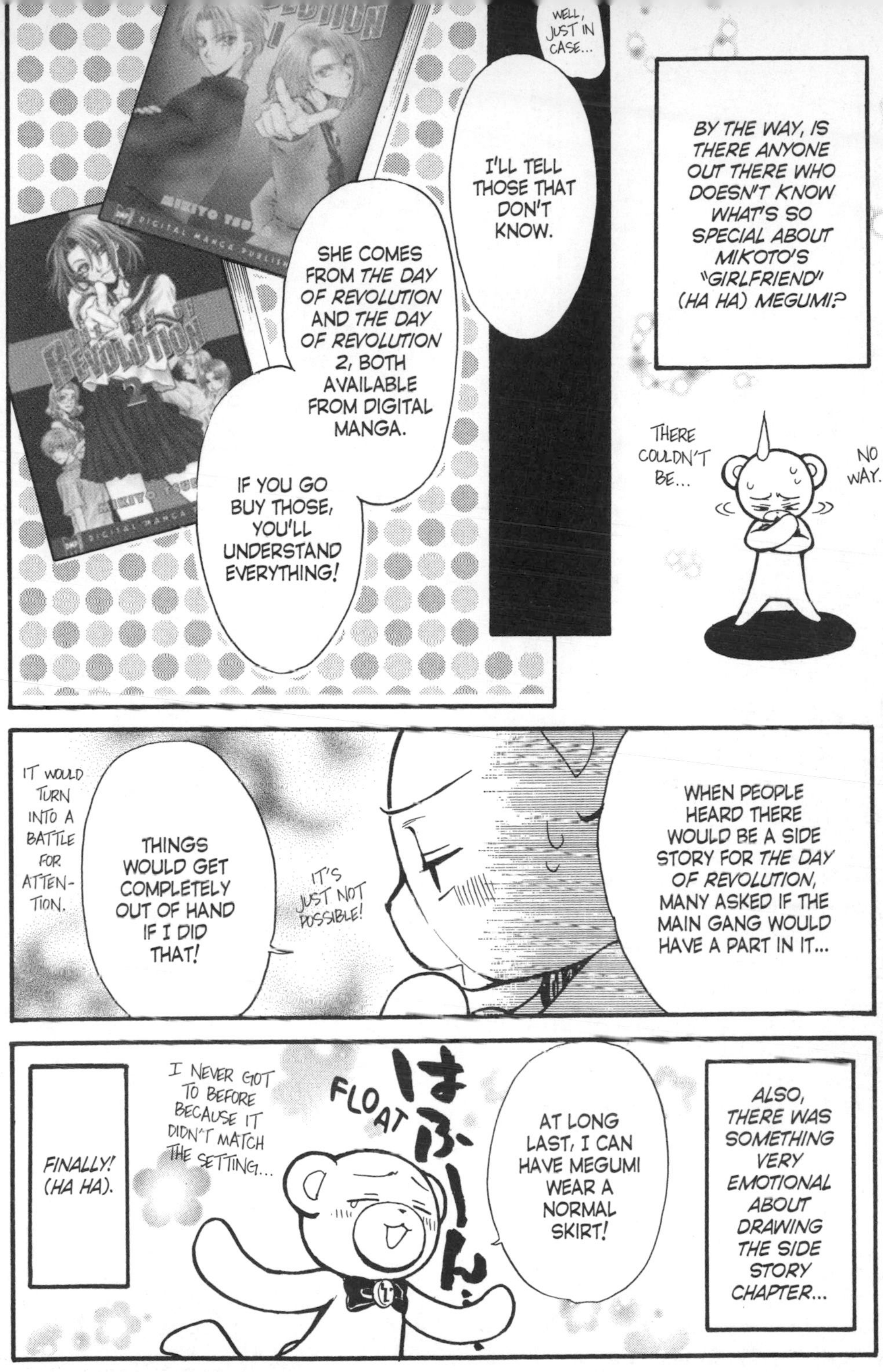
BY THE WAY, IS THERE ANYONE OUT THERE WHO DOESN'T KNOW WHAT'S SO SPECIAL ABOUT MIKOTO'S "GIRLFRIEND" (HA HA) MEGUMI?
THERE COULDN'T BE...
NO WAY...
WELL, JUST IN CASE...
I'LL TELL THOSE THAT DON'T KNOW.
SHE COMES FROM *THE DAY OF REVOLUTION* AND *THE DAY OF REVOLUTION 2*, BOTH AVAILABLE FROM DIGITAL MANGA.
IF YOU GO BUY THOSE, YOU'LL UNDERSTAND EVERYTHING!
WHEN PEOPLE HEARD THERE WOULD BE A SIDE STORY FOR *THE DAY OF REVOLUTION*, MANY ASKED IF THE MAIN GANG WOULD HAVE A PART IN IT...
IT'S JUST NOT POSSIBLE!
THINGS WOULD GET COMPLETELY OUT OF HAND IF I DID THAT!
IT WOULD TURN INTO A BATTLE FOR ATTENTION.
ALSO, THERE WAS SOMETHING VERY EMOTIONAL ABOUT DRAWING THE SIDE STORY CHAPTER...
AT LONG LAST, I CAN HAVE MEGUMI WEAR A NORMAL SKIRT!
はふーん
FLOAT
I NEVER GOT TO BEFORE BECAUSE IT DIDN'T MATCH THE SETTING...
FINALLY! (HA HA).

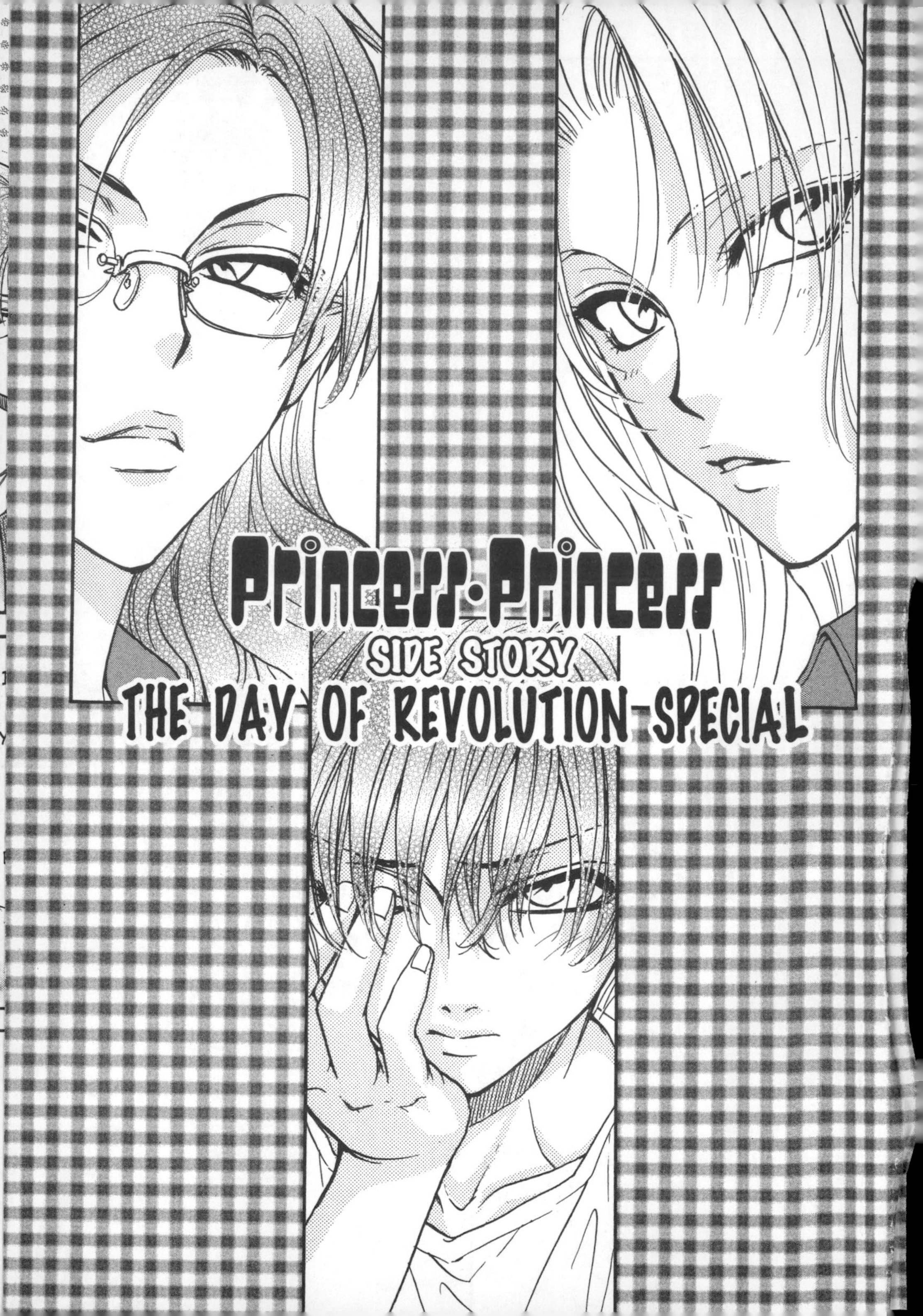
Princess·Princess
SIDE STORY
THE DAY OF REVOLUTION SPECIAL

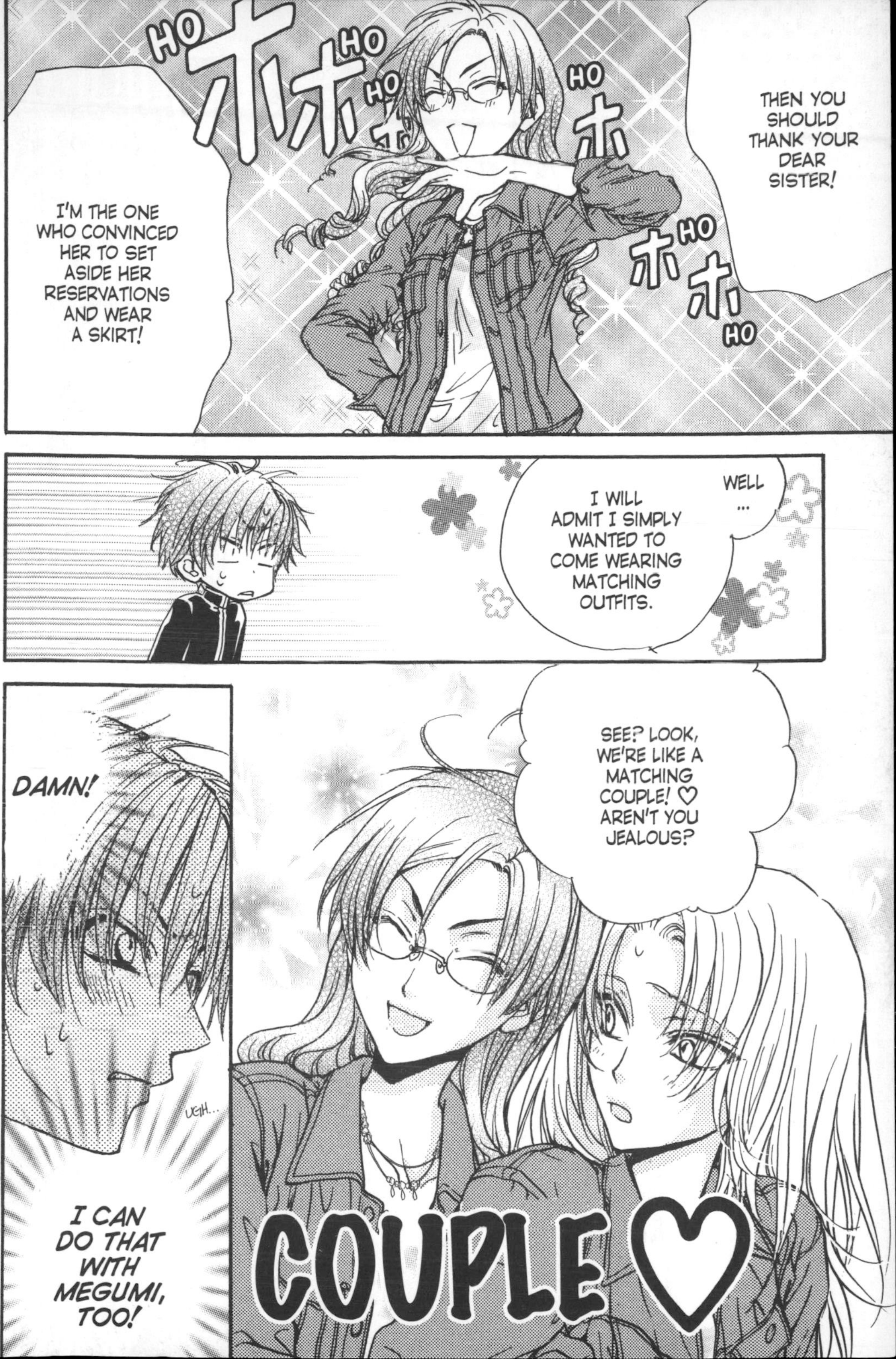
THEN YOU SHOULD THANK YOUR DEAR SISTER!
HO ホ HO ホ HO ホ HO
HO ホ HO ホ HO ホ HO ホ
I'M THE ONE WHO CONVINCED HER TO SET ASIDE HER RESERVATIONS AND WEAR A SKIRT!
WELL...
I WILL ADMIT I SIMPLY WANTED TO COME WEARING MATCHING OUTFITS.
SEE? LOOK, WE'RE LIKE A MATCHING COUPLE! ♡ AREN'T YOU JEALOUS?
COUPLE ♡
DAMN!
UGH...
I CAN DO THAT WITH MEGUMI, TOO!

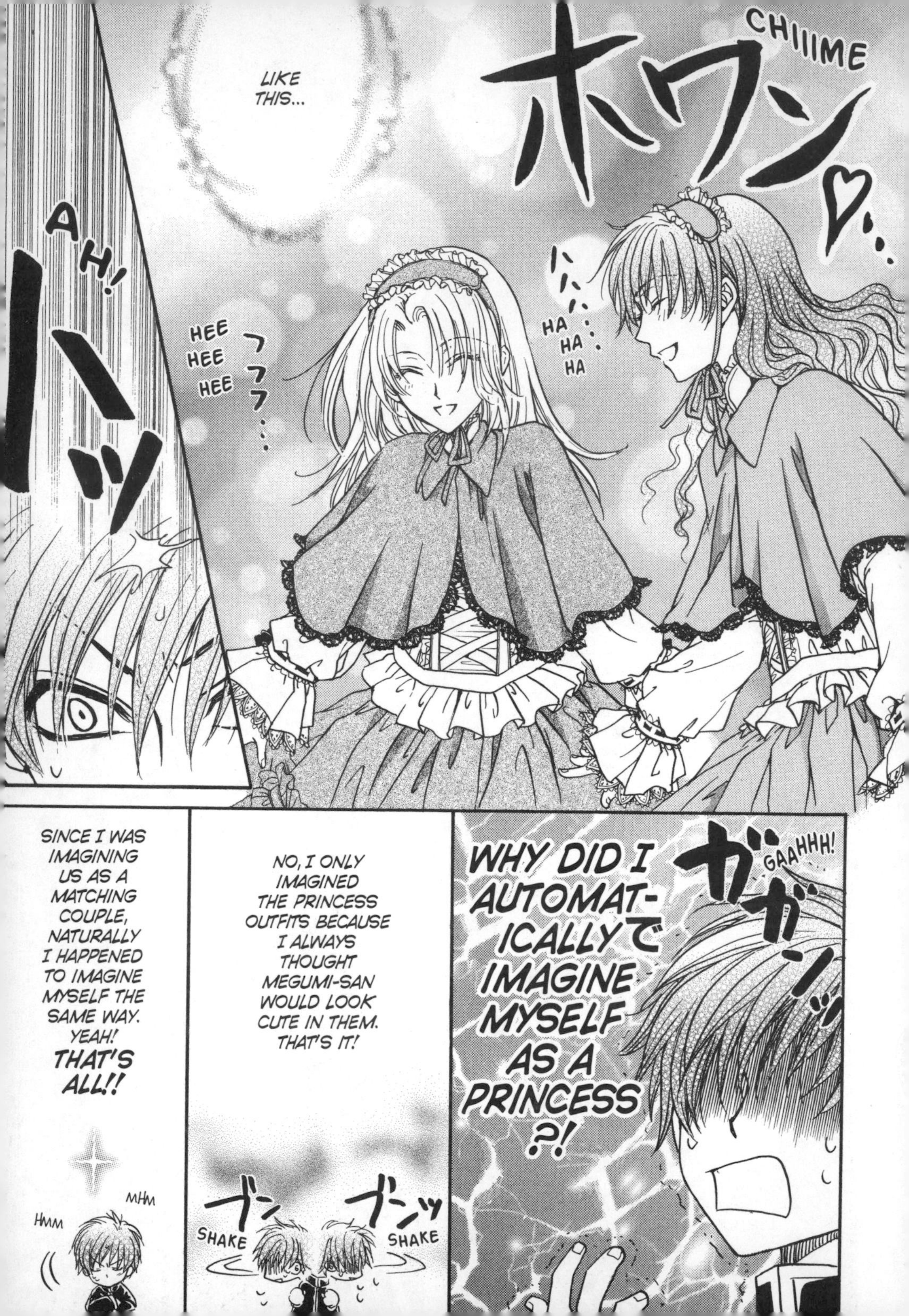

ホワン
CHIIIME
LIKE THIS...
ハハハ
HA HA HA
HEE HEE HEE
フフフ…
AH!
ハッ
WHY DID I AUTOMATICALLY IMAGINE MYSELF AS A PRINCESS?!
ガーン
GAAHHH!
NO, I ONLY IMAGINED THE PRINCESS OUTFITS BECAUSE I ALWAYS THOUGHT MEGUMI-SAN WOULD LOOK CUTE IN THEM. THAT'S IT!
ブン
SHAKE
ブンッ
SHAKE
SINCE I WAS IMAGINING US AS A MATCHING COUPLE, NATURALLY I HAPPENED TO IMAGINE MYSELF THE SAME WAY. YEAH! THAT'S ALL!!
MHM
HMM

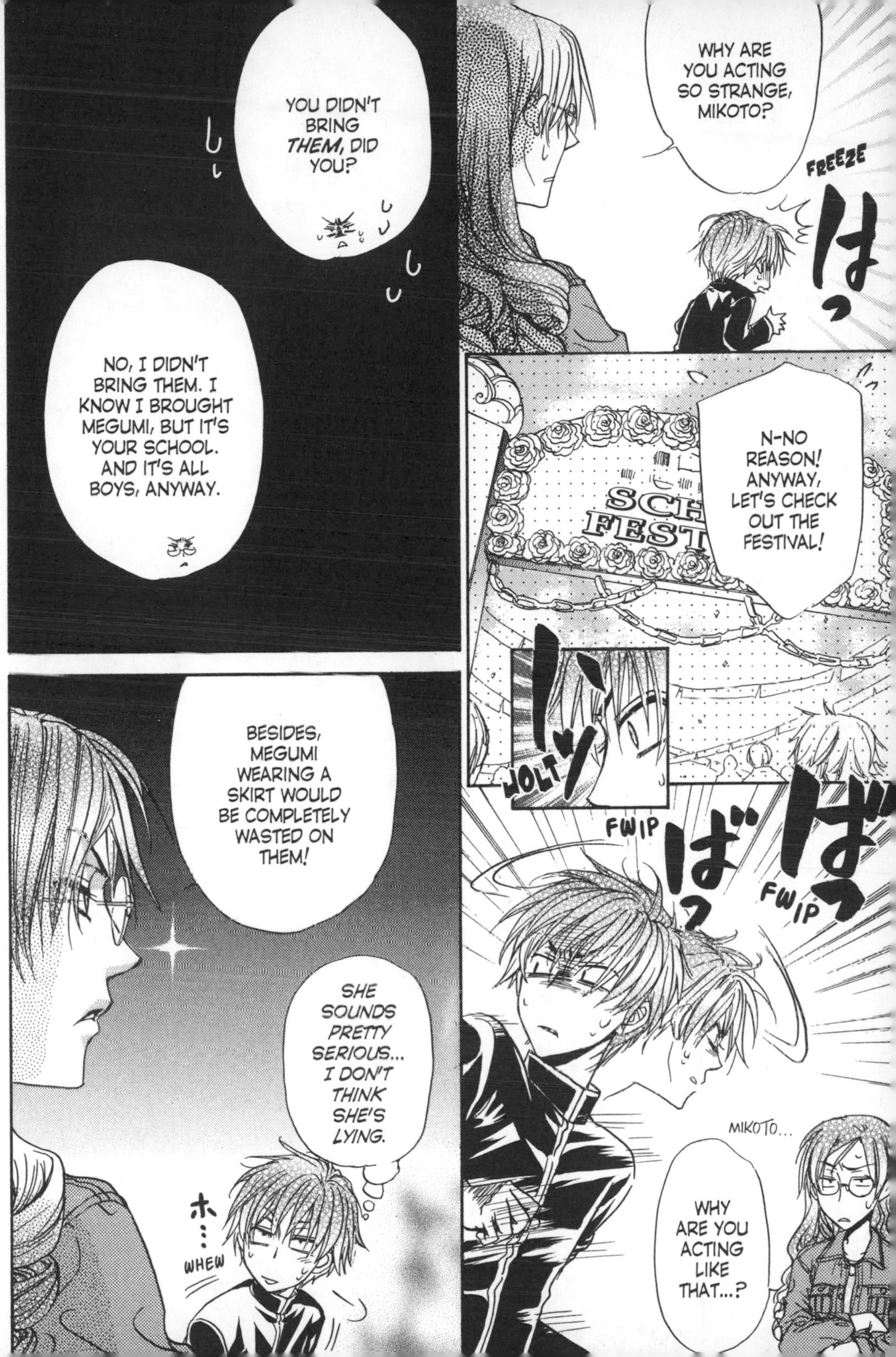
WHY ARE YOU ACTING SO STRANGE, MIKOTO?
FREEZE
はっ
N-NO REASON! ANYWAY, LET'S CHECK OUT THE FESTIVAL!
JOLT
ばっ
ばっ
FWIP
FWIP
MIKOTO...
WHY ARE YOU ACTING LIKE THAT...?
YOU DIDN'T BRING THEM, DID YOU?
NO, I DIDN'T BRING THEM. I KNOW I BROUGHT MEGUMI, BUT IT'S YOUR SCHOOL. AND IT'S ALL BOYS, ANYWAY.
BESIDES, MEGUMI WEARING A SKIRT WOULD BE COMPLETELY WASTED ON THEM!
SHE SOUNDS PRETTY SERIOUS... I DON'T THINK SHE'S LYING.
WHEW

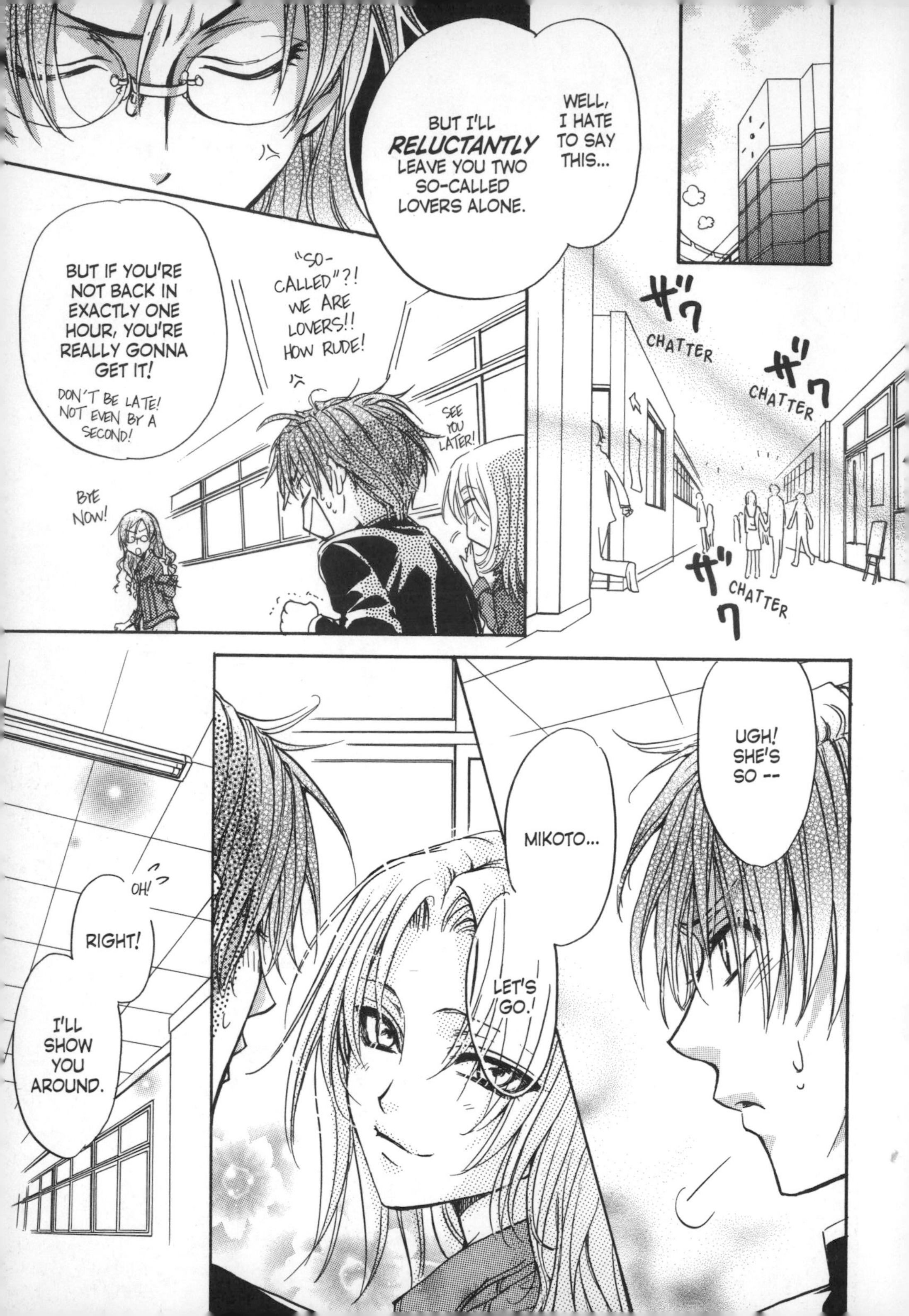
WELL, I HATE TO SAY THIS...
BUT I'LL *RELUCTANTLY* LEAVE YOU TWO SO-CALLED LOVERS ALONE.
ザワ CHATTER
ザワ CHATTER
ザワ CHATTER
"SO-CALLED"?! WE ARE LOVERS!! HOW RUDE!
SEE YOU LATER!
BUT IF YOU'RE NOT BACK IN EXACTLY ONE HOUR, YOU'RE REALLY GONNA GET IT!
DON'T BE LATE! NOT EVEN BY A SECOND!
BYE NOW!
UGH! SHE'S SO --
MIKOTO...
LET'S GO!
OH!
RIGHT!
I'LL SHOW YOU AROUND.

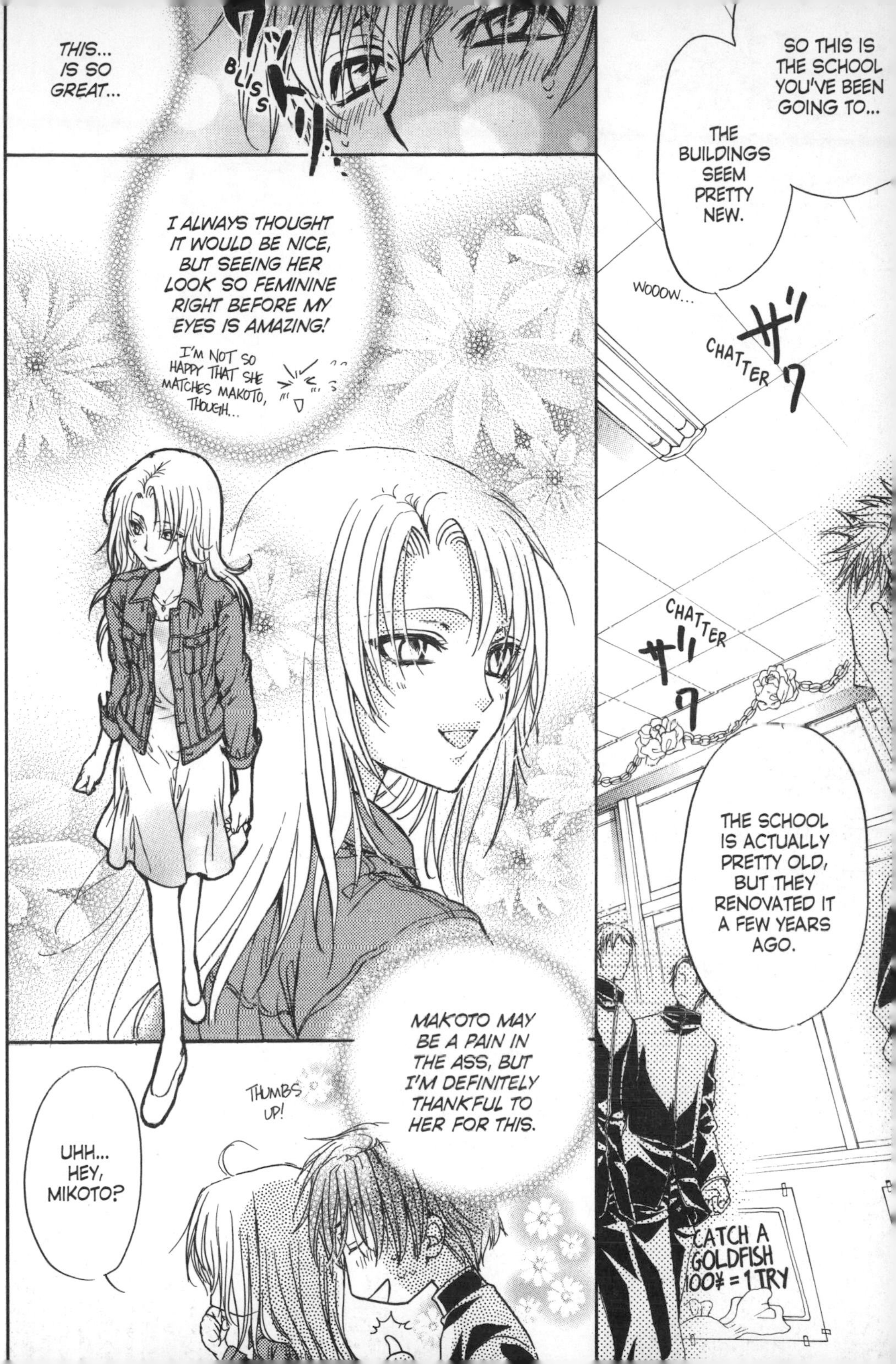
SO THIS IS THE SCHOOL YOU'VE BEEN GOING TO...
THE BUILDINGS SEEM PRETTY NEW.
WOOOW...
CHATTER
CHATTER
THE SCHOOL IS ACTUALLY PRETTY OLD, BUT THEY RENOVATED IT A FEW YEARS AGO.
CATCH A GOLDFISH 100¥ = 1 TRY
THIS... IS SO GREAT...
BLISS
I ALWAYS THOUGHT IT WOULD BE NICE, BUT SEEING HER LOOK SO FEMININE RIGHT BEFORE MY EYES IS AMAZING!
I'M NOT SO HAPPY THAT SHE MATCHES MAKOTO, THOUGH...
MAKOTO MAY BE A PAIN IN THE ASS, BUT I'M DEFINITELY THANKFUL TO HER FOR THIS.
THUMBS UP!
UHH... HEY, MIKOTO?

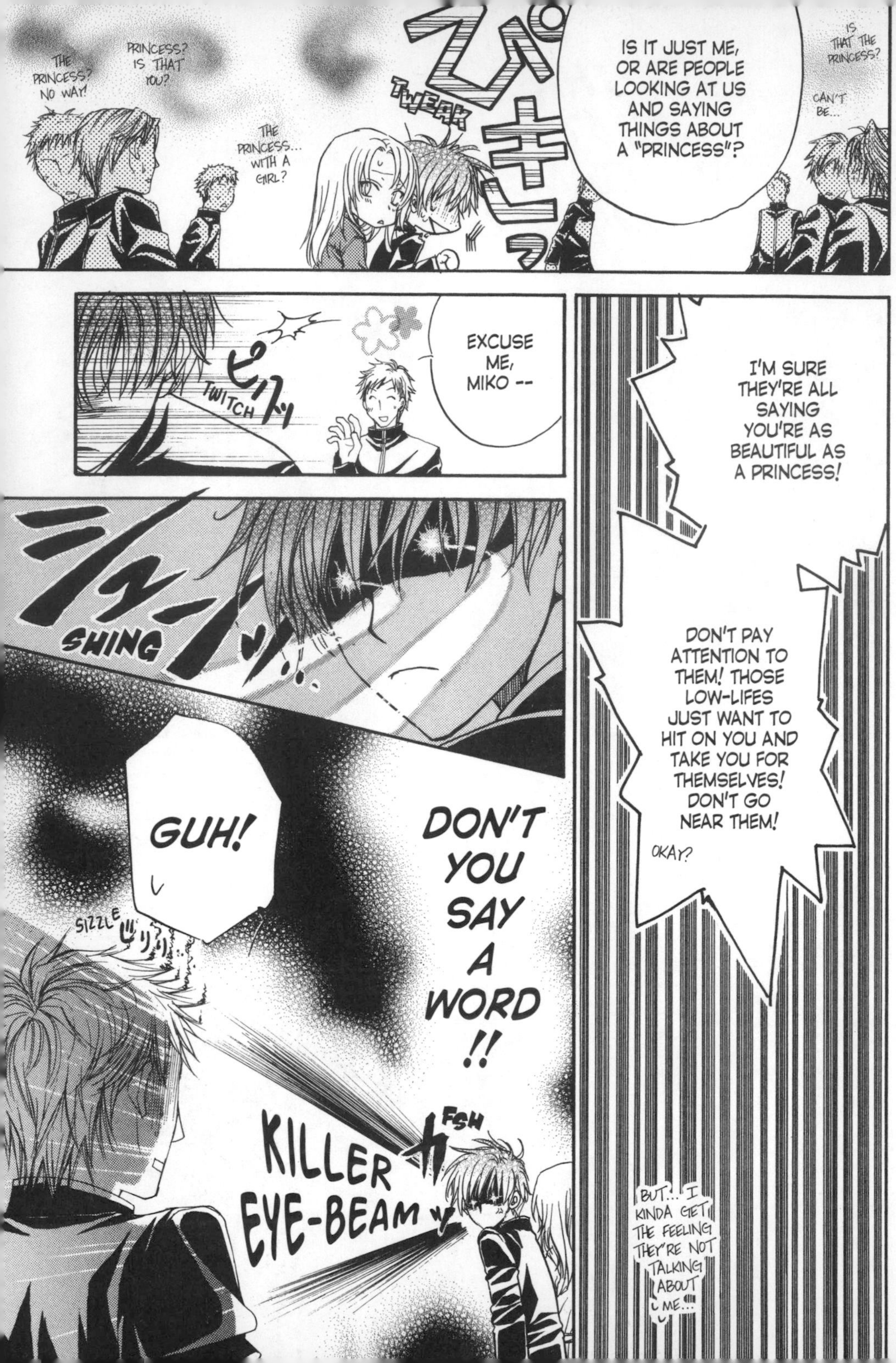
IS THAT THE PRINCESS?
CAN'T BE...
IS IT JUST ME, OR ARE PEOPLE LOOKING AT US AND SAYING THINGS ABOUT A "PRINCESS"?
TWEAK
THE PRINCESS... WITH A GIRL?
PRINCESS? IS THAT YOU?
THE PRINCESS? NO WAY!
I'M SURE THEY'RE ALL SAYING YOU'RE AS BEAUTIFUL AS A PRINCESS!
DON'T PAY ATTENTION TO THEM! THOSE LOW-LIFES JUST WANT TO HIT ON YOU AND TAKE YOU FOR THEMSELVES! DON'T GO NEAR THEM!
OKAY?
BUT... I KINDA GET THE FEELING THEY'RE NOT TALKING ABOUT ME...
EXCUSE ME, MIKO --
TWITCH
SHING
DON'T YOU SAY A WORD!!
GUH!
SIZZLE
FSH
KILLER EYE-BEAM

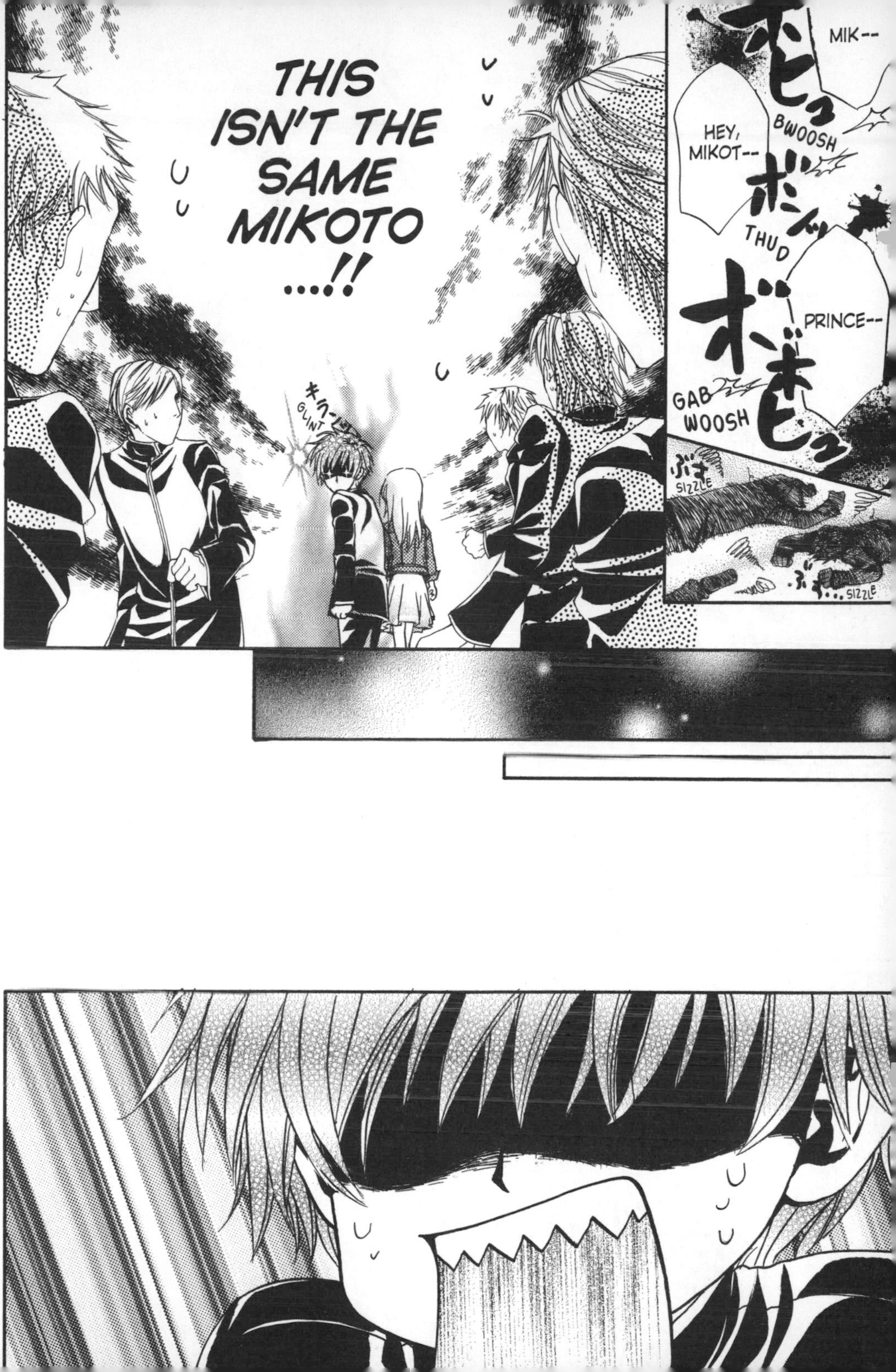
MIK--
HEY, MIKOT--
BWOOSH
THUD
PRINCE--
GAB WOOSH
SIZZLE
SIZZLE
THIS ISN'T THE SAME MIKOTO ...!!
GLINT

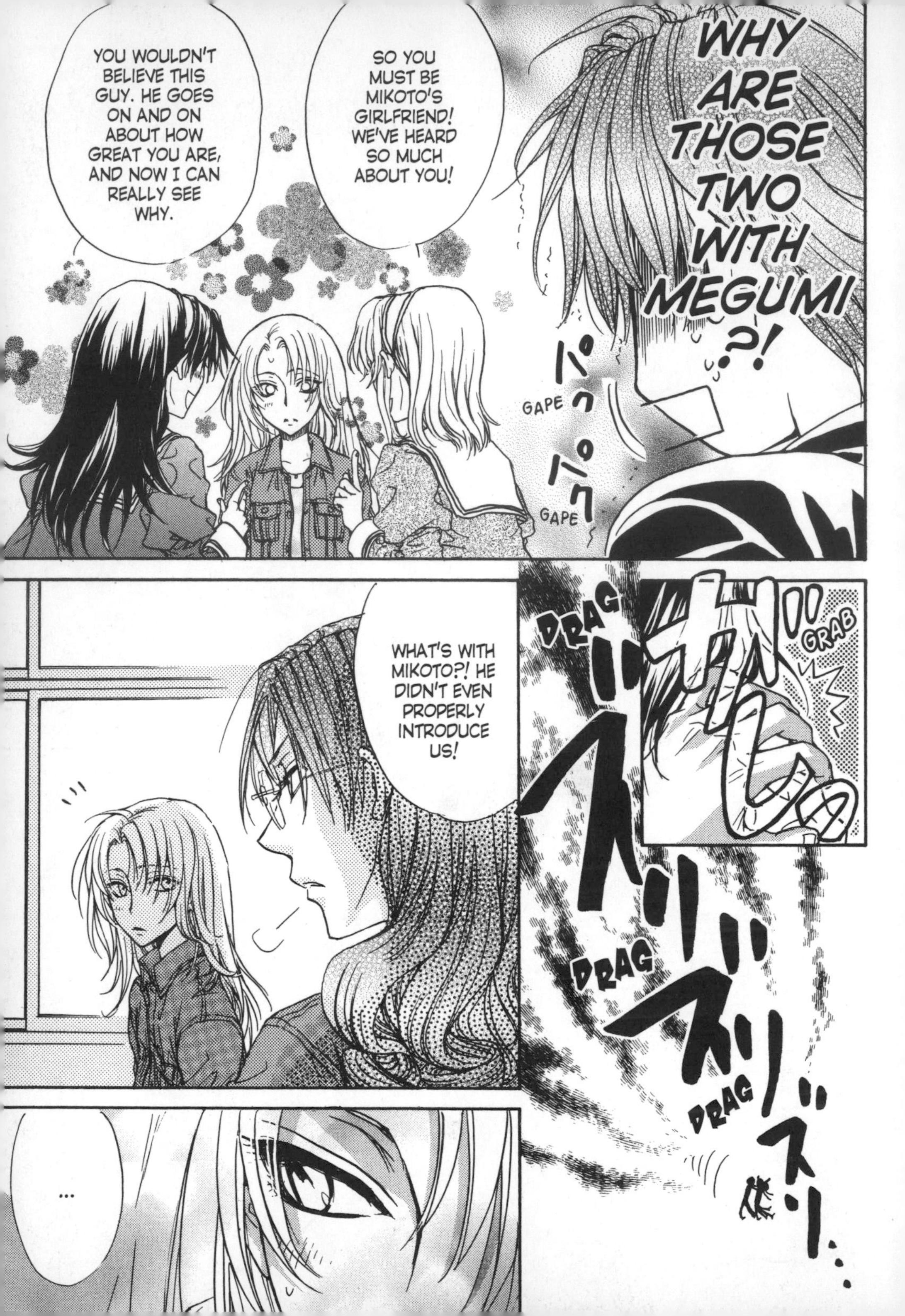
WHY ARE THOSE TWO WITH MEGUMI?!
GAPE
GAPE
SO YOU MUST BE MIKOTO'S GIRLFRIEND! WE'VE HEARD SO MUCH ABOUT YOU!
YOU WOULDN'T BELIEVE THIS GUY. HE GOES ON AND ON ABOUT HOW GREAT YOU ARE, AND NOW I CAN REALLY SEE WHY.
GRAB
DRAG
DRAG
DRAG
WHAT'S WITH MIKOTO?! HE DIDN'T EVEN PROPERLY INTRODUCE US!
...

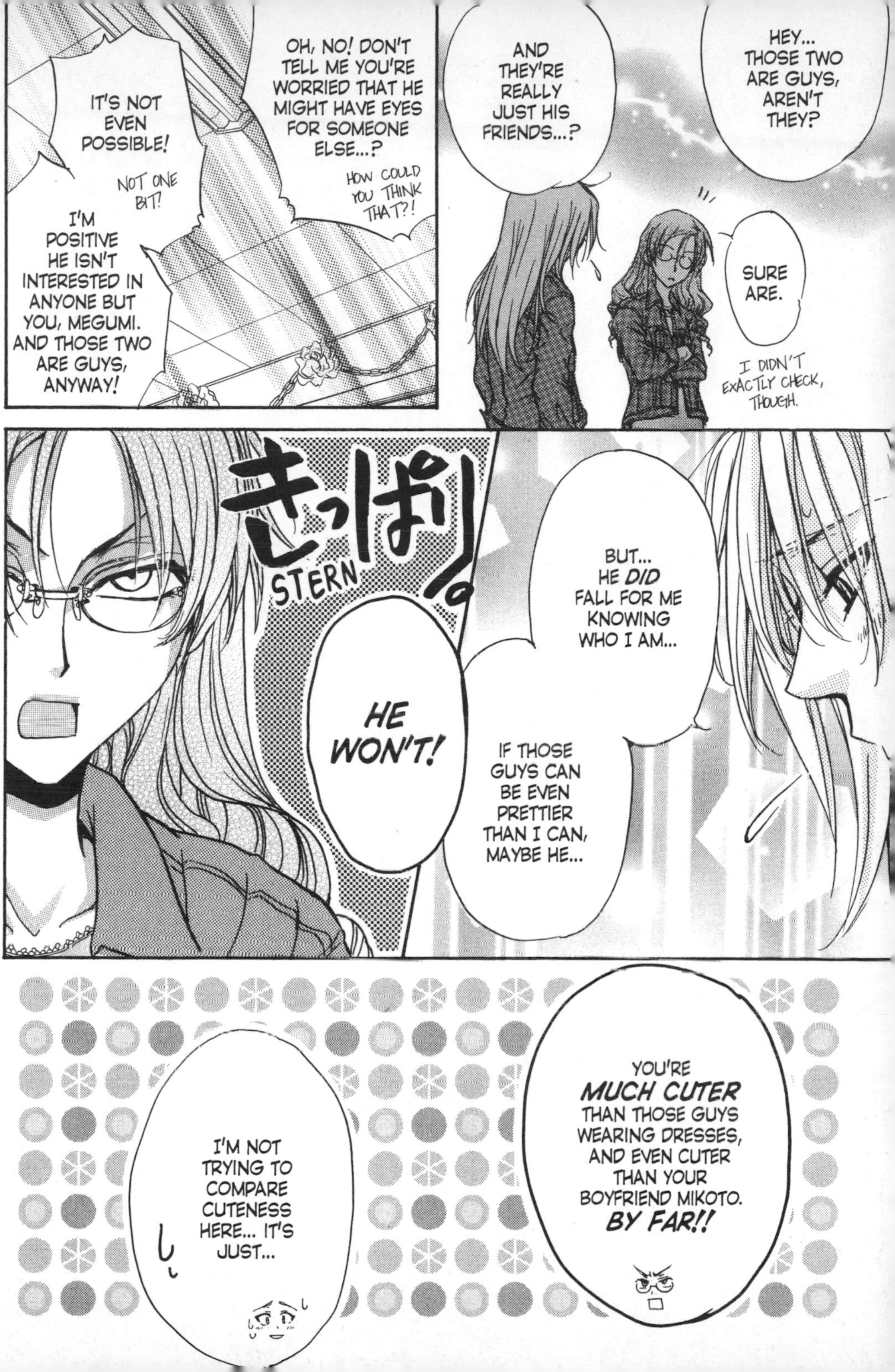
HEY... THOSE TWO ARE GUYS, AREN'T THEY?
AND THEY'RE REALLY JUST HIS FRIENDS...?
SURE ARE.
I DIDN'T EXACTLY CHECK, THOUGH.
OH, NO! DON'T TELL ME YOU'RE WORRIED THAT HE MIGHT HAVE EYES FOR SOMEONE ELSE...?
HOW COULD YOU THINK THAT?!
IT'S NOT EVEN POSSIBLE!
NOT ONE BIT!
I'M POSITIVE HE ISN'T INTERESTED IN ANYONE BUT YOU, MEGUMI. AND THOSE TWO ARE GUYS, ANYWAY!
BUT... HE *DID* FALL FOR ME KNOWING WHO I AM...
IF THOSE GUYS CAN BE EVEN PRETTIER THAN I CAN, MAYBE HE...
きっぱり
STERN
HE WON'T!
YOU'RE **MUCH CUTER** THAN THOSE GUYS WEARING DRESSES, AND EVEN CUTER THAN YOUR BOYFRIEND MIKOTO. **BY FAR!!**
I'M NOT TRYING TO COMPARE CUTENESS HERE... IT'S JUST...

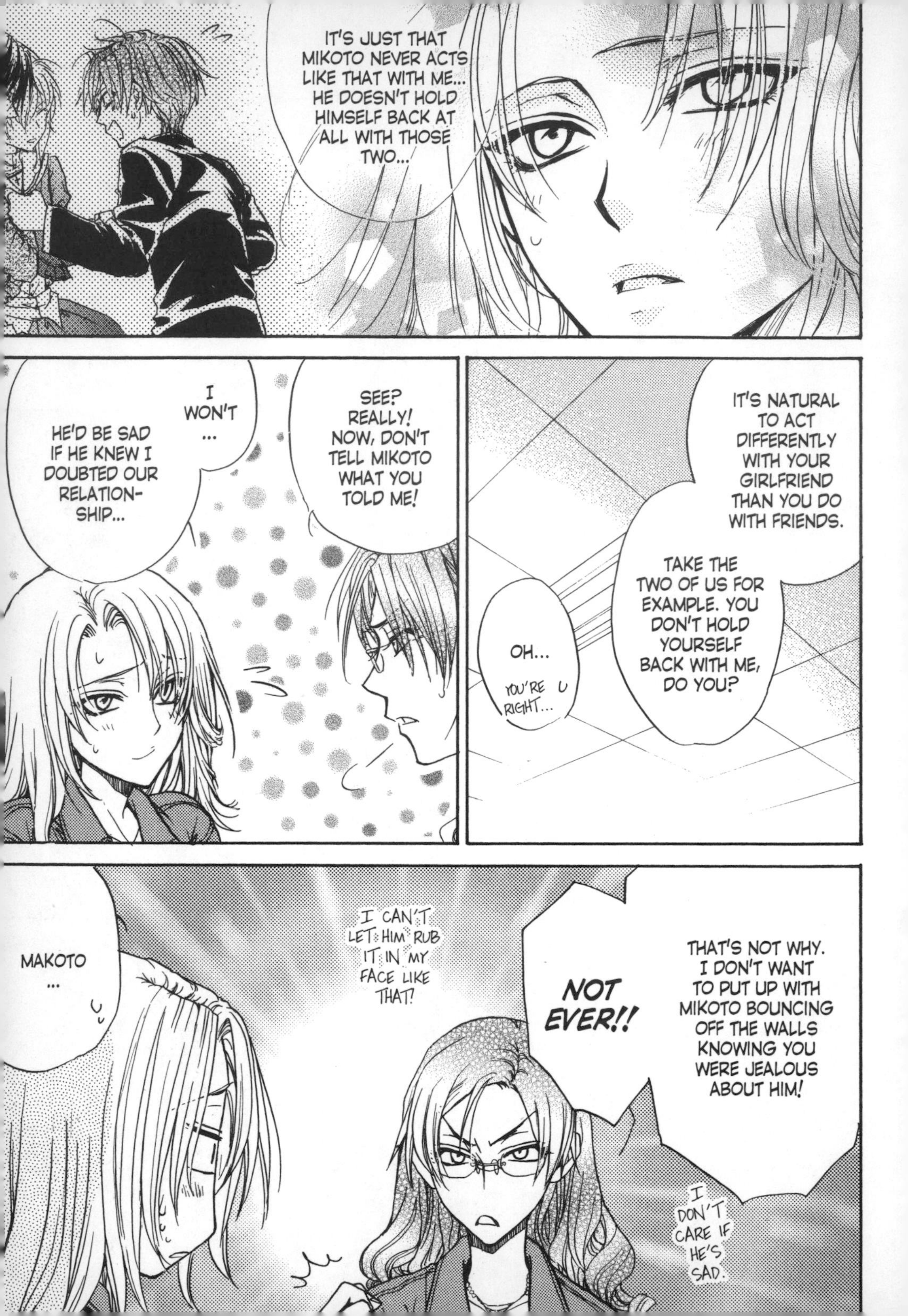
IT'S JUST THAT MIKOTO NEVER ACTS LIKE THAT WITH ME... HE DOESN'T HOLD HIMSELF BACK AT ALL WITH THOSE TWO...
IT'S NATURAL TO ACT DIFFERENTLY WITH YOUR GIRLFRIEND THAN YOU DO WITH FRIENDS.
TAKE THE TWO OF US FOR EXAMPLE. YOU DON'T HOLD YOURSELF BACK WITH ME, DO YOU?
OH...
YOU'RE RIGHT...
SEE? REALLY! NOW, DON'T TELL MIKOTO WHAT YOU TOLD ME!
I WON'T ...
HE'D BE SAD IF HE KNEW I DOUBTED OUR RELATION-SHIP...
THAT'S NOT WHY. I DON'T WANT TO PUT UP WITH MIKOTO BOUNCING OFF THE WALLS KNOWING YOU WERE JEALOUS ABOUT HIM!
NOT EVER!!
I DON'T CARE IF HE'S SAD.
I CAN'T LET HIM RUB IT IN MY FACE LIKE THAT!
MAKOTO ...

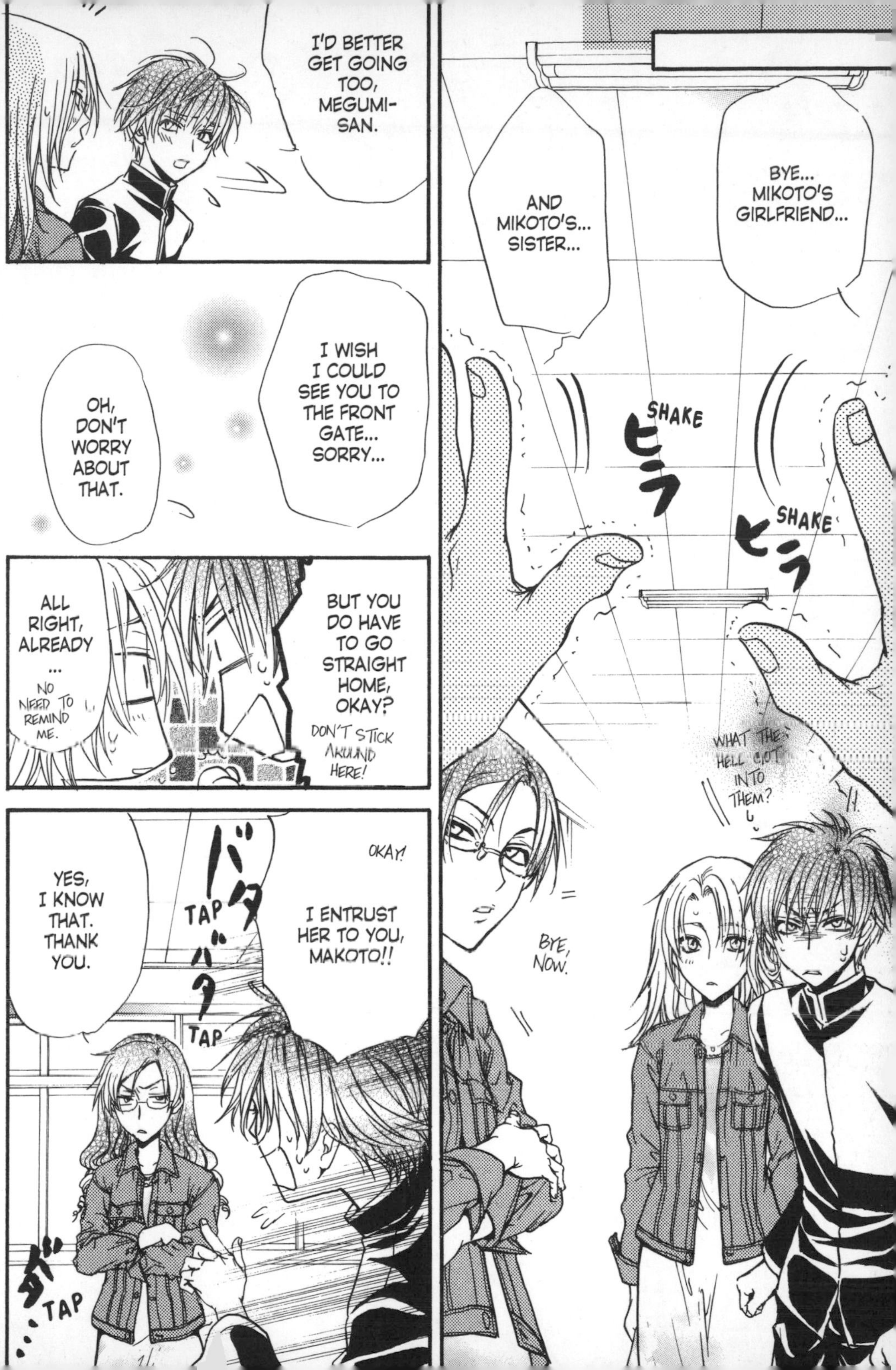
BYE... MIKOTO'S GIRLFRIEND...
AND MIKOTO'S... SISTER...
SHAKE ヒラ
SHAKE ヒラ
WHAT THE HELL GOT INTO THEM?
BYE, NOW.
I'D BETTER GET GOING TOO, MEGUMI-SAN.
I WISH I COULD SEE YOU TO THE FRONT GATE... SORRY...
OH, DON'T WORRY ABOUT THAT.
BUT YOU DO HAVE TO GO STRAIGHT HOME, OKAY?
DON'T STICK AROUND HERE!
ALL RIGHT, ALREADY...
NO NEED TO REMIND ME.
OKAY!
I ENTRUST HER TO YOU, MAKOTO!!
バタ TAP
バタ TAP
YES, I KNOW THAT. THANK YOU.
ダ TAP

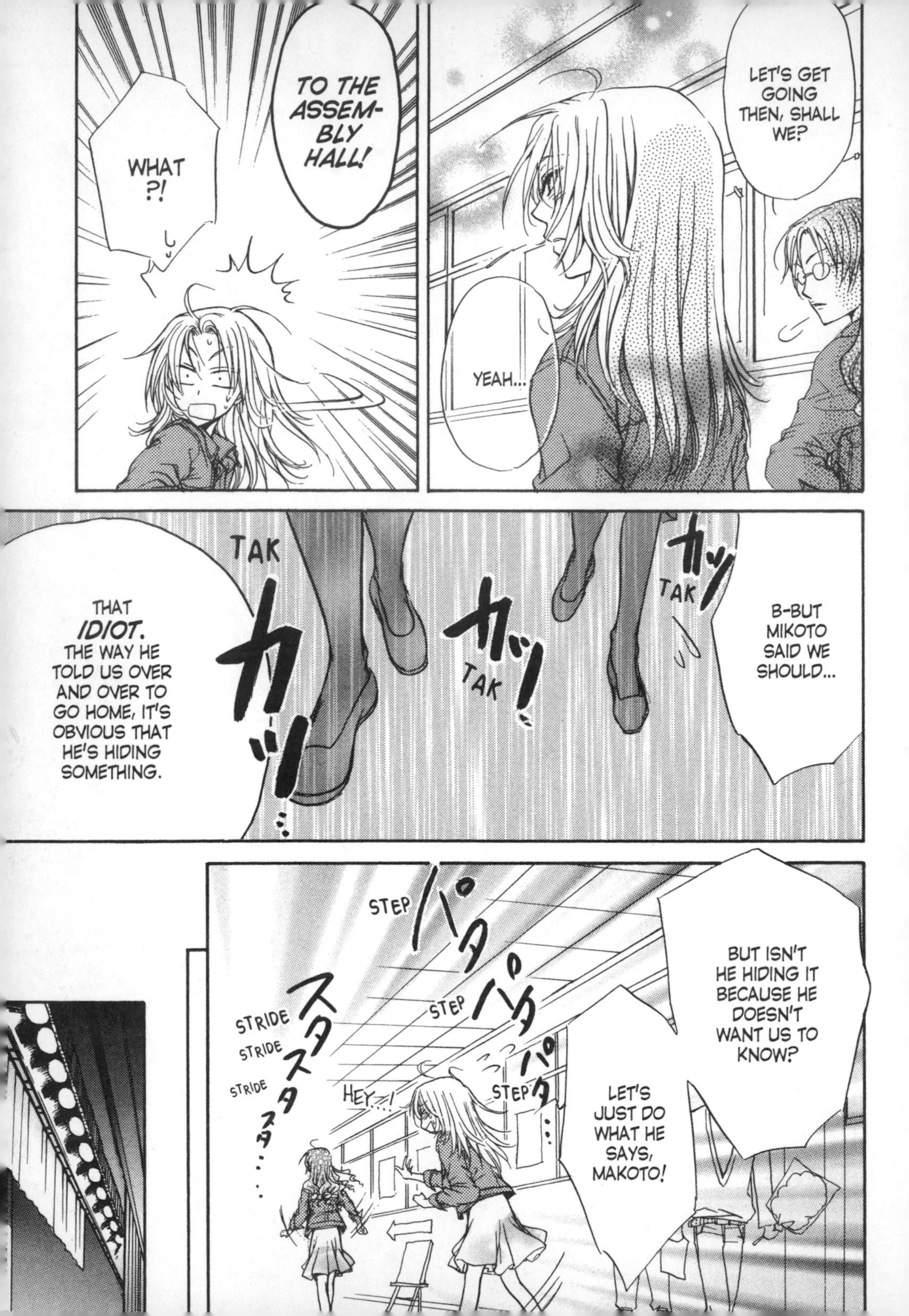

LET'S GET GOING THEN, SHALL WE?
YEAH...
TO THE ASSEM-BLY HALL!
WHAT ?!
B-BUT MIKOTO SAID WE SHOULD...
TAK
TAK
TAK
THAT *IDIOT*. THE WAY HE TOLD US OVER AND OVER TO GO HOME, IT'S OBVIOUS THAT HE'S HIDING SOMETHING.
BUT ISN'T HE HIDING IT BECAUSE HE DOESN'T WANT US TO KNOW?
LET'S JUST DO WHAT HE SAYS, MAKOTO!
STEP
STEP
STEP
STRIDE
STRIDE
STRIDE
HEY...!

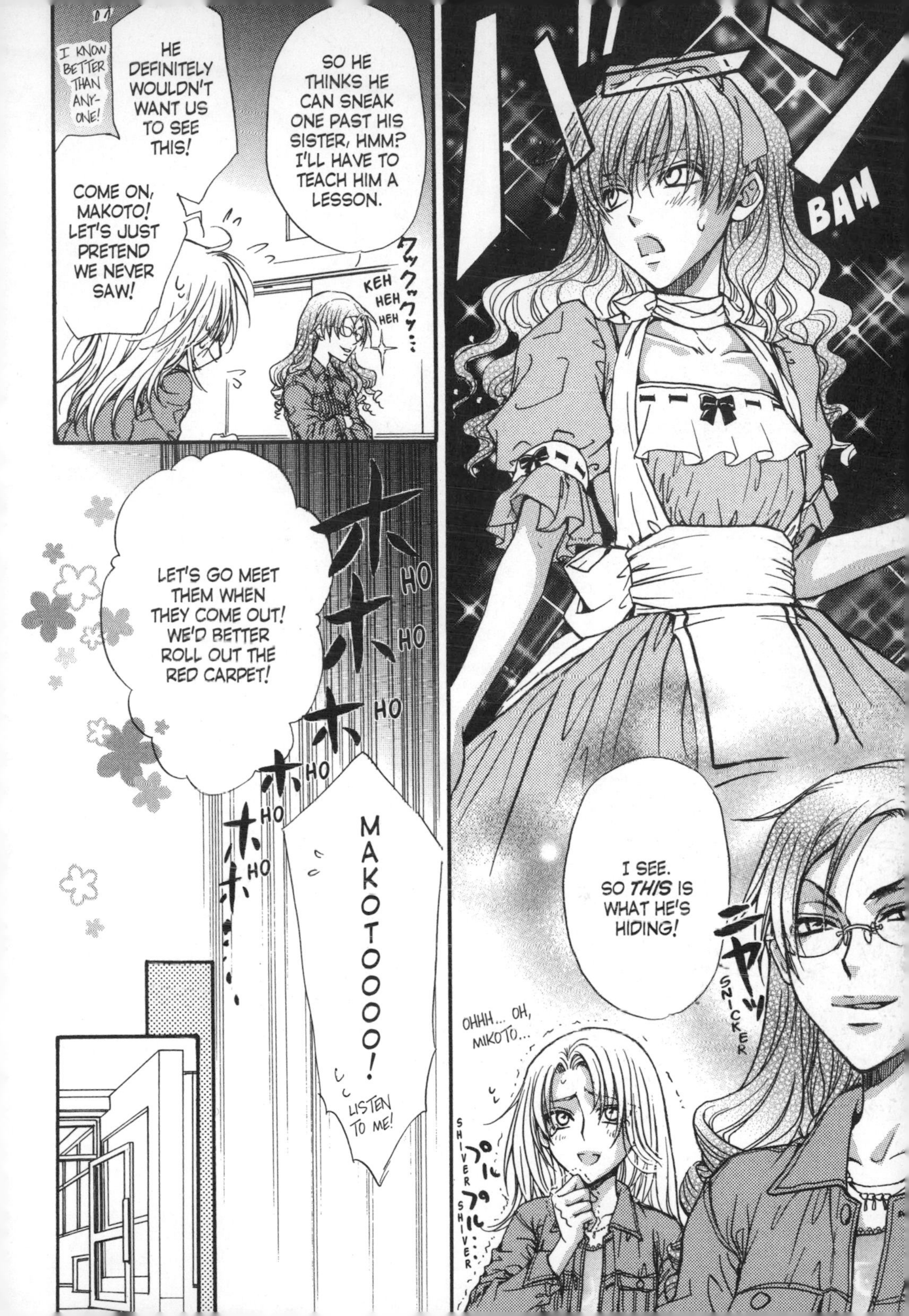
BAM
I SEE. SO THIS IS WHAT HE'S HIDING!
SNICKER
OHHH... OH, MIKOTO...
SHIVER SHIVER
SO HE THINKS HE CAN SNEAK ONE PAST HIS SISTER, HMM? I'LL HAVE TO TEACH HIM A LESSON.
HE DEFINITELY WOULDN'T WANT US TO SEE THIS!
I KNOW BETTER THAN ANY-ONE!
KEH HEH HEH
COME ON, MAKOTO! LET'S JUST PRETEND WE NEVER SAW!
HO HO HO HO HO HO
LET'S GO MEET THEM WHEN THEY COME OUT! WE'D BETTER ROLL OUT THE RED CARPET!
MAKOTOOOOO!
LISTEN TO ME!

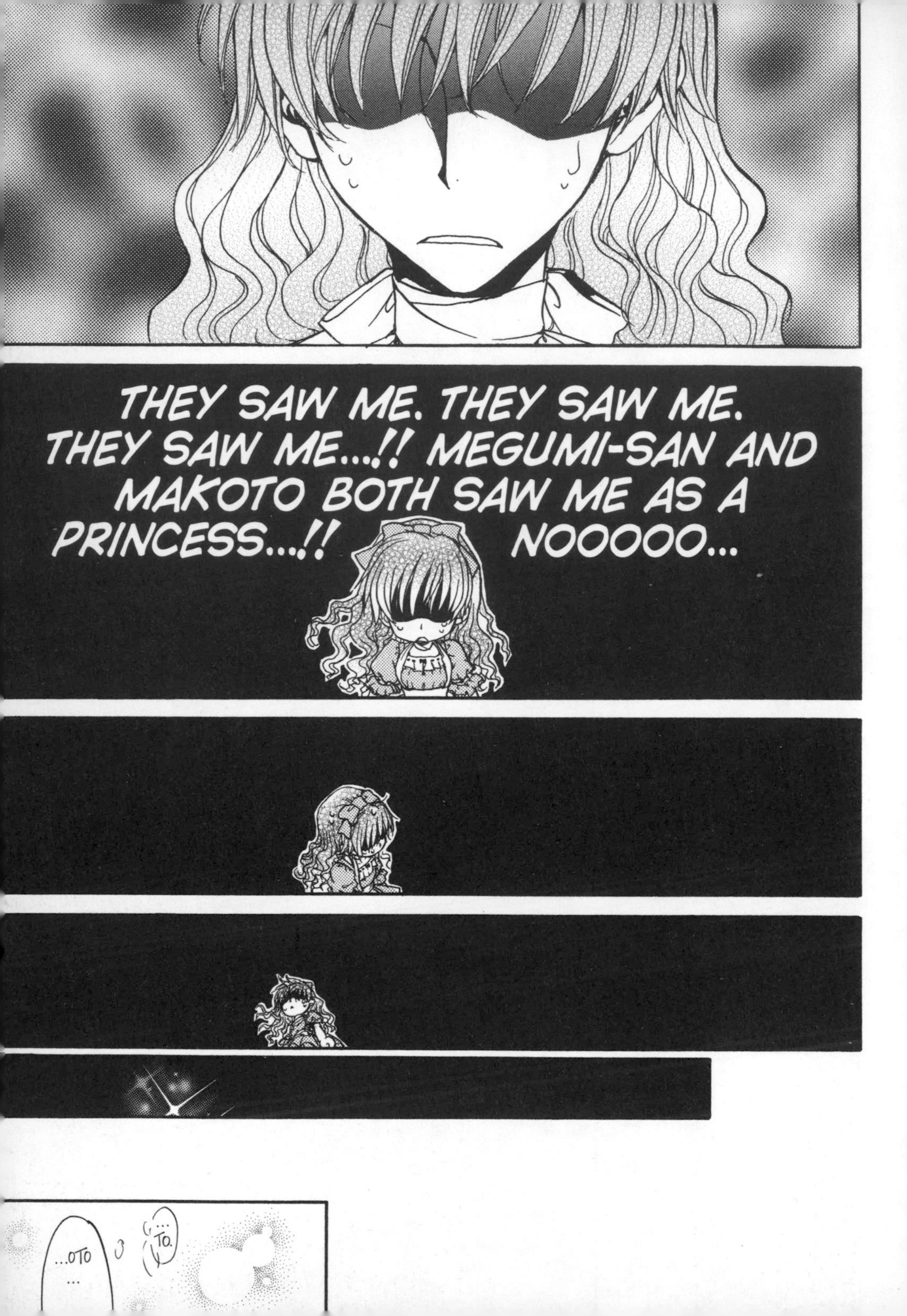
THEY SAW ME. THEY SAW ME. THEY SAW ME...!! MEGUMI-SAN AND MAKOTO BOTH SAW ME AS A PRINCESS...!! NOOOOO...
...TO.
...OTO ...

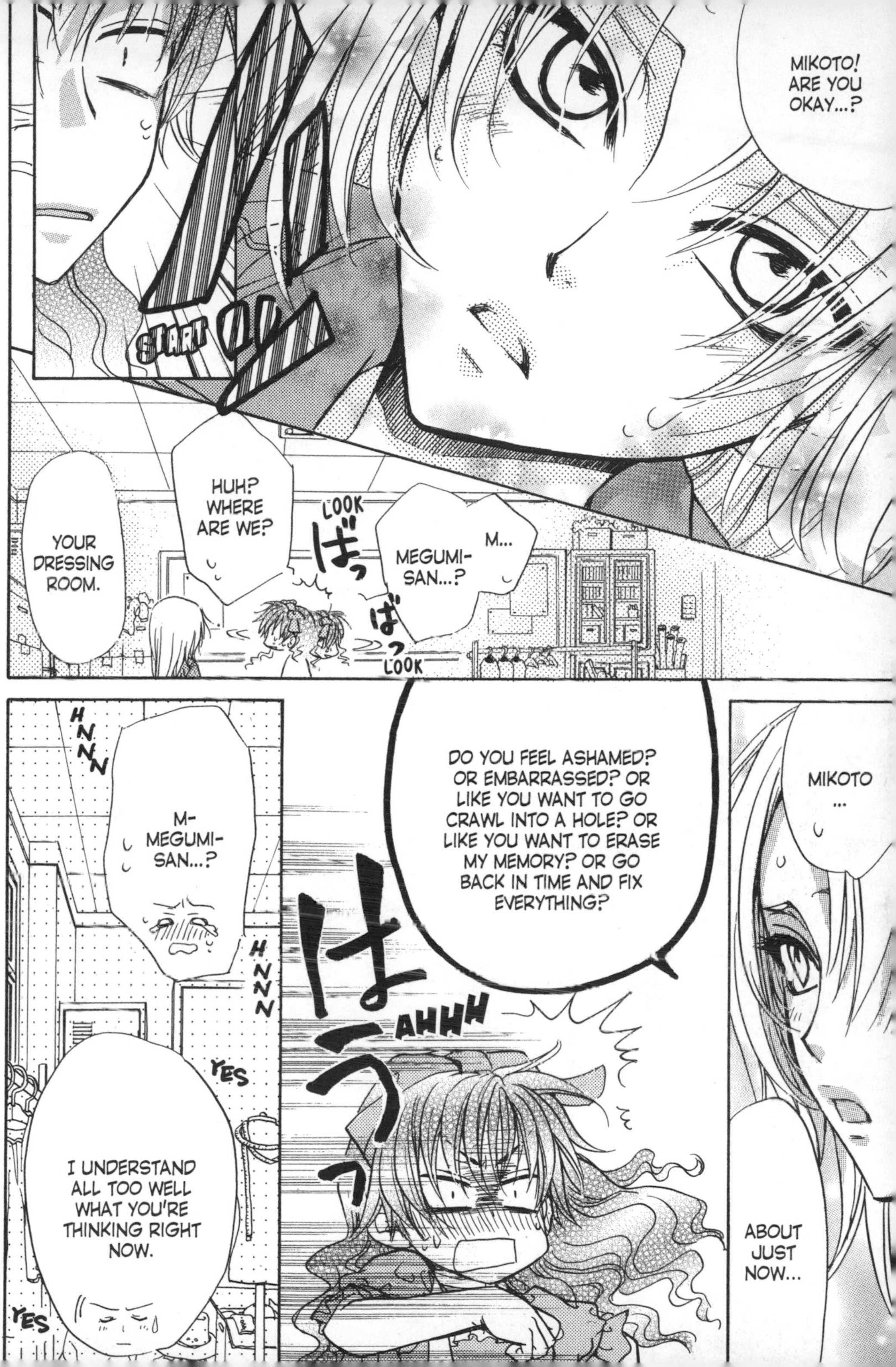
MIKOTO! ARE YOU OKAY...?
START
M... MEGUMI-SAN...?
ばっ
LOOK
ばっ
LOOK
HUH? WHERE ARE WE?
YOUR DRESSING ROOM.
MIKOTO ...
ABOUT JUST NOW...
DO YOU FEEL ASHAMED? OR EMBARRASSED? OR LIKE YOU WANT TO GO CRAWL INTO A HOLE? OR LIKE YOU WANT TO ERASE MY MEMORY? OR GO BACK IN TIME AND FIX EVERYTHING?
はっ
AHHH
HNNN
M- MEGUMI-SAN...?
HNNN
YES
I UNDERSTAND ALL TOO WELL WHAT YOU'RE THINKING RIGHT NOW.
YES

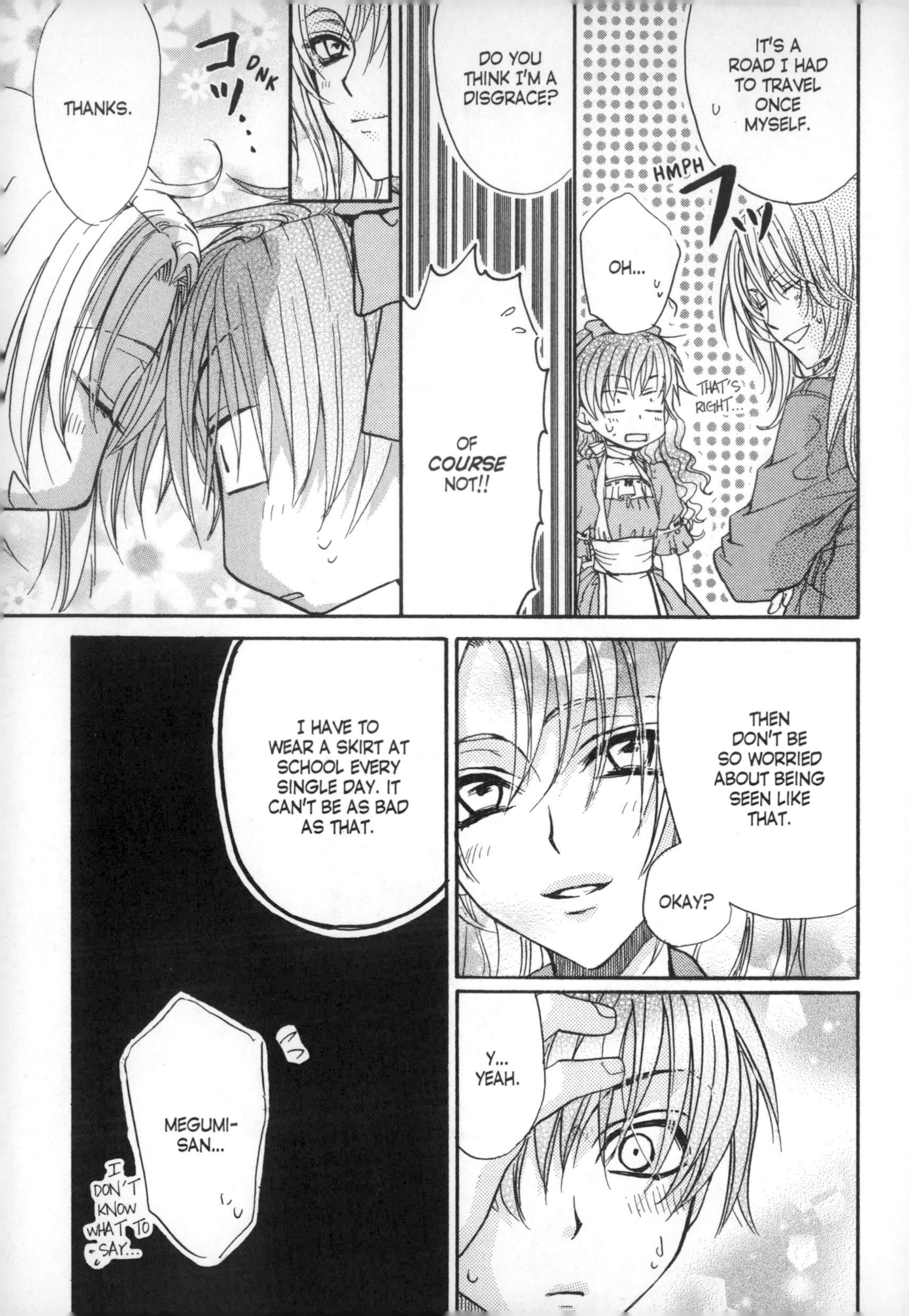
IT'S A ROAD I HAD TO TRAVEL ONCE MYSELF.
HMPH
OH...
THAT'S RIGHT...
DO YOU THINK I'M A DISGRACE?
OF COURSE NOT!!
DNK
THANKS.
THEN DON'T BE SO WORRIED ABOUT BEING SEEN LIKE THAT.
OKAY?
Y... YEAH.
I HAVE TO WEAR A SKIRT AT SCHOOL EVERY SINGLE DAY. IT CAN'T BE AS BAD AS THAT.
MEGUMI-SAN...
I DON'T KNOW WHAT TO SAY...

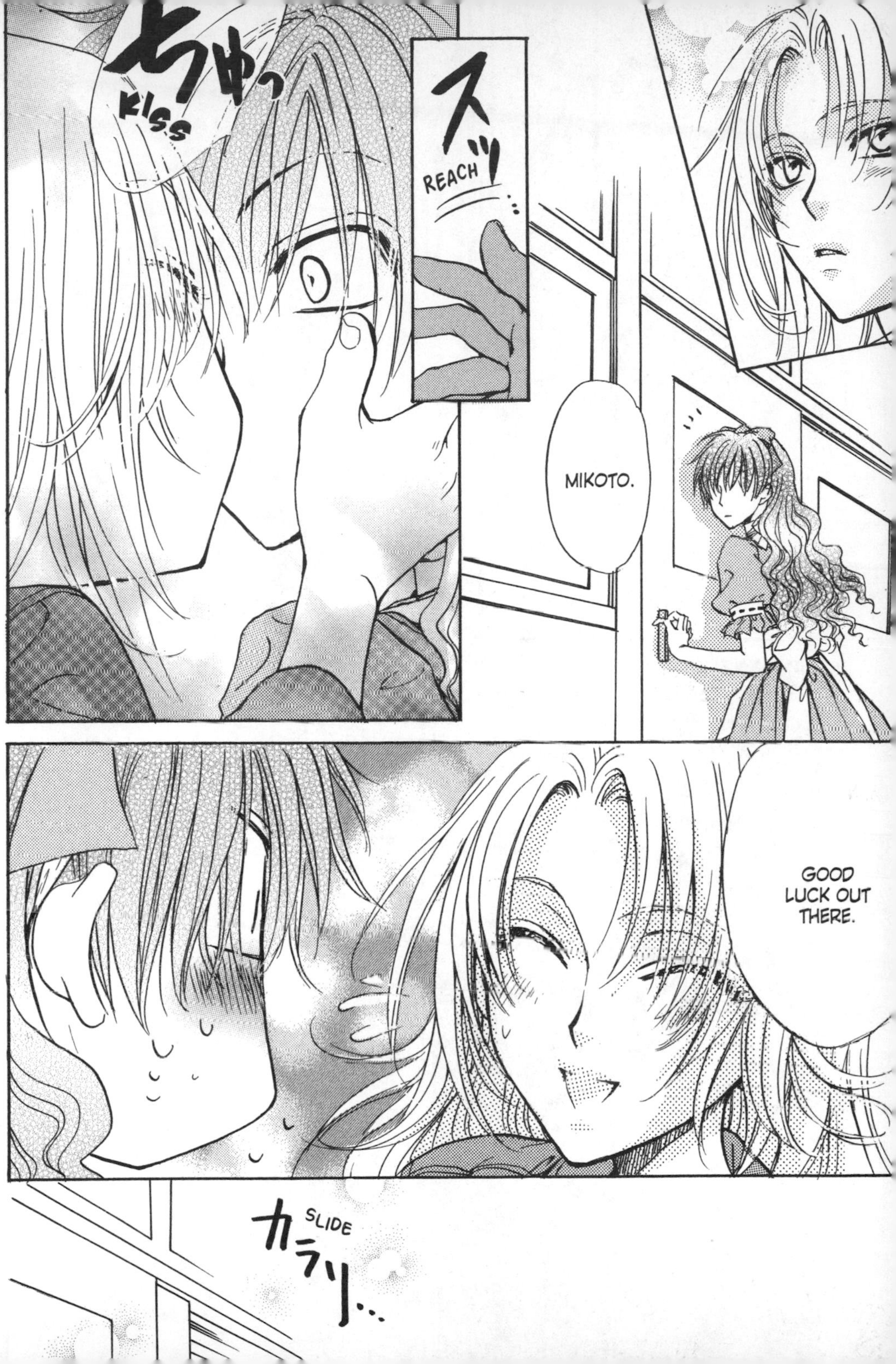

MIKOTO.
ちゅっ
KISS
スッ
REACH
GOOD LUCK OUT THERE.
カラリ…
SLIDE

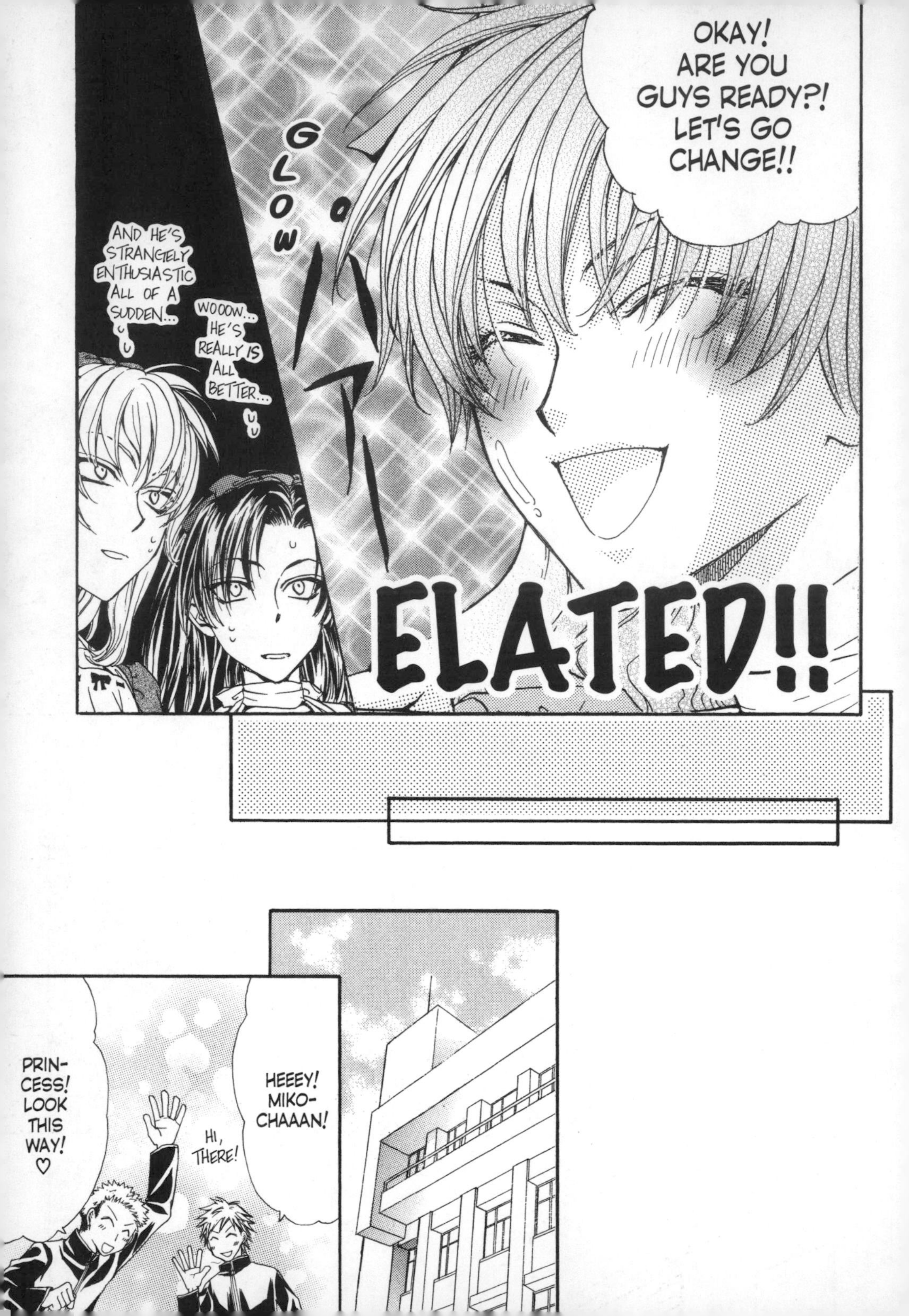
OKAY! ARE YOU GUYS READY?! LET'S GO CHANGE!!
GLOW
ELATED!!
WOOOW... HE'S REALLY IS ALL BETTER...
AND HE'S STRANGELY ENTHUSIASTIC ALL OF A SUDDEN...
HEEEY! MIKO-CHAAAN!
HI, THERE!
PRIN-CESS! LOOK THIS WAY! ♡

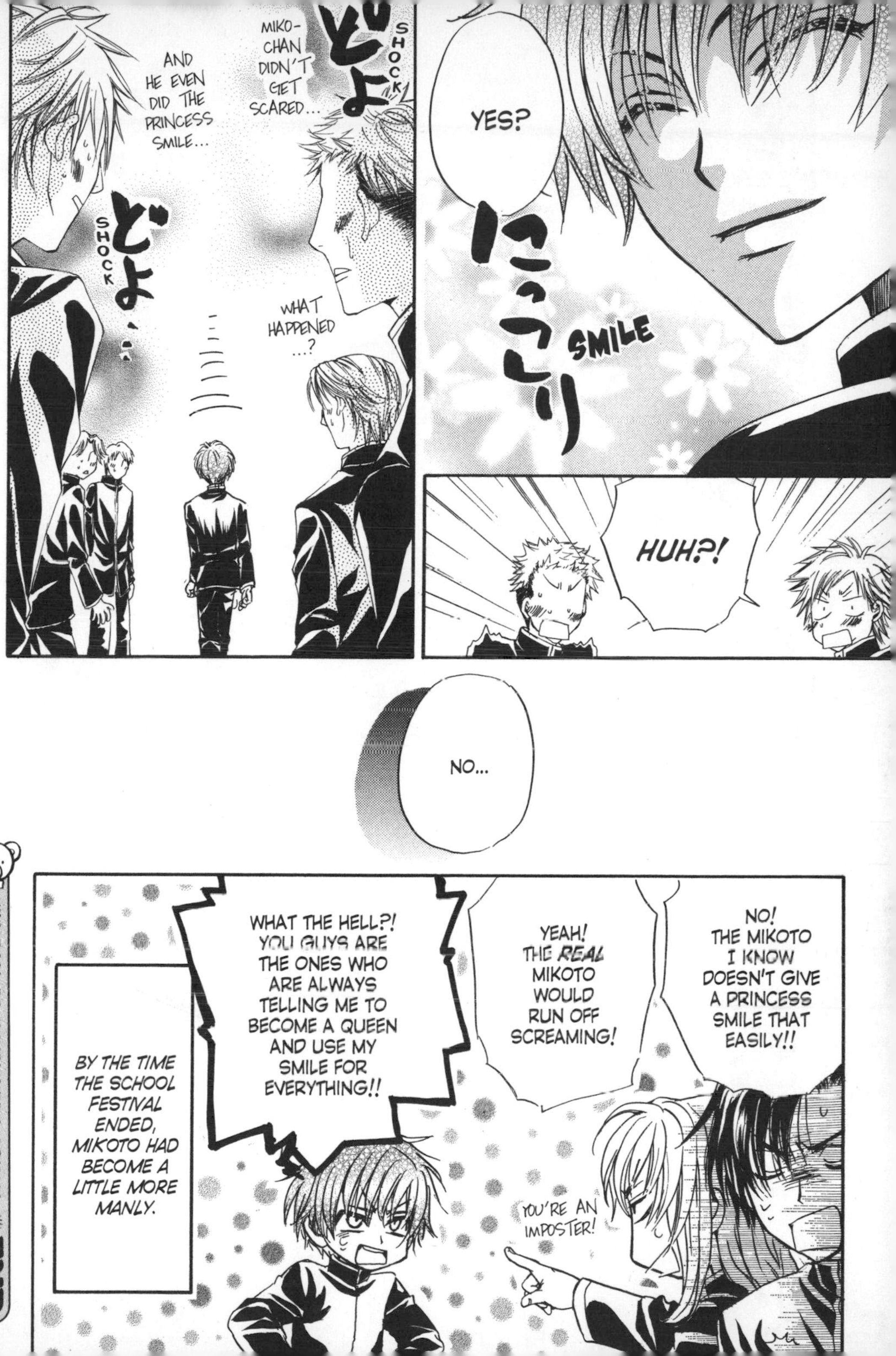
YES?
にっこり
SMILE
HUH?!
どよ
SHOCK
MIKO-CHAN DIDN'T GET SCARED...
AND HE EVEN DID THE PRINCESS SMILE...
どよ
SHOCK
WHAT HAPPENED ...?
NO...
NO! THE MIKOTO I KNOW DOESN'T GIVE A PRINCESS SMILE THAT EASILY!!
YEAH! THE *REAL* MIKOTO WOULD RUN OFF SCREAMING!
WHAT THE HELL?! YOU GUYS ARE THE ONES WHO ARE ALWAYS TELLING ME TO BECOME A QUEEN AND USE MY SMILE FOR EVERYTHING!!
YOU'RE AN IMPOSTER!
BY THE TIME THE SCHOOL FESTIVAL ENDED, MIKOTO HAD BECOME A LITTLE MORE MANLY.

THE JAY OF REVOLUTION SPECIAL ✸ END

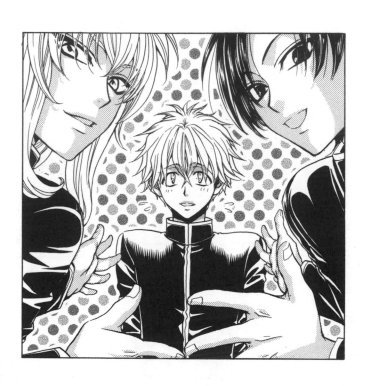

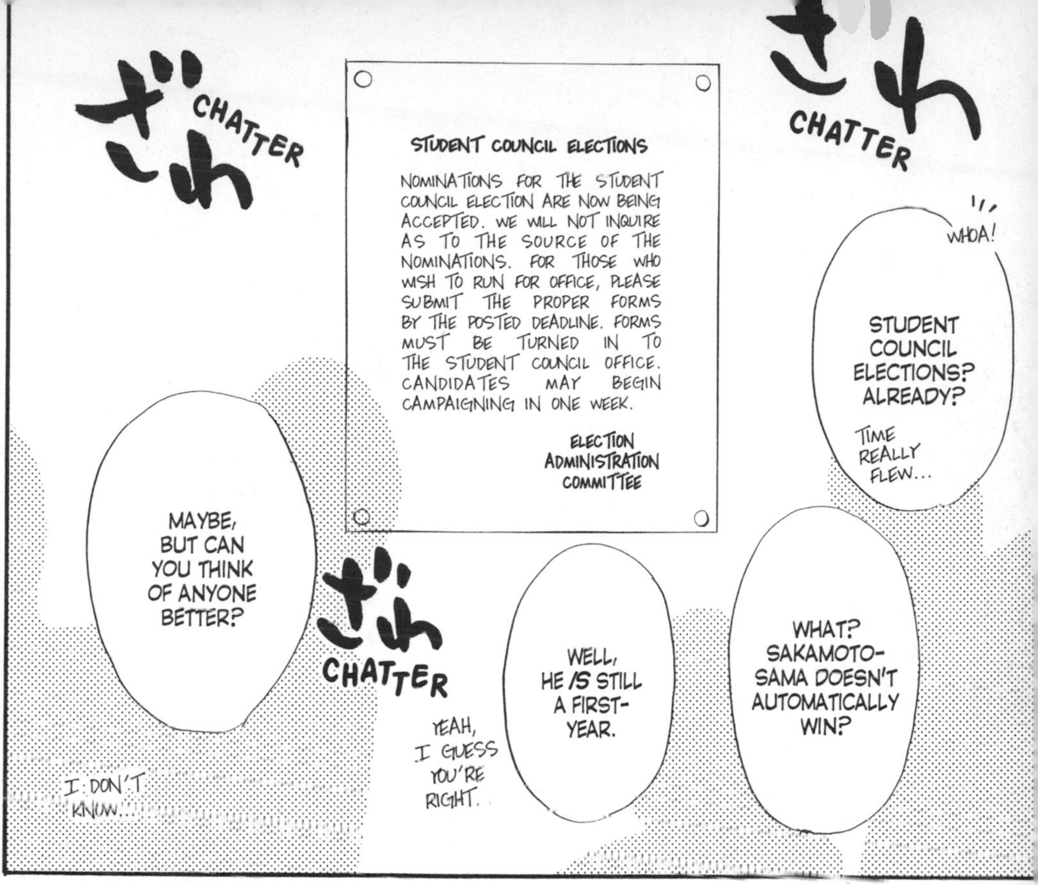
さわ CHATTER
WHOA!
STUDENT COUNCIL ELECTIONS? ALREADY?
TIME REALLY FLEW...
STUDENT COUNCIL ELECTIONS
NOMINATIONS FOR THE STUDENT COUNCIL ELECTION ARE NOW BEING ACCEPTED. WE WILL NOT INQUIRE AS TO THE SOURCE OF THE NOMINATIONS. FOR THOSE WHO WISH TO RUN FOR OFFICE, PLEASE SUBMIT THE PROPER FORMS BY THE POSTED DEADLINE. FORMS MUST BE TURNED IN TO THE STUDENT COUNCIL OFFICE. CANDIDATES MAY BEGIN CAMPAIGNING IN ONE WEEK.
ELECTION ADMINISTRATION COMMITTEE
ざわ CHATTER
WHAT? SAKAMOTO-SAMA DOESN'T AUTOMATICALLY WIN?
WELL, HE *IS* STILL A FIRST-YEAR.
YEAH, I GUESS YOU'RE RIGHT.
ざわ CHATTER
MAYBE, BUT CAN YOU THINK OF ANYONE BETTER?
I DON'T KNOW...
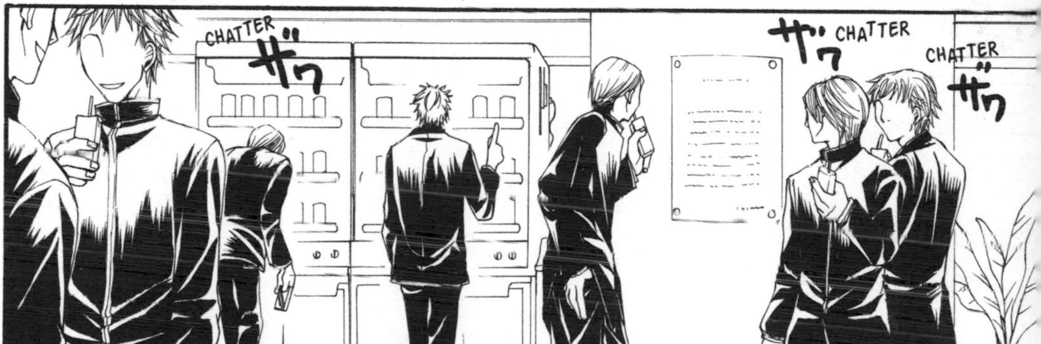
ザワ CHATTER
ザワ CHATTER
ザワ CHATTER
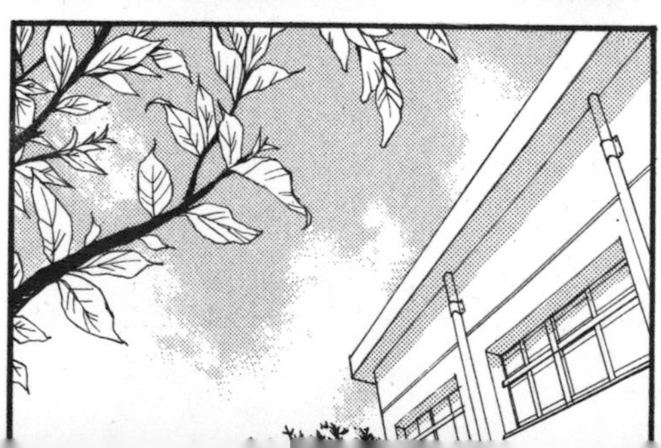

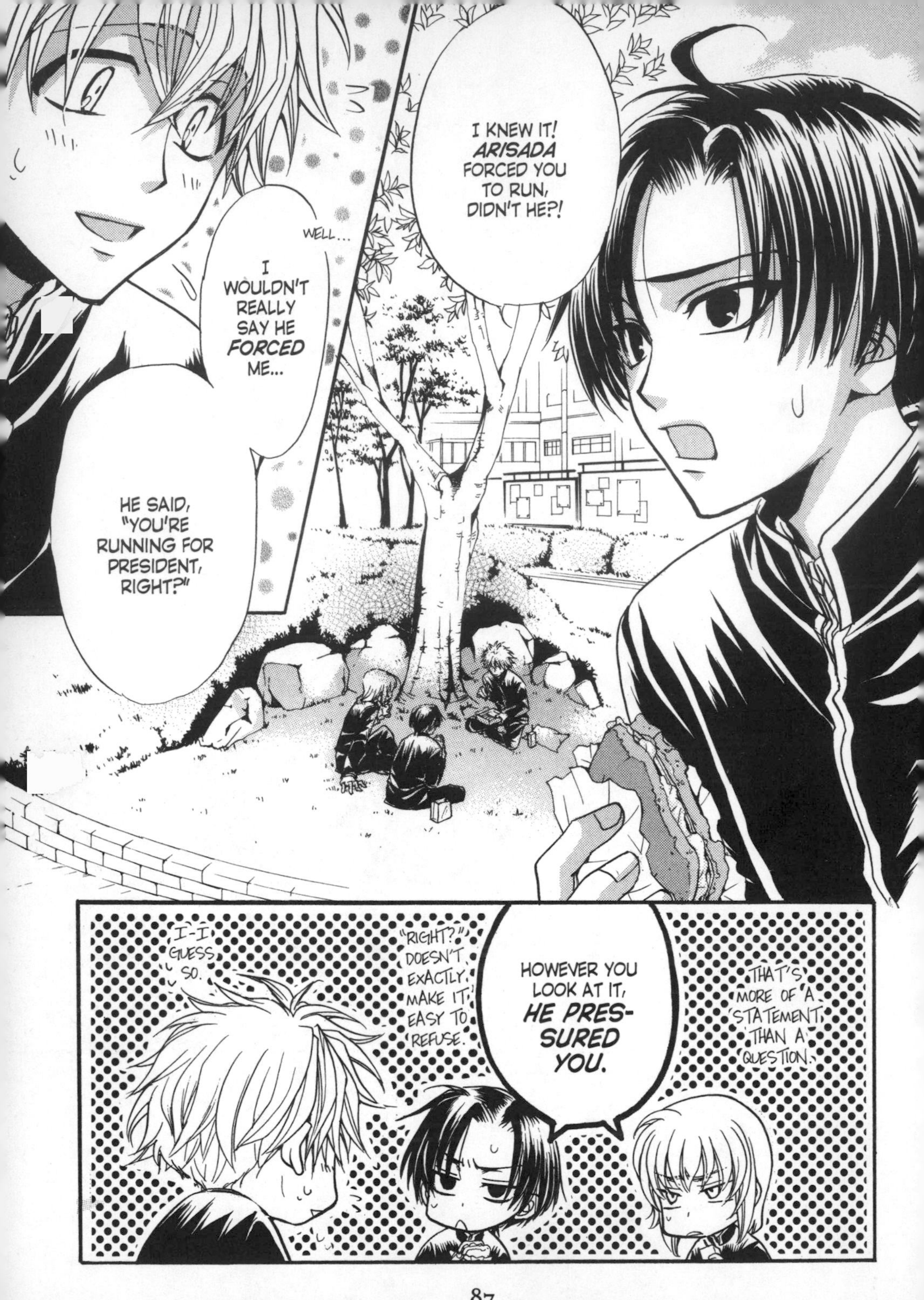
I KNEW IT! ARISADA FORCED YOU TO RUN, DIDN'T HE?!
WELL...
I WOULDN'T REALLY SAY HE FORCED ME...
HE SAID, "YOU'RE RUNNING FOR PRESIDENT, RIGHT?"
THAT'S MORE OF A STATEMENT THAN A QUESTION.
HOWEVER YOU LOOK AT IT, HE PRES-SURED YOU.
"RIGHT?" DOESN'T EXACTLY MAKE IT EASY TO REFUSE.
I-I GUESS SO.

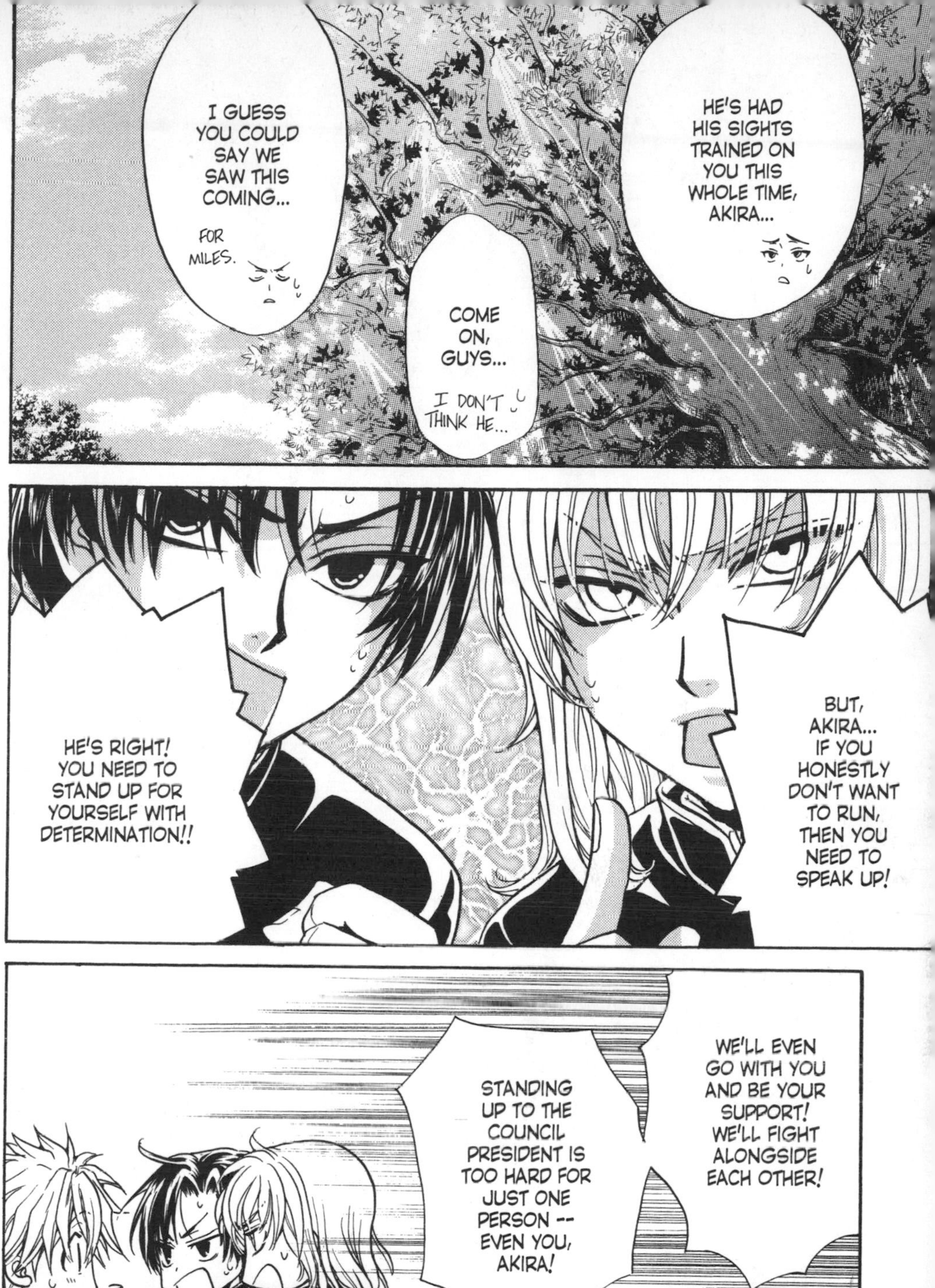
HE'S HAD HIS SIGHTS TRAINED ON YOU THIS WHOLE TIME, AKIRA...
COME ON, GUYS...
I DON'T THINK HE...
I GUESS YOU COULD SAY WE SAW THIS COMING...
FOR MILES.
BUT, AKIRA... IF YOU HONESTLY DON'T WANT TO RUN, THEN YOU NEED TO SPEAK UP!
HE'S RIGHT! YOU NEED TO STAND UP FOR YOURSELF WITH DETERMINATION!!
WE'LL EVEN GO WITH YOU AND BE YOUR SUPPORT! WE'LL FIGHT ALONGSIDE EACH OTHER!
STANDING UP TO THE COUNCIL PRESIDENT IS TOO HARD FOR JUST ONE PERSON -- EVEN YOU, AKIRA!

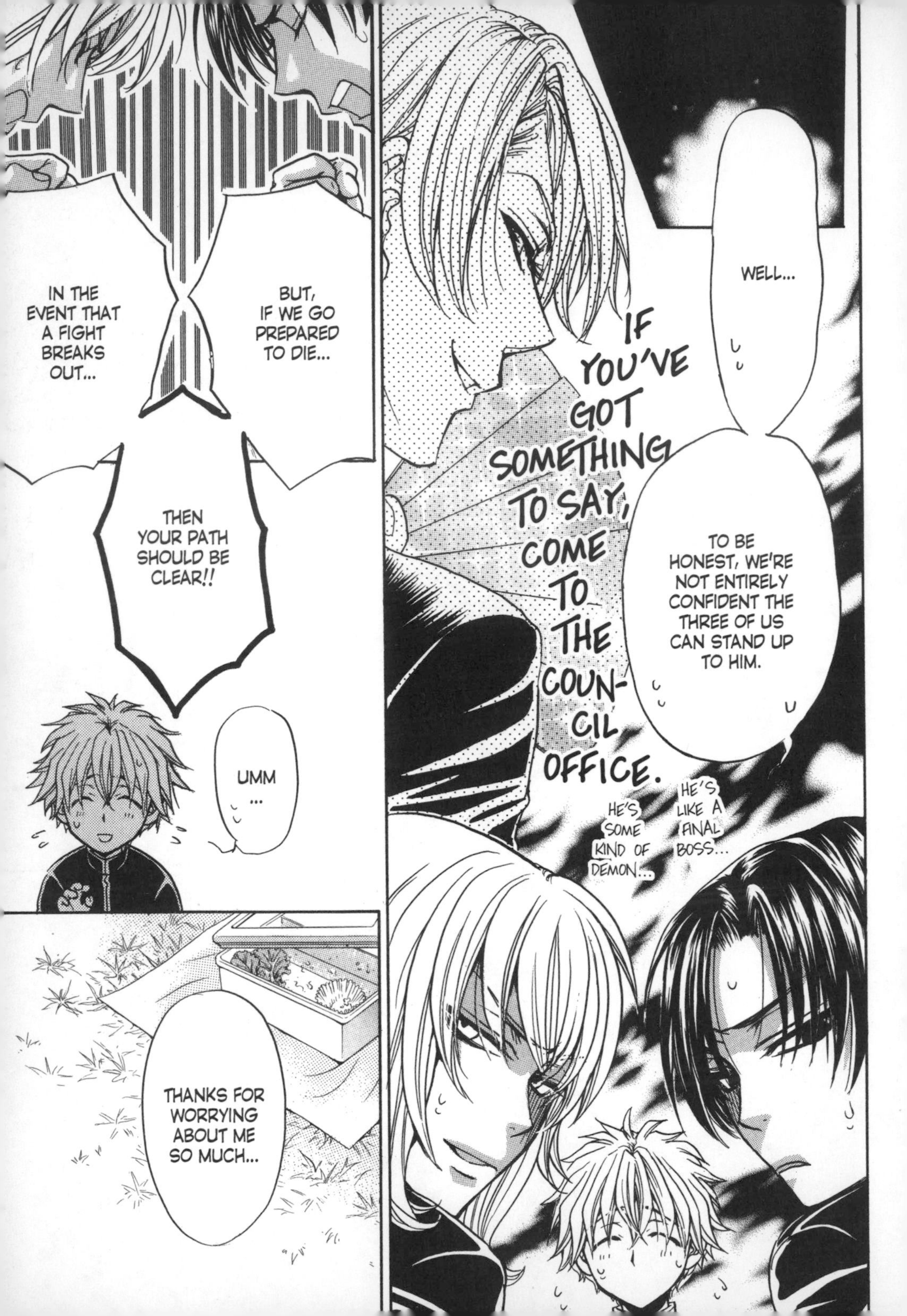
WELL...
TO BE HONEST, WE'RE NOT ENTIRELY CONFIDENT THE THREE OF US CAN STAND UP TO HIM.
IF YOU'VE GOT SOMETHING TO SAY, COME TO THE COUN-CIL OFFICE.
HE'S LIKE A FINAL BOSS...
HE'S SOME KIND OF DEMON...
BUT, IF WE GO PREPARED TO DIE...
IN THE EVENT THAT A FIGHT BREAKS OUT...
THEN YOUR PATH SHOULD BE CLEAR!!
UMM ...
THANKS FOR WORRYING ABOUT ME SO MUCH...

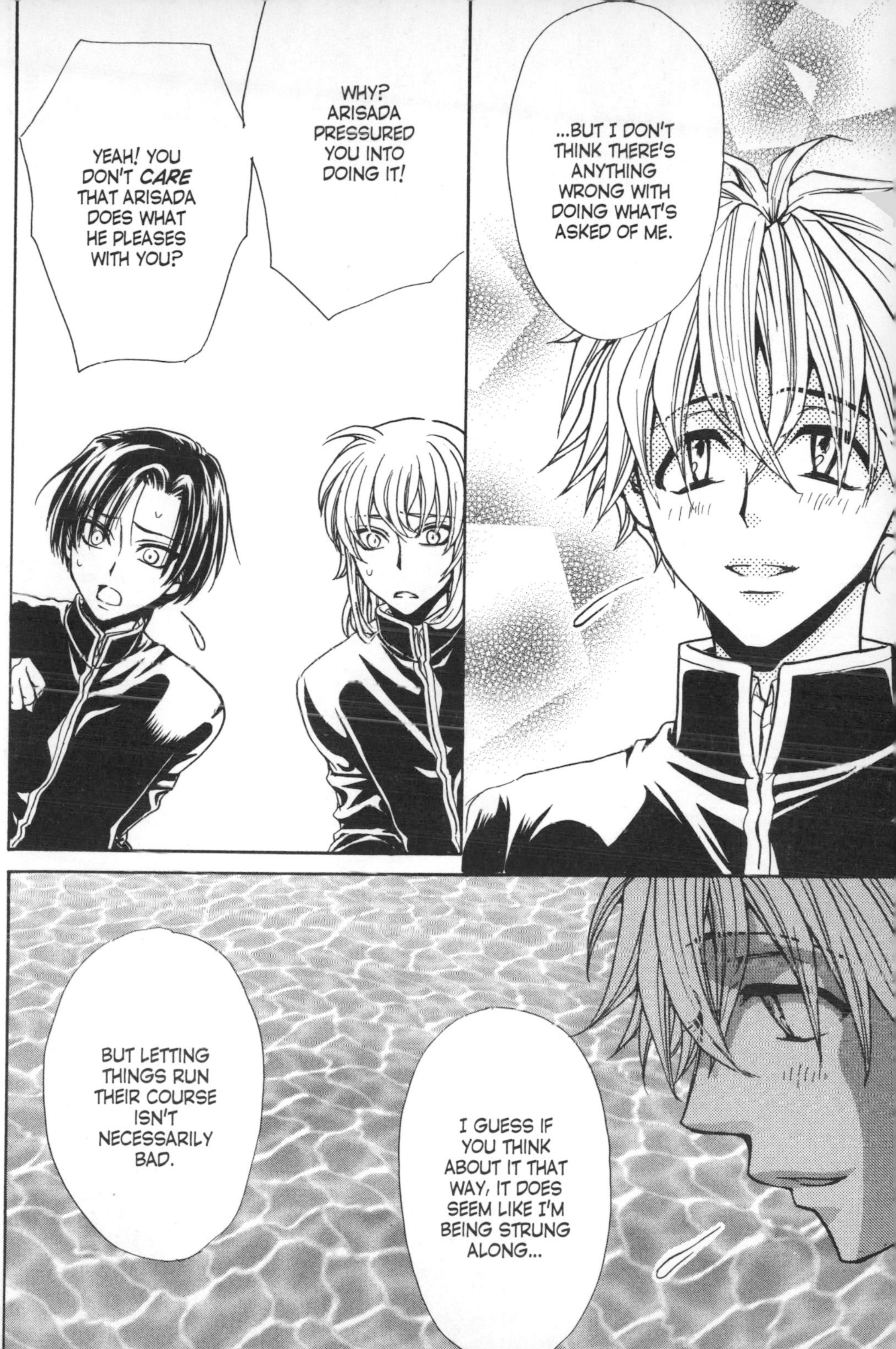
...BUT I DON'T THINK THERE'S ANYTHING WRONG WITH DOING WHAT'S ASKED OF ME.
WHY? ARISADA PRESSURED YOU INTO DOING IT!
YEAH! YOU DON'T *CARE* THAT ARISADA DOES WHAT HE PLEASES WITH YOU?
I GUESS IF YOU THINK ABOUT IT THAT WAY, IT DOES SEEM LIKE I'M BEING STRUNG ALONG...
BUT LETTING THINGS RUN THEIR COURSE ISN'T NECESSARILY BAD.

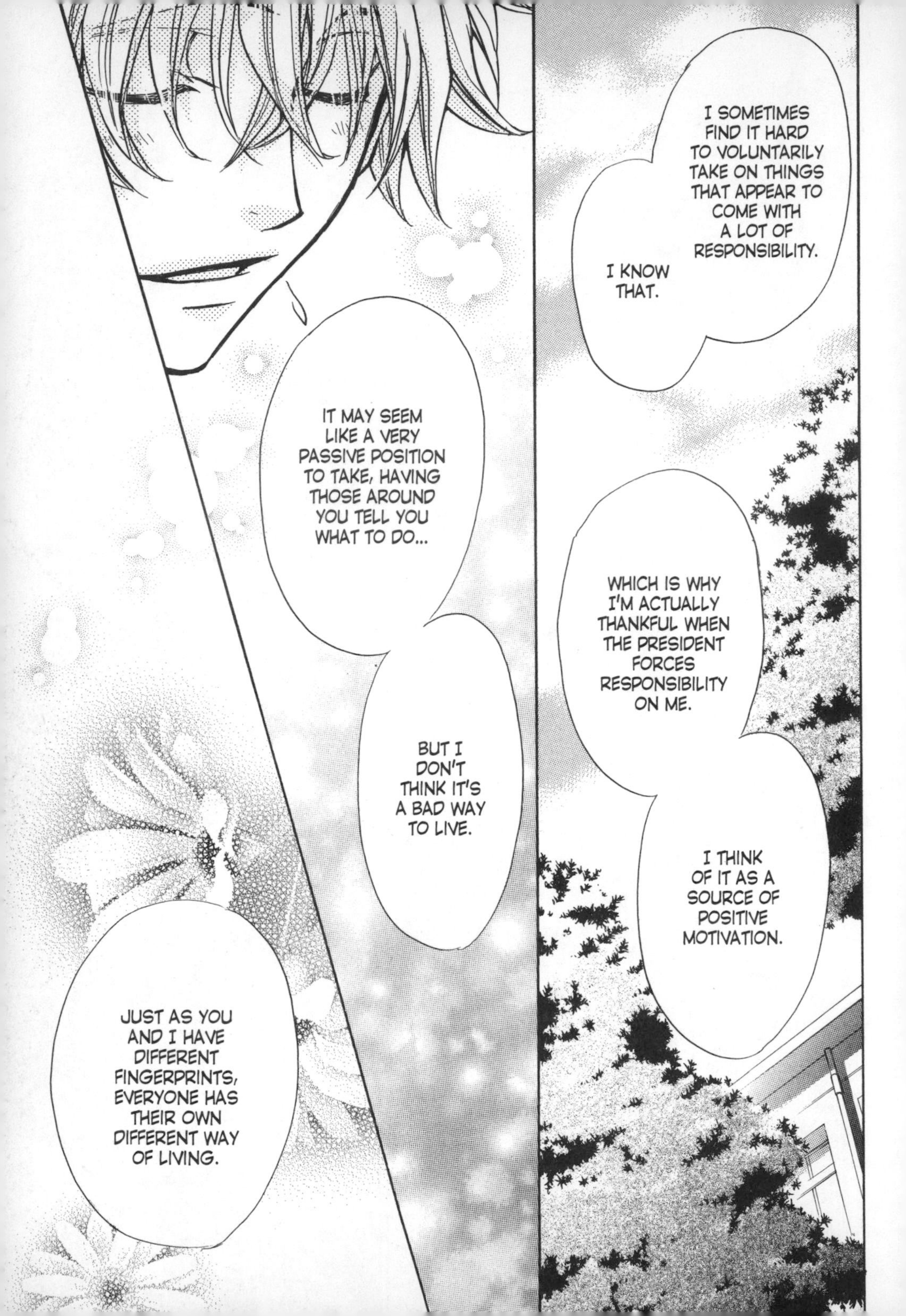
I SOMETIMES FIND IT HARD TO VOLUNTARILY TAKE ON THINGS THAT APPEAR TO COME WITH A LOT OF RESPONSIBILITY.
I KNOW THAT.
WHICH IS WHY I'M ACTUALLY THANKFUL WHEN THE PRESIDENT FORCES RESPONSIBILITY ON ME.
I THINK OF IT AS A SOURCE OF POSITIVE MOTIVATION.
IT MAY SEEM LIKE A VERY PASSIVE POSITION TO TAKE, HAVING THOSE AROUND YOU TELL YOU WHAT TO DO...
BUT I DON'T THINK IT'S A BAD WAY TO LIVE.
JUST AS YOU AND I HAVE DIFFERENT FINGERPRINTS, EVERYONE HAS THEIR OWN DIFFERENT WAY OF LIVING.

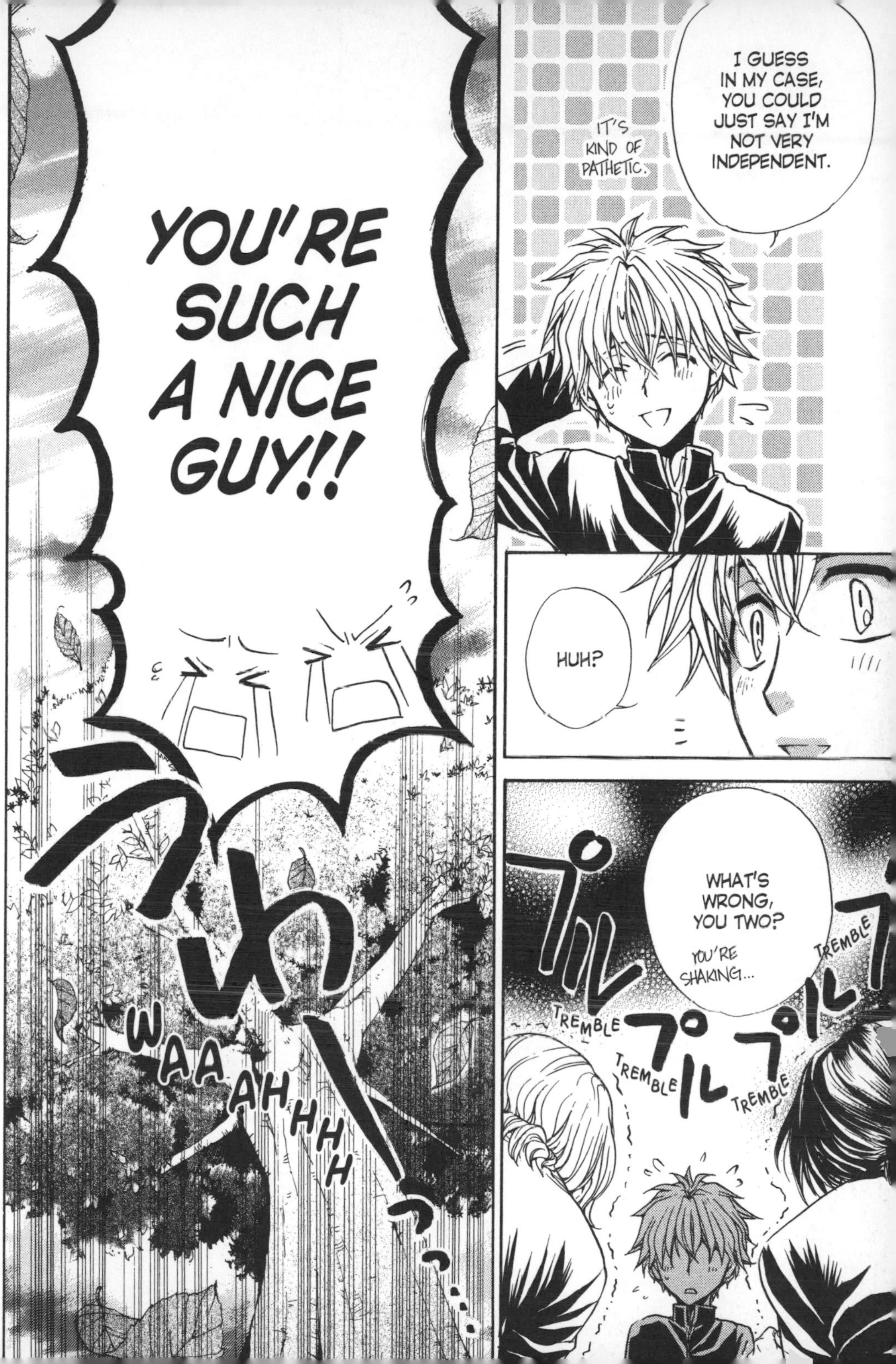
I GUESS IN MY CASE, YOU COULD JUST SAY I'M NOT VERY INDEPENDENT.
IT'S KIND OF PATHETIC.
HUH?
WHAT'S WRONG, YOU TWO?
YOU'RE SHAKING...
TREMBLE
TREMBLE
TREMBLE
TREMBLE
YOU'RE SUCH A NICE GUY!!
WAAAAHHHHH

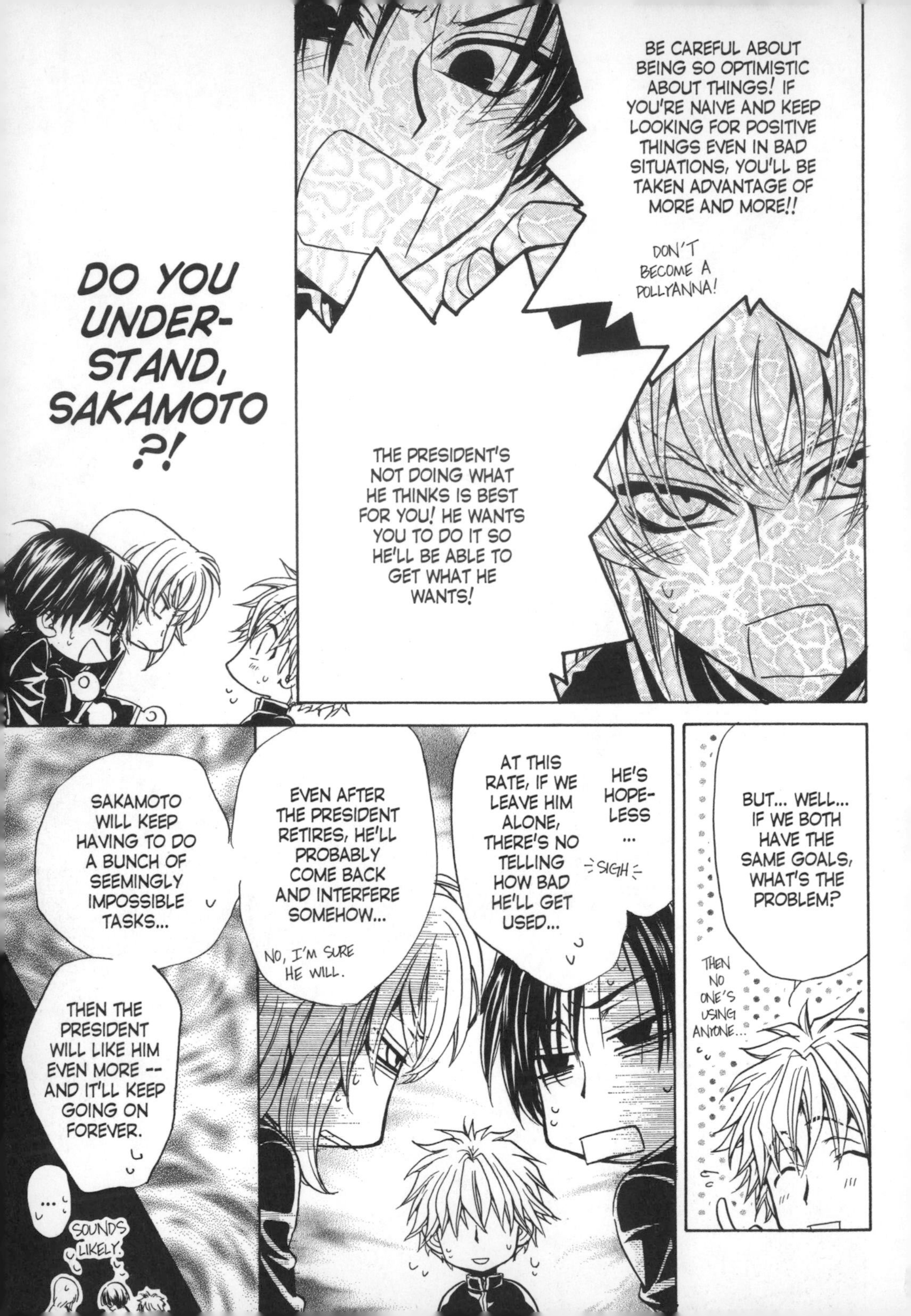
BE CAREFUL ABOUT BEING SO OPTIMISTIC ABOUT THINGS! IF YOU'RE NAIVE AND KEEP LOOKING FOR POSITIVE THINGS EVEN IN BAD SITUATIONS, YOU'LL BE TAKEN ADVANTAGE OF MORE AND MORE!!
DON'T BECOME A POLLYANNA!
THE PRESIDENT'S NOT DOING WHAT HE THINKS IS BEST FOR YOU! HE WANTS YOU TO DO IT SO HE'LL BE ABLE TO GET WHAT HE WANTS!
DO YOU UNDER-STAND, SAKAMOTO?!
BUT... WELL... IF WE BOTH HAVE THE SAME GOALS, WHAT'S THE PROBLEM?
THEN NO ONE'S USING ANYONE...
HE'S HOPE-LESS...
SIGH
AT THIS RATE, IF WE LEAVE HIM ALONE, THERE'S NO TELLING HOW BAD HE'LL GET USED...
EVEN AFTER THE PRESIDENT RETIRES, HE'LL PROBABLY COME BACK AND INTERFERE SOMEHOW...
NO, I'M SURE HE WILL.
SAKAMOTO WILL KEEP HAVING TO DO A BUNCH OF SEEMINGLY IMPOSSIBLE TASKS...
THEN THE PRESIDENT WILL LIKE HIM EVEN MORE -- AND IT'LL KEEP GOING ON FOREVER.
...
SOUNDS LIKELY.

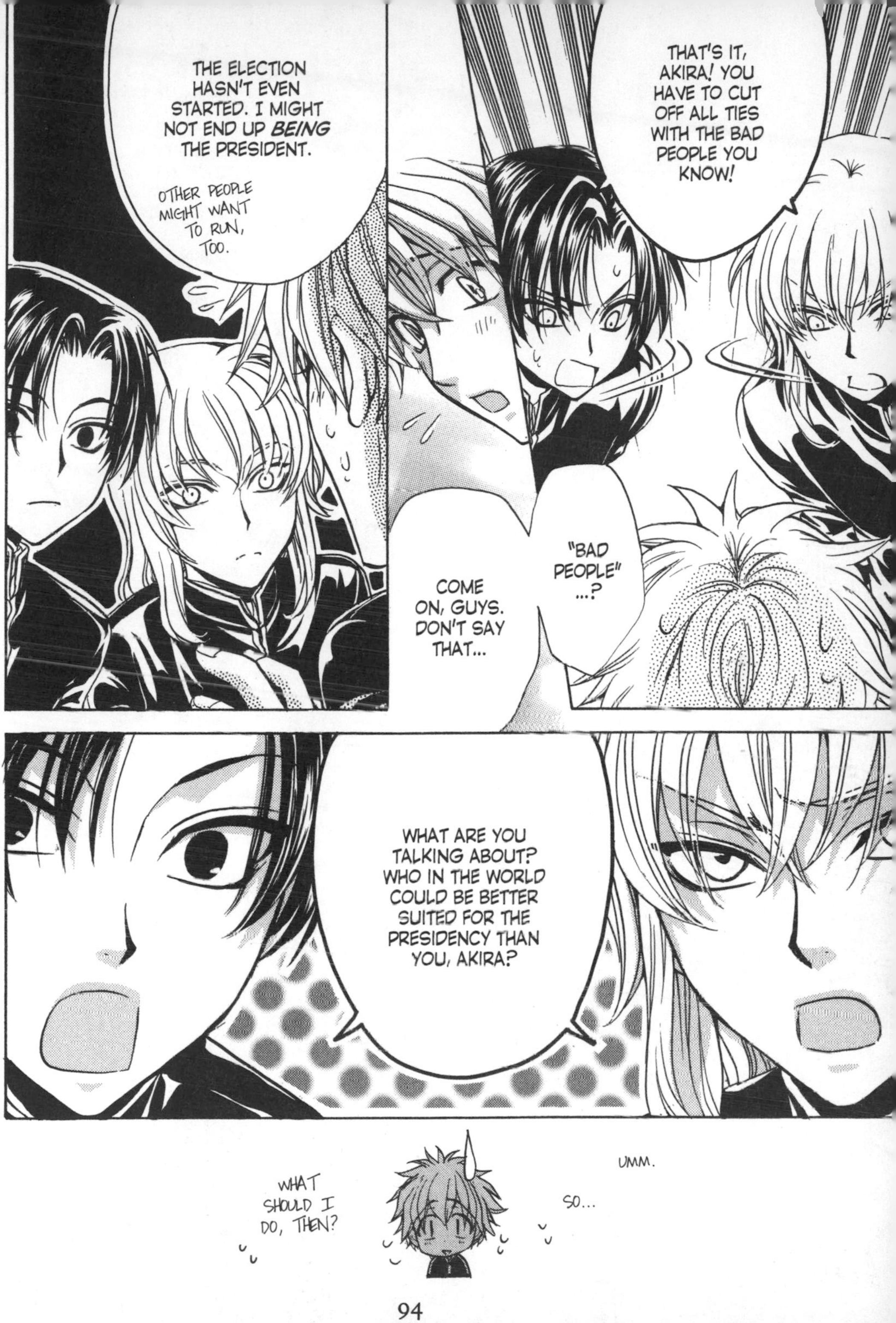
THAT'S IT, AKIRA! YOU HAVE TO CUT OFF ALL TIES WITH THE BAD PEOPLE YOU KNOW!
"BAD PEOPLE" ...?
COME ON, GUYS. DON'T SAY THAT...
THE ELECTION HASN'T EVEN STARTED. I MIGHT NOT END UP *BEING* THE PRESIDENT.
OTHER PEOPLE MIGHT WANT TO RUN, TOO.
WHAT ARE YOU TALKING ABOUT? WHO IN THE WORLD COULD BE BETTER SUITED FOR THE PRESIDENCY THAN YOU, AKIRA?
UMM.
SO...
WHAT SHOULD I DO, THEN?

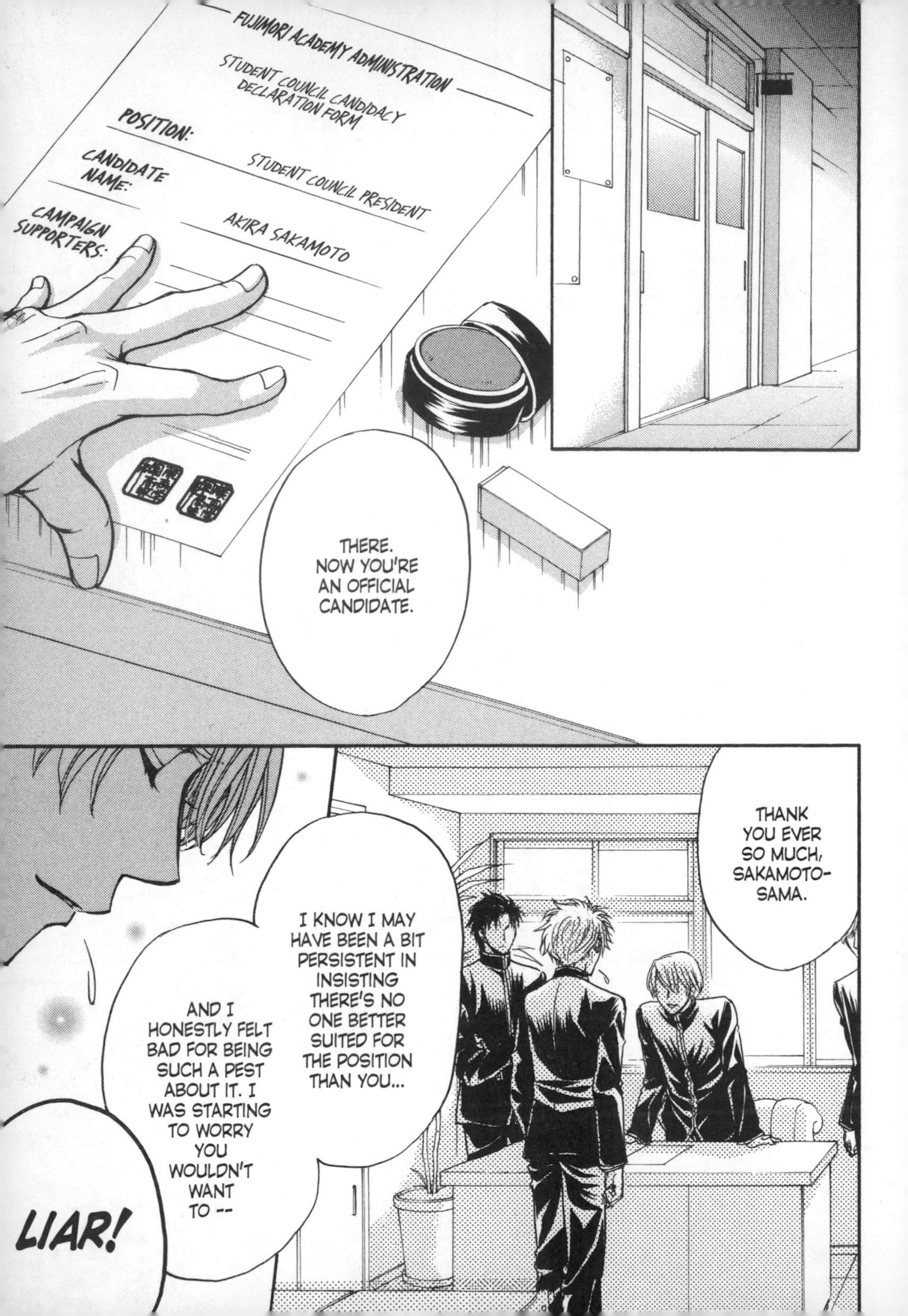
FUJIMORI ACADEMY ADMINISTRATION
STUDENT COUNCIL CANDIDACY DECLARATION FORM
POSITION: STUDENT COUNCIL PRESIDENT
CANDIDATE NAME: AKIRA SAKAMOTO
CAMPAIGN SUPPORTERS:
THERE. NOW YOU'RE AN OFFICIAL CANDIDATE.
THANK YOU EVER SO MUCH, SAKAMOTO-SAMA.
I KNOW I MAY HAVE BEEN A BIT PERSISTENT IN INSISTING THERE'S NO ONE BETTER SUITED FOR THE POSITION THAN YOU...
AND I HONESTLY FELT BAD FOR BEING SUCH A PEST ABOUT IT. I WAS STARTING TO WORRY YOU WOULDN'T WANT TO --
LIAR!

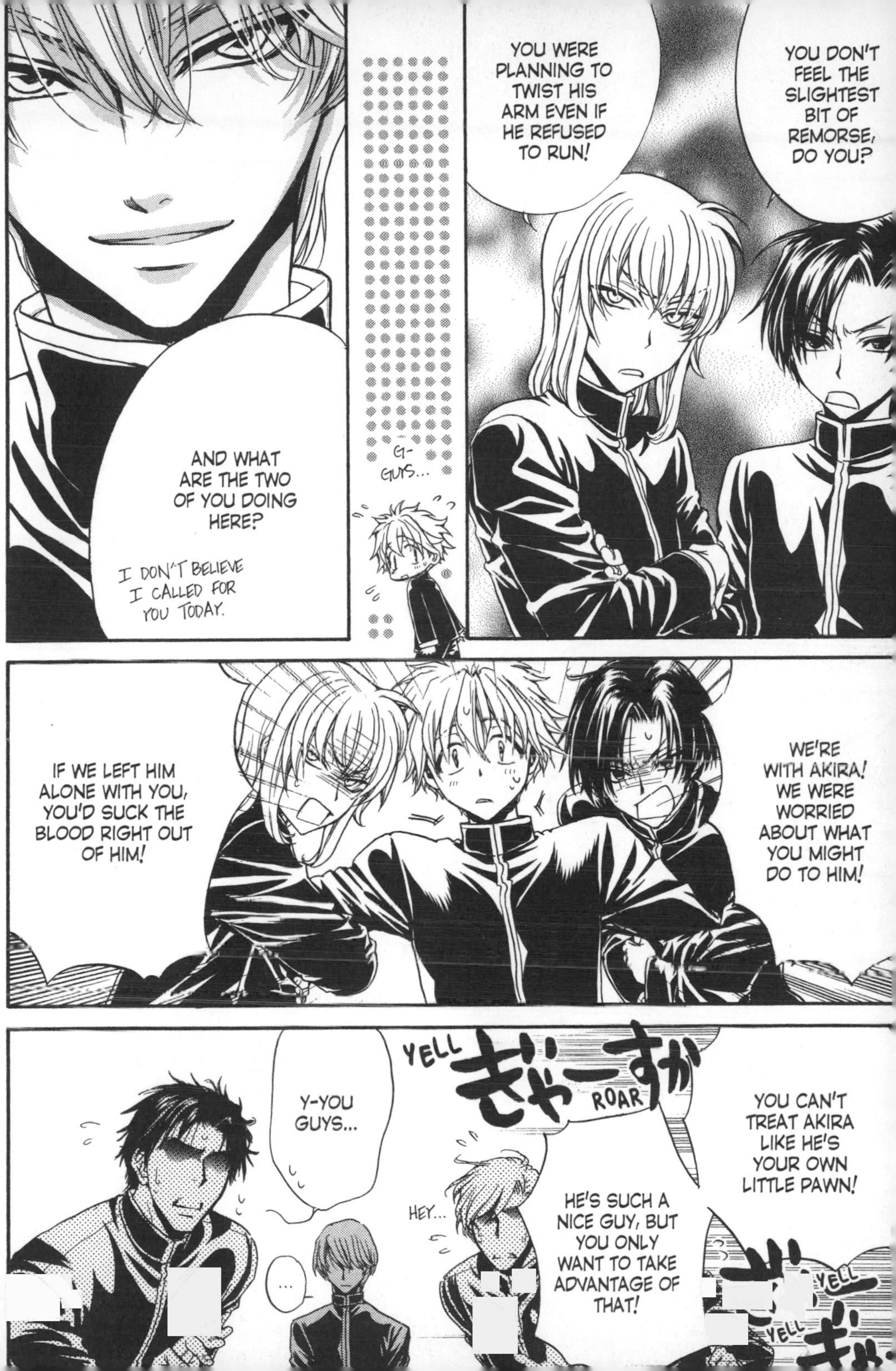
YOU DON'T FEEL THE SLIGHTEST BIT OF REMORSE, DO YOU?
YOU WERE PLANNING TO TWIST HIS ARM EVEN IF HE REFUSED TO RUN!
G-GUYS...
AND WHAT ARE THE TWO OF YOU DOING HERE?
I DON'T BELIEVE I CALLED FOR YOU TODAY.
WE'RE WITH AKIRA! WE WERE WORRIED ABOUT WHAT YOU MIGHT DO TO HIM!
IF WE LEFT HIM ALONE WITH YOU, YOU'D SUCK THE BLOOD RIGHT OUT OF HIM!
YOU CAN'T TREAT AKIRA LIKE HE'S YOUR OWN LITTLE PAWN!
YELL
YELL
HE'S SUCH A NICE GUY, BUT YOU ONLY WANT TO TAKE ADVANTAGE OF THAT!
YELL ぎゃーすか ROAR
HEY...
Y-YOU GUYS...
...

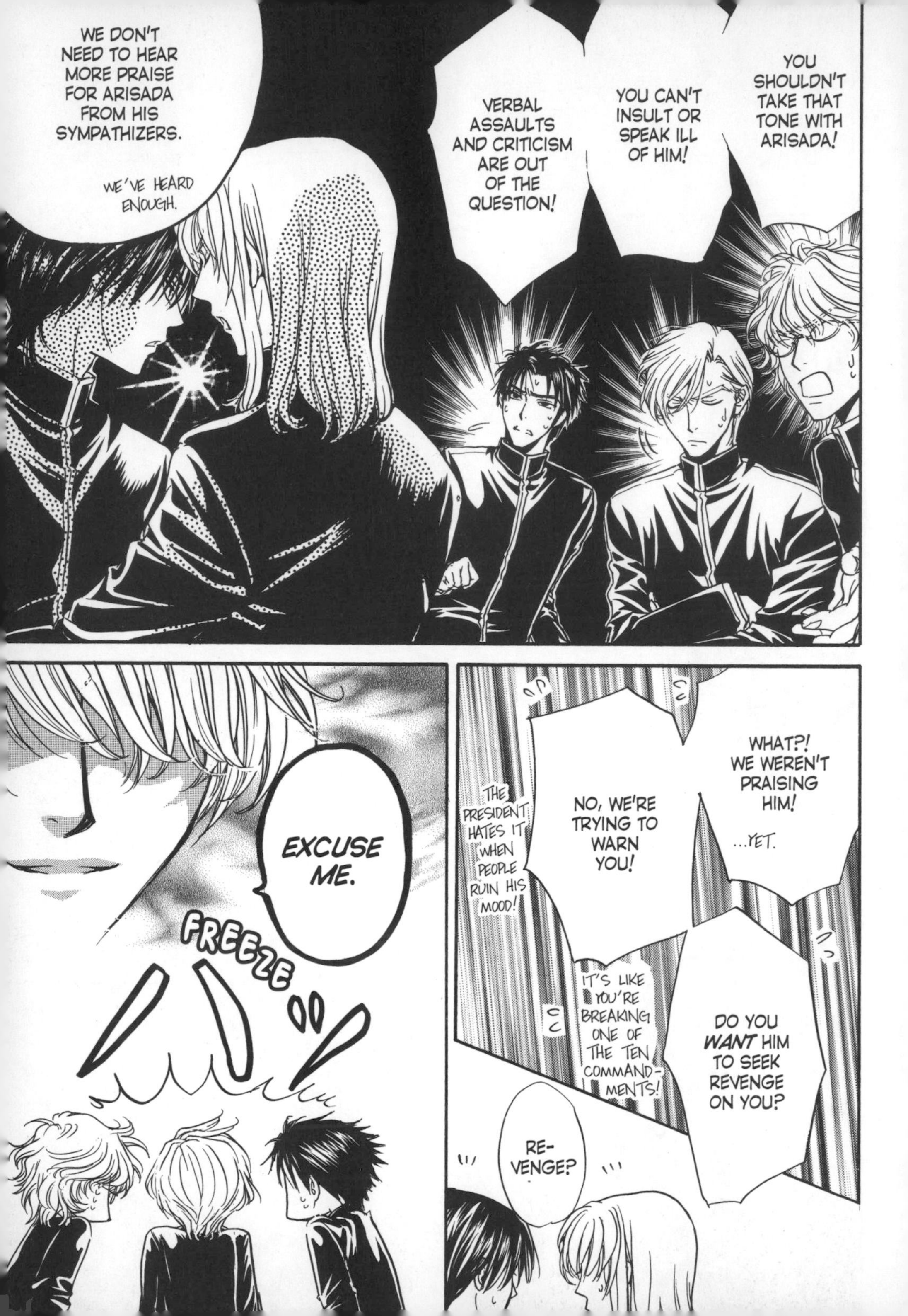
YOU SHOULDN'T TAKE THAT TONE WITH ARISADA!
YOU CAN'T INSULT OR SPEAK ILL OF HIM!
VERBAL ASSAULTS AND CRITICISM ARE OUT OF THE QUESTION!
WE DON'T NEED TO HEAR MORE PRAISE FOR ARISADA FROM HIS SYMPATHIZERS.
WE'VE HEARD ENOUGH.
WHAT?! WE WEREN'T PRAISING HIM!
...YET.
NO, WE'RE TRYING TO WARN YOU!
THE PRESIDENT HATES IT WHEN PEOPLE RUIN HIS MOOD!
DO YOU *WANT* HIM TO SEEK REVENGE ON YOU?
IT'S LIKE YOU'RE BREAKING ONE OF THE TEN COMMAND-MENTS!
RE-VENGE?
EXCUSE ME.
FREEZE

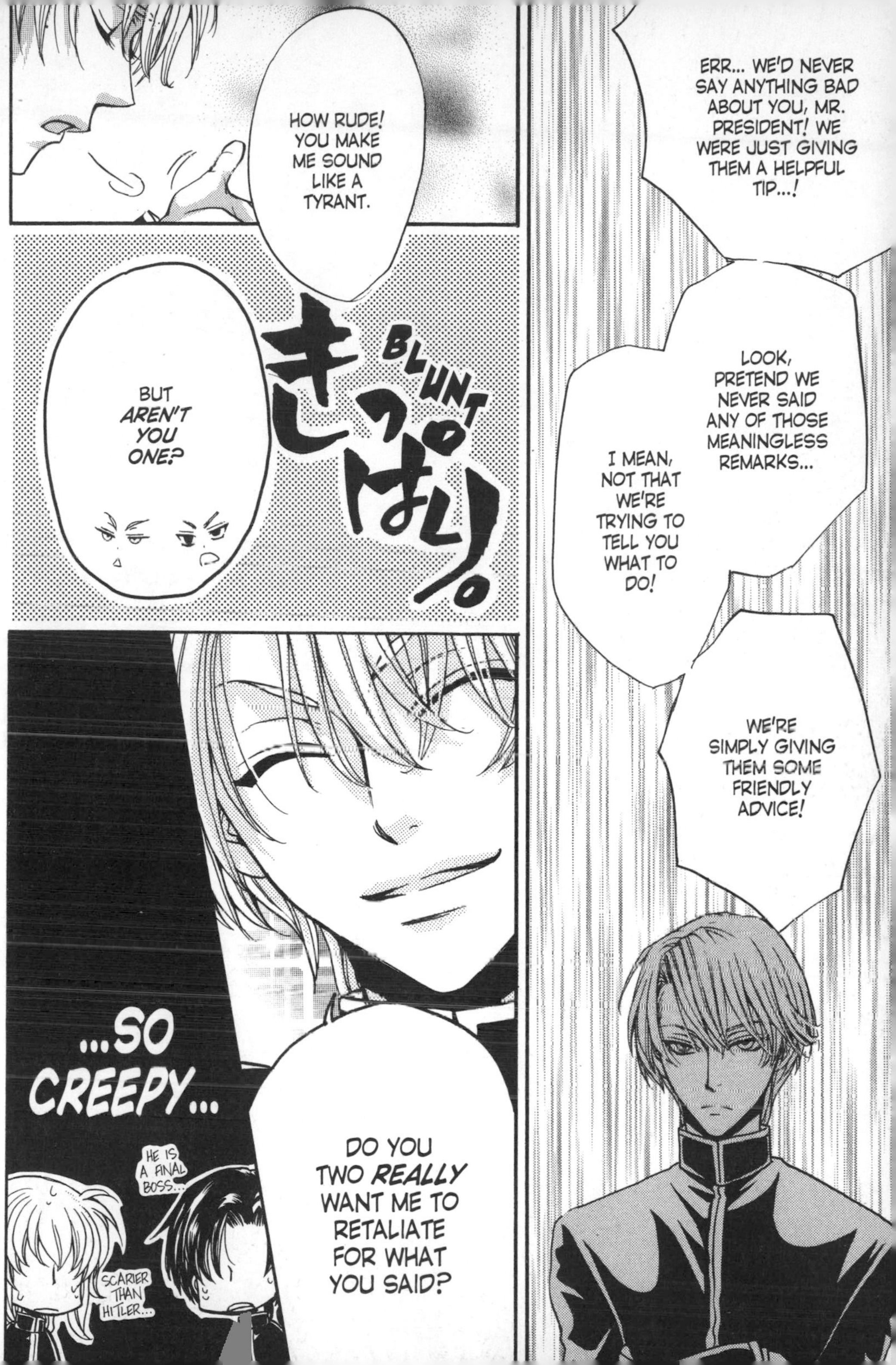
ERR... WE'D NEVER SAY ANYTHING BAD ABOUT YOU, MR. PRESIDENT! WE WERE JUST GIVING THEM A HELPFUL TIP...!
LOOK, PRETEND WE NEVER SAID ANY OF THOSE MEANINGLESS REMARKS...
I MEAN, NOT THAT WE'RE TRYING TO TELL YOU WHAT TO DO!
WE'RE SIMPLY GIVING THEM SOME FRIENDLY ADVICE!
HOW RUDE! YOU MAKE ME SOUND LIKE A TYRANT.
きっぱり。
BLUNT
BUT *AREN'T YOU* ONE?
DO YOU TWO ***REALLY*** WANT ME TO RETALIATE FOR WHAT YOU SAID?
...SO CREEPY...
HE IS A FINAL BOSS...
SCARIER THAN HITLER...

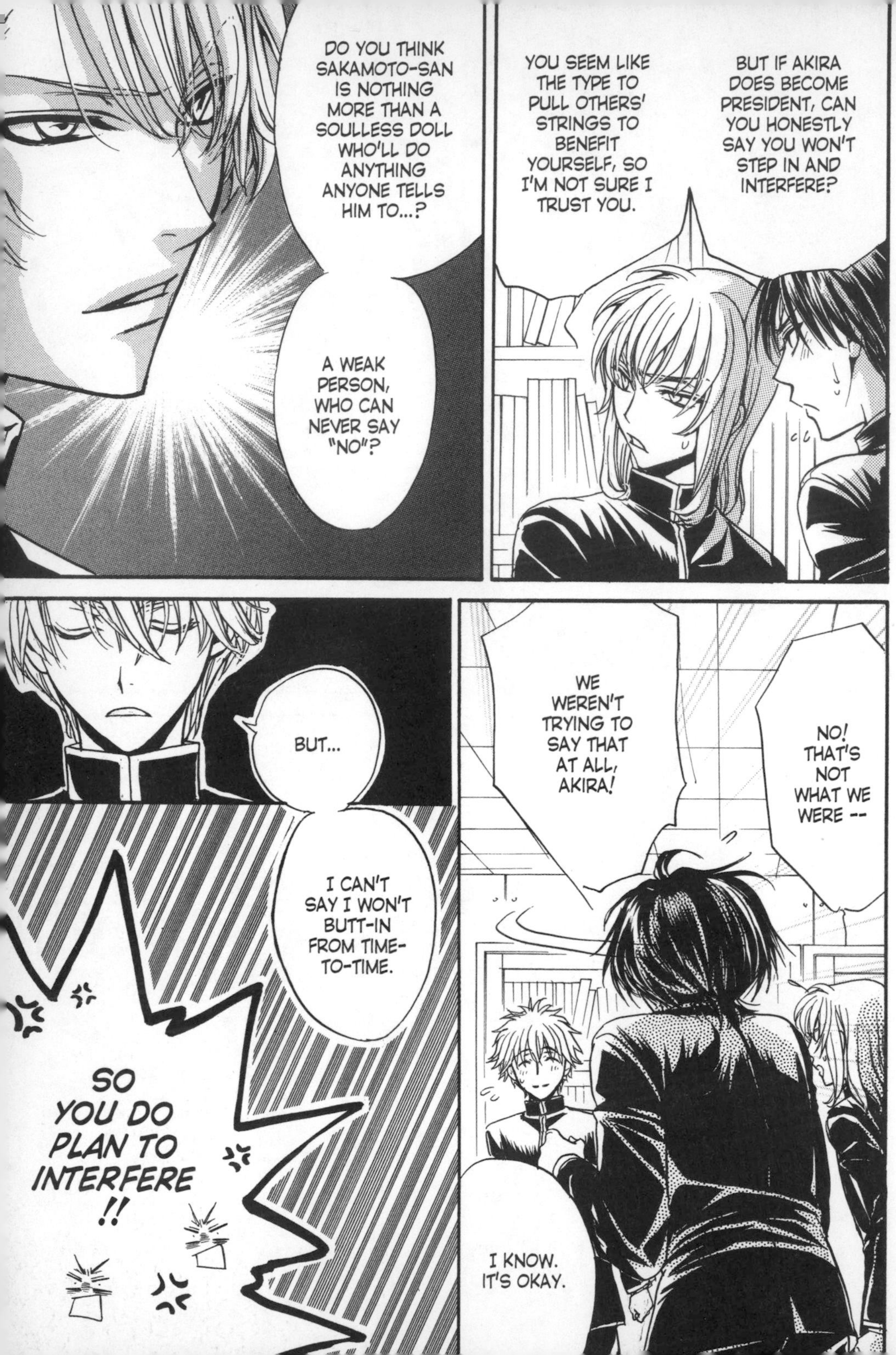
BUT IF AKIRA DOES BECOME PRESIDENT, CAN YOU HONESTLY SAY YOU WON'T STEP IN AND INTERFERE?
YOU SEEM LIKE THE TYPE TO PULL OTHERS' STRINGS TO BENEFIT YOURSELF, SO I'M NOT SURE I TRUST YOU.
DO YOU THINK SAKAMOTO-SAN IS NOTHING MORE THAN A SOULLESS DOLL WHO'LL DO ANYTHING ANYONE TELLS HIM TO...?
A WEAK PERSON, WHO CAN NEVER SAY "NO"?
NO! THAT'S NOT WHAT WE WERE --
WE WEREN'T TRYING TO SAY THAT AT ALL, AKIRA!
I KNOW. IT'S OKAY.
BUT...
I CAN'T SAY I WON'T BUTT-IN FROM TIME-TO-TIME.
SO YOU DO PLAN TO INTERFERE !!

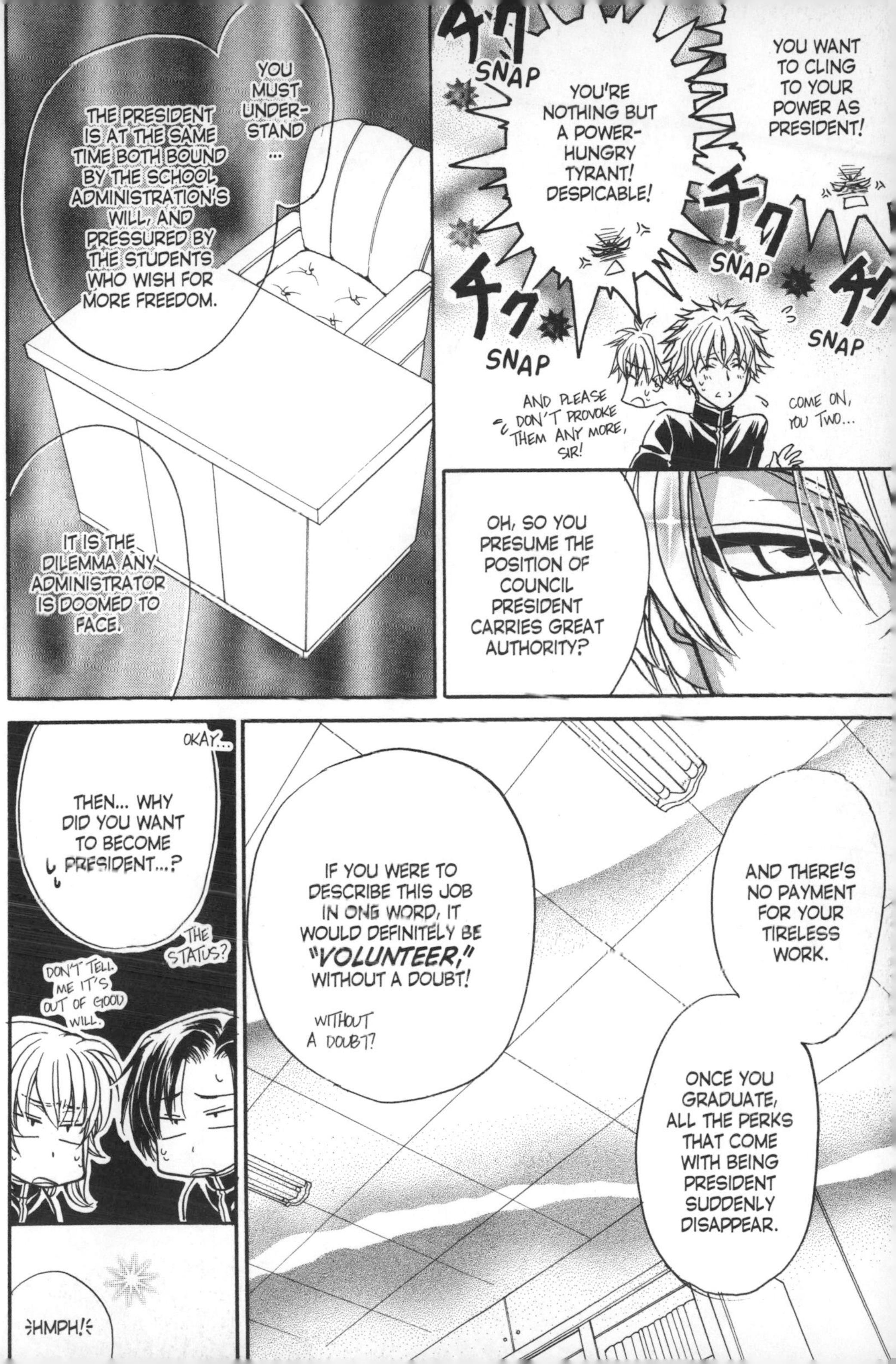
YOU WANT TO CLING TO YOUR POWER AS PRESIDENT!
YOU'RE NOTHING BUT A POWER-HUNGRY TYRANT! DESPICABLE!
SNAP
チク
SNAP
SNAP
チク
SNAP
COME ON, YOU TWO...
AND PLEASE DON'T PROVOKE THEM ANY MORE, SIR!
OH, SO YOU PRESUME THE POSITION OF COUNCIL PRESIDENT CARRIES GREAT AUTHORITY?
YOU MUST UNDERSTAND...
THE PRESIDENT IS AT THE SAME TIME BOTH BOUND BY THE SCHOOL ADMINISTRATION'S WILL, AND PRESSURED BY THE STUDENTS WHO WISH FOR MORE FREEDOM.
IT IS THE DILEMMA ANY ADMINISTRATOR IS DOOMED TO FACE.
IF YOU WERE TO DESCRIBE THIS JOB IN ONE WORD, IT WOULD DEFINITELY BE "VOLUNTEER," WITHOUT A DOUBT!
WITHOUT A DOUBT?
AND THERE'S NO PAYMENT FOR YOUR TIRELESS WORK.
ONCE YOU GRADUATE, ALL THE PERKS THAT COME WITH BEING PRESIDENT SUDDENLY DISAPPEAR.
OKAY...
THEN... WHY DID YOU WANT TO BECOME PRESIDENT...?
THE STATUS?
DON'T TELL ME IT'S OUT OF GOOD WILL.
HMPH!

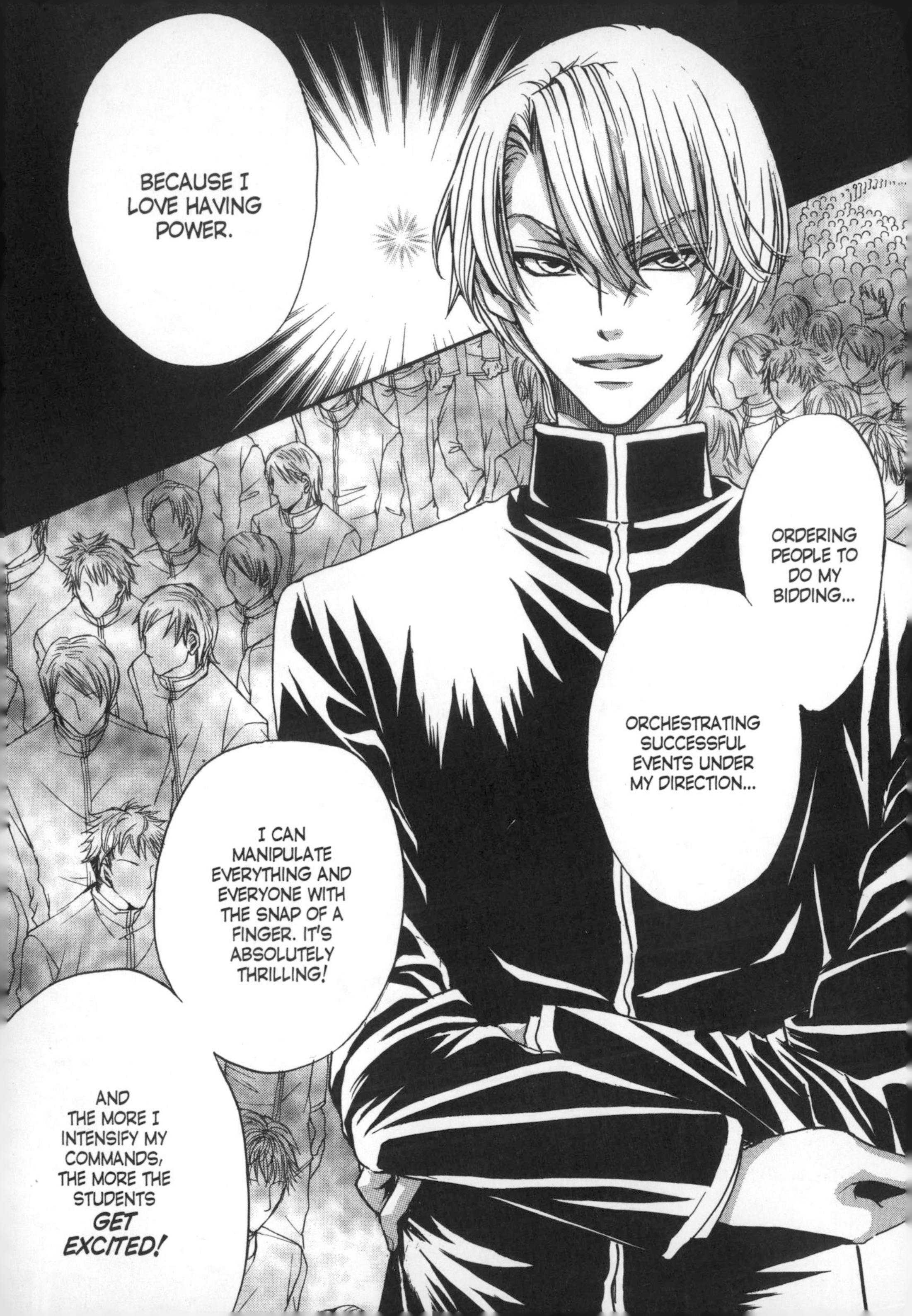
BECAUSE I LOVE HAVING POWER.
ORDERING PEOPLE TO DO MY BIDDING...
ORCHESTRATING SUCCESSFUL EVENTS UNDER MY DIRECTION...
I CAN MANIPULATE EVERYTHING AND EVERYONE WITH THE SNAP OF A FINGER. IT'S ABSOLUTELY THRILLING!
AND THE MORE I INTENSIFY MY COMMANDS, THE MORE THE STUDENTS GET EXCITED!

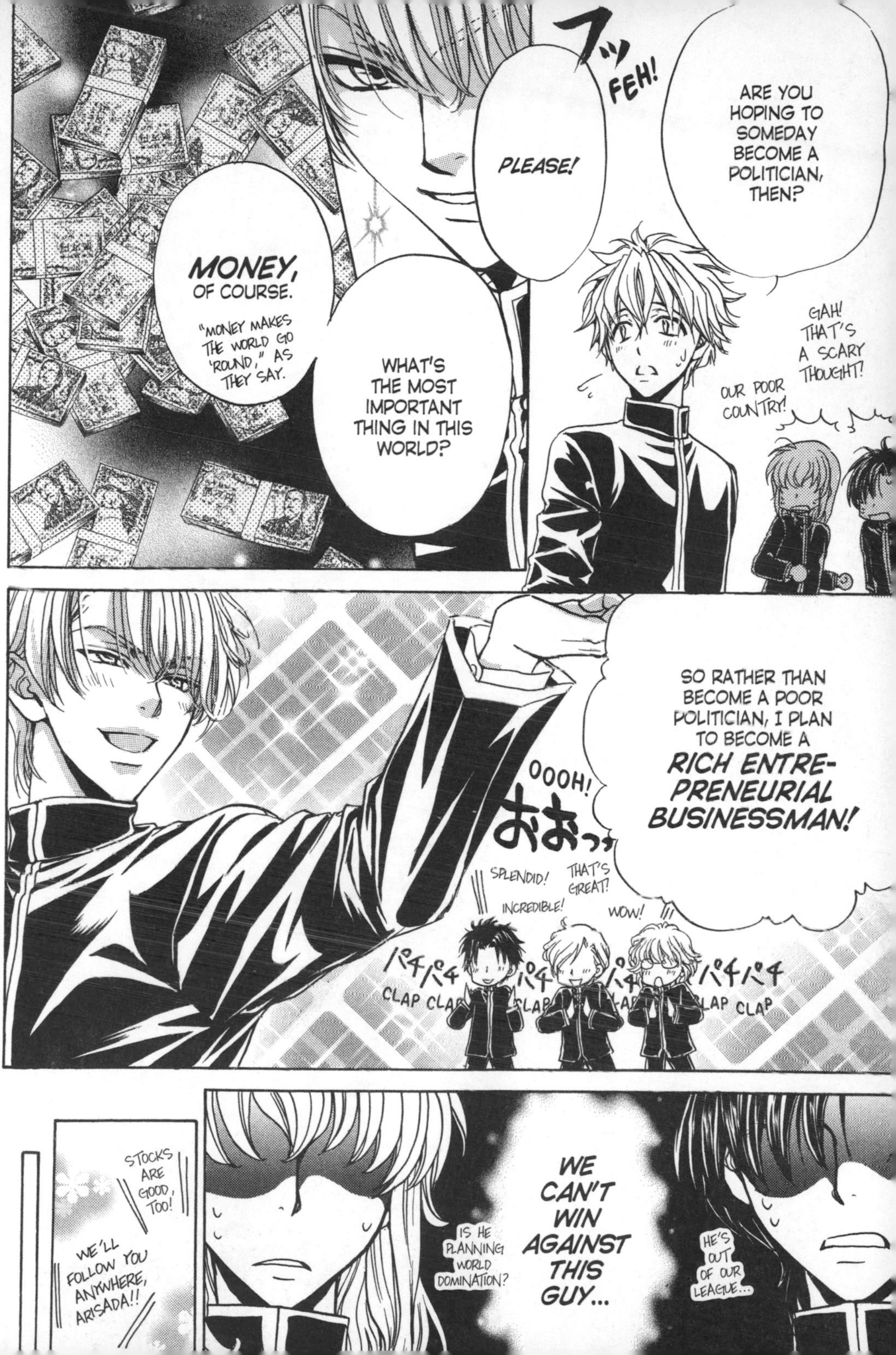
ARE YOU HOPING TO SOMEDAY BECOME A POLITICIAN, THEN?
フッ FEH!
PLEASE!
GAH! THAT'S A SCARY THOUGHT!
OUR POOR COUNTRY!
WHAT'S THE MOST IMPORTANT THING IN THIS WORLD?
MONEY, OF COURSE.
"MONEY MAKES THE WORLD GO 'ROUND," AS THEY SAY.
SO RATHER THAN BECOME A POOR POLITICIAN, I PLAN TO BECOME A RICH ENTRE-PRENEURIAL BUSINESSMAN!
おおっ OOOH!
THAT'S GREAT!
SPLENDID!
WOW!
INCREDIBLE!
パチパチ CLAP CLAP
WE CAN'T WIN AGAINST THIS GUY...
HE'S OUT OF OUR LEAGUE...
IS HE PLANNING WORLD DOMINATION?
STOCKS ARE GOOD, TOO!
WE'LL FOLLOW YOU ANYWHERE, ARISADA!!

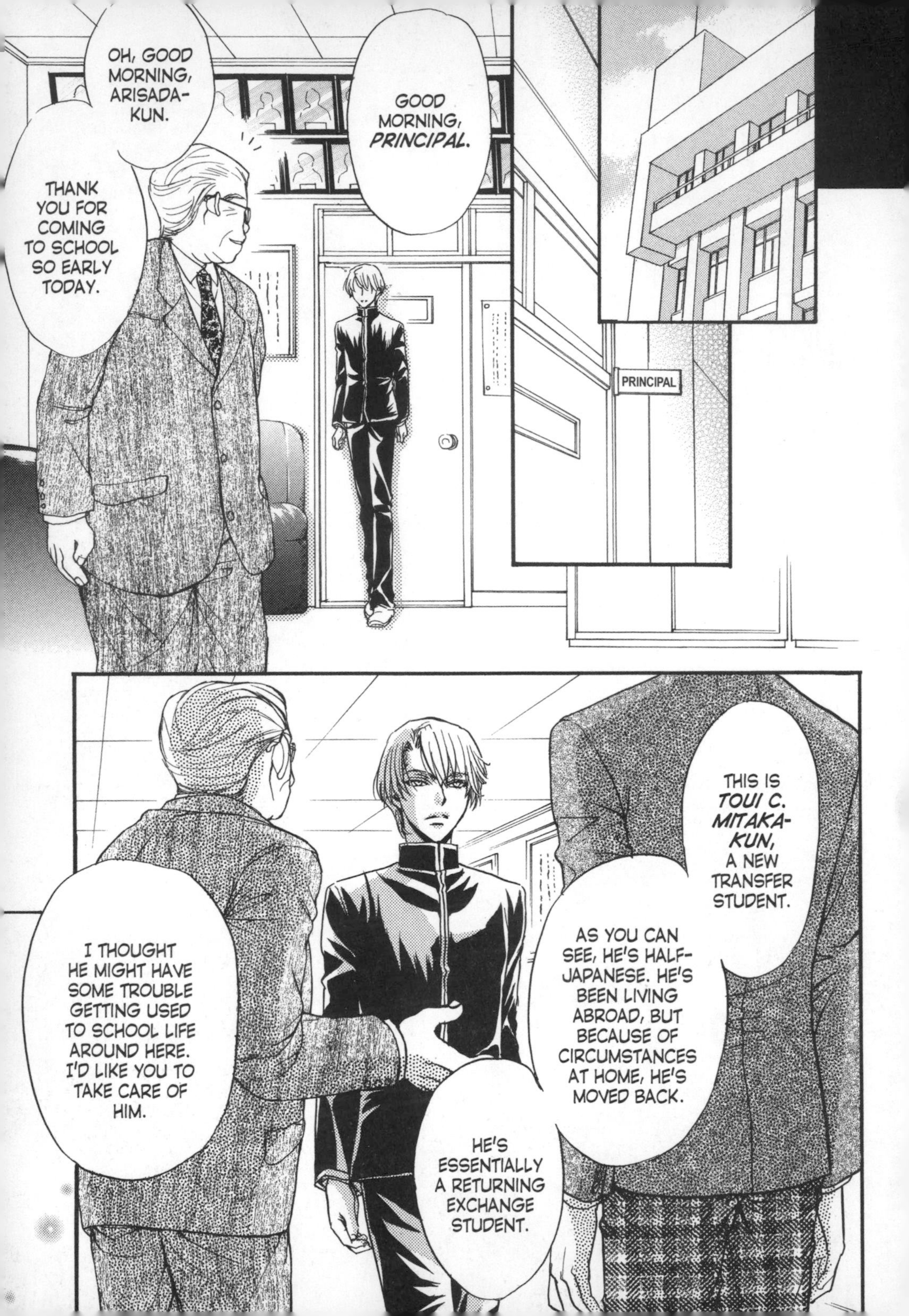
GOOD MORNING, PRINCIPAL.
OH, GOOD MORNING, ARISADA-KUN.
THANK YOU FOR COMING TO SCHOOL SO EARLY TODAY.
PRINCIPAL
THIS IS TOUI C. MITAKA-KUN, A NEW TRANSFER STUDENT.
AS YOU CAN SEE, HE'S HALF-JAPANESE. HE'S BEEN LIVING ABROAD, BUT BECAUSE OF CIRCUMSTANCES AT HOME, HE'S MOVED BACK.
HE'S ESSENTIALLY A RETURNING EXCHANGE STUDENT.
I THOUGHT HE MIGHT HAVE SOME TROUBLE GETTING USED TO SCHOOL LIFE AROUND HERE. I'D LIKE YOU TO TAKE CARE OF HIM.

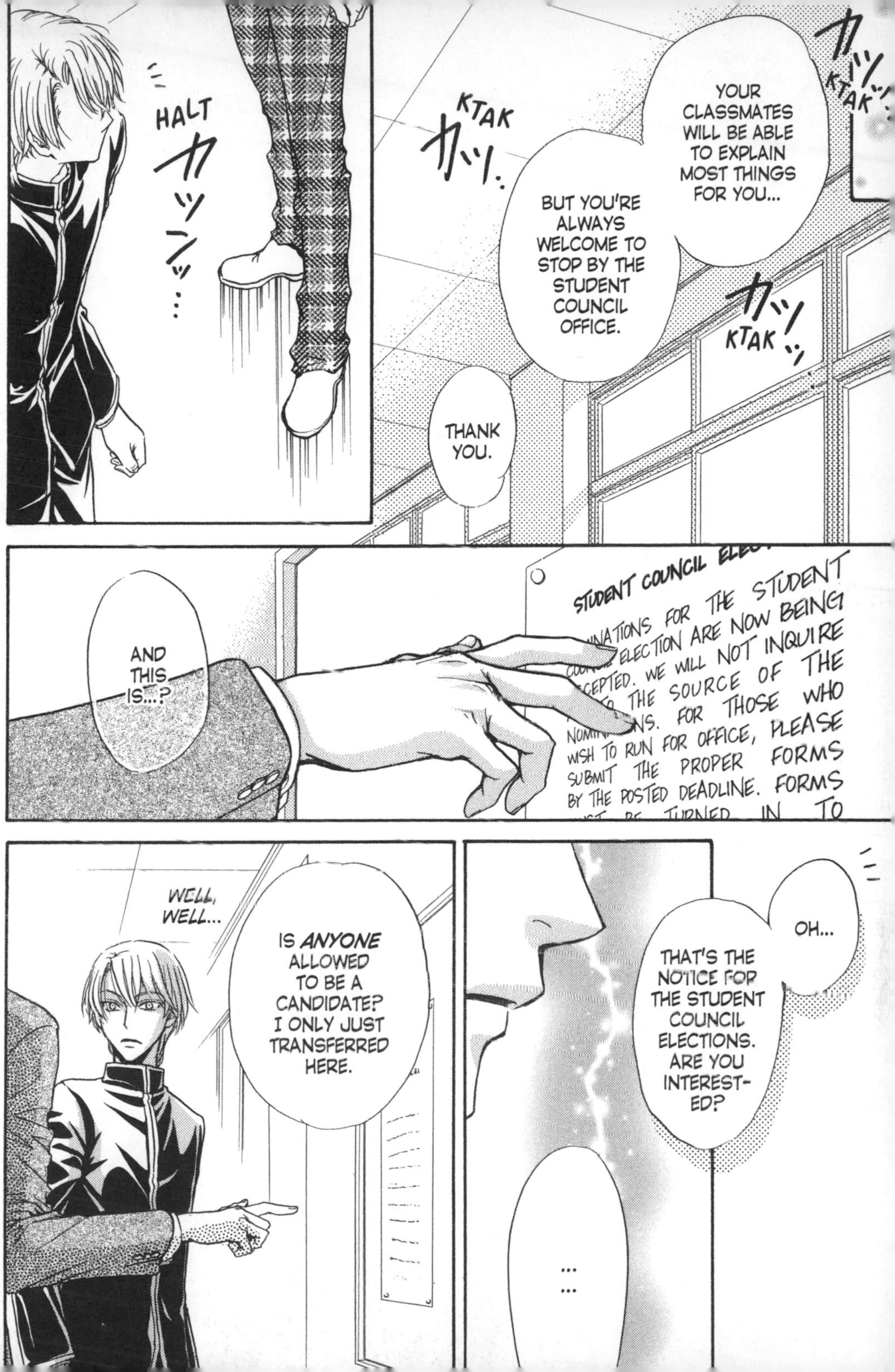
KTAK
YOUR CLASSMATES WILL BE ABLE TO EXPLAIN MOST THINGS FOR YOU...
KTAK
BUT YOU'RE ALWAYS WELCOME TO STOP BY THE STUDENT COUNCIL OFFICE.
KTAK
THANK YOU.
HALT
AND THIS IS...?
STUDENT COUNCIL
FOR THE STUDENT
ELECTION ARE NOW BEING
WE WILL NOT INQUIRE
THE SOURCE OF THE
FOR THOSE WHO
WISH TO RUN FOR OFFICE, PLEASE
SUBMIT THE PROPER FORMS
BY THE POSTED DEADLINE. FORMS
OH...
THAT'S THE NOTICE FOR THE STUDENT COUNCIL ELECTIONS. ARE YOU INTEREST-ED?
......
WELL, WELL...
IS ANYONE ALLOWED TO BE A CANDIDATE? I ONLY JUST TRANSFERRED HERE.

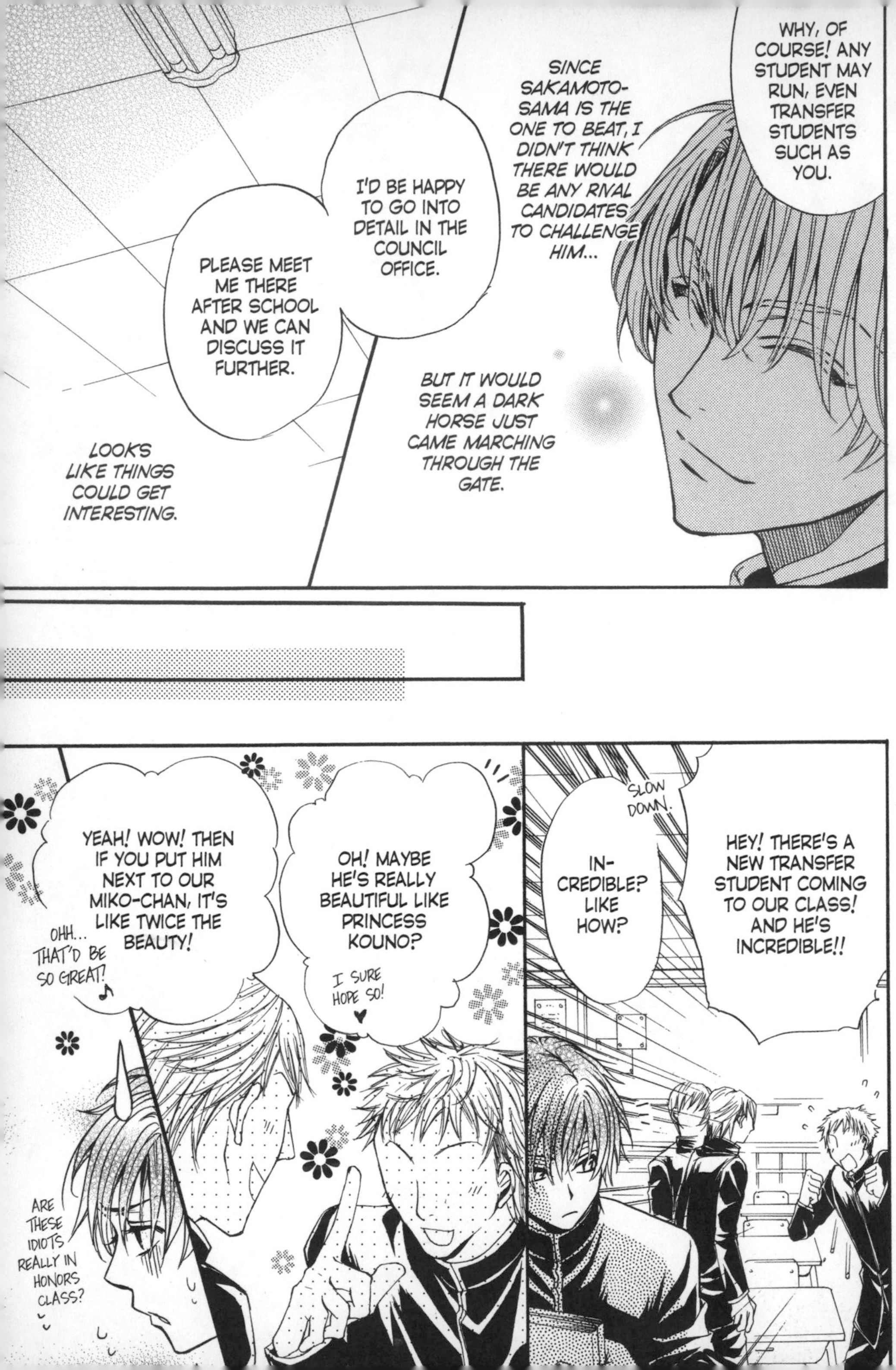
WHY, OF COURSE! ANY STUDENT MAY RUN, EVEN TRANSFER STUDENTS SUCH AS YOU.
SINCE SAKAMOTO-SAMA IS THE ONE TO BEAT, I DIDN'T THINK THERE WOULD BE ANY RIVAL CANDIDATES TO CHALLENGE HIM...
BUT IT WOULD SEEM A DARK HORSE JUST CAME MARCHING THROUGH THE GATE.
I'D BE HAPPY TO GO INTO DETAIL IN THE COUNCIL OFFICE.
PLEASE MEET ME THERE AFTER SCHOOL AND WE CAN DISCUSS IT FURTHER.
LOOKS LIKE THINGS COULD GET INTERESTING.
HEY! THERE'S A NEW TRANSFER STUDENT COMING TO OUR CLASS! AND HE'S INCREDIBLE!!
SLOW DOWN.
IN-CREDIBLE? LIKE HOW?
OH! MAYBE HE'S REALLY BEAUTIFUL LIKE PRINCESS KOUNO?
I SURE HOPE SO!
YEAH! WOW! THEN IF YOU PUT HIM NEXT TO OUR MIKO-CHAN, IT'S LIKE TWICE THE BEAUTY!
OHH... THAT'D BE SO GREAT!
ARE THESE IDIOTS REALLY IN HONORS CLASS?

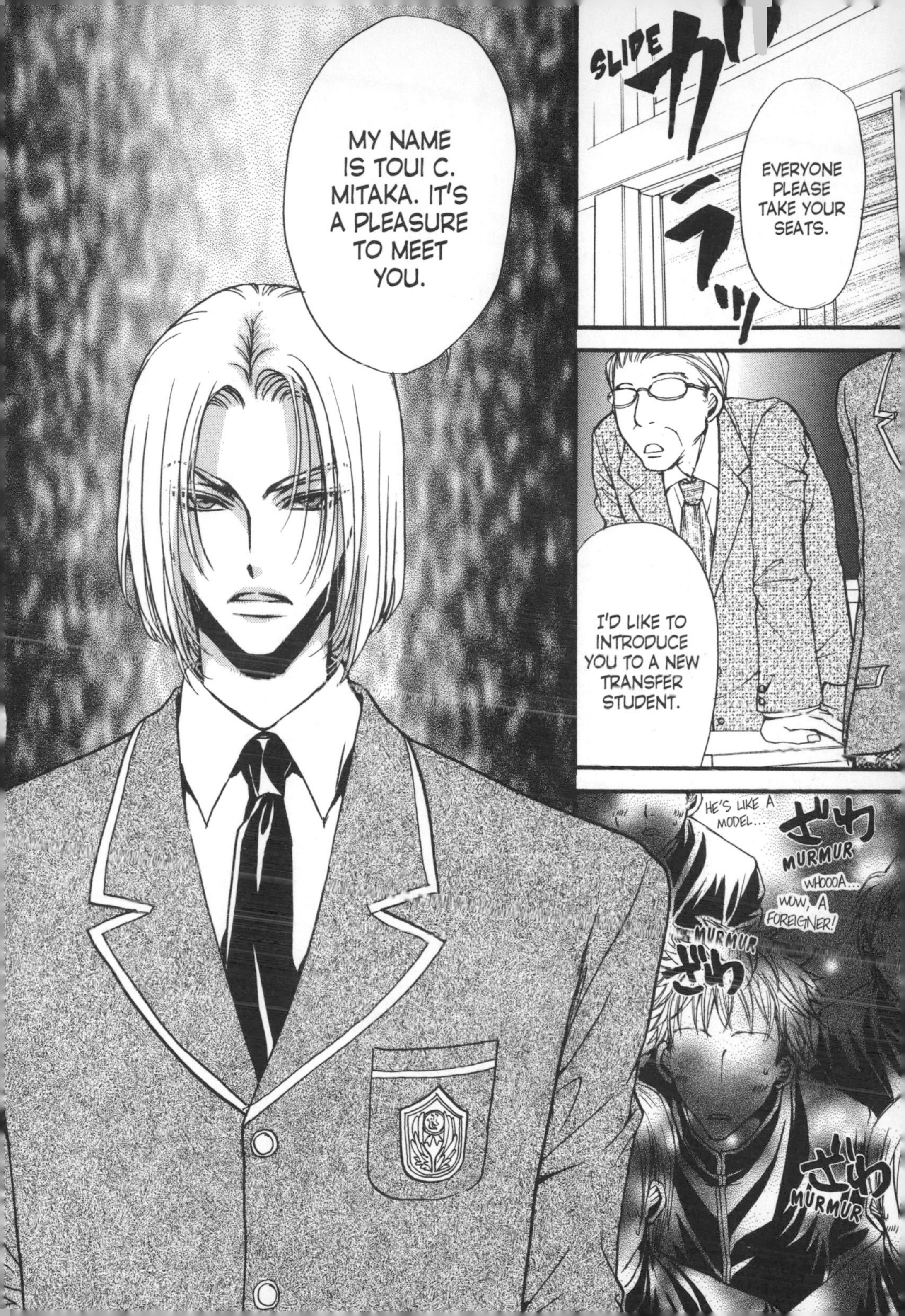
SLIDE
カラッ
EVERYONE PLEASE TAKE YOUR SEATS.
I'D LIKE TO INTRODUCE YOU TO A NEW TRANSFER STUDENT.
HE'S LIKE A MODEL...
ざわ
MURMUR
WHOOOA...
WOW, A FOREIGNER!
MURMUR
ざわ
ざわ
MURMUR
MY NAME IS TOUI C. MITAKA. IT'S A PLEASURE TO MEET YOU.

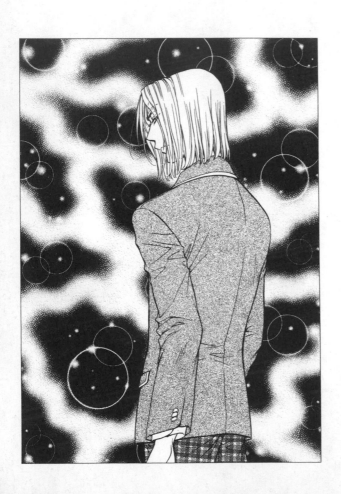

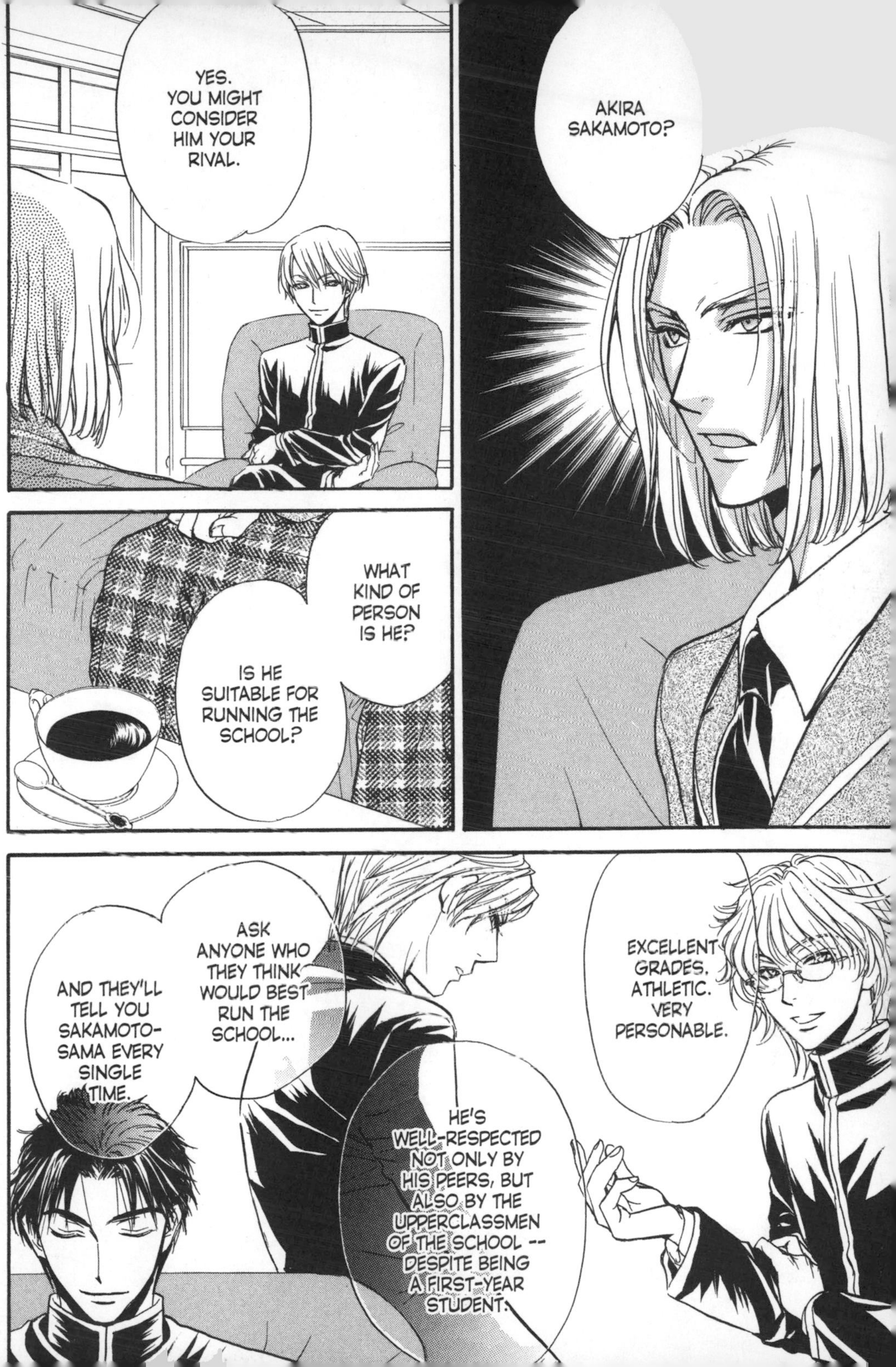
AKIRA SAKAMOTO?
YES. YOU MIGHT CONSIDER HIM YOUR RIVAL.
WHAT KIND OF PERSON IS HE?
IS HE SUITABLE FOR RUNNING THE SCHOOL?
EXCELLENT GRADES. ATHLETIC. VERY PERSONABLE.
HE'S WELL-RESPECTED NOT ONLY BY HIS PEERS, BUT ALSO BY THE UPPERCLASSMEN OF THE SCHOOL -- DESPITE BEING A FIRST-YEAR STUDENT.
ASK ANYONE WHO THEY THINK WOULD BEST RUN THE SCHOOL...
AND THEY'LL TELL YOU SAKAMOTO-SAMA EVERY SINGLE TIME.

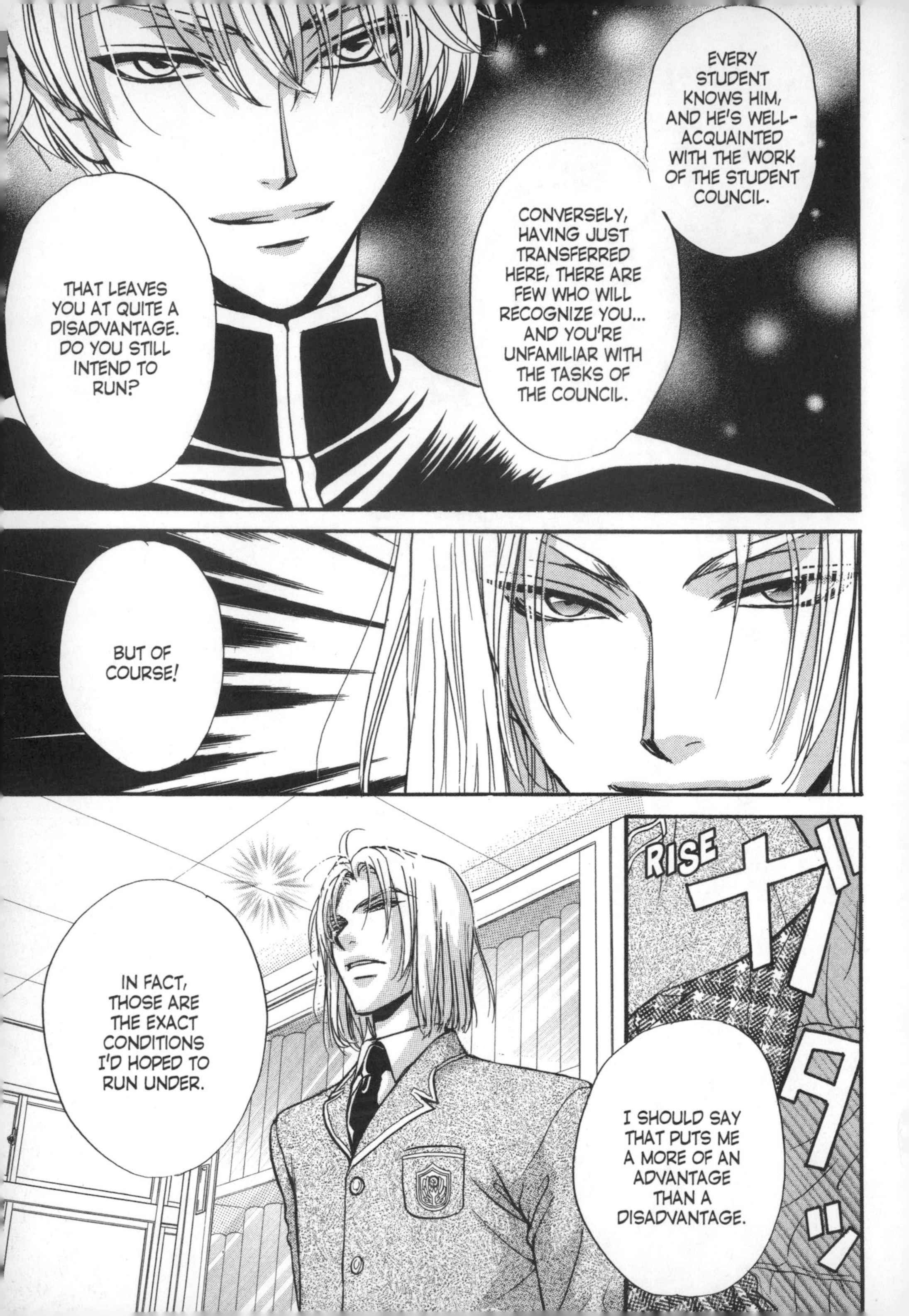
EVERY STUDENT KNOWS HIM, AND HE'S WELL-ACQUAINTED WITH THE WORK OF THE STUDENT COUNCIL.
CONVERSELY, HAVING JUST TRANSFERRED HERE, THERE ARE FEW WHO WILL RECOGNIZE YOU... AND YOU'RE UNFAMILIAR WITH THE TASKS OF THE COUNCIL.
THAT LEAVES YOU AT QUITE A DISADVANTAGE. DO YOU STILL INTEND TO RUN?
BUT OF COURSE!
RISE
IN FACT, THOSE ARE THE EXACT CONDITIONS I'D HOPED TO RUN UNDER.
I SHOULD SAY THAT PUTS ME A MORE OF AN ADVANTAGE THAN A DISADVANTAGE.

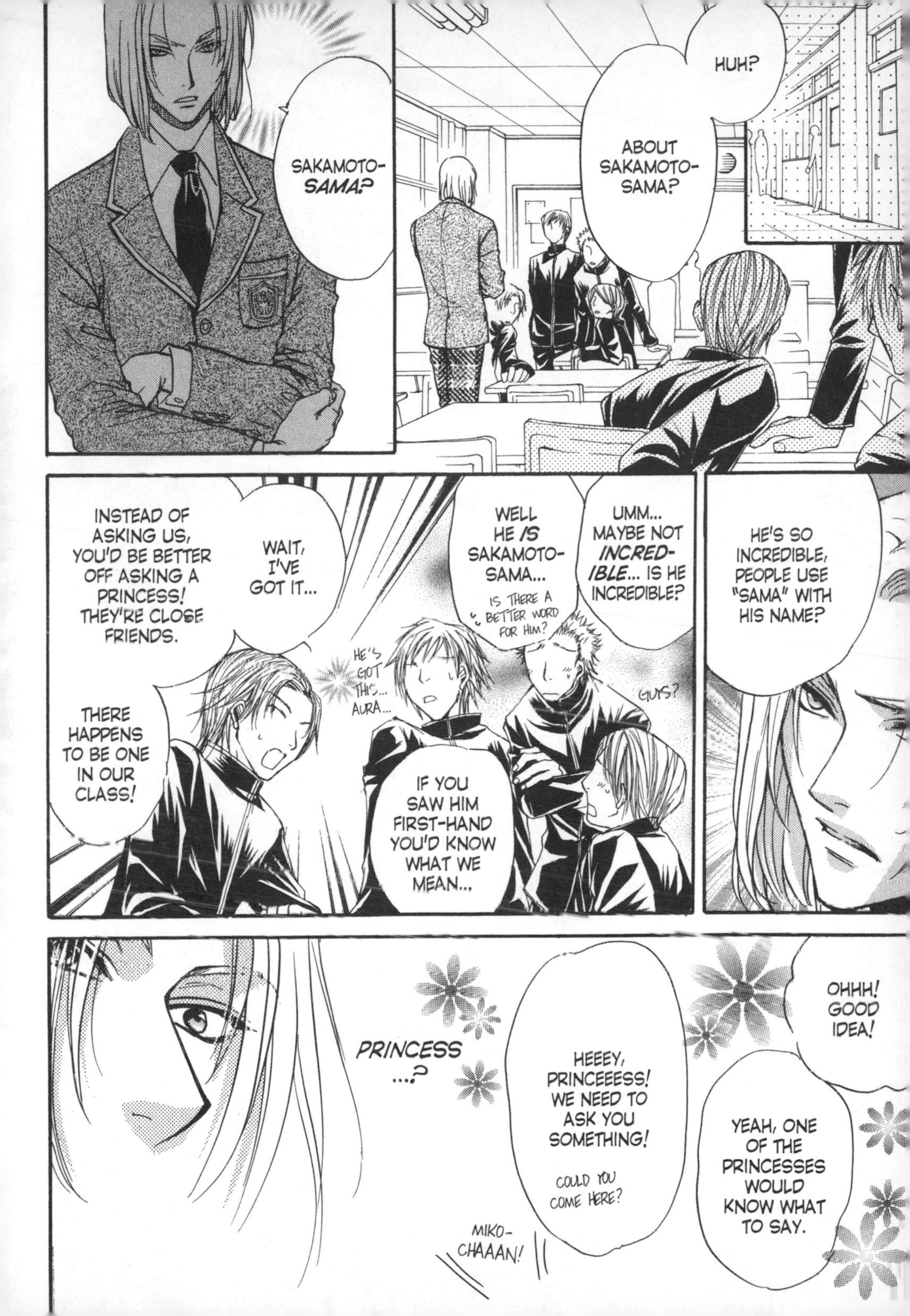
HUH?
ABOUT SAKAMOTO-SAMA?
SAKAMOTO-*SAMA*?
HE'S SO INCREDIBLE, PEOPLE USE "SAMA" WITH HIS NAME?
UMM... MAYBE NOT *INCREDIBLE*... IS HE INCREDIBLE?
WELL HE *IS* SAKAMOTO-SAMA...
IS THERE A BETTER WORD FOR HIM?
GUYS?
HE'S GOT THIS... AURA...
IF YOU SAW HIM FIRST-HAND YOU'D KNOW WHAT WE MEAN...
WAIT, I'VE GOT IT...
INSTEAD OF ASKING US, YOU'D BE BETTER OFF ASKING A PRINCESS! THEY'RE CLOSE FRIENDS.
THERE HAPPENS TO BE ONE IN OUR CLASS!
OHHH! GOOD IDEA!
YEAH, ONE OF THE PRINCESSES WOULD KNOW WHAT TO SAY.
HEEEY, PRINCEEEESS! WE NEED TO ASK YOU SOMETHING!
COULD YOU COME HERE?
MIKO-CHAAAN!
PRINCESS ...?

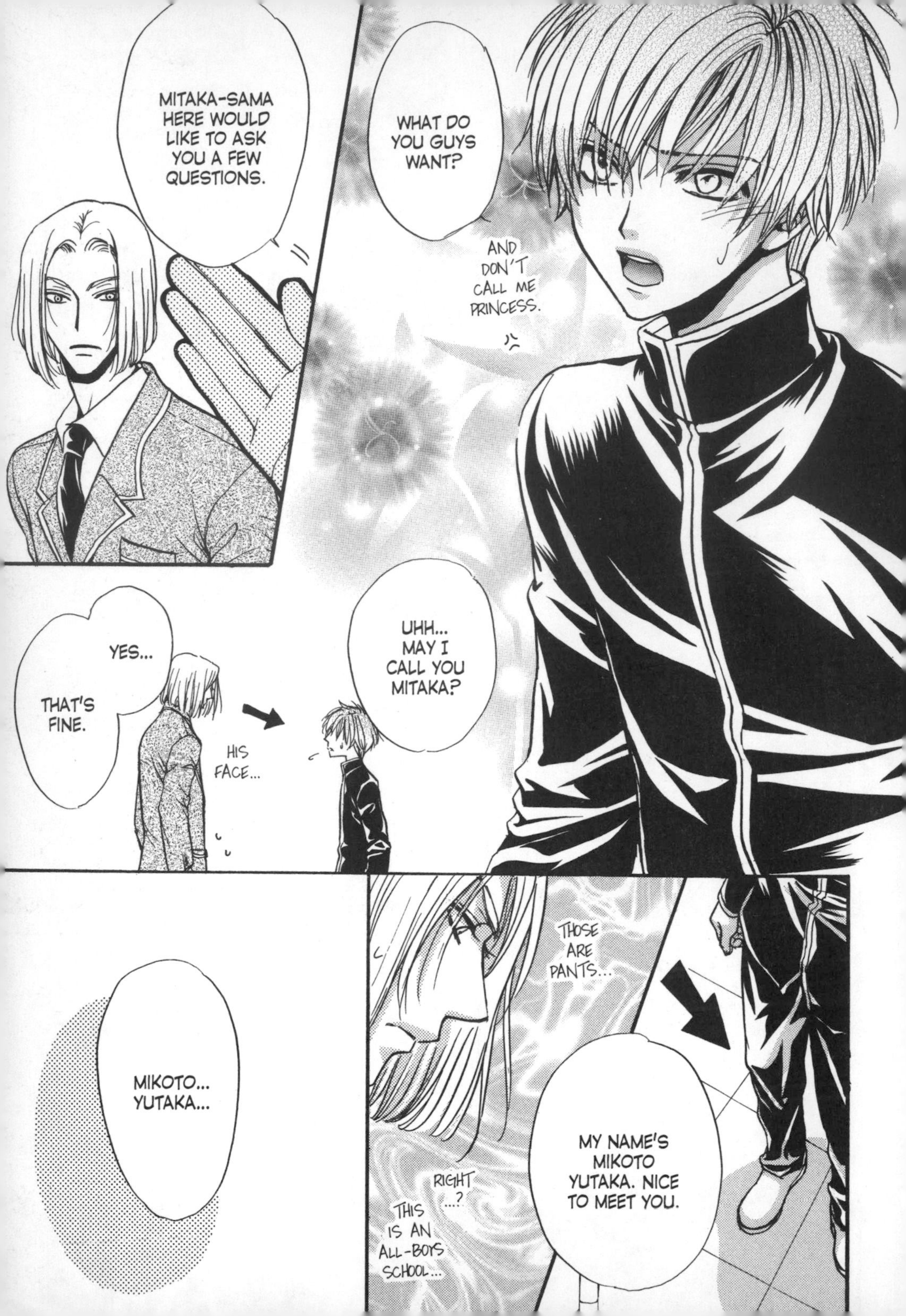
WHAT DO YOU GUYS WANT?
AND DON'T CALL ME PRINCESS.
MITAKA-SAMA HERE WOULD LIKE TO ASK YOU A FEW QUESTIONS.
UHH... MAY I CALL YOU MITAKA?
HIS FACE...
YES...
THAT'S FINE.
THOSE ARE PANTS...
MY NAME'S MIKOTO YUTAKA. NICE TO MEET YOU.
RIGHT ...?
THIS IS AN ALL-BOYS SCHOOL...
MIKOTO... YUTAKA...

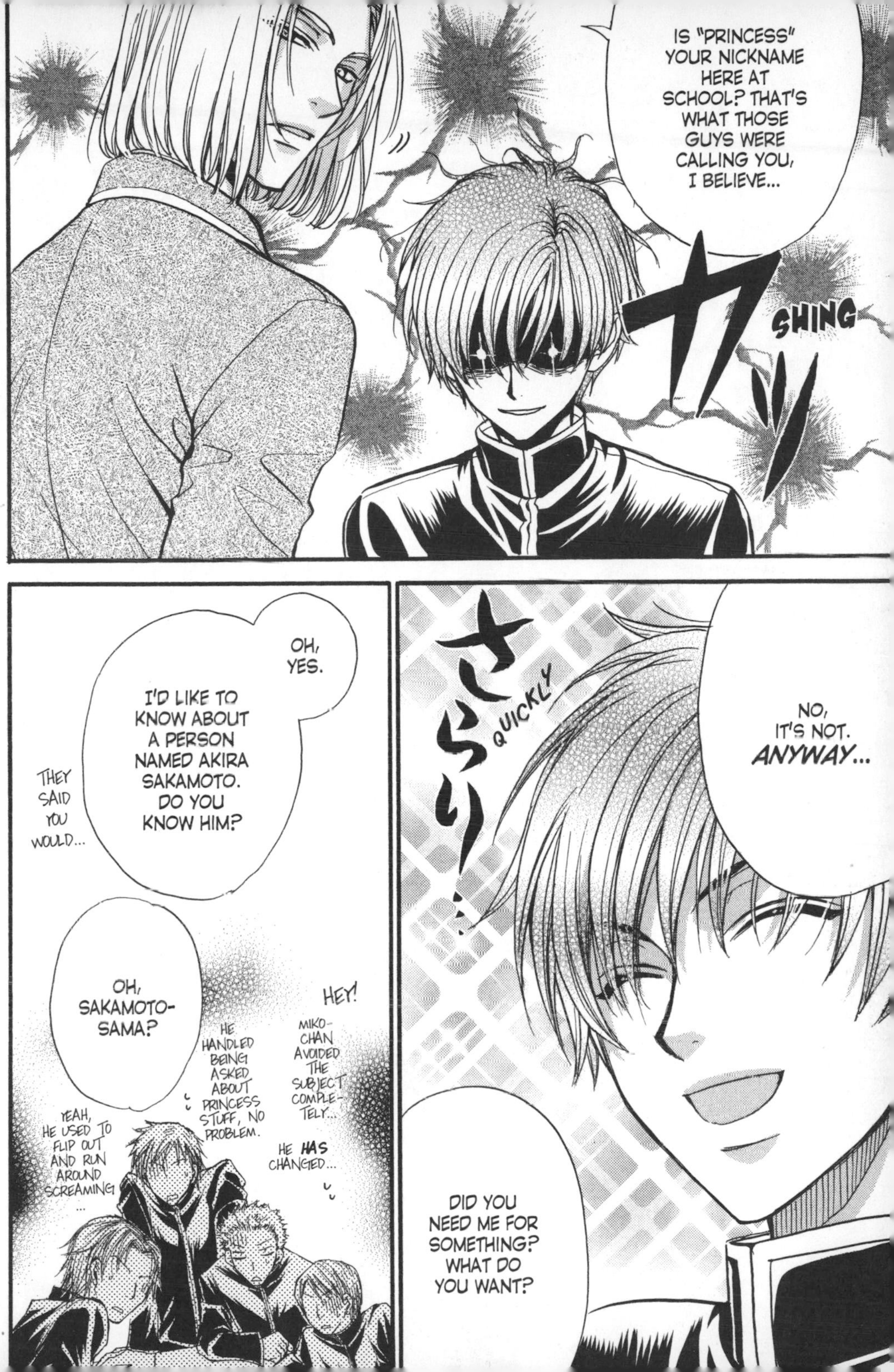
IS "PRINCESS" YOUR NICKNAME HERE AT SCHOOL? THAT'S WHAT THOSE GUYS WERE CALLING YOU, I BELIEVE...
カッ
SHING
さらり!
QUICKLY
NO, IT'S NOT. ANYWAY...
DID YOU NEED ME FOR SOMETHING? WHAT DO YOU WANT?
OH, YES.
I'D LIKE TO KNOW ABOUT A PERSON NAMED AKIRA SAKAMOTO. DO YOU KNOW HIM?
THEY SAID YOU WOULD...
OH, SAKAMOTO-SAMA?
HEY!
MIKO-CHAN AVOIDED THE SUBJECT COMPLETELY...
HE HANDLED BEING ASKED ABOUT PRINCESS STUFF, NO PROBLEM.
HE HAS CHANGED...
YEAH, HE USED TO FLIP OUT AND RUN AROUND SCREAMING...

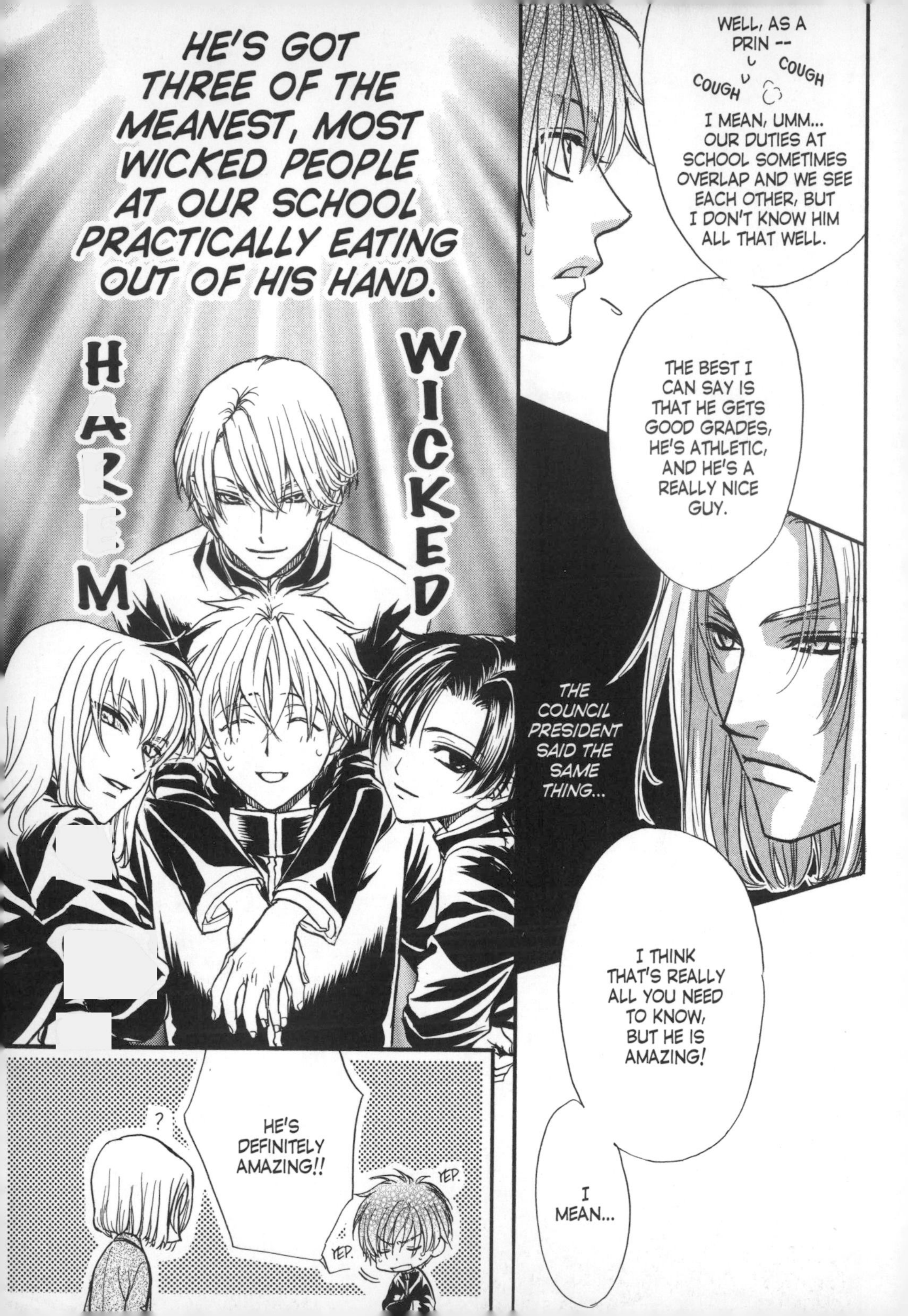
WELL, AS A PRIN --
COUGH
COUGH
I MEAN, UMM... OUR DUTIES AT SCHOOL SOMETIMES OVERLAP AND WE SEE EACH OTHER, BUT I DON'T KNOW HIM ALL THAT WELL.
THE BEST I CAN SAY IS THAT HE GETS GOOD GRADES, HE'S ATHLETIC, AND HE'S A REALLY NICE GUY.
THE COUNCIL PRESIDENT SAID THE SAME THING...
I THINK THAT'S REALLY ALL YOU NEED TO KNOW, BUT HE IS AMAZING!
I MEAN...
HE'S GOT THREE OF THE MEANEST, MOST WICKED PEOPLE AT OUR SCHOOL PRACTICALLY EATING OUT OF HIS HAND.
WICKED
HAREM
HE'S DEFINITELY AMAZING!!
?
YEP.
YEP.

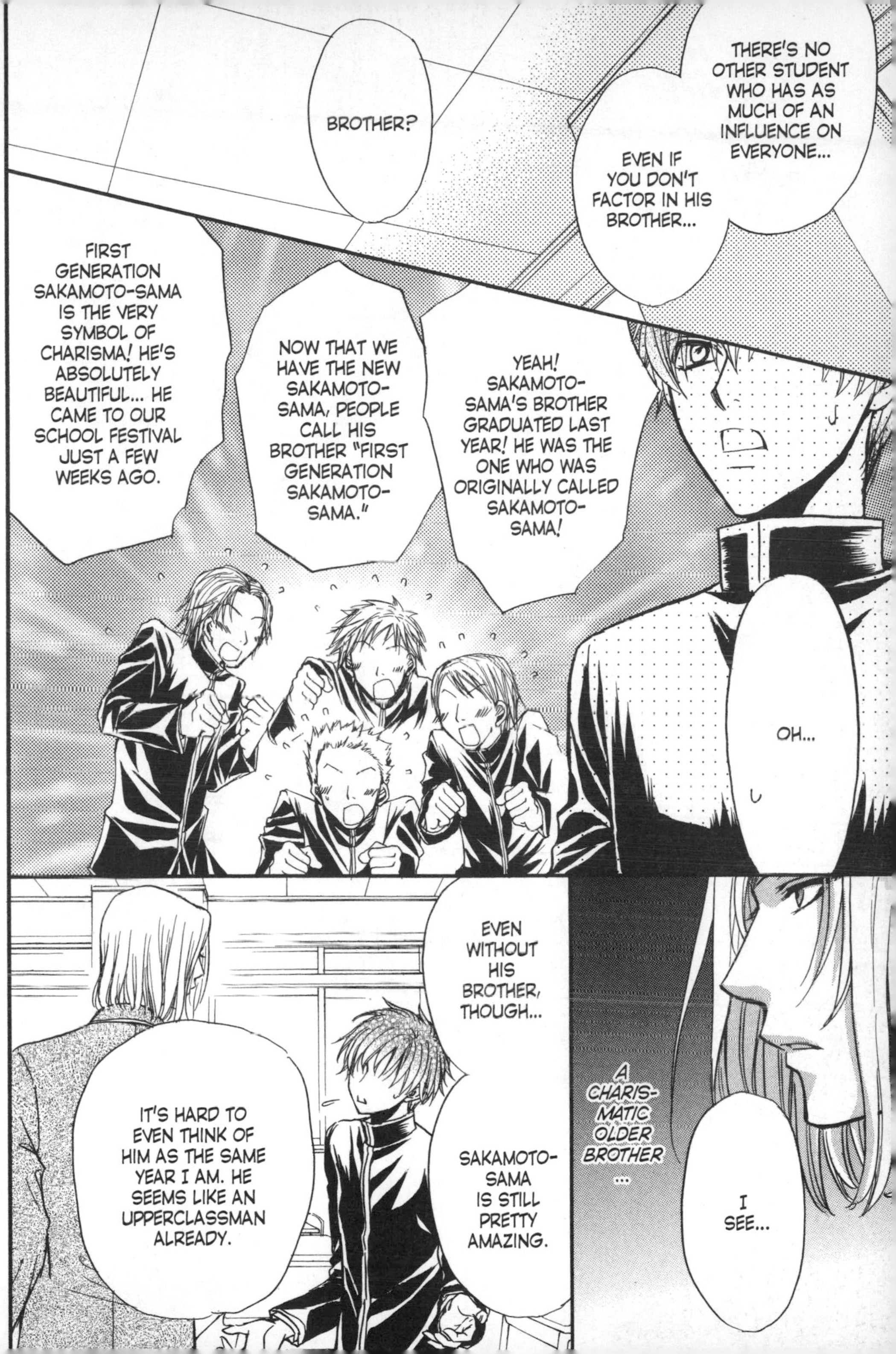
THERE'S NO OTHER STUDENT WHO HAS AS MUCH OF AN INFLUENCE ON EVERYONE...
EVEN IF YOU DON'T FACTOR IN HIS BROTHER...
BROTHER?
YEAH! SAKAMOTO-SAMA'S BROTHER GRADUATED LAST YEAR! HE WAS THE ONE WHO WAS ORIGINALLY CALLED SAKAMOTO-SAMA!
NOW THAT WE HAVE THE NEW SAKAMOTO-SAMA, PEOPLE CALL HIS BROTHER "FIRST GENERATION SAKAMOTO-SAMA."
FIRST GENERATION SAKAMOTO-SAMA IS THE VERY SYMBOL OF CHARISMA! HE'S ABSOLUTELY BEAUTIFUL... HE CAME TO OUR SCHOOL FESTIVAL JUST A FEW WEEKS AGO.
OH...
I SEE...
A CHARIS-MATIC OLDER BROTHER ...
EVEN WITHOUT HIS BROTHER, THOUGH...
SAKAMOTO-SAMA IS STILL PRETTY AMAZING.
IT'S HARD TO EVEN THINK OF HIM AS THE SAME YEAR I AM. HE SEEMS LIKE AN UPPERCLASSMAN ALREADY.

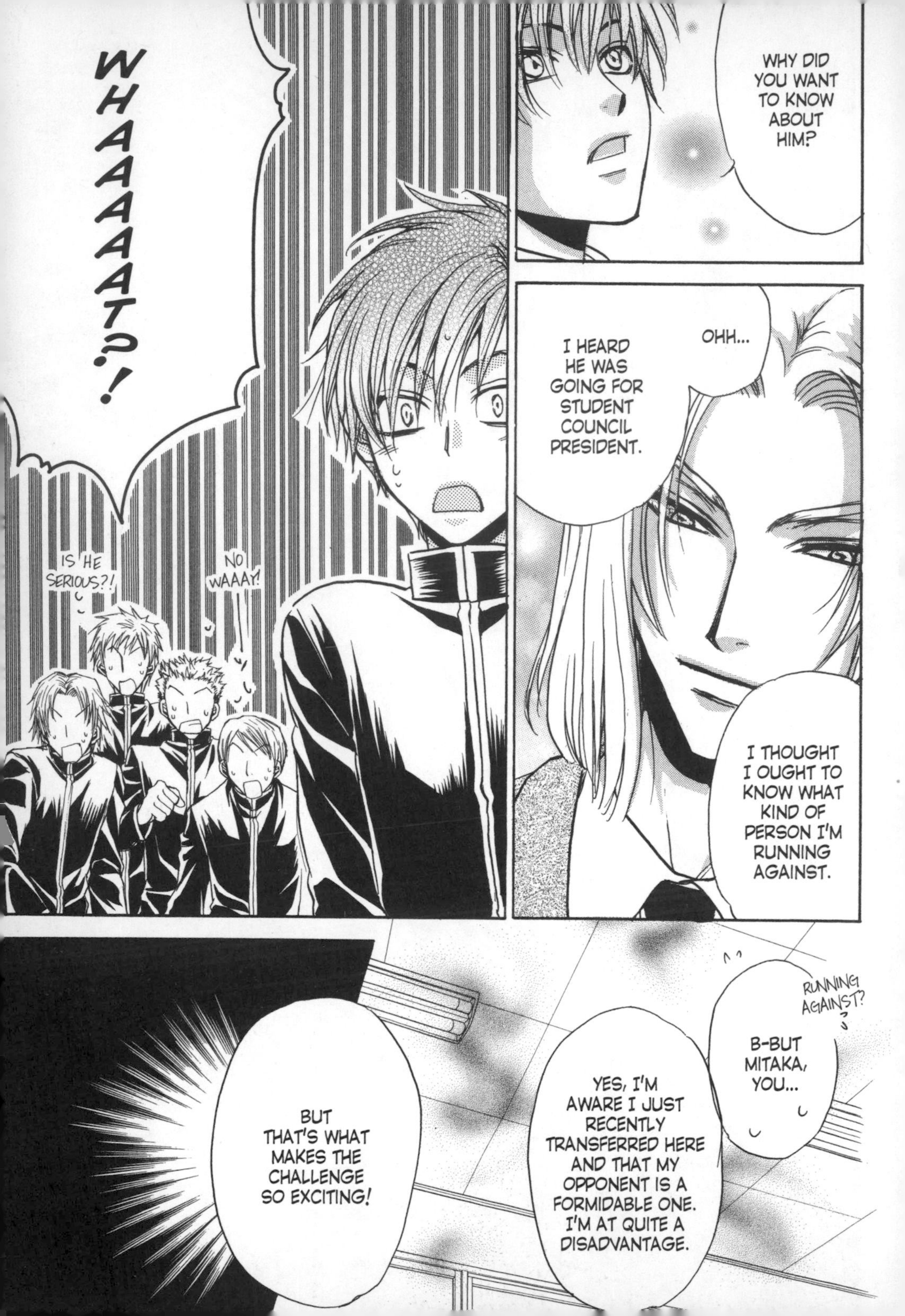
WHY DID YOU WANT TO KNOW ABOUT HIM?
OHH...
I HEARD HE WAS GOING FOR STUDENT COUNCIL PRESIDENT.
I THOUGHT I OUGHT TO KNOW WHAT KIND OF PERSON I'M RUNNING AGAINST.
WHAAAAAAT?!
NO WAAAY!
IS HE SERIOUS?!
RUNNING AGAINST?
B-BUT MITAKA, YOU...
YES, I'M AWARE I JUST RECENTLY TRANSFERRED HERE AND THAT MY OPPONENT IS A FORMIDABLE ONE. I'M AT QUITE A DISADVANTAGE.
BUT THAT'S WHAT MAKES THE CHALLENGE SO EXCITING!

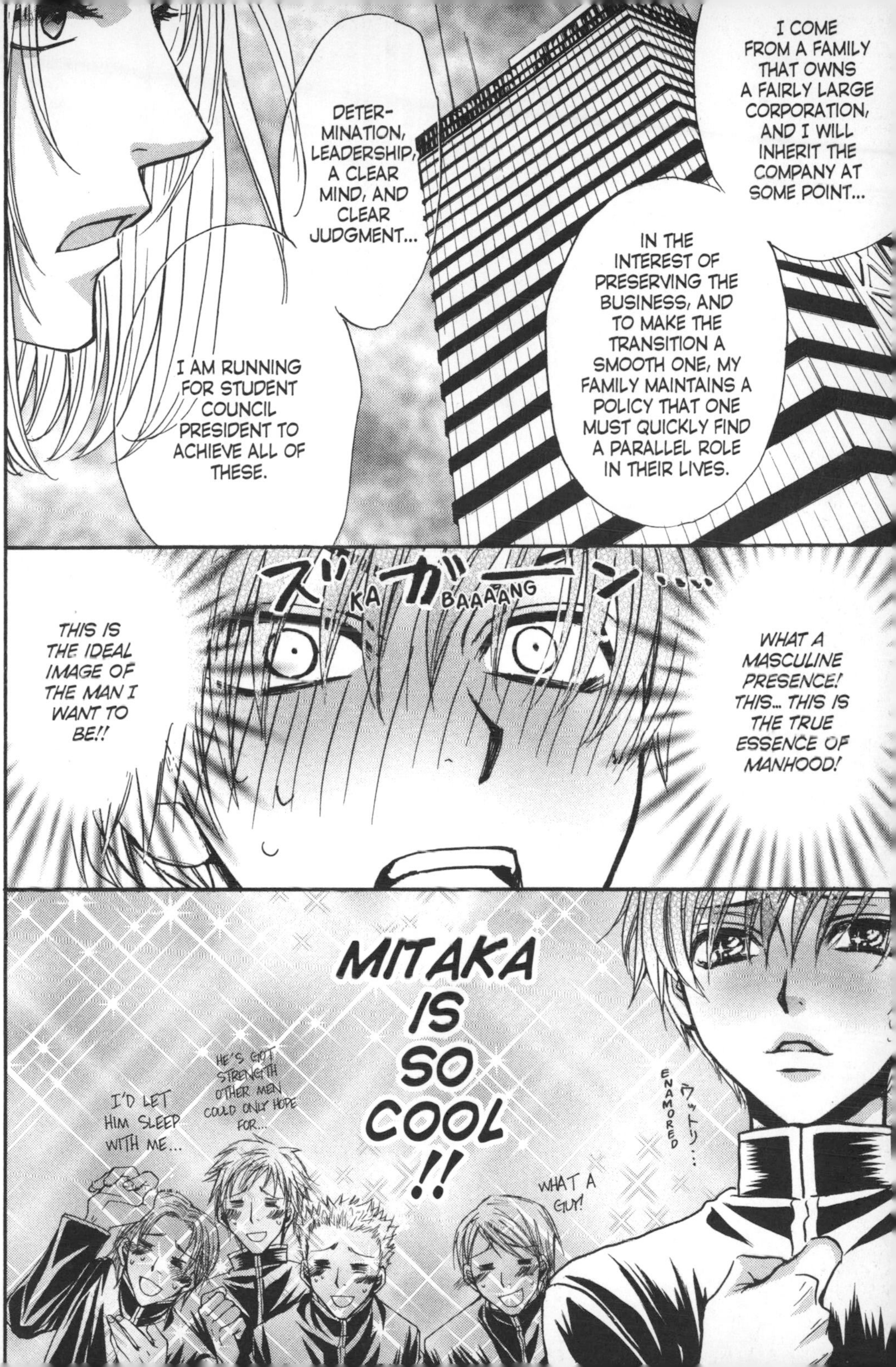
I COME FROM A FAMILY THAT OWNS A FAIRLY LARGE CORPORATION, AND I WILL INHERIT THE COMPANY AT SOME POINT...
IN THE INTEREST OF PRESERVING THE BUSINESS, AND TO MAKE THE TRANSITION A SMOOTH ONE, MY FAMILY MAINTAINS A POLICY THAT ONE MUST QUICKLY FIND A PARALLEL ROLE IN THEIR LIVES.
DETER-MINATION, LEADERSHIP, A CLEAR MIND, AND CLEAR JUDGMENT...
I AM RUNNING FOR STUDENT COUNCIL PRESIDENT TO ACHIEVE ALL OF THESE.
ズガーーン...
KA BAAAANG
WHAT A MASCULINE PRESENCE! THIS... THIS IS THE TRUE ESSENCE OF MANHOOD!
THIS IS THE IDEAL IMAGE OF THE MAN I WANT TO BE!!
MITAKA IS SO COOL!!
ウットリ...
ENAMORED
WHAT A GUY!
HE'S GOT STRENGTH OTHER MEN COULD ONLY HOPE FOR...
I'D LET HIM SLEEP WITH ME...

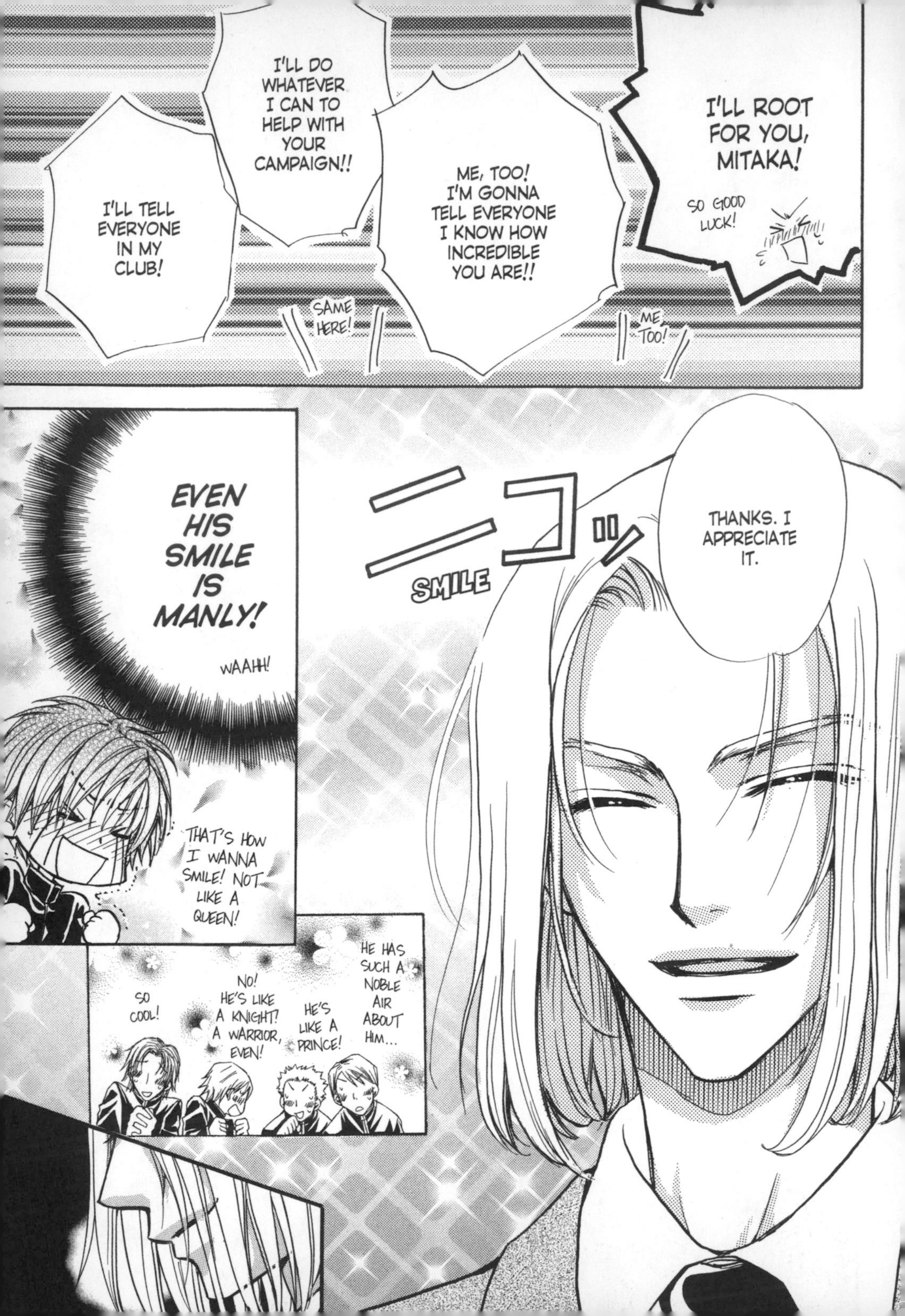
I'LL ROOT FOR YOU, MITAKA!
SO GOOD LUCK!
ME, TOO! I'M GONNA TELL EVERYONE I KNOW HOW INCREDIBLE YOU ARE!!
I'LL DO WHATEVER I CAN TO HELP WITH YOUR CAMPAIGN!!
I'LL TELL EVERYONE IN MY CLUB!
ME TOO!
SAME HERE!
THANKS. I APPRECIATE IT.
ニコッ
SMILE
EVEN HIS SMILE IS MANLY!
WAAHH!
THAT'S HOW I WANNA SMILE! NOT LIKE A QUEEN!
HE HAS SUCH A NOBLE AIR ABOUT HIM...
HE'S LIKE A PRINCE!
NO! HE'S LIKE A KNIGHT! A WARRIOR, EVEN!
SO COOL!

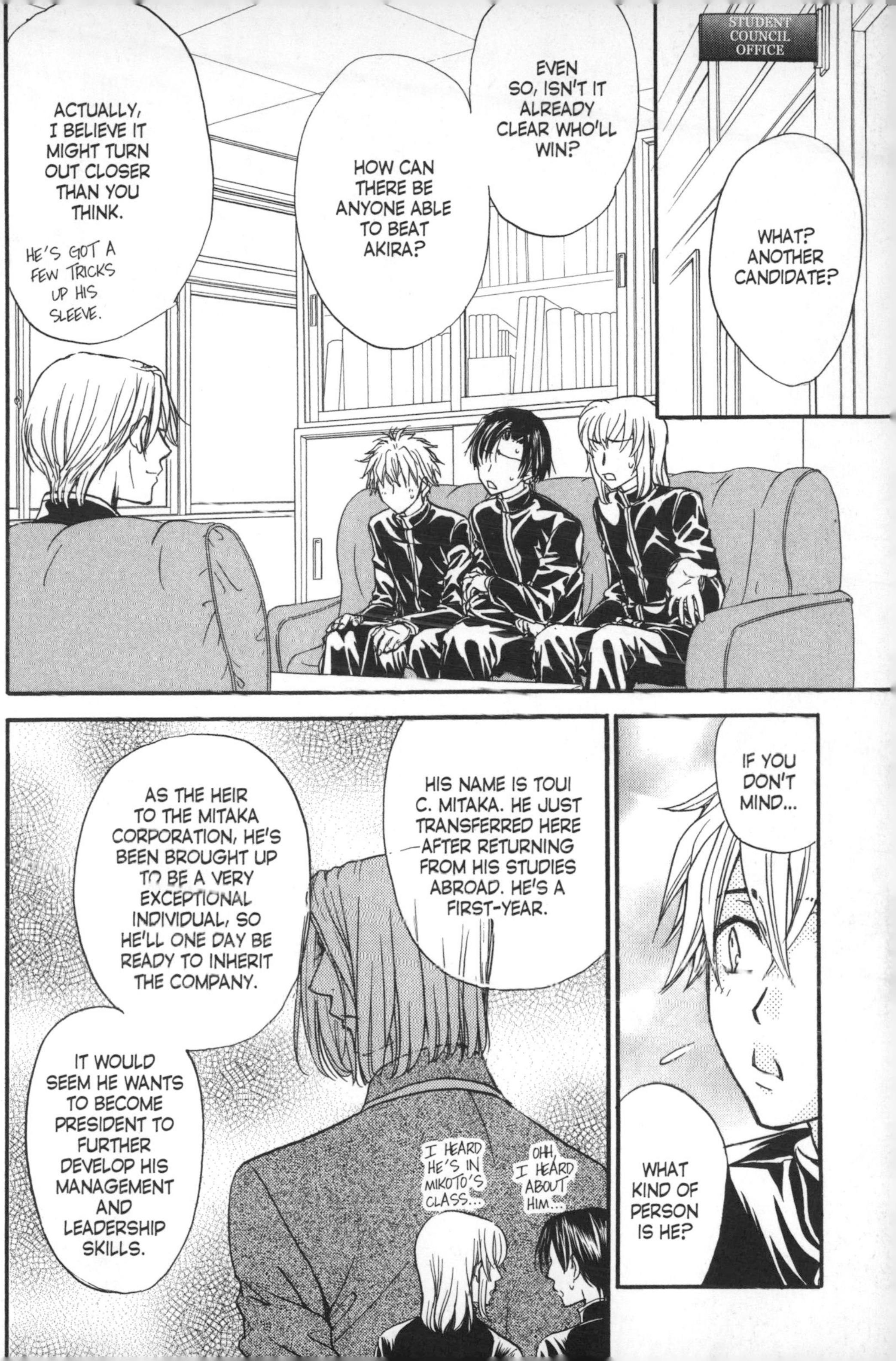
STUDENT COUNCIL OFFICE
WHAT? ANOTHER CANDIDATE?
EVEN SO, ISN'T IT ALREADY CLEAR WHO'LL WIN?
HOW CAN THERE BE ANYONE ABLE TO BEAT AKIRA?
ACTUALLY, I BELIEVE IT MIGHT TURN OUT CLOSER THAN YOU THINK.
HE'S GOT A FEW TRICKS UP HIS SLEEVE.
IF YOU DON'T MIND...
WHAT KIND OF PERSON IS HE?
HIS NAME IS TOUI C. MITAKA. HE JUST TRANSFERRED HERE AFTER RETURNING FROM HIS STUDIES ABROAD. HE'S A FIRST-YEAR.
AS THE HEIR TO THE MITAKA CORPORATION, HE'S BEEN BROUGHT UP TO BE A VERY EXCEPTIONAL INDIVIDUAL, SO HE'LL ONE DAY BE READY TO INHERIT THE COMPANY.
IT WOULD SEEM HE WANTS TO BECOME PRESIDENT TO FURTHER DEVELOP HIS MANAGEMENT AND LEADERSHIP SKILLS.
OHH, I HEARD ABOUT HIM...
I HEARD HE'S IN MIKOTO'S CLASS...

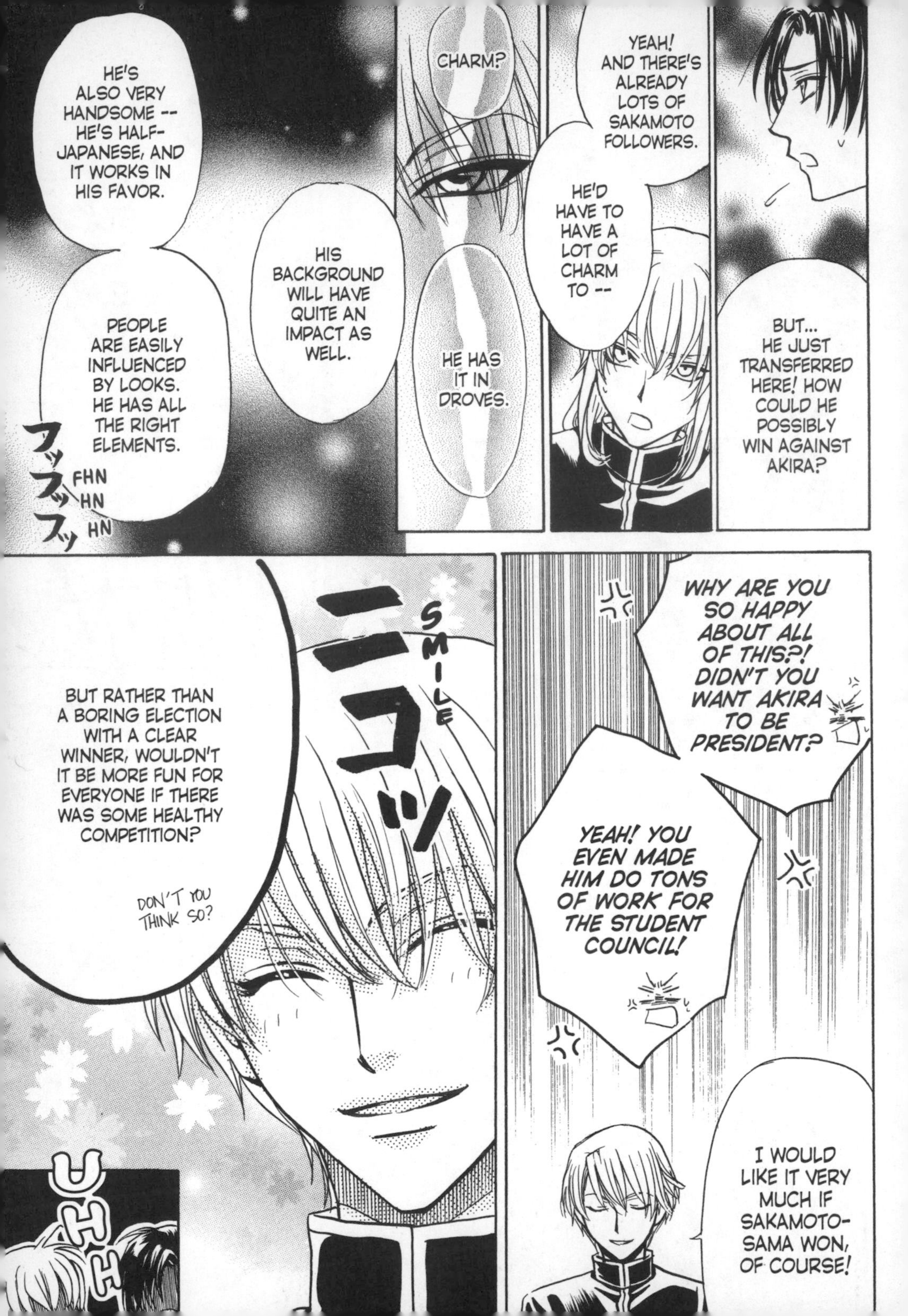
BUT... HE JUST TRANSFERRED HERE! HOW COULD HE POSSIBLY WIN AGAINST AKIRA?
YEAH! AND THERE'S ALREADY LOTS OF SAKAMOTO FOLLOWERS.
HE'D HAVE TO HAVE A LOT OF CHARM TO --
CHARM?
HE HAS IT IN DROVES.
HIS BACKGROUND WILL HAVE QUITE AN IMPACT AS WELL.
HE'S ALSO VERY HANDSOME -- HE'S HALF-JAPANESE, AND IT WORKS IN HIS FAVOR.
PEOPLE ARE EASILY INFLUENCED BY LOOKS. HE HAS ALL THE RIGHT ELEMENTS.
FHN HN HN
WHY ARE YOU SO HAPPY ABOUT ALL OF THIS?! DIDN'T YOU WANT AKIRA TO BE PRESIDENT?
YEAH! YOU EVEN MADE HIM DO TONS OF WORK FOR THE STUDENT COUNCIL!
I WOULD LIKE IT VERY MUCH IF SAKAMOTO-SAMA WON, OF COURSE!
SMILE
BUT RATHER THAN A BORING ELECTION WITH A CLEAR WINNER, WOULDN'T IT BE MORE FUN FOR EVERYONE IF THERE WAS SOME HEALTHY COMPETITION?
DON'T YOU THINK SO?
UHH

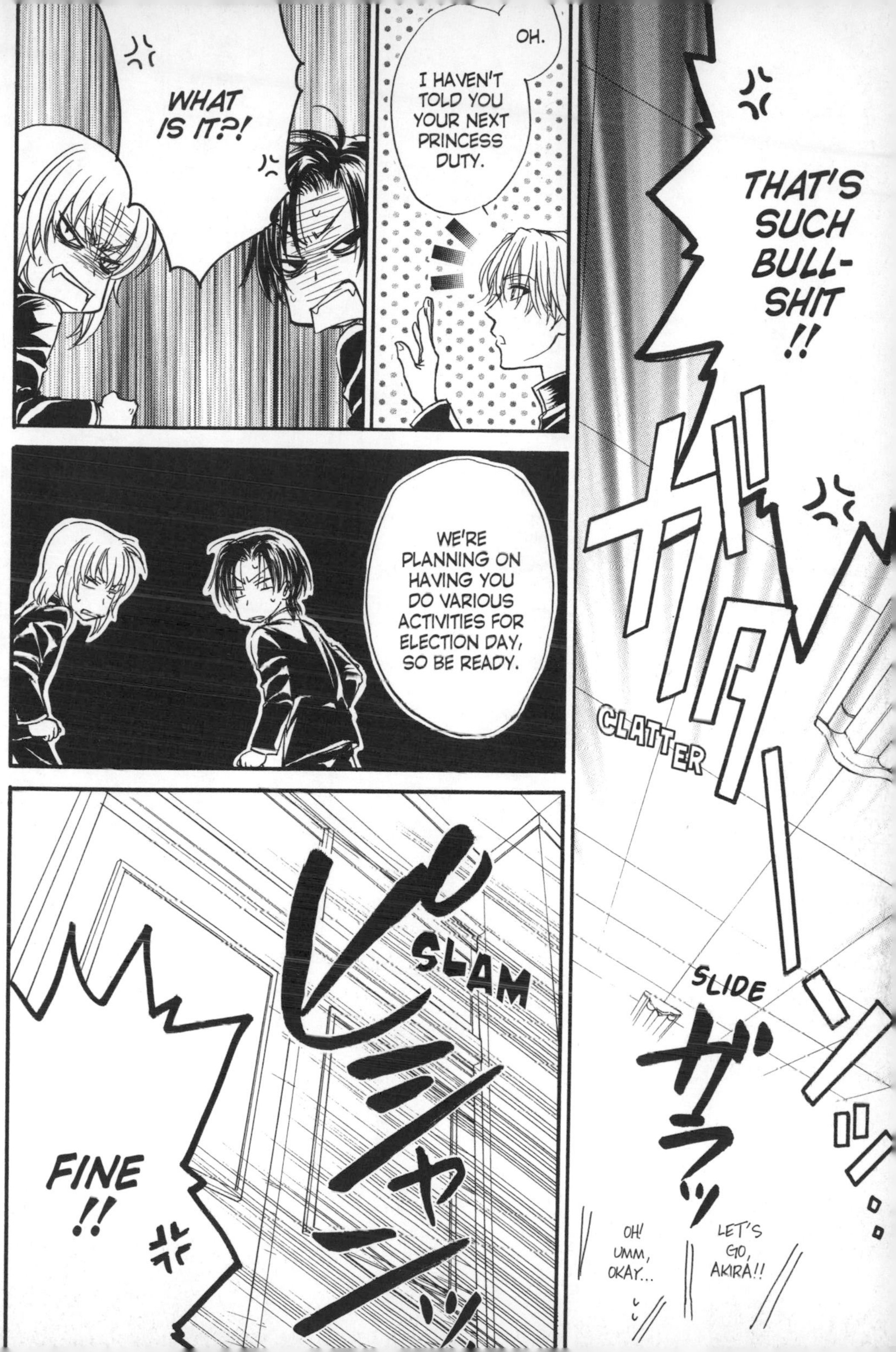
THAT'S SUCH BULL-SHIT!!
CLATTER
SLIDE
LET'S GO, AKIRA!!
OH! UMM, OKAY...
OH.
I HAVEN'T TOLD YOU YOUR NEXT PRINCESS DUTY.
WHAT IS IT?!
WE'RE PLANNING ON HAVING YOU DO VARIOUS ACTIVITIES FOR ELECTION DAY, SO BE READY.
SLAM
FINE!!

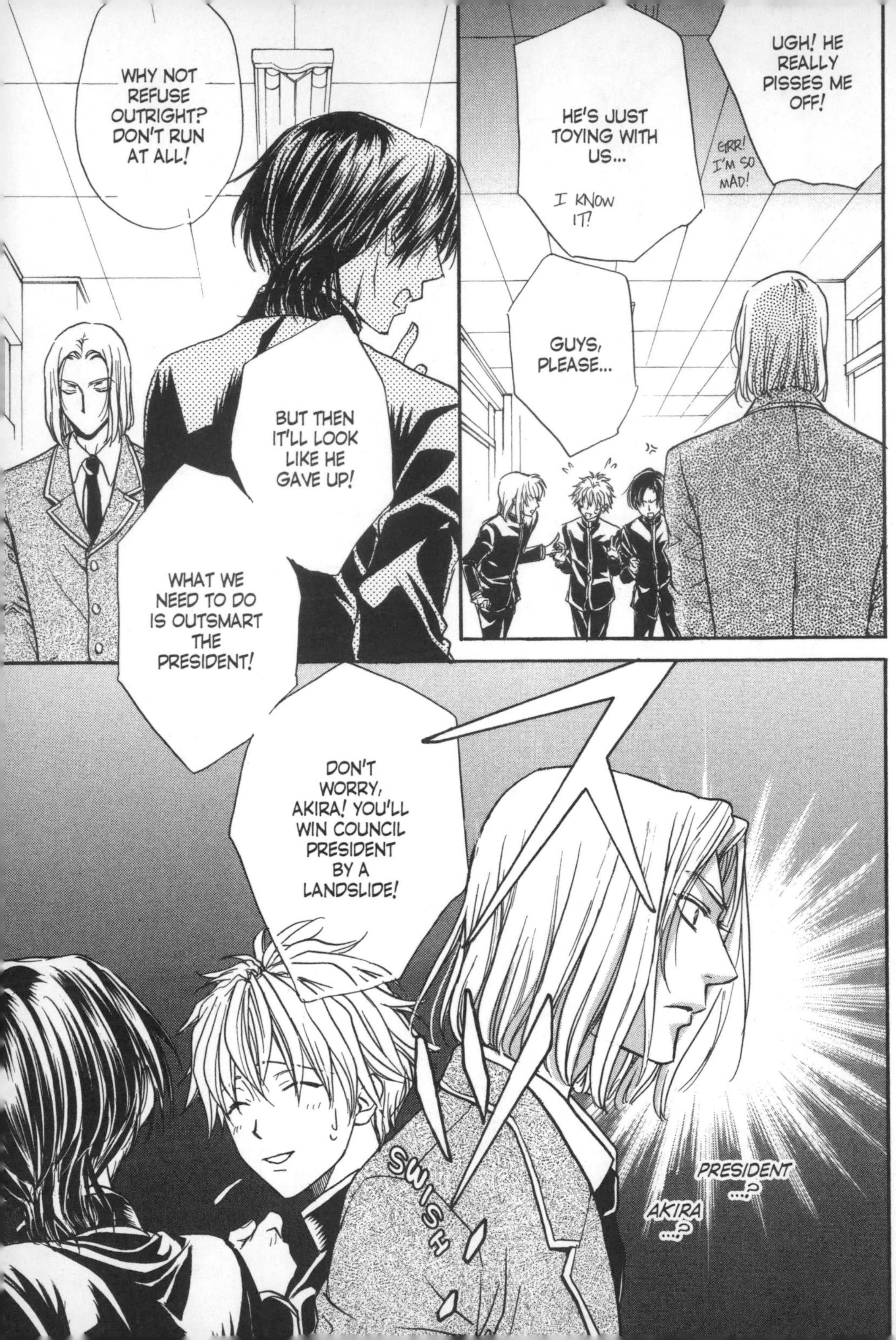
UGH! HE REALLY PISSES ME OFF!
GRR! I'M SO MAD!
HE'S JUST TOYING WITH US...
I KNOW IT!
GUYS, PLEASE...
WHY NOT REFUSE OUTRIGHT? DON'T RUN AT ALL!
BUT THEN IT'LL LOOK LIKE HE GAVE UP!
WHAT WE NEED TO DO IS OUTSMART THE PRESIDENT!
DON'T WORRY, AKIRA! YOU'LL WIN COUNCIL PRESIDENT BY A LANDSLIDE!
SWISH
PRESIDENT ...?
AKIRA ...?

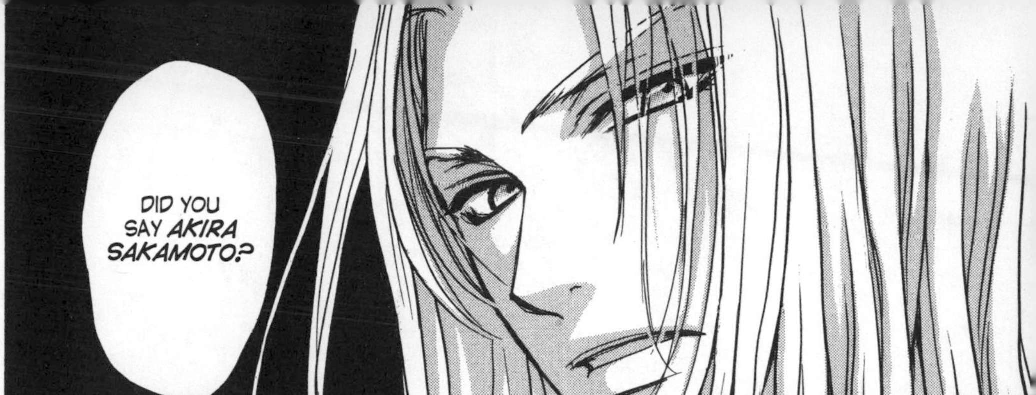
DID YOU SAY AKIRA SAKAMOTO?

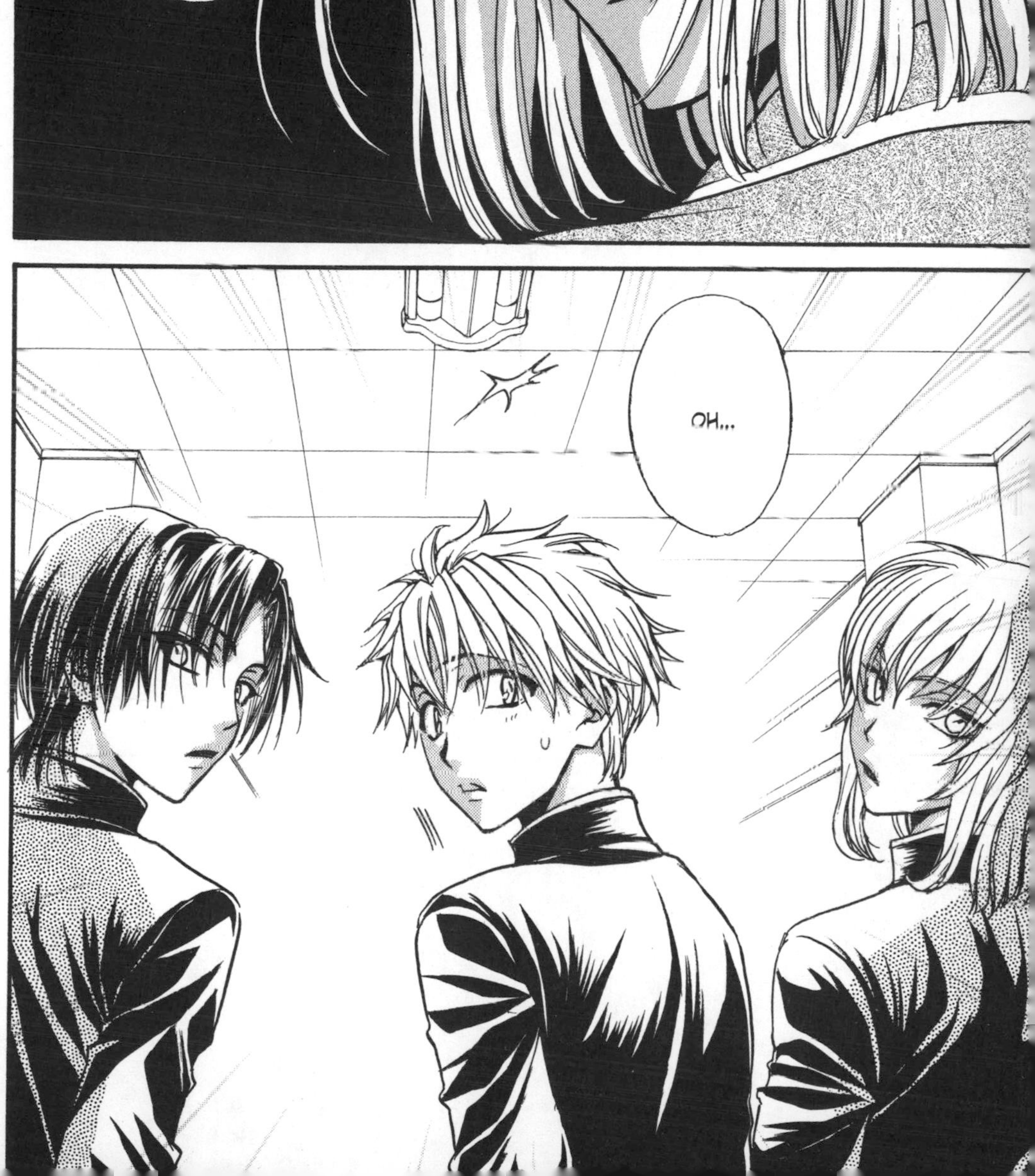
OH...

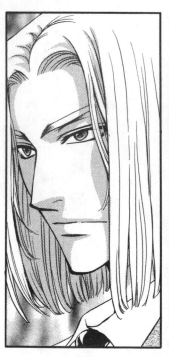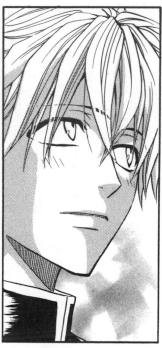

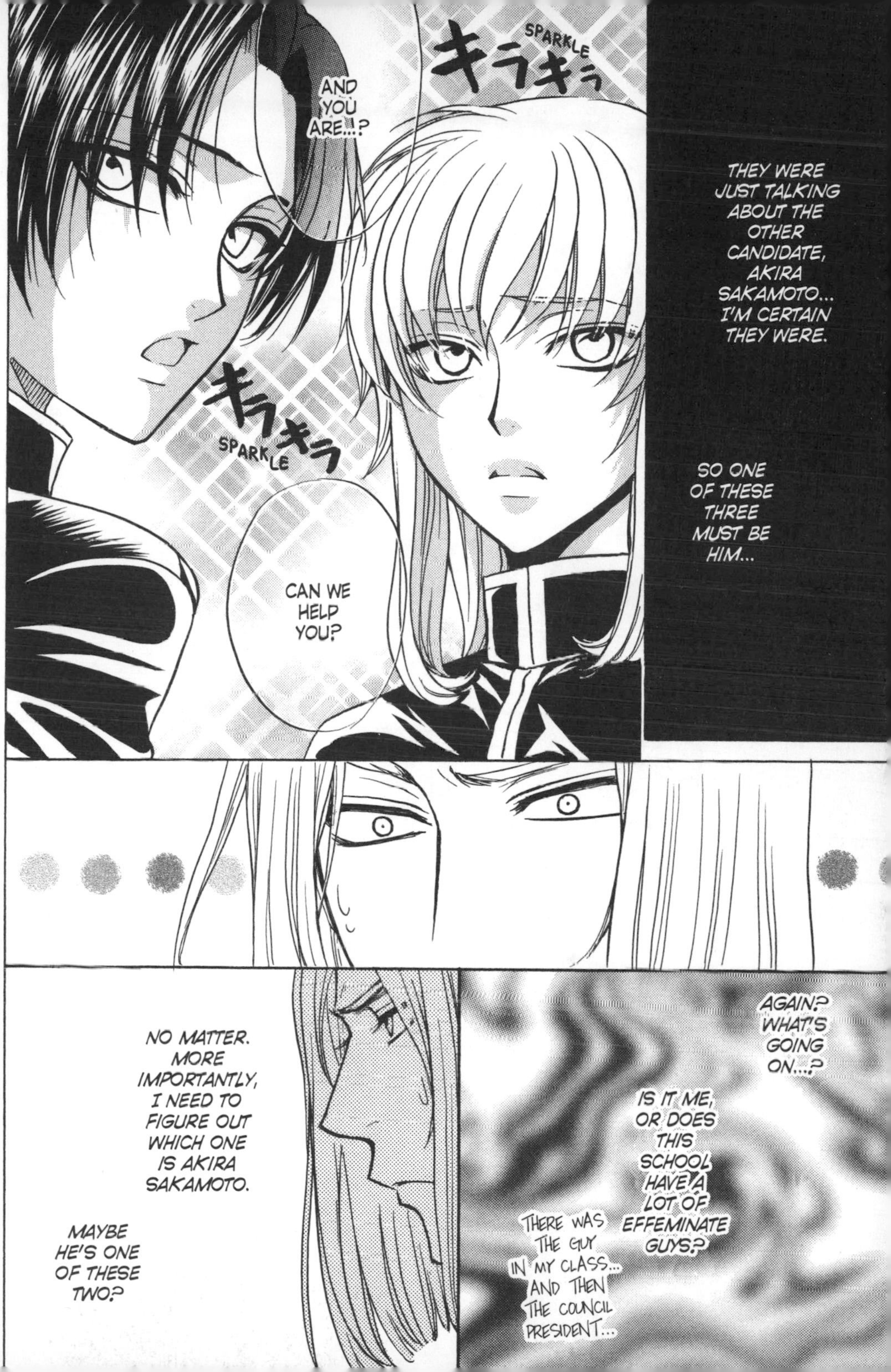
THEY WERE JUST TALKING ABOUT THE OTHER CANDIDATE, AKIRA SAKAMOTO... I'M CERTAIN THEY WERE.
SO ONE OF THESE THREE MUST BE HIM...
キラキラ SPARKLE
AND YOU ARE...?
キラキラ SPARKLE
CAN WE HELP YOU?
AGAIN? WHAT'S GOING ON...?
IS IT ME, OR DOES THIS SCHOOL HAVE A LOT OF EFFEMINATE GUYS?
THERE WAS THE GUY IN MY CLASS... AND THEN THE COUNCIL PRESIDENT...
NO MATTER. MORE IMPORTANTLY, I NEED TO FIGURE OUT WHICH ONE IS AKIRA SAKAMOTO.
MAYBE HE'S ONE OF THESE TWO?

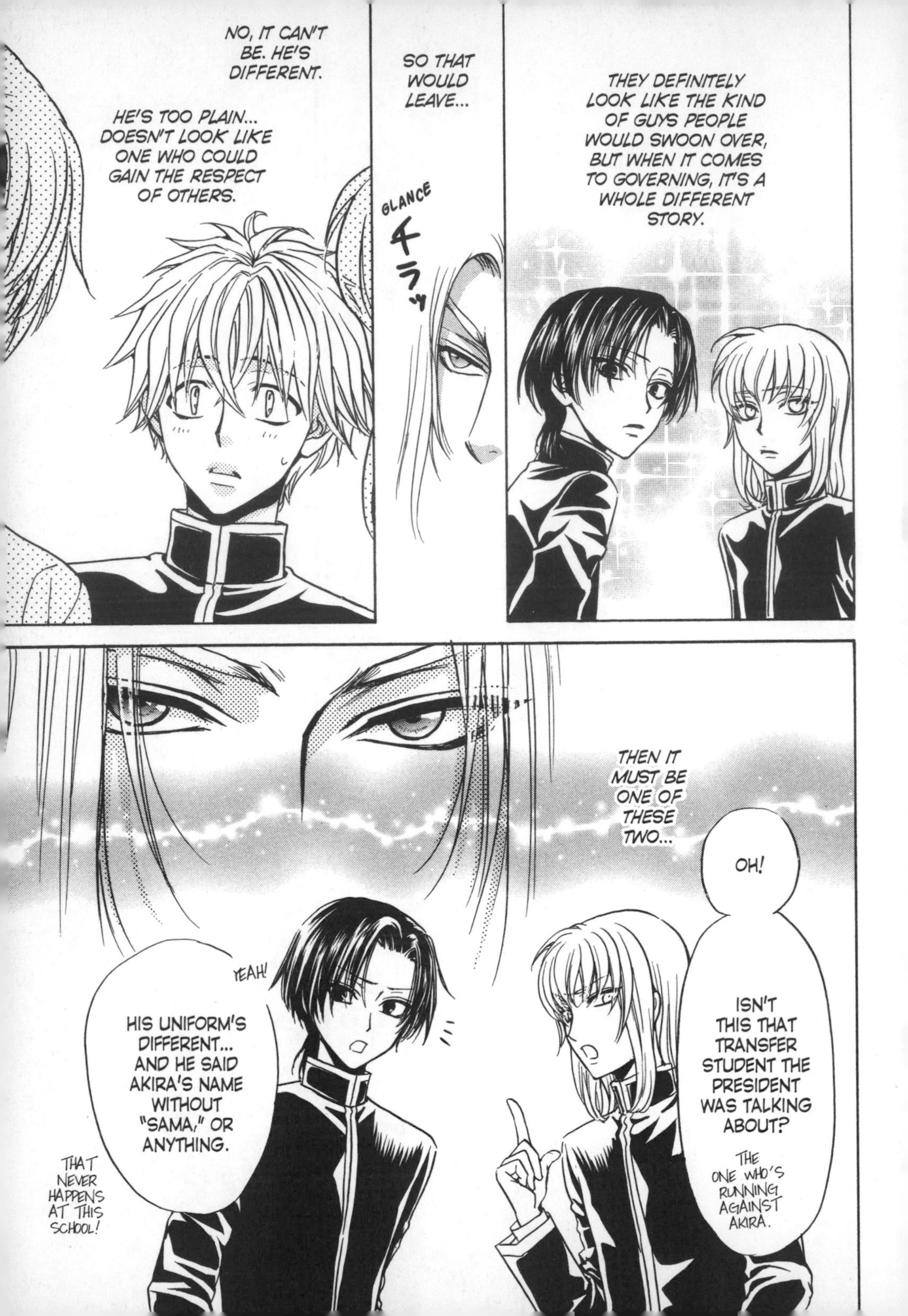
THEY DEFINITELY LOOK LIKE THE KIND OF GUYS PEOPLE WOULD SWOON OVER, BUT WHEN IT COMES TO GOVERNING, IT'S A WHOLE DIFFERENT STORY.
SO THAT WOULD LEAVE...
GLANCE
チラッ
NO, IT CAN'T BE. HE'S DIFFERENT.
HE'S TOO PLAIN... DOESN'T LOOK LIKE ONE WHO COULD GAIN THE RESPECT OF OTHERS.
THEN IT MUST BE ONE OF THESE TWO...
OH!
ISN'T THIS THAT TRANSFER STUDENT THE PRESIDENT WAS TALKING ABOUT?
THE ONE WHO'S RUNNING AGAINST AKIRA.
YEAH!
HIS UNIFORM'S DIFFERENT... AND HE SAID AKIRA'S NAME WITHOUT "SAMA," OR ANYTHING.
THAT NEVER HAPPENS AT THIS SCHOOL!

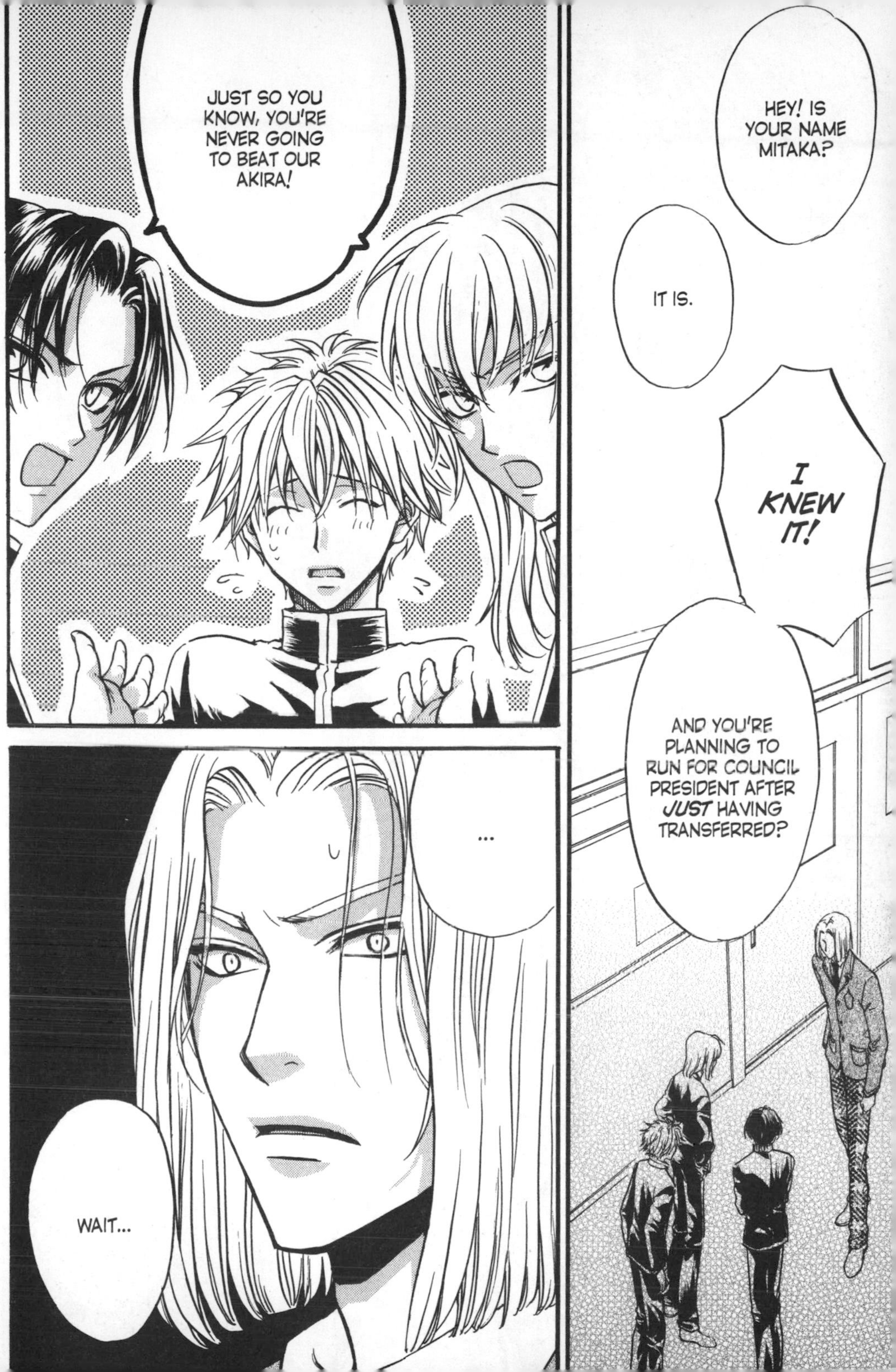
HEY! IS YOUR NAME MITAKA?
IT IS.
I KNEW IT!
AND YOU'RE PLANNING TO RUN FOR COUNCIL PRESIDENT AFTER JUST HAVING TRANSFERRED?
JUST SO YOU KNOW, YOU'RE NEVER GOING TO BEAT OUR AKIRA!
...
WAIT...

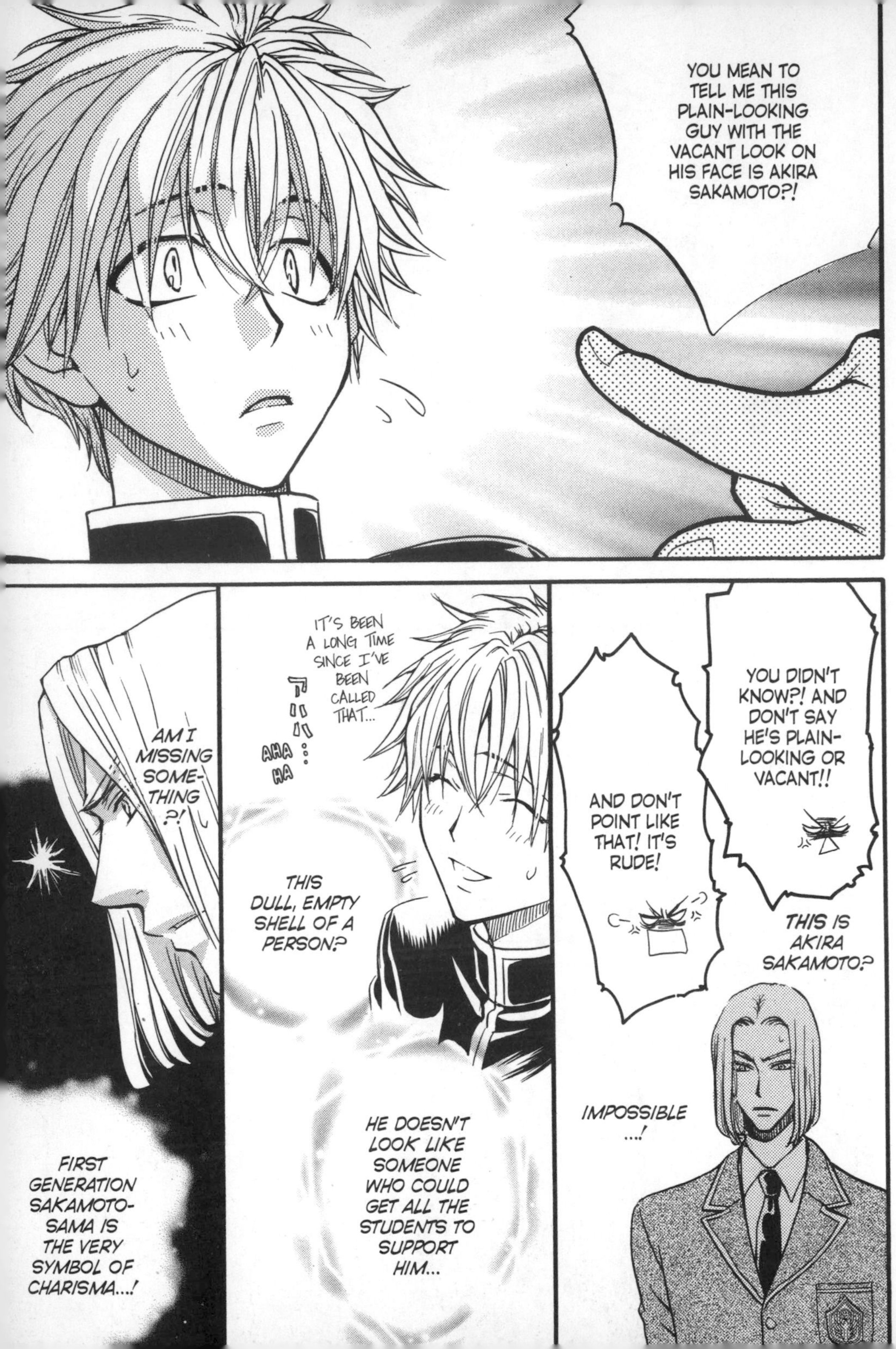
YOU MEAN TO TELL ME THIS PLAIN-LOOKING GUY WITH THE VACANT LOOK ON HIS FACE IS AKIRA SAKAMOTO?!
YOU DIDN'T KNOW?! AND DON'T SAY HE'S PLAIN-LOOKING OR VACANT!!
AND DON'T POINT LIKE THAT! IT'S RUDE!
THIS IS AKIRA SAKAMOTO?
IMPOSSIBLE ...!
IT'S BEEN A LONG TIME SINCE I'VE BEEN CALLED THAT...
AHA HA
THIS DULL, EMPTY SHELL OF A PERSON?
HE DOESN'T LOOK LIKE SOMEONE WHO COULD GET ALL THE STUDENTS TO SUPPORT HIM...
AM I MISSING SOME-THING?!
FIRST GENERATION SAKAMOTO-SAMA IS THE VERY SYMBOL OF CHARISMA...!

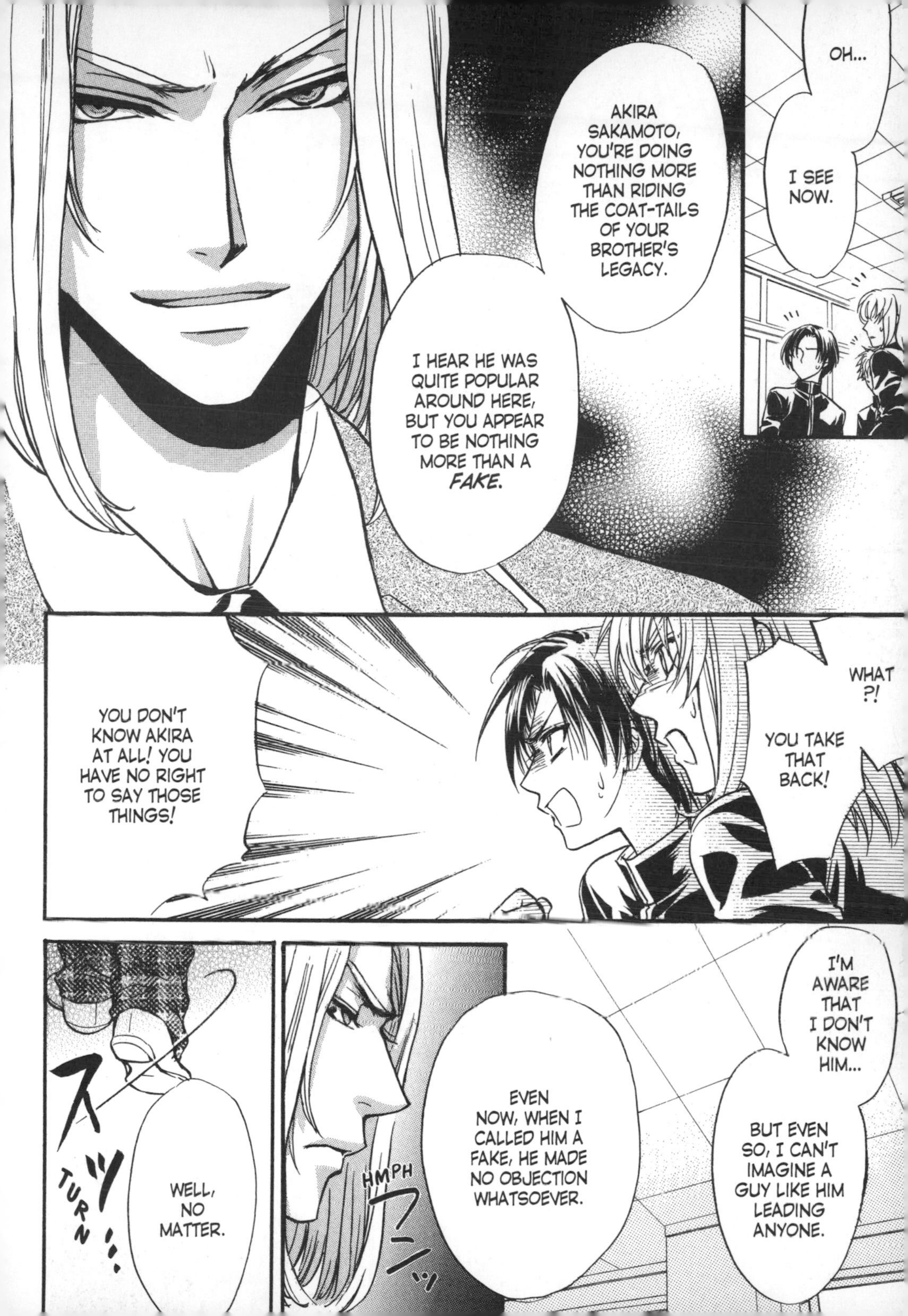
OH...
I SEE NOW.
AKIRA SAKAMOTO, YOU'RE DOING NOTHING MORE THAN RIDING THE COAT-TAILS OF YOUR BROTHER'S LEGACY.
I HEAR HE WAS QUITE POPULAR AROUND HERE, BUT YOU APPEAR TO BE NOTHING MORE THAN A *FAKE*.
WHAT ?!
YOU TAKE THAT BACK!
YOU DON'T KNOW AKIRA AT ALL! YOU HAVE NO RIGHT TO SAY THOSE THINGS!
I'M AWARE THAT I DON'T KNOW HIM...
BUT EVEN SO, I CAN'T IMAGINE A GUY LIKE HIM LEADING ANYONE.
HMPH
EVEN NOW, WHEN I CALLED HIM A FAKE, HE MADE NO OBJECTION WHATSOEVER.
WELL, NO MATTER.
TURN

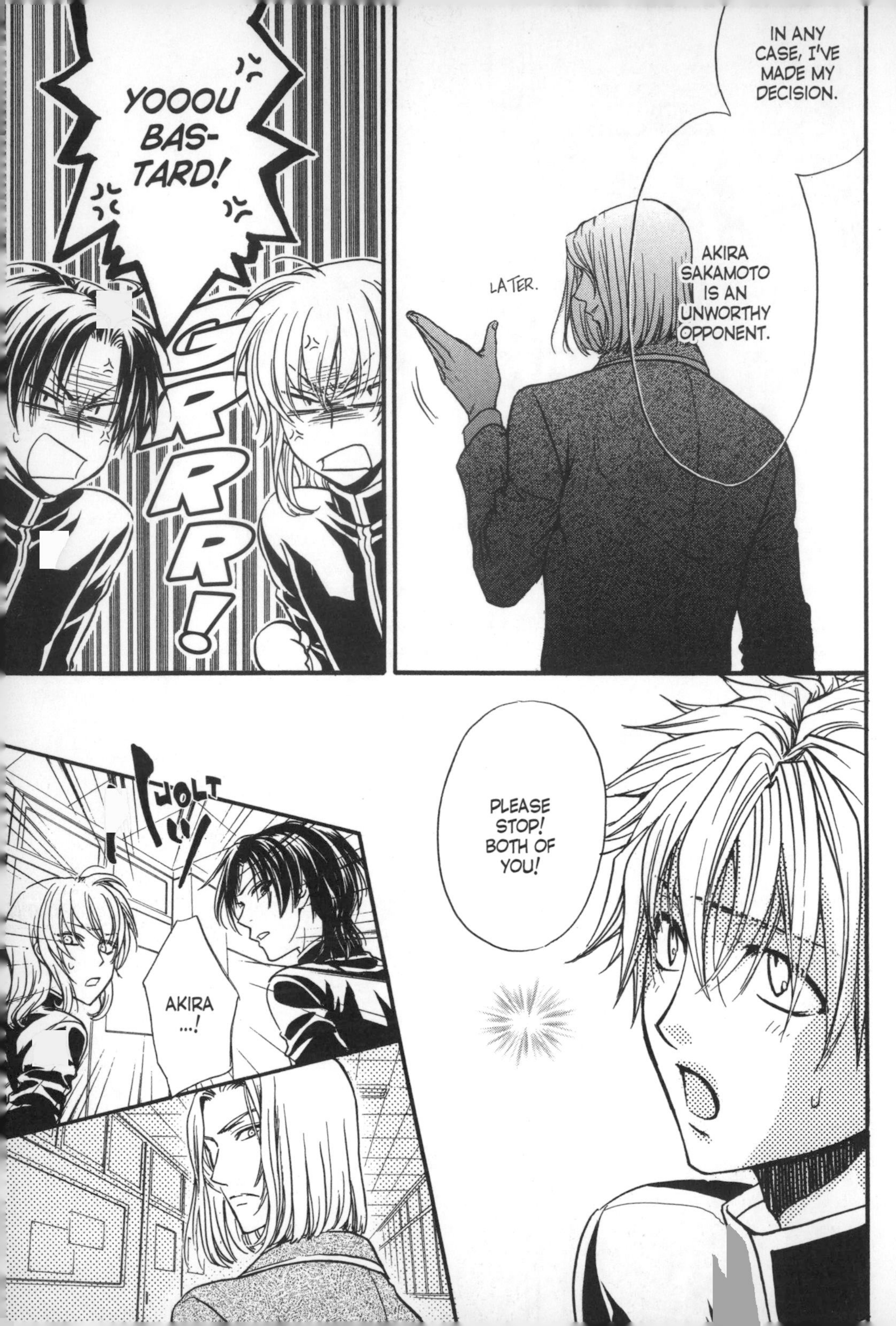

IN ANY CASE, I'VE MADE MY DECISION.
AKIRA SAKAMOTO IS AN UNWORTHY OPPONENT.
LATER.
YOOOU BAS-TARD!
GRRR!
PLEASE STOP! BOTH OF YOU!
JOLT
AKIRA ...!

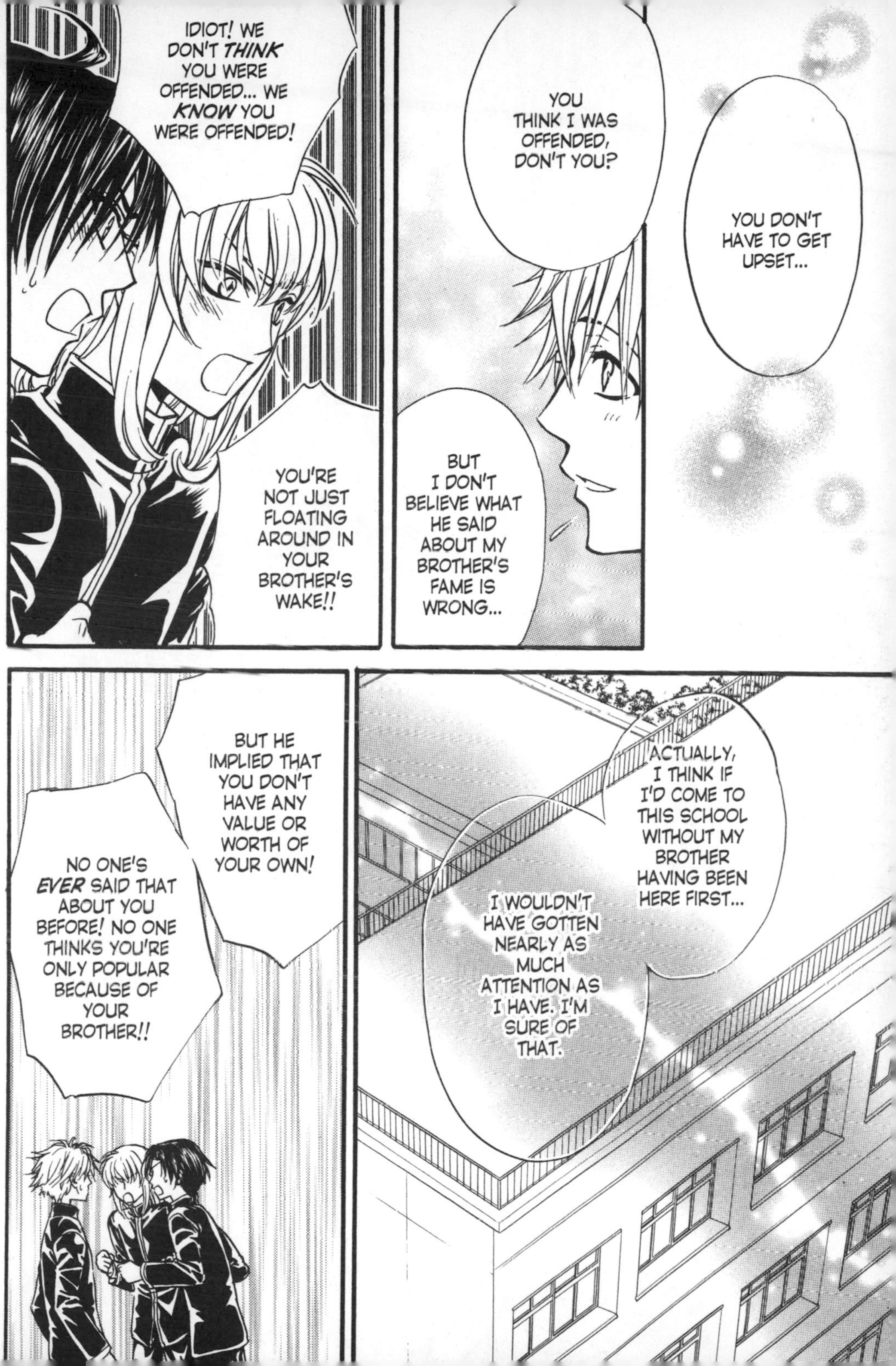
YOU THINK I WAS OFFENDED, DON'T YOU?
YOU DON'T HAVE TO GET UPSET...
BUT I DON'T BELIEVE WHAT HE SAID ABOUT MY BROTHER'S FAME IS WRONG...
IDIOT! WE DON'T THINK YOU WERE OFFENDED... WE KNOW YOU WERE OFFENDED!
YOU'RE NOT JUST FLOATING AROUND IN YOUR BROTHER'S WAKE!!
ACTUALLY, I THINK IF I'D COME TO THIS SCHOOL WITHOUT MY BROTHER HAVING BEEN HERE FIRST...
I WOULDN'T HAVE GOTTEN NEARLY AS MUCH ATTENTION AS I HAVE. I'M SURE OF THAT.
BUT HE IMPLIED THAT YOU DON'T HAVE ANY VALUE OR WORTH OF YOUR OWN!
NO ONE'S EVER SAID THAT ABOUT YOU BEFORE! NO ONE THINKS YOU'RE ONLY POPULAR BECAUSE OF YOUR BROTHER!!

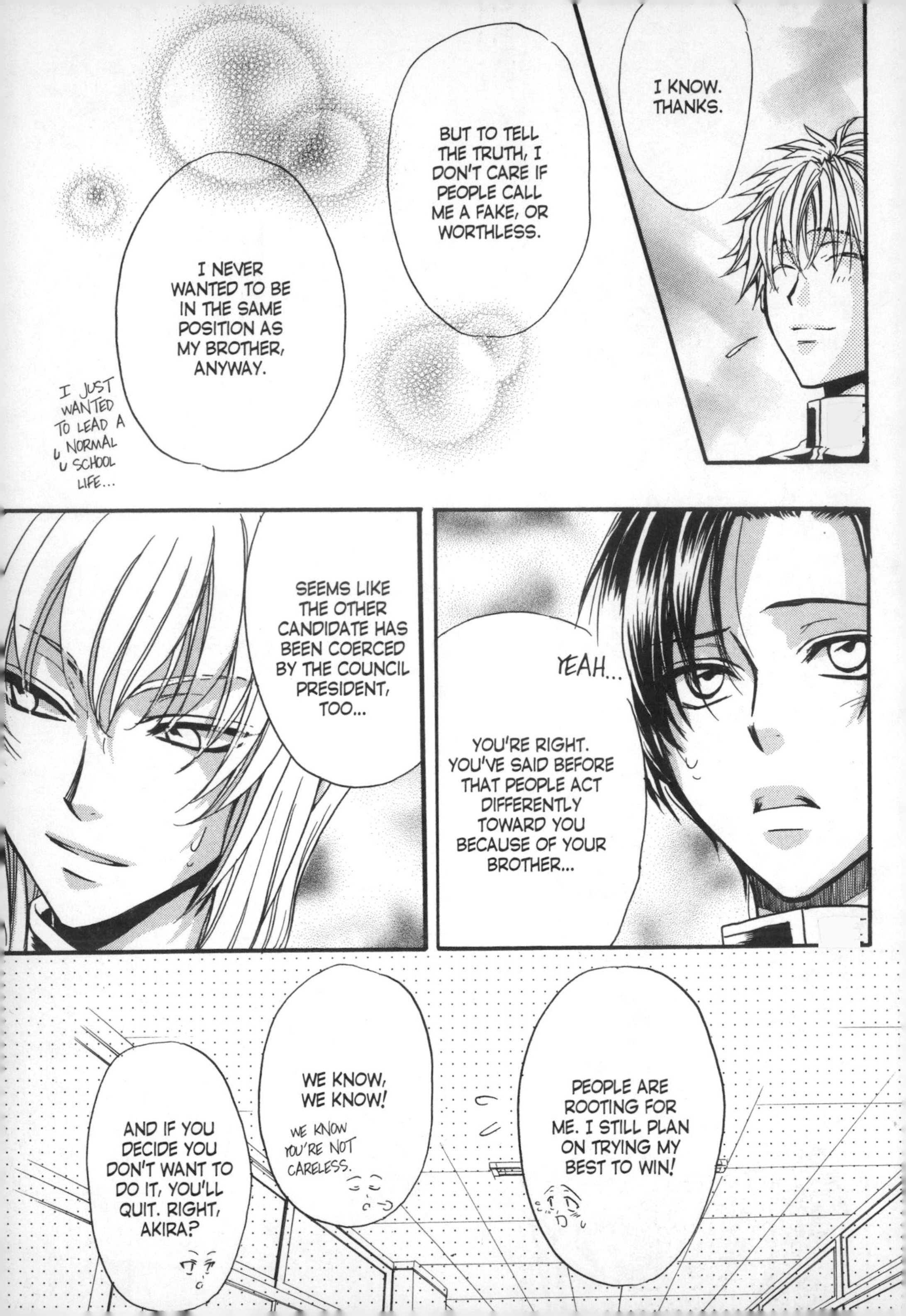
I KNOW. THANKS.
BUT TO TELL THE TRUTH, I DON'T CARE IF PEOPLE CALL ME A FAKE, OR WORTHLESS.
I NEVER WANTED TO BE IN THE SAME POSITION AS MY BROTHER, ANYWAY.
I JUST WANTED TO LEAD A NORMAL SCHOOL LIFE...
YEAH...
YOU'RE RIGHT. YOU'VE SAID BEFORE THAT PEOPLE ACT DIFFERENTLY TOWARD YOU BECAUSE OF YOUR BROTHER...
SEEMS LIKE THE OTHER CANDIDATE HAS BEEN COERCED BY THE COUNCIL PRESIDENT, TOO...
PEOPLE ARE ROOTING FOR ME. I STILL PLAN ON TRYING MY BEST TO WIN!
WE KNOW, WE KNOW!
WE KNOW YOU'RE NOT CARELESS.
AND IF YOU DECIDE YOU DON'T WANT TO DO IT, YOU'LL QUIT. RIGHT, AKIRA?

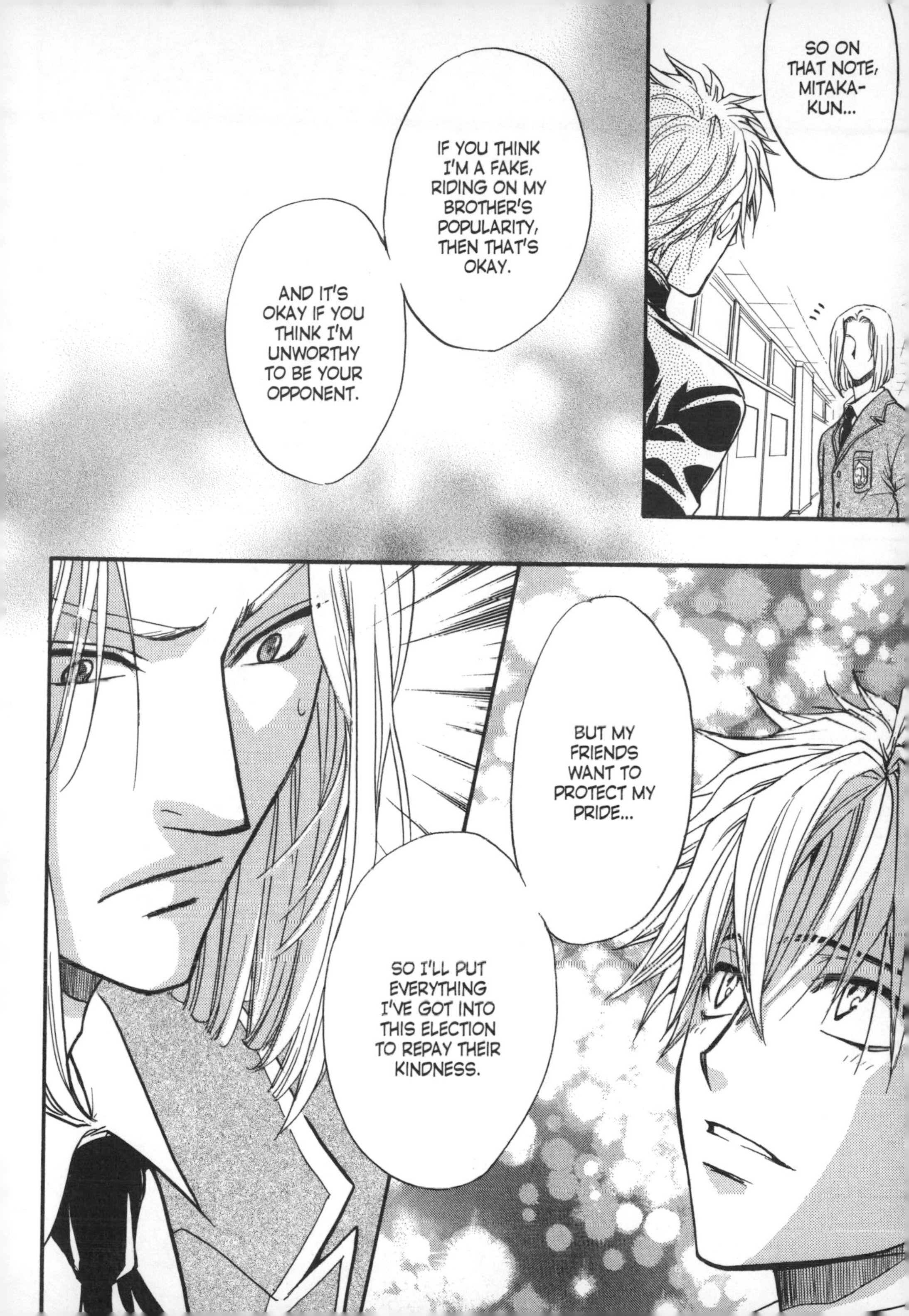
SO ON THAT NOTE, MITAKA-KUN...
IF YOU THINK I'M A FAKE, RIDING ON MY BROTHER'S POPULARITY, THEN THAT'S OKAY.
AND IT'S OKAY IF YOU THINK I'M UNWORTHY TO BE YOUR OPPONENT.
BUT MY FRIENDS WANT TO PROTECT MY PRIDE...
SO I'LL PUT EVERYTHING I'VE GOT INTO THIS ELECTION TO REPAY THEIR KINDNESS.

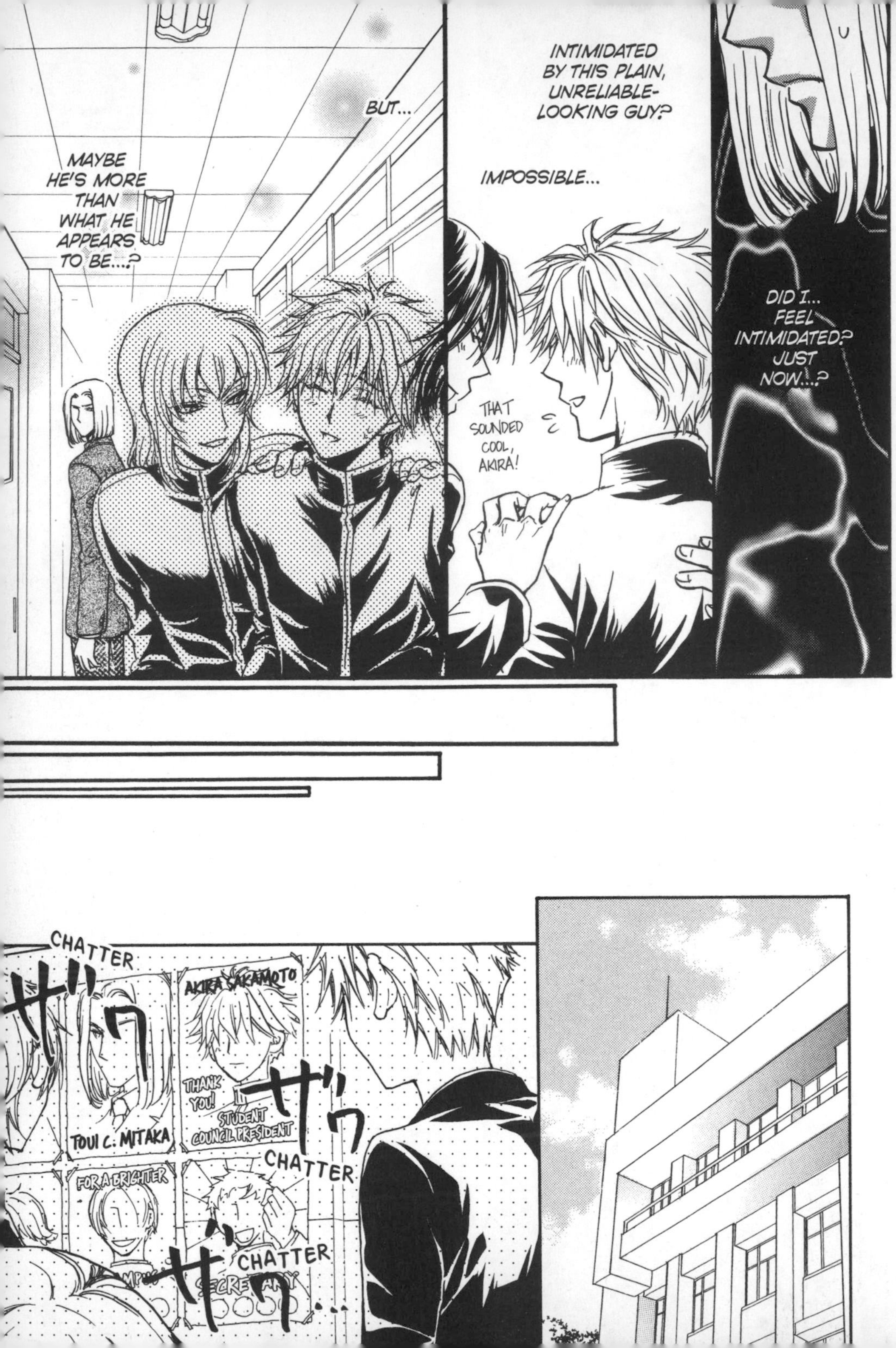
DID I... FEEL INTIMIDATED? JUST NOW...?
INTIMIDATED BY THIS PLAIN, UNRELIABLE-LOOKING GUY?
IMPOSSIBLE...
THAT SOUNDED COOL, AKIRA!
BUT...
MAYBE HE'S MORE THAN WHAT HE APPEARS TO BE...?
CHATTER
ザワ
AKIRA SAKAMOTO
THANK YOU!
STUDENT COUNCIL PRESIDENT
TOUI C. MITAKA
ザワ
CHATTER
FOR A BRIGHTER
CHATTER
ザワ...

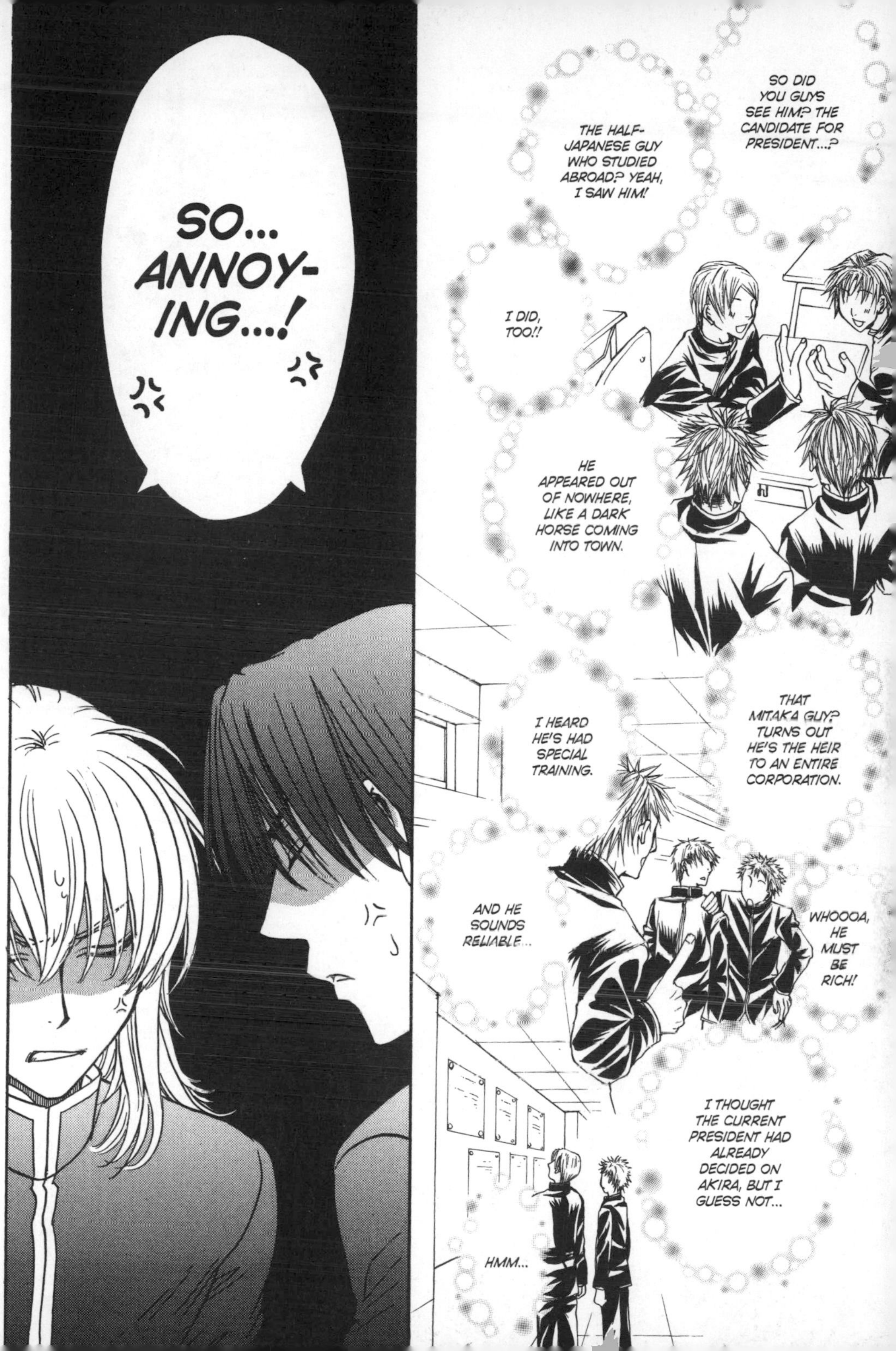
SO DID YOU GUYS SEE HIM? THE CANDIDATE FOR PRESIDENT...?
THE HALF-JAPANESE GUY WHO STUDIED ABROAD? YEAH, I SAW HIM!
I DID, TOO!!
HE APPEARED OUT OF NOWHERE, LIKE A DARK HORSE COMING INTO TOWN.
THAT MITAKA GUY? TURNS OUT HE'S THE HEIR TO AN ENTIRE CORPORATION.
I HEARD HE'S HAD SPECIAL TRAINING.
WHOOOA, HE MUST BE RICH!
AND HE SOUNDS RELIABLE...
I THOUGHT THE CURRENT PRESIDENT HAD ALREADY DECIDED ON AKIRA, BUT I GUESS NOT...
HMM...
SO... ANNOY-ING...!

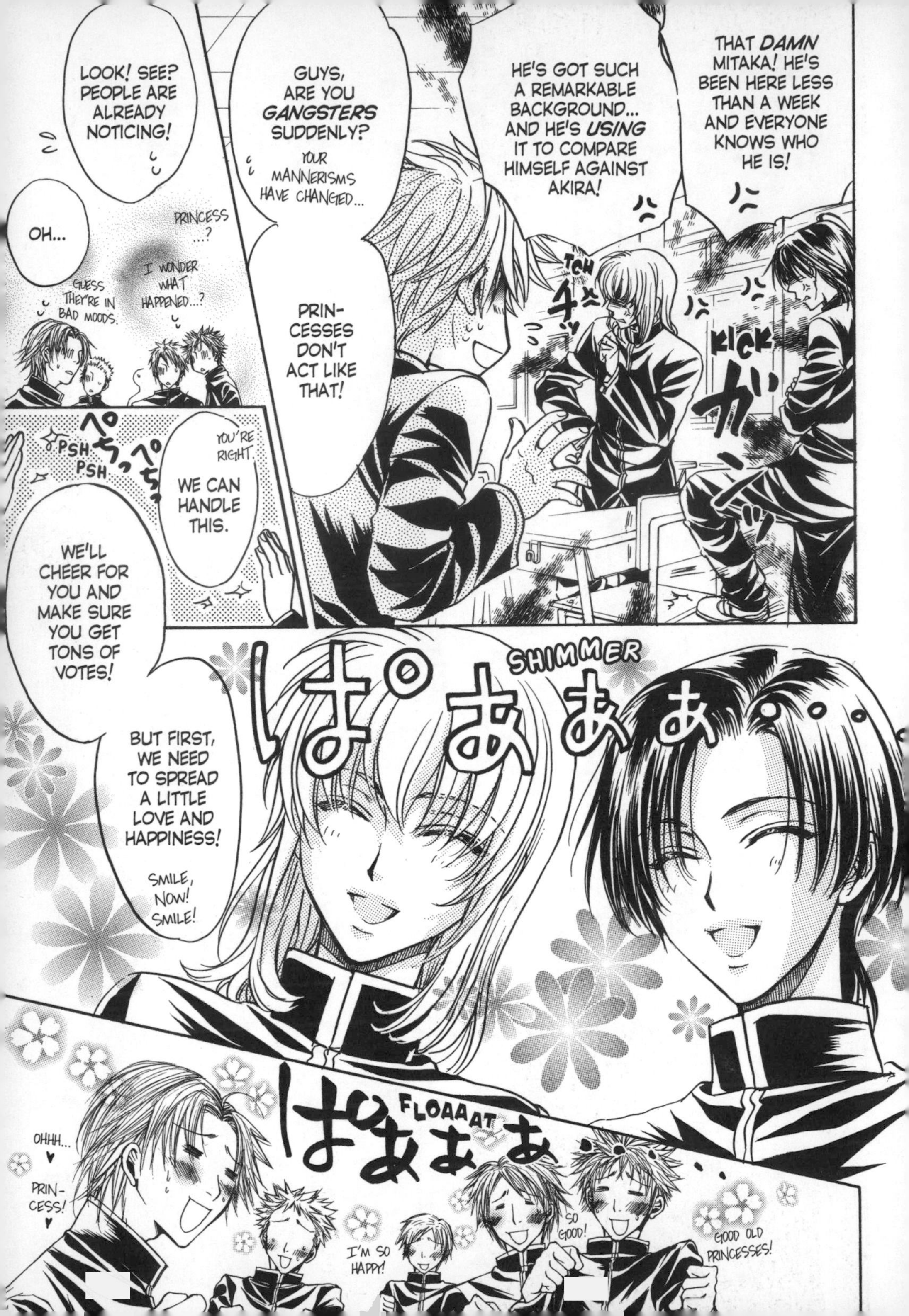
THAT DAMN MITAKA! HE'S BEEN HERE LESS THAN A WEEK AND EVERYONE KNOWS WHO HE IS!
HE'S GOT SUCH A REMARKABLE BACKGROUND... AND HE'S USING IT TO COMPARE HIMSELF AGAINST AKIRA!
KICK
ガッ
TCH
チッ
GUYS, ARE YOU GANGSTERS SUDDENLY?
YOUR MANNERISMS HAVE CHANGED...
PRIN-CESSES DON'T ACT LIKE THAT!
LOOK! SEE? PEOPLE ARE ALREADY NOTICING!
OH...
PRINCESS ...?
I WONDER WHAT HAPPENED...?
GUESS THEY'RE IN BAD MOODS.
YOU'RE RIGHT.
WE CAN HANDLE THIS.
PSH PSH
ぺちっぺちっ
WE'LL CHEER FOR YOU AND MAKE SURE YOU GET TONS OF VOTES!
SHIMMER
ぱあああ
BUT FIRST, WE NEED TO SPREAD A LITTLE LOVE AND HAPPINESS!
SMILE, NOW! SMILE!
FLOAAAT
ぱあああ
GOOD OLD PRINCESSES!
SO GOOD!
I'M SO HAPPY!
OHHH...
PRIN-CESS!

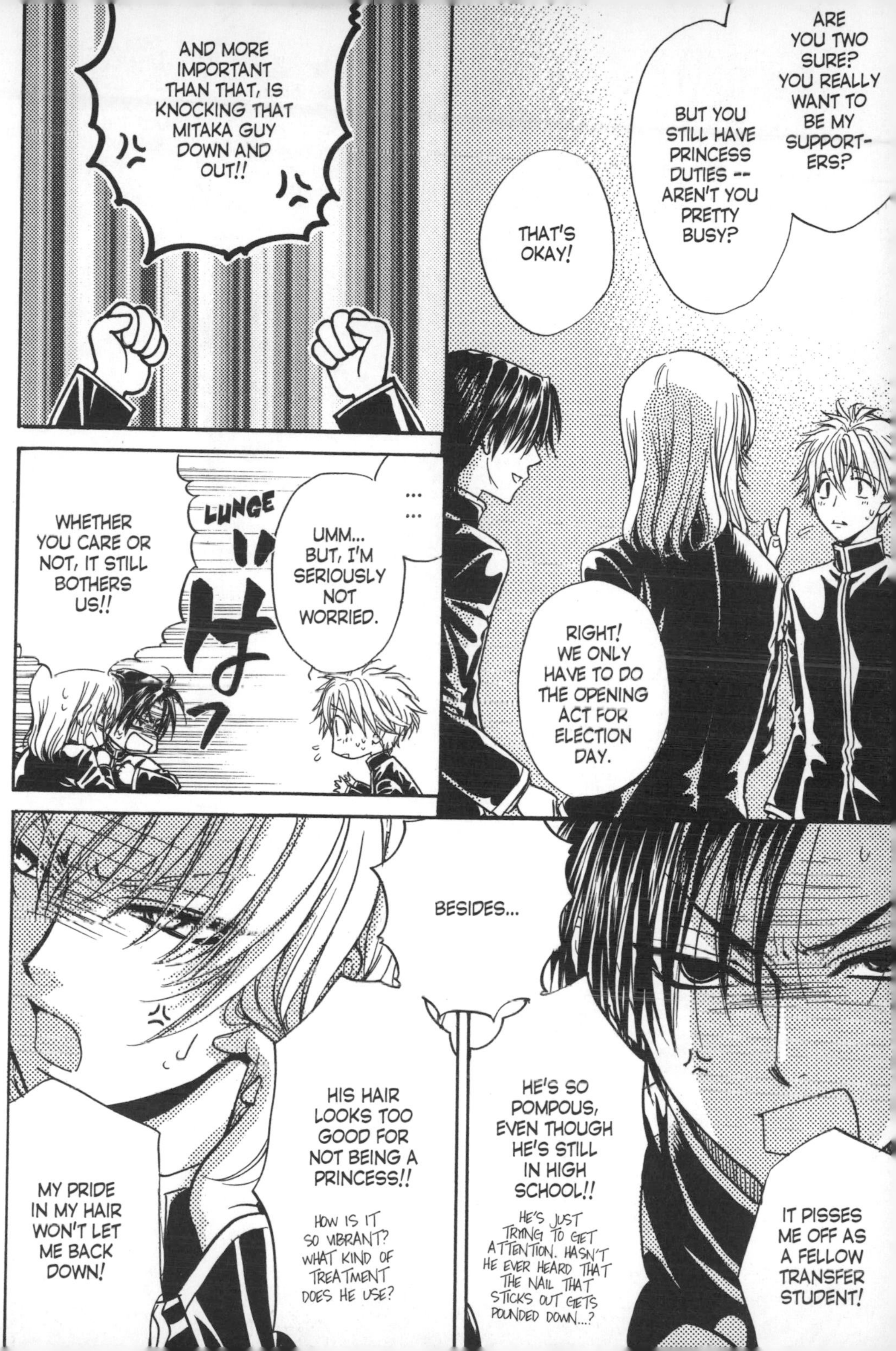
ARE YOU TWO SURE? YOU REALLY WANT TO BE MY SUPPORTERS?
BUT YOU STILL HAVE PRINCESS DUTIES -- AREN'T YOU PRETTY BUSY?
THAT'S OKAY!
RIGHT! WE ONLY HAVE TO DO THE OPENING ACT FOR ELECTION DAY.
AND MORE IMPORTANT THAN THAT, IS KNOCKING THAT MITAKA GUY DOWN AND OUT!!
...
...
UMM... BUT, I'M SERIOUSLY NOT WORRIED.
LUNGE
WHETHER YOU CARE OR NOT, IT STILL BOTHERS US!!
BESIDES...
IT PISSES ME OFF AS A FELLOW TRANSFER STUDENT!
HE'S SO POMPOUS, EVEN THOUGH HE'S STILL IN HIGH SCHOOL!!
HE'S JUST TRYING TO GET ATTENTION. HASN'T HE EVER HEARD THAT THE NAIL THAT STICKS OUT GETS POUNDED DOWN...?
HIS HAIR LOOKS TOO GOOD FOR NOT BEING A PRINCESS!!
HOW IS IT SO VIBRANT? WHAT KIND OF TREATMENT DOES HE USE?
MY PRIDE IN MY HAIR WON'T LET ME BACK DOWN!

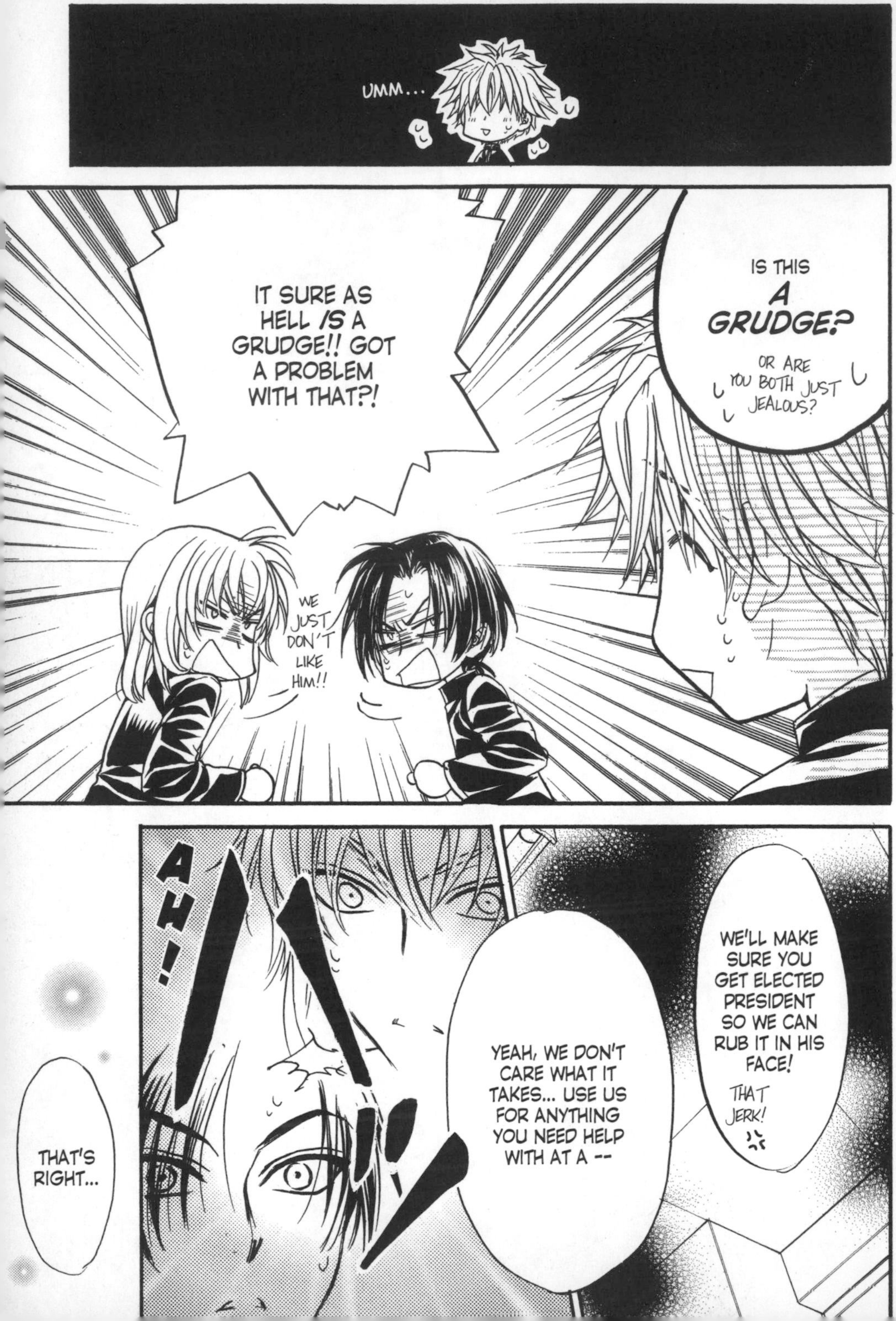
UMM...
IS THIS A GRUDGE?
OR ARE YOU BOTH JUST JEALOUS?
IT SURE AS HELL IS A GRUDGE!! GOT A PROBLEM WITH THAT?!
WE JUST DON'T LIKE HIM!!
WE'LL MAKE SURE YOU GET ELECTED PRESIDENT SO WE CAN RUB IT IN HIS FACE!
THAT JERK!
YEAH, WE DON'T CARE WHAT IT TAKES... USE US FOR ANYTHING YOU NEED HELP WITH AT A --
AH!
THAT'S RIGHT...

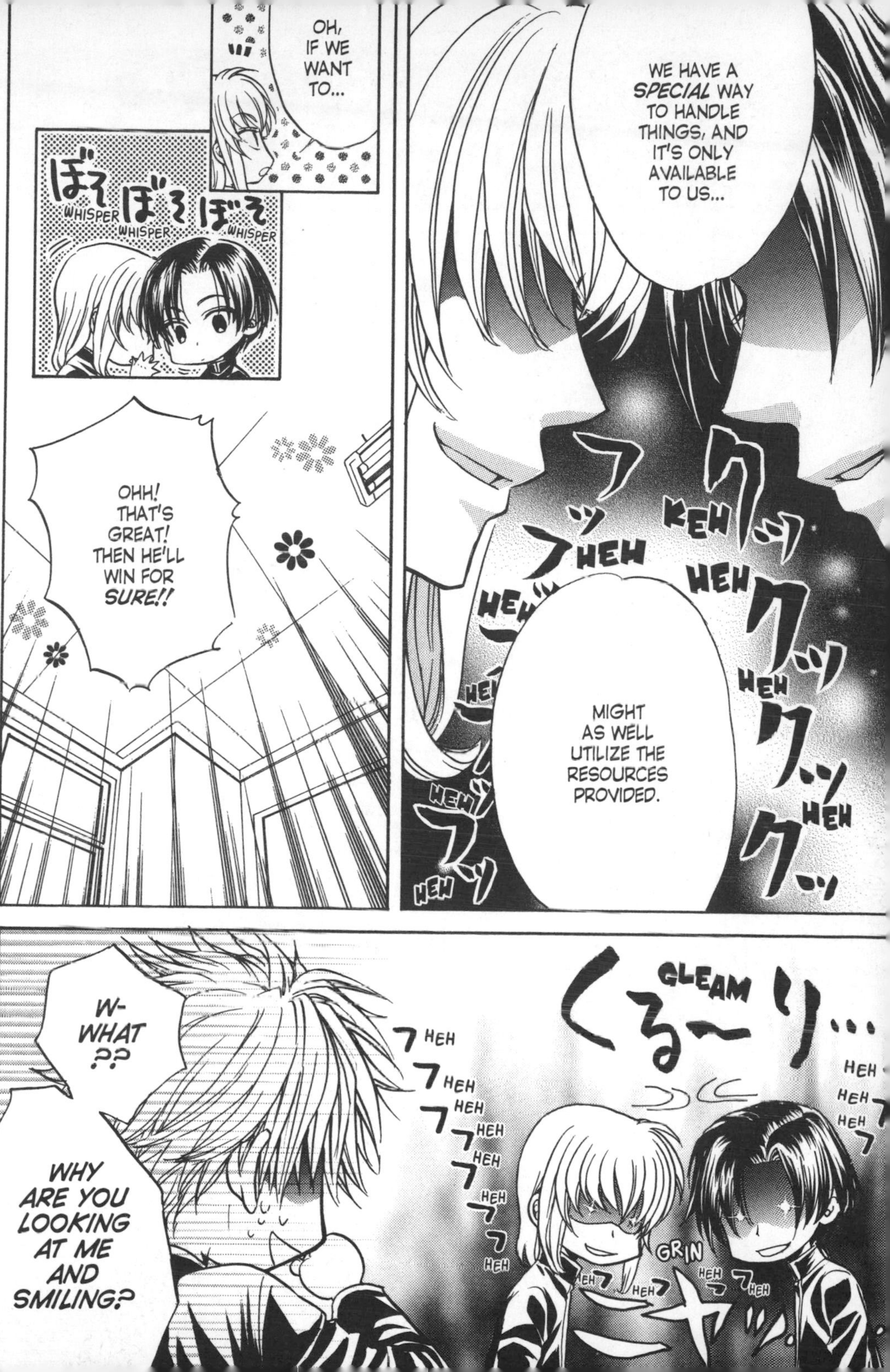
WE HAVE A *SPECIAL* WAY TO HANDLE THINGS, AND IT'S ONLY AVAILABLE TO US...
KEH HEH HEH HEH HEH
HEH HEH HEH HEH HEH
MIGHT AS WELL UTILIZE THE RESOURCES PROVIDED.
OH, IF WE WANT TO...
WHISPER WHISPER WHISPER
OHH! THAT'S GREAT! THEN HE'LL WIN FOR *SURE!!*
GLEAM
くる〜り…
HEH HEH HEH
HEH HEH HEH HEH HEH HEH HEH
GRIN
HEH HEH HEH HEH
W-WHAT??
WHY ARE YOU LOOKING AT ME AND SMILING?

TO BE CONTINUED IN PRINCESS • PRINCESS 5

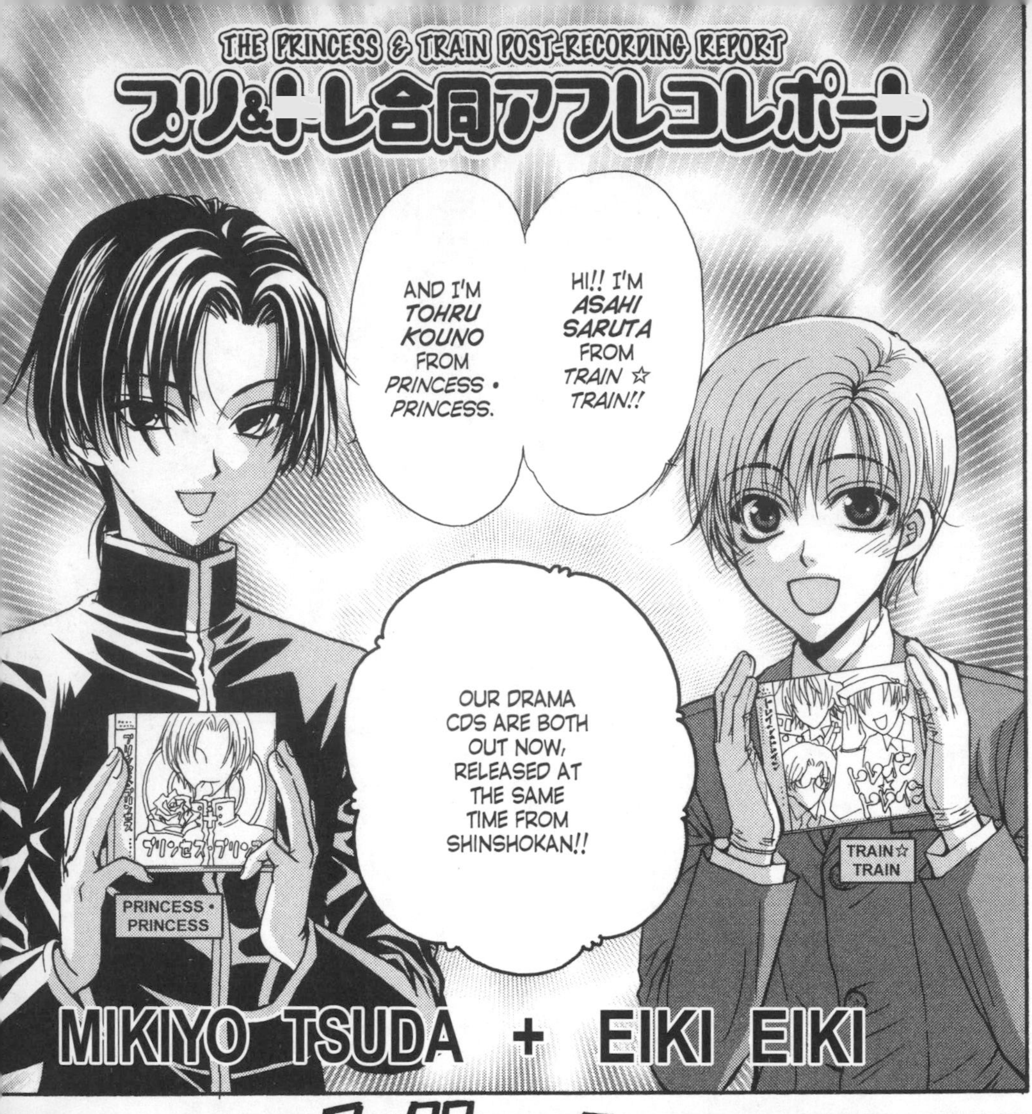
THE PRINCESS & TRAIN POST-RECORDING REPORT
プリ&トレ合同アフレコレポート
HI!! I'M ASAHI SARUTA FROM TRAIN ☆ TRAIN!!
AND I'M TOHRU KOUNO FROM PRINCESS • PRINCESS.
OUR DRAMA CDS ARE BOTH OUT NOW, RELEASED AT THE SAME TIME FROM SHINSHOKAN!!
TRAIN☆ TRAIN
PRINCESS • PRINCESS
MIKIYO TSUDA + EIKI EIKI
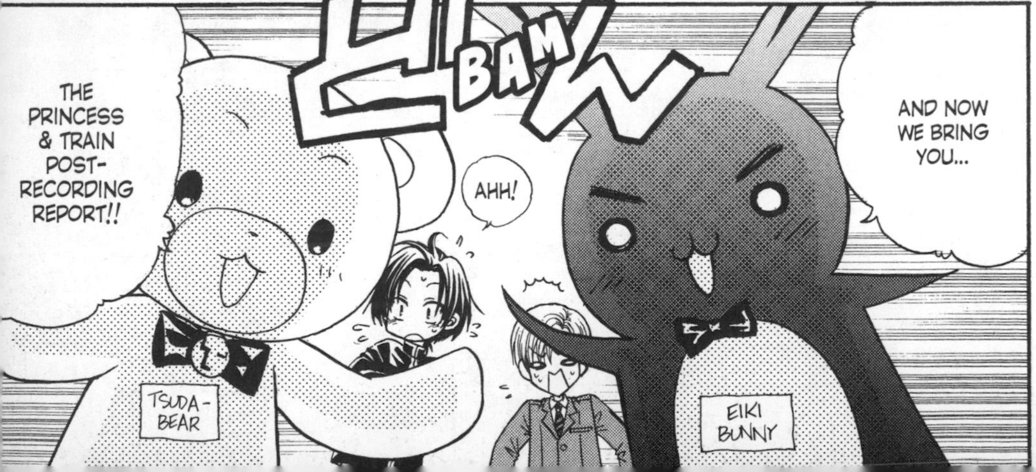
AND NOW WE BRING YOU...
BAM
THE PRINCESS & TRAIN POST-RECORDING REPORT!!
AHH!
EIKI BUNNY
TSUDA-BEAR

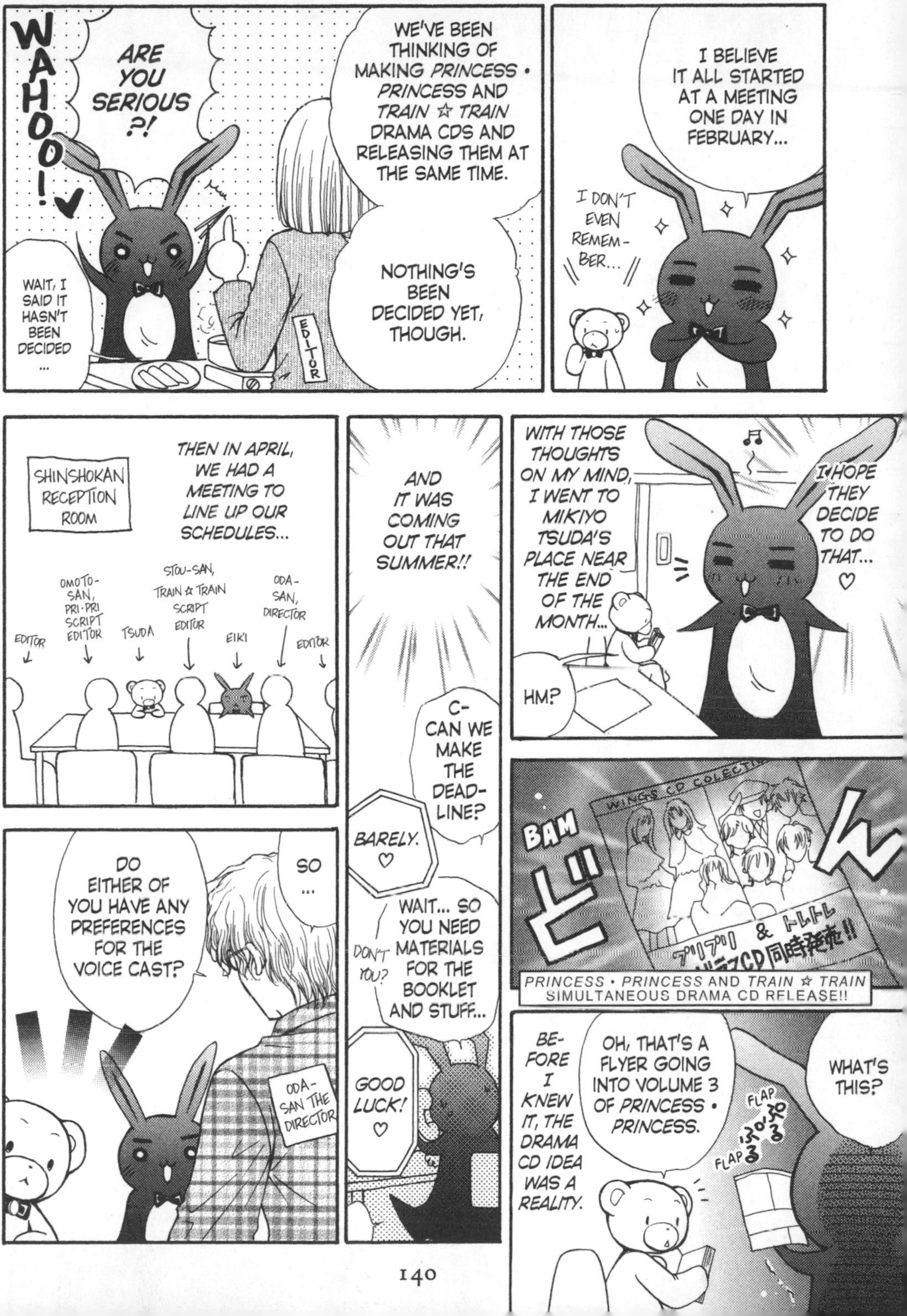
I BELIEVE IT ALL STARTED AT A MEETING ONE DAY IN FEBRUARY...
I DON'T EVEN REMEMBER...
WE'VE BEEN THINKING OF MAKING PRINCESS • PRINCESS AND TRAIN ☆ TRAIN DRAMA CDS AND RELEASING THEM AT THE SAME TIME.
ARE YOU SERIOUS ?!
WAHOO!
NOTHING'S BEEN DECIDED YET, THOUGH.
EDITOR
WAIT, I SAID IT HASN'T BEEN DECIDED ...
WITH THOSE THOUGHTS ON MY MIND, I WENT TO MIKIYO TSUDA'S PLACE NEAR THE END OF THE MONTH...
I HOPE THEY DECIDE TO DO THAT...
HM?
BAM
WINGS CD COLLECTI
プリプリ & トレトレ
PRINCESS • PRINCESS AND TRAIN ☆ TRAIN SIMULTANEOUS DRAMA CD RELEASE!!
WHAT'S THIS?
OH, THAT'S A FLYER GOING INTO VOLUME 3 OF PRINCESS • PRINCESS.
FLAP FLAP FLAP
BEFORE I KNEW IT, THE DRAMA CD IDEA WAS A REALITY.
AND IT WAS COMING OUT THAT SUMMER!!
C-CAN WE MAKE THE DEADLINE?
BARELY.
WAIT... SO YOU NEED MATERIALS FOR THE BOOKLET AND STUFF...
DON'T YOU?
GOOD LUCK!
THEN IN APRIL, WE HAD A MEETING TO LINE UP OUR SCHEDULES...
SHINSHOKAN RECEPTION ROOM
EDITOR
OMOTO-SAN, PRI-PRI SCRIPT EDITOR
TSUDA
STOU-SAN, TRAIN ☆ TRAIN SCRIPT EDITOR
EIKI
ODA-SAN, DIRECTOR
EDITOR
SO ...
DO EITHER OF YOU HAVE ANY PREFERENCES FOR THE VOICE CAST?
ODA-SAN THE DIRECTOR

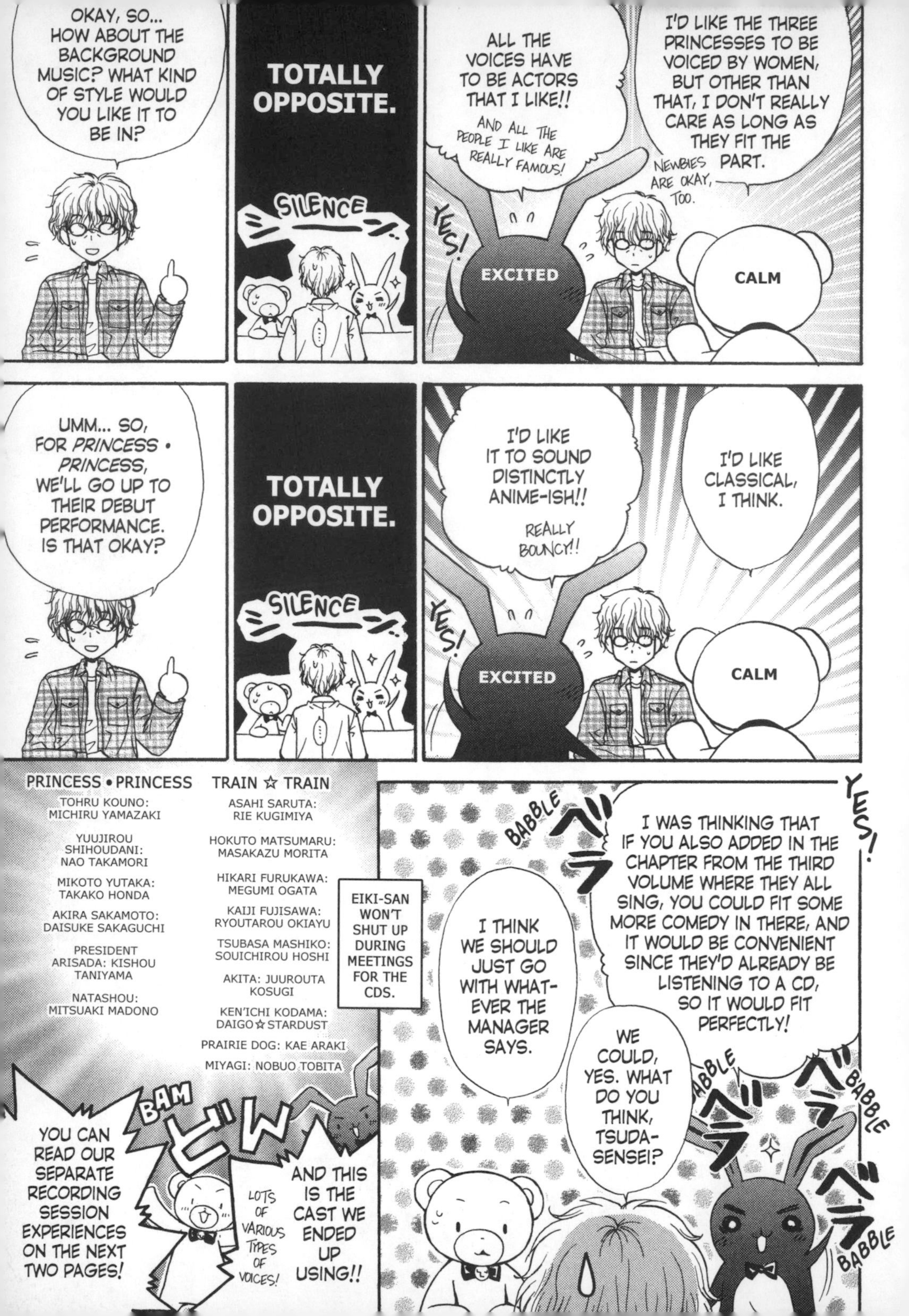
I'D LIKE THE THREE PRINCESSES TO BE VOICED BY WOMEN, BUT OTHER THAN THAT, I DON'T REALLY CARE AS LONG AS THEY FIT THE PART.
NEWBIES ARE OKAY, TOO.
ALL THE VOICES HAVE TO BE ACTORS THAT I LIKE!!
AND ALL THE PEOPLE I LIKE ARE REALLY FAMOUS!
YES!
CALM
EXCITED
TOTALLY OPPOSITE.
SILENCE
OKAY, SO... HOW ABOUT THE BACKGROUND MUSIC? WHAT KIND OF STYLE WOULD YOU LIKE IT TO BE IN?
I'D LIKE CLASSICAL, I THINK.
I'D LIKE IT TO SOUND DISTINCTLY ANIME-ISH!!
REALLY BOUNCY!!
YES!
CALM
EXCITED
TOTALLY OPPOSITE.
SILENCE
UMM... SO, FOR *PRINCESS • PRINCESS*, WE'LL GO UP TO THEIR DEBUT PERFORMANCE. IS THAT OKAY?
YES!
I WAS THINKING THAT IF YOU ALSO ADDED IN THE CHAPTER FROM THE THIRD VOLUME WHERE THEY ALL SING, YOU COULD FIT SOME MORE COMEDY IN THERE, AND IT WOULD BE CONVENIENT SINCE THEY'D ALREADY BE LISTENING TO A CD, SO IT WOULD FIT PERFECTLY!
BABBLE
I THINK WE SHOULD JUST GO WITH WHAT-EVER THE MANAGER SAYS.
WE COULD, YES. WHAT DO YOU THINK, TSUDA-SENSEI?
BABBLE
BABBLE
BABBLE
PRINCESS • PRINCESS
TOHRU KOUNO: MICHIRU YAMAZAKI
YUUJIROU SHIHOUDANI: NAO TAKAMORI
MIKOTO YUTAKA: TAKAKO HONDA
AKIRA SAKAMOTO: DAISUKE SAKAGUCHI
PRESIDENT ARISADA: KISHOU TANIYAMA
NATASHOU: MITSUAKI MADONO
TRAIN ☆ TRAIN
ASAHI SARUTA: RIE KUGIMIYA
HOKUTO MATSUMARU: MASAKAZU MORITA
HIKARI FURUKAWA: MEGUMI OGATA
KAIJI FUJISAWA: RYOUTAROU OKIAYU
TSUBASA MASHIKO: SOUICHIROU HOSHI
AKITA: JUUROUTA KOSUGI
KEN'ICHI KODAMA: DAIGO☆STARDUST
PRAIRIE DOG: KAE ARAKI
MIYAGI: NOBUO TOBITA
EIKI-SAN WON'T SHUT UP DURING MEETINGS FOR THE CDS.
BAM
AND THIS IS THE CAST WE ENDED UP USING!!
LOTS OF VARIOUS TYPES OF VOICES!
YOU CAN READ OUR SEPARATE RECORDING SESSION EXPERIENCES ON THE NEXT TWO PAGES!

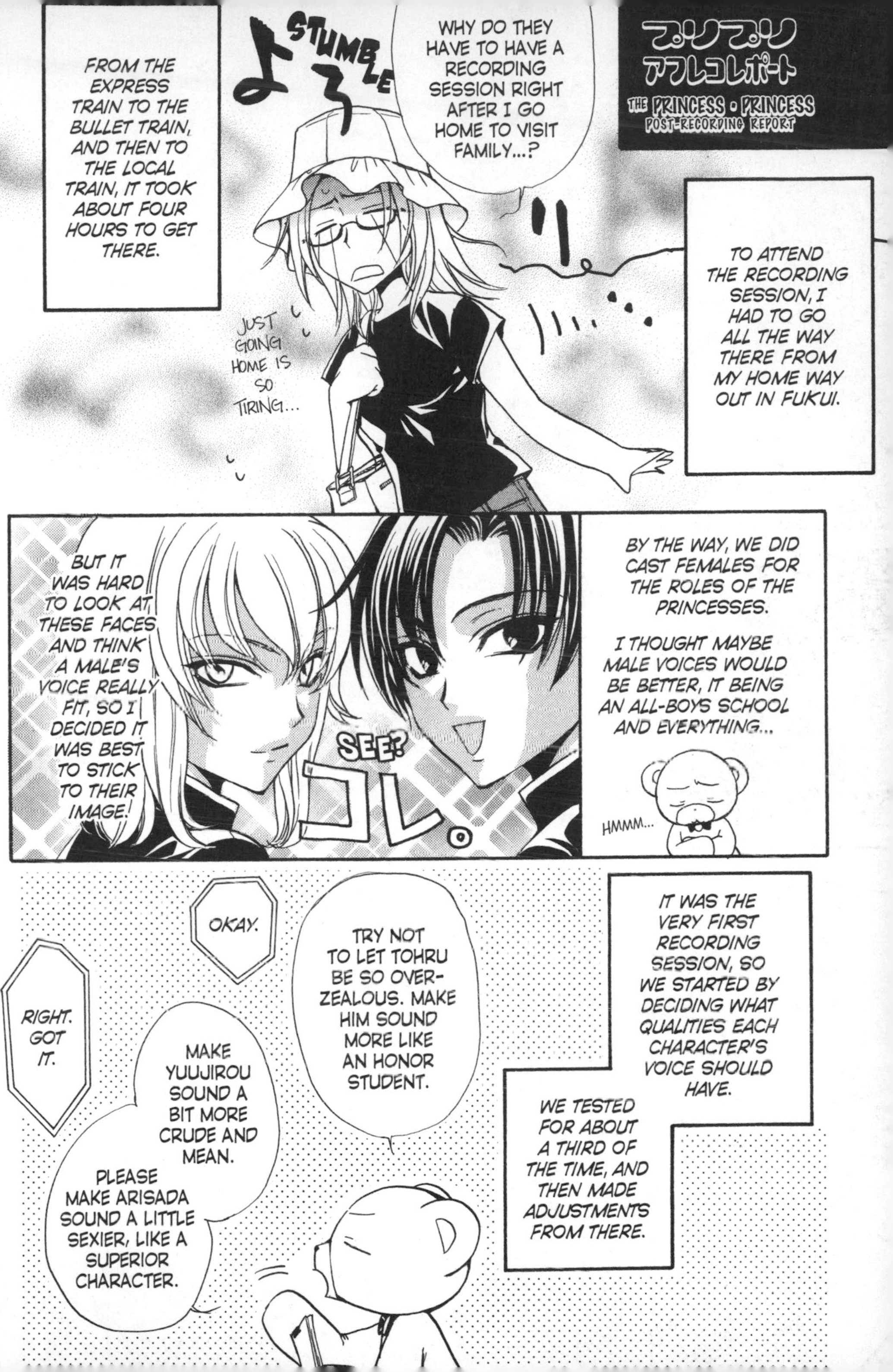
プリプリ アフレコレポート
THE PRINCESS • PRINCESS POST-RECORDING REPORT
WHY DO THEY HAVE TO HAVE A RECORDING SESSION RIGHT AFTER I GO HOME TO VISIT FAMILY...?
STUMBLE
FROM THE EXPRESS TRAIN TO THE BULLET TRAIN, AND THEN TO THE LOCAL TRAIN, IT TOOK ABOUT FOUR HOURS TO GET THERE.
TO ATTEND THE RECORDING SESSION, I HAD TO GO ALL THE WAY THERE FROM MY HOME WAY OUT IN FUKUI.
JUST GOING HOME IS SO TIRING...
BY THE WAY, WE DID CAST FEMALES FOR THE ROLES OF THE PRINCESSES.
I THOUGHT MAYBE MALE VOICES WOULD BE BETTER, IT BEING AN ALL-BOYS SCHOOL AND EVERYTHING...
HMMM...
BUT IT WAS HARD TO LOOK AT THESE FACES AND THINK A MALE'S VOICE REALLY FIT, SO I DECIDED IT WAS BEST TO STICK TO THEIR IMAGE.
SEE?
コレ。
IT WAS THE VERY FIRST RECORDING SESSION, SO WE STARTED BY DECIDING WHAT QUALITIES EACH CHARACTER'S VOICE SHOULD HAVE.
TRY NOT TO LET TOHRU BE SO OVER-ZEALOUS. MAKE HIM SOUND MORE LIKE AN HONOR STUDENT.
OKAY.
MAKE YUUJIROU SOUND A BIT MORE CRUDE AND MEAN.
RIGHT. GOT IT.
PLEASE MAKE ARISADA SOUND A LITTLE SEXIER, LIKE A SUPERIOR CHARACTER.
WE TESTED FOR ABOUT A THIRD OF THE TIME, AND THEN MADE ADJUSTMENTS FROM THERE.

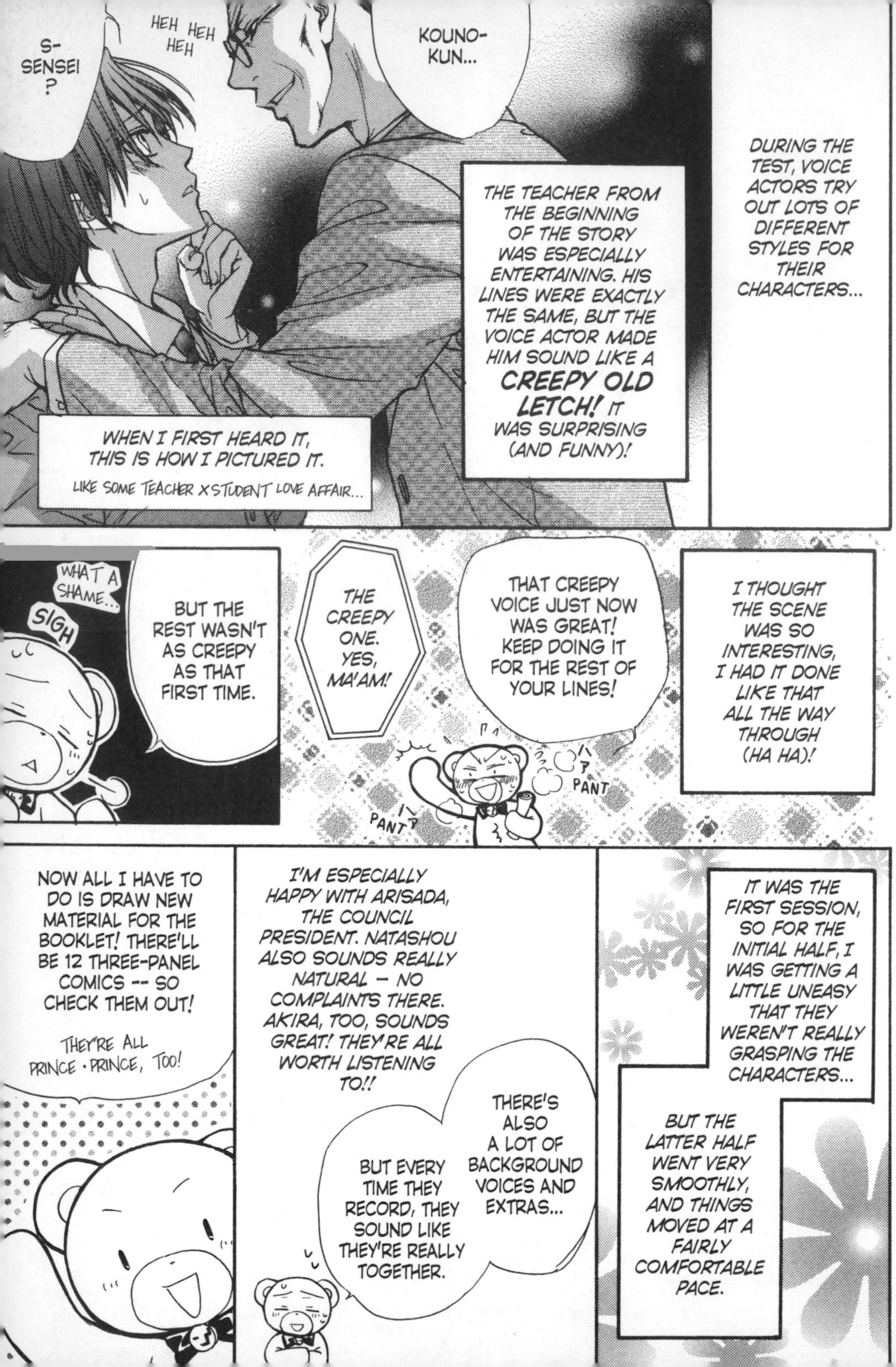
DURING THE TEST, VOICE ACTORS TRY OUT LOTS OF DIFFERENT STYLES FOR THEIR CHARACTERS...
KOUNO-KUN...
THE TEACHER FROM THE BEGINNING OF THE STORY WAS ESPECIALLY ENTERTAINING. HIS LINES WERE EXACTLY THE SAME, BUT THE VOICE ACTOR MADE HIM SOUND LIKE A CREEPY OLD LETCH! IT WAS SURPRISING (AND FUNNY)!
HEH HEH HEH
S-SENSEI?
WHEN I FIRST HEARD IT, THIS IS HOW I PICTURED IT.
LIKE SOME TEACHER X STUDENT LOVE AFFAIR...
I THOUGHT THE SCENE WAS SO INTERESTING, I HAD IT DONE LIKE THAT ALL THE WAY THROUGH (HA HA)!
THAT CREEPY VOICE JUST NOW WAS GREAT! KEEP DOING IT FOR THE REST OF YOUR LINES!
PANT
PANT
THE CREEPY ONE. YES, MA'AM!
BUT THE REST WASN'T AS CREEPY AS THAT FIRST TIME.
WHAT A SHAME...
SIGH
IT WAS THE FIRST SESSION, SO FOR THE INITIAL HALF, I WAS GETTING A LITTLE UNEASY THAT THEY WEREN'T REALLY GRASPING THE CHARACTERS...
BUT THE LATTER HALF WENT VERY SMOOTHLY, AND THINGS MOVED AT A FAIRLY COMFORTABLE PACE.
I'M ESPECIALLY HAPPY WITH ARISADA, THE COUNCIL PRESIDENT. NATASHOU ALSO SOUNDS REALLY NATURAL – NO COMPLAINTS THERE. AKIRA, TOO, SOUNDS GREAT! THEY'RE ALL WORTH LISTENING TO!!
THERE'S ALSO A LOT OF BACKGROUND VOICES AND EXTRAS...
BUT EVERY TIME THEY RECORD, THEY SOUND LIKE THEY'RE REALLY TOGETHER.
NOW ALL I HAVE TO DO IS DRAW NEW MATERIAL FOR THE BOOKLET! THERE'LL BE 12 THREE-PANEL COMICS -- SO CHECK THEM OUT!
THEY'RE ALL PRINCE・PRINCE, TOO!

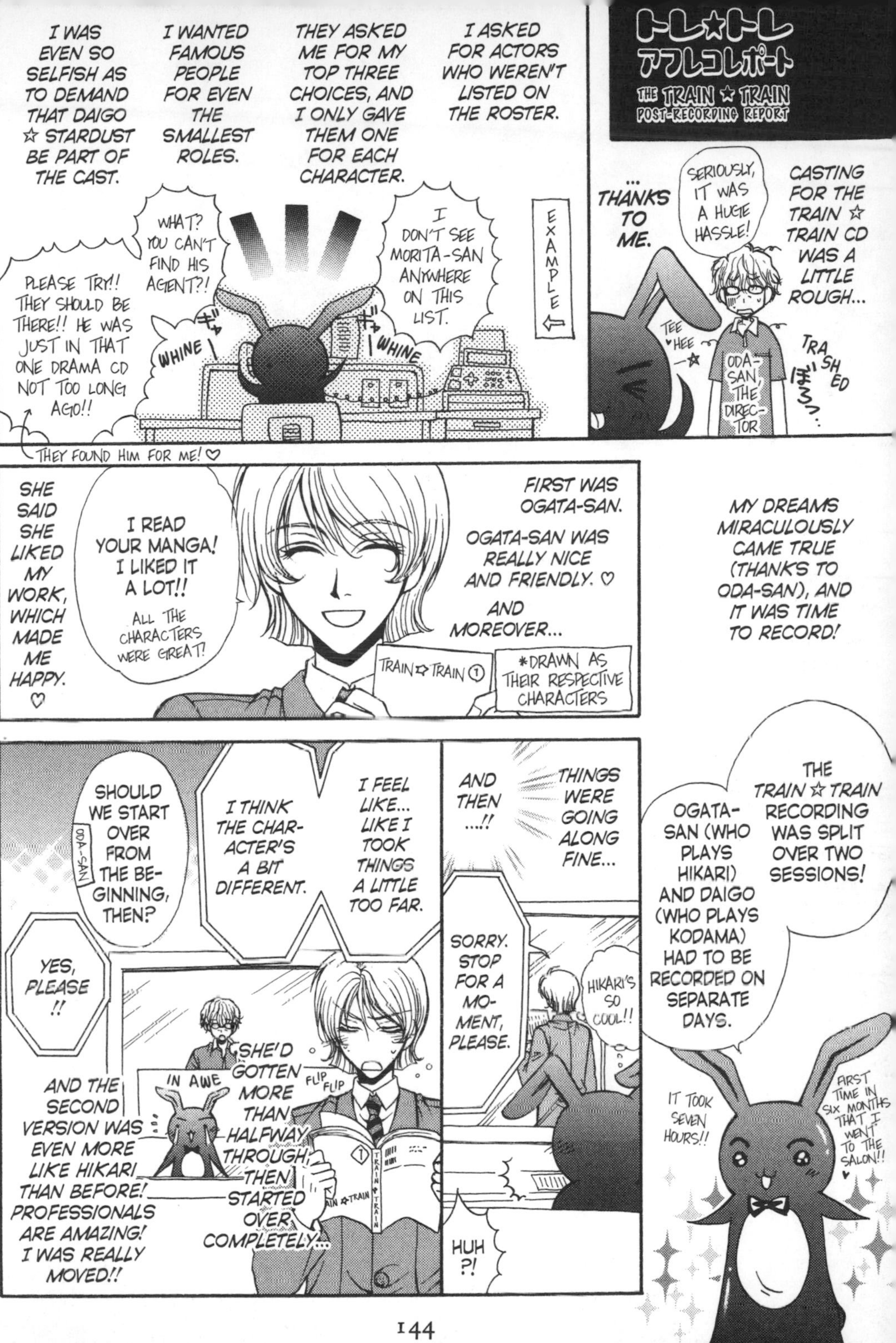
トレ☆トレ アフレコレポート
THE TRAIN ☆ TRAIN POST-RECORDING REPORT
CASTING FOR THE TRAIN ☆ TRAIN CD WAS A LITTLE ROUGH...
SERIOUSLY, IT WAS A HUGE HASSLE!
... THANKS TO ME.
TEE HEE ☆
ODA-SAN, THE DIRECTOR
TRASHED
I ASKED FOR ACTORS WHO WEREN'T LISTED ON THE ROSTER.
THEY ASKED ME FOR MY TOP THREE CHOICES, AND I ONLY GAVE THEM ONE FOR EACH CHARACTER.
I WANTED FAMOUS PEOPLE FOR EVEN THE SMALLEST ROLES.
I WAS EVEN SO SELFISH AS TO DEMAND THAT DAIGO ☆ STARDUST BE PART OF THE CAST.
EXAMPLE
I DON'T SEE MORITA-SAN ANYWHERE ON THIS LIST.
WHAT? YOU CAN'T FIND HIS AGENT?!
WHINE
WHINE
PLEASE TRY!! THEY SHOULD BE THERE!! HE WAS JUST IN THAT ONE DRAMA CD NOT TOO LONG AGO!!
THEY FOUND HIM FOR ME! ♡
MY DREAMS MIRACULOUSLY CAME TRUE (THANKS TO ODA-SAN), AND IT WAS TIME TO RECORD!
FIRST WAS OGATA-SAN.
OGATA-SAN WAS REALLY NICE AND FRIENDLY. ♡
AND MOREOVER...
*DRAWN AS THEIR RESPECTIVE CHARACTERS
TRAIN ☆ TRAIN 1
I READ YOUR MANGA! I LIKED IT A LOT!! ALL THE CHARACTERS WERE GREAT!
SHE SAID SHE LIKED MY WORK, WHICH MADE ME HAPPY. ♡
THE TRAIN ☆ TRAIN RECORDING WAS SPLIT OVER TWO SESSIONS!
OGATA-SAN (WHO PLAYS HIKARI) AND DAIGO (WHO PLAYS KODAMA) HAD TO BE RECORDED ON SEPARATE DAYS.
IT TOOK SEVEN HOURS!!
FIRST TIME IN SIX MONTHS THAT I WENT TO THE SALON!!
THINGS WERE GOING ALONG FINE...
AND THEN ....!!
SORRY. STOP FOR A MOMENT, PLEASE.
HIKARI'S SO COOL!!
HUH ?!
I FEEL LIKE... LIKE I TOOK THINGS A LITTLE TOO FAR.
I THINK THE CHARACTER'S A BIT DIFFERENT.
SHOULD WE START OVER FROM THE BEGINNING, THEN?
ODA-SAN
YES, PLEASE !!
SHE'D GOTTEN MORE THAN HALFWAY THROUGH, THEN STARTED OVER COMPLETELY...
FLIP FLIP
IN AWE
TRAIN ☆ TRAIN
AND THE SECOND VERSION WAS EVEN MORE LIKE HIKARI THAN BEFORE! PROFESSIONALS ARE AMAZING! I WAS REALLY MOVED!!

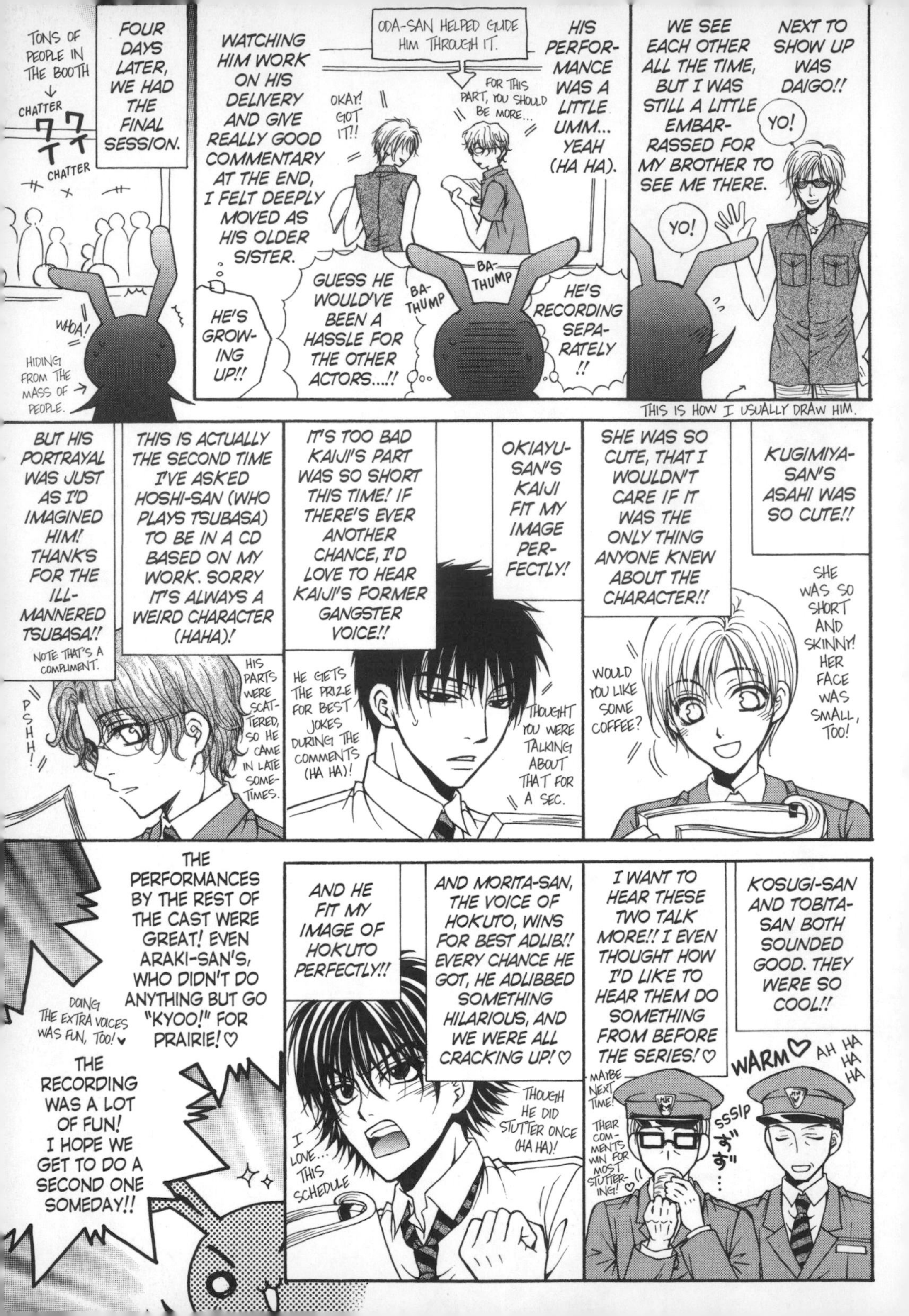
NEXT TO SHOW UP WAS DAIGO!!
WE SEE EACH OTHER ALL THE TIME, BUT I WAS STILL A LITTLE EMBARRASSED FOR MY BROTHER TO SEE ME THERE.
YO!
YO!
THIS IS HOW I USUALLY DRAW HIM.
HIS PERFORMANCE WAS A LITTLE UMM... YEAH (HA HA).
ODA-SAN HELPED GUIDE HIM THROUGH IT.
FOR THIS PART, YOU SHOULD BE MORE...
OKAY! GOT IT!!
WATCHING HIM WORK ON HIS DELIVERY AND GIVE REALLY GOOD COMMENTARY AT THE END, I FELT DEEPLY MOVED AS HIS OLDER SISTER.
BA-THUMP
BA-THUMP
HE'S RECORDING SEPARATELY!!
GUESS HE WOULD'VE BEEN A HASSLE FOR THE OTHER ACTORS...!!
HE'S GROWING UP!!
FOUR DAYS LATER, WE HAD THE FINAL SESSION.
TONS OF PEOPLE IN THE BOOTH
CHATTER
CHATTER
WHOA!
HIDING FROM THE MASS OF PEOPLE.
KUGIMIYA-SAN'S ASAHI WAS SO CUTE!!
SHE WAS SO CUTE, THAT I WOULDN'T CARE IF IT WAS THE ONLY THING ANYONE KNEW ABOUT THE CHARACTER!!
SHE WAS SO SHORT AND SKINNY! HER FACE WAS SMALL, TOO!
WOULD YOU LIKE SOME COFFEE?
OKIAYU-SAN'S KAIJI FIT MY IMAGE PERFECTLY!
IT'S TOO BAD KAIJI'S PART WAS SO SHORT THIS TIME! IF THERE'S EVER ANOTHER CHANCE, I'D LOVE TO HEAR KAIJI'S FORMER GANGSTER VOICE!!
THOUGHT YOU WERE TALKING ABOUT THAT FOR A SEC.
HE GETS THE PRIZE FOR BEST JOKES DURING THE COMMENTS (HA HA)!
THIS IS ACTUALLY THE SECOND TIME I'VE ASKED HOSHI-SAN (WHO PLAYS TSUBASA) TO BE IN A CD BASED ON MY WORK. SORRY IT'S ALWAYS A WEIRD CHARACTER (HAHA)!
BUT HIS PORTRAYAL WAS JUST AS I'D IMAGINED HIM! THANKS FOR THE ILL-MANNERED TSUBASA!!
NOTE THAT'S A COMPLIMENT.
HIS PARTS WERE SCATTERED, SO HE CAME IN LATE SOMETIMES.
PSHH!
KOSUGI-SAN AND TOBITA-SAN BOTH SOUNDED GOOD. THEY WERE SO COOL!!
I WANT TO HEAR THESE TWO TALK MORE!! I EVEN THOUGHT HOW I'D LIKE TO HEAR THEM DO SOMETHING FROM BEFORE THE SERIES! ♡
WARM♡
AH HA HA HA
MAYBE NEXT TIME!
SSSIP
THEIR COMMENTS WIN FOR MOST STUTTERING! ♡
AND MORITA-SAN, THE VOICE OF HOKUTO, WINS FOR BEST ADLIB!! EVERY CHANCE HE GOT, HE ADLIBBED SOMETHING HILARIOUS, AND WE WERE ALL CRACKING UP! ♡
AND HE FIT MY IMAGE OF HOKUTO PERFECTLY!!
THOUGH HE DID STUTTER ONCE (HA HA)!
I LOVE... THIS SCHEDULE
THE PERFORMANCES BY THE REST OF THE CAST WERE GREAT! EVEN ARAKI-SAN'S, WHO DIDN'T DO ANYTHING BUT GO "KYOO!" FOR PRAIRIE! ♡
DOING THE EXTRA VOICES WAS FUN, TOO! ♥
THE RECORDING WAS A LOT OF FUN! I HOPE WE GET TO DO A SECOND ONE SOMEDAY!!

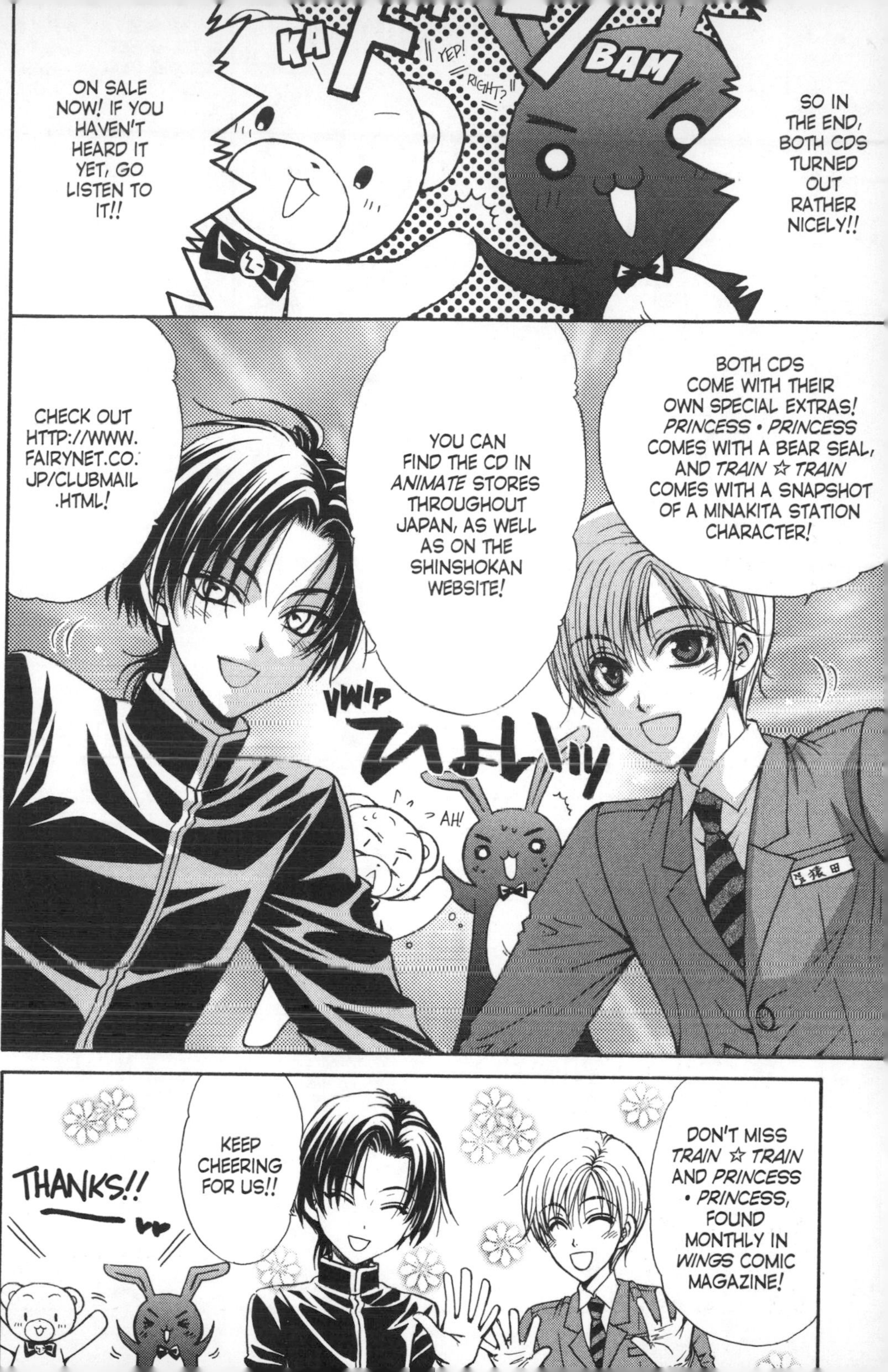
SO IN THE END, BOTH CDS TURNED OUT RATHER NICELY!!
BAM
KA
YEP!
RIGHT?
ON SALE NOW! IF YOU HAVEN'T HEARD IT YET, GO LISTEN TO IT!!
BOTH CDS COME WITH THEIR OWN SPECIAL EXTRAS! *PRINCESS • PRINCESS* COMES WITH A BEAR SEAL, AND *TRAIN ☆ TRAIN* COMES WITH A SNAPSHOT OF A MINAKITA STATION CHARACTER!
YOU CAN FIND THE CD IN *ANIMATE* STORES THROUGHOUT JAPAN, AS WELL AS ON THE SHINSHOKAN WEBSITE!
CHECK OUT HTTP://WWW.FAIRYNET.CO.JP/CLUBMAIL.HTML!
VWIP
AH!
DON'T MISS *TRAIN ☆ TRAIN* AND *PRINCESS • PRINCESS*, FOUND MONTHLY IN *WINGS COMIC MAGAZINE*!
KEEP CHEERING FOR US!!
THANKS!!

PRINCESS & TRAIN POST-RECORDING REPORT ✱ END

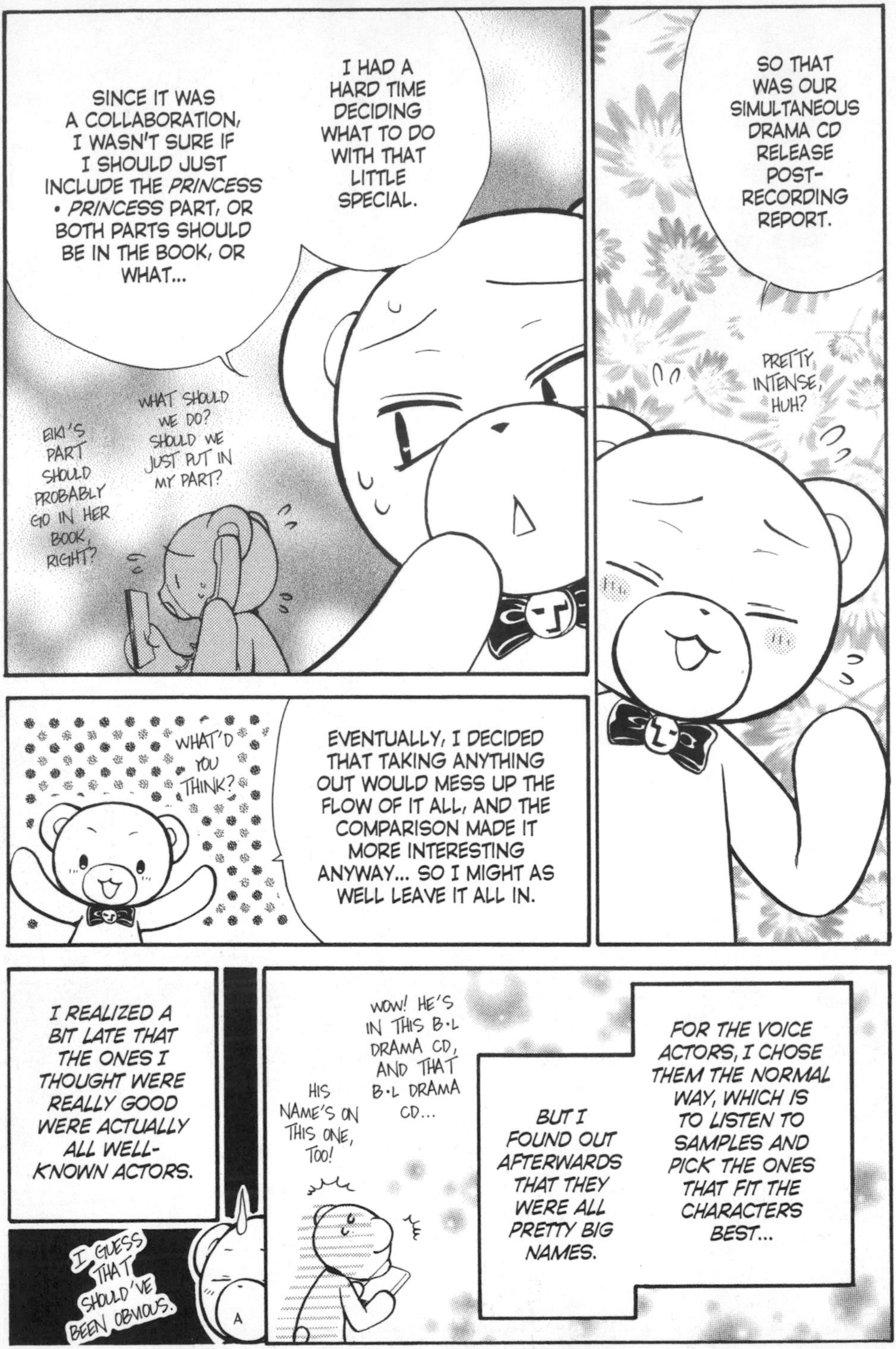
SO THAT WAS OUR SIMULTANEOUS DRAMA CD RELEASE POST-RECORDING REPORT.
PRETTY INTENSE, HUH?
I HAD A HARD TIME DECIDING WHAT TO DO WITH THAT LITTLE SPECIAL.
SINCE IT WAS A COLLABORATION, I WASN'T SURE IF I SHOULD JUST INCLUDE THE *PRINCESS • PRINCESS* PART, OR BOTH PARTS SHOULD BE IN THE BOOK, OR WHAT...
WHAT SHOULD WE DO? SHOULD WE JUST PUT IN MY PART?
EIKI'S PART SHOULD PROBABLY GO IN HER BOOK, RIGHT?
EVENTUALLY, I DECIDED THAT TAKING ANYTHING OUT WOULD MESS UP THE FLOW OF IT ALL, AND THE COMPARISON MADE IT MORE INTERESTING ANYWAY... SO I MIGHT AS WELL LEAVE IT ALL IN.
WHAT'D YOU THINK?
FOR THE VOICE ACTORS, I CHOSE THEM THE NORMAL WAY, WHICH IS TO LISTEN TO SAMPLES AND PICK THE ONES THAT FIT THE CHARACTERS BEST...
BUT I FOUND OUT AFTERWARDS THAT THEY WERE ALL PRETTY BIG NAMES.
WOW! HE'S IN THIS B·L DRAMA CD, AND THAT B·L DRAMA CD...
HIS NAME'S ON THIS ONE, TOO!
I REALIZED A BIT LATE THAT THE ONES I THOUGHT WERE REALLY GOOD WERE ACTUALLY ALL WELL-KNOWN ACTORS.
I GUESS THAT SHOULD'VE BEEN OBVIOUS.

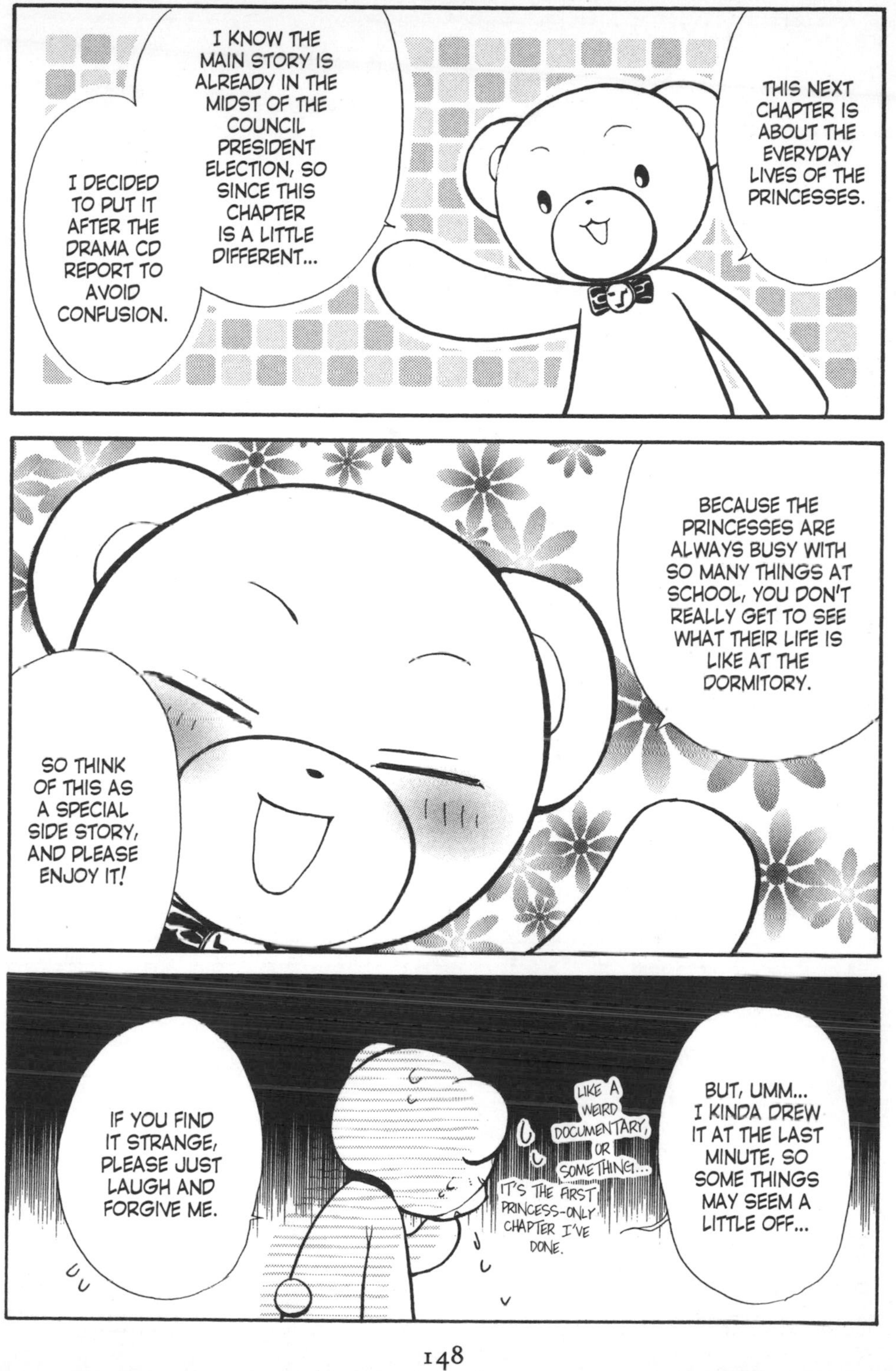
THIS NEXT CHAPTER IS ABOUT THE EVERYDAY LIVES OF THE PRINCESSES.
I KNOW THE MAIN STORY IS ALREADY IN THE MIDST OF THE COUNCIL PRESIDENT ELECTION, SO SINCE THIS CHAPTER IS A LITTLE DIFFERENT...
I DECIDED TO PUT IT AFTER THE DRAMA CD REPORT TO AVOID CONFUSION.
BECAUSE THE PRINCESSES ARE ALWAYS BUSY WITH SO MANY THINGS AT SCHOOL, YOU DON'T REALLY GET TO SEE WHAT THEIR LIFE IS LIKE AT THE DORMITORY.
SO THINK OF THIS AS A SPECIAL SIDE STORY, AND PLEASE ENJOY IT!
BUT, UMM... I KINDA DREW IT AT THE LAST MINUTE, SO SOME THINGS MAY SEEM A LITTLE OFF...
LIKE A WEIRD DOCUMENTARY, OR SOMETHING...
IT'S THE FIRST PRINCESS-ONLY CHAPTER I'VE DONE.
IF YOU FIND IT STRANGE, PLEASE JUST LAUGH AND FORGIVE ME.

Princess·Princess
EVERYDAY LIFE
A DAY IN THE LIFE OF A PRINCESS

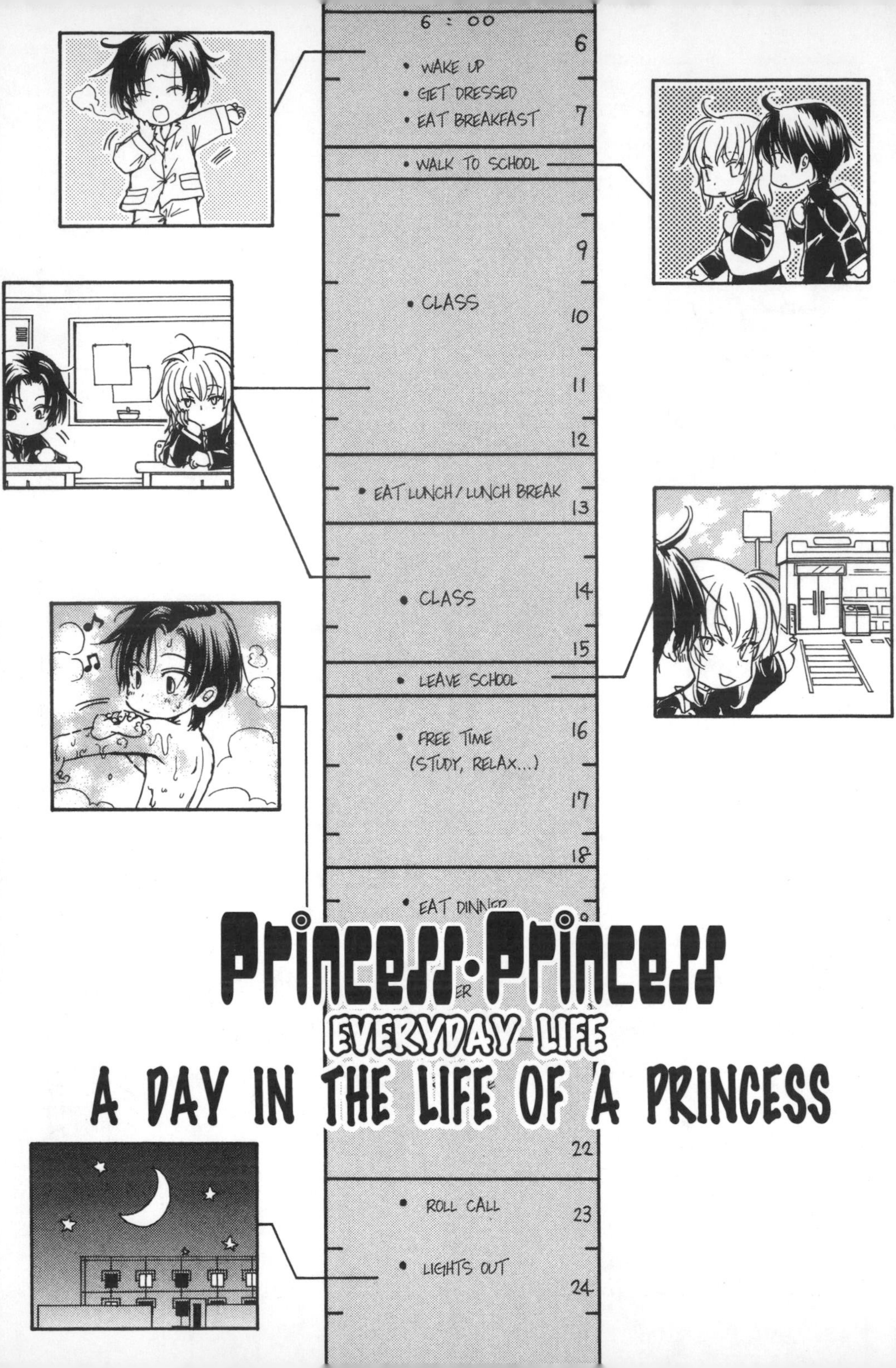

6:00
6
• WAKE UP
• GET DRESSED
• EAT BREAKFAST
7
• WALK TO SCHOOL
9
• CLASS
10
11
12
• EAT LUNCH / LUNCH BREAK
13
14
• CLASS
15
• LEAVE SCHOOL
16
• FREE TIME
(STUDY, RELAX...)
17
18
• EAT DINNER
22
• ROLL CALL
23
• LIGHTS OUT
24

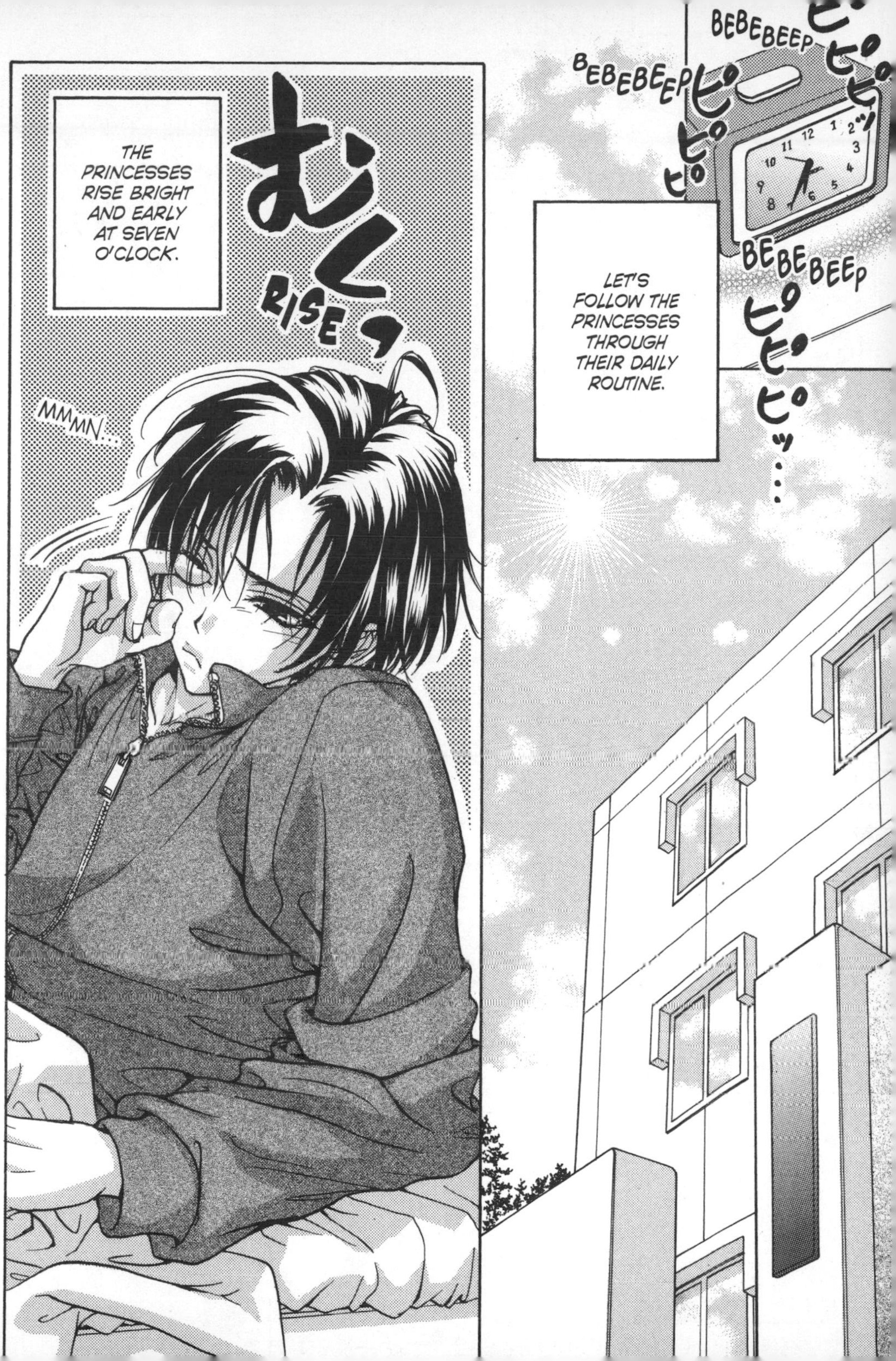

BEBEBEEP ピピピッ
BEBEBEEP ピピピ
LET'S FOLLOW THE PRINCESSES THROUGH THEIR DAILY ROUTINE.
BEBEBEEP ピピピッ…
THE PRINCESSES RISE BRIGHT AND EARLY AT SEVEN O'CLOCK.
むく RISE
MMMN…

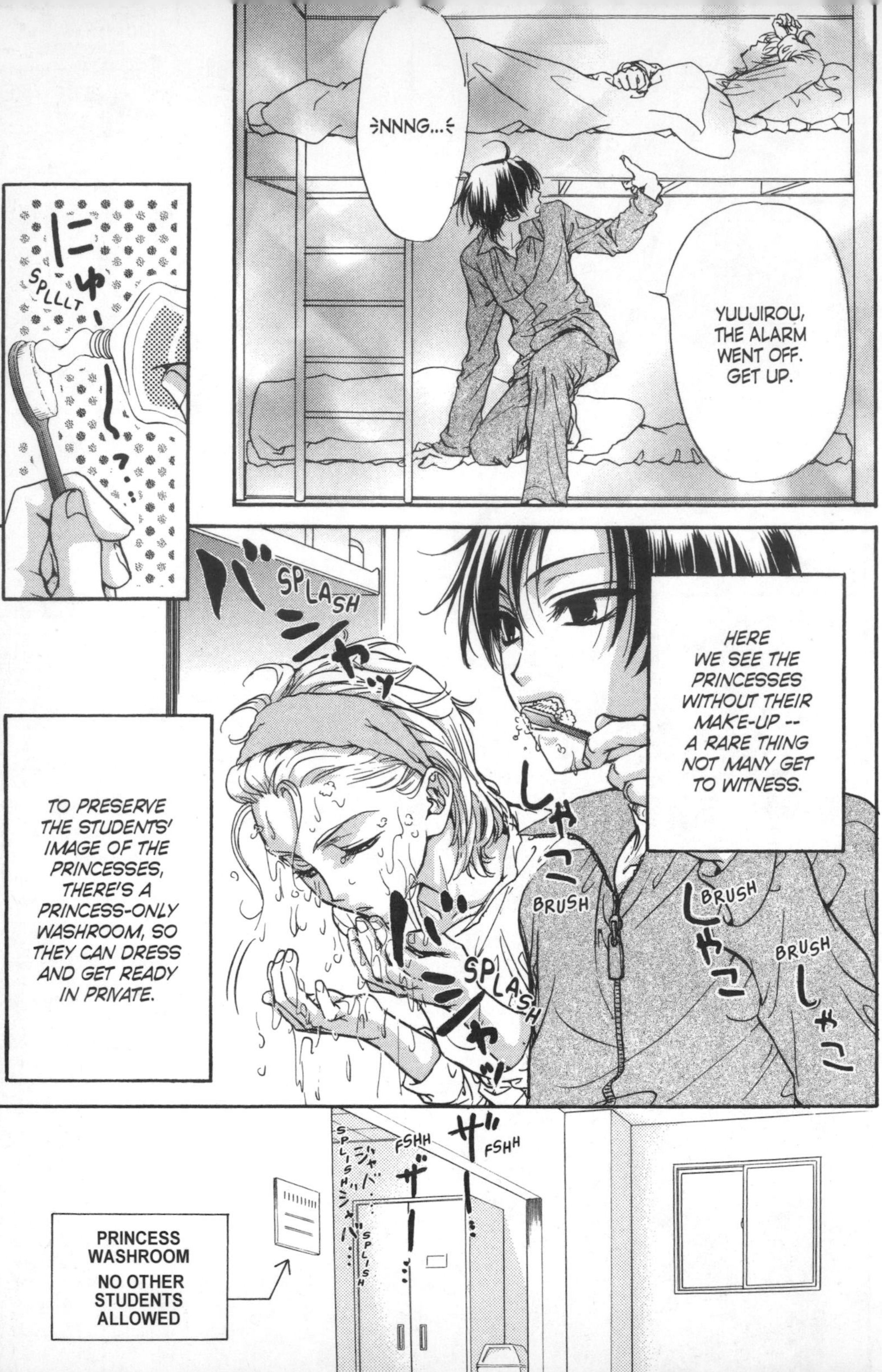
YUUJIROU, THE ALARM WENT OFF. GET UP.
NNNG...
にゅ〜〜っ…
SPLLLT
HERE WE SEE THE PRINCESSES WITHOUT THEIR MAKE-UP -- A RARE THING NOT MANY GET TO WITNESS.
しゃこ
BRUSH
しゃこ
BRUSH
しゃこ
BRUSH
バシャッ
SPLASH
バシャッ
SPLASH
TO PRESERVE THE STUDENTS' IMAGE OF THE PRINCESSES, THERE'S A PRINCESS-ONLY WASHROOM, SO THEY CAN DRESS AND GET READY IN PRIVATE.
ザー…
FSHH
ザー…
FSHH
ジャバ…
SPLISH
ジャバ…
SPLISH
PRINCESS WASHROOM
NO OTHER STUDENTS ALLOWED

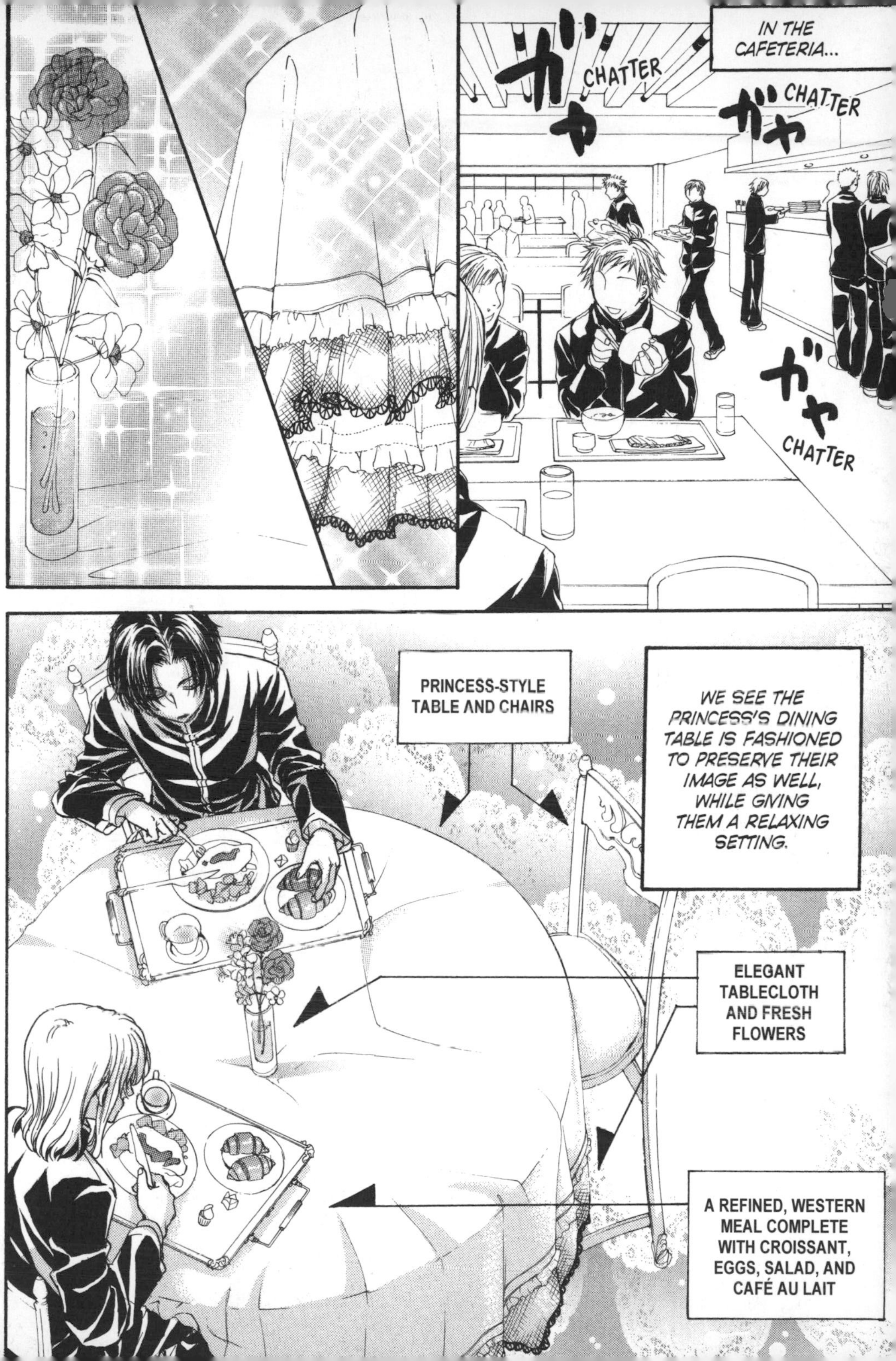
IN THE CAFETERIA...
ガヤ
CHATTER
ガヤ
CHATTER
ガヤ
CHATTER
WE SEE THE PRINCESS'S DINING TABLE IS FASHIONED TO PRESERVE THEIR IMAGE AS WELL, WHILE GIVING THEM A RELAXING SETTING.
PRINCESS-STYLE TABLE AND CHAIRS
ELEGANT TABLECLOTH AND FRESH FLOWERS
A REFINED, WESTERN MEAL COMPLETE WITH CROISSANT, EGGS, SALAD, AND CAFÉ AU LAIT

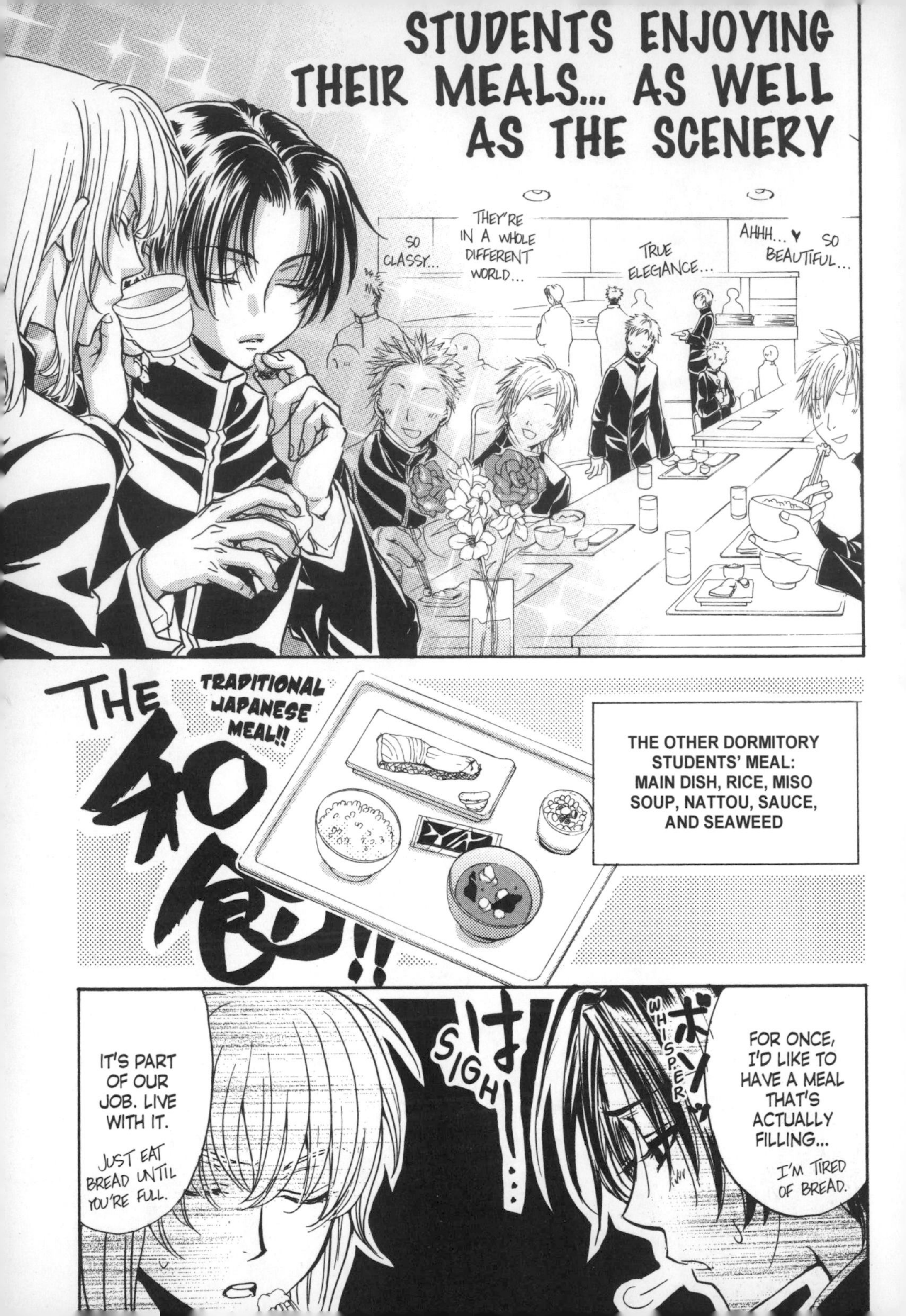
STUDENTS ENJOYING THEIR MEALS... AS WELL AS THE SCENERY
AHHH... ♥ SO BEAUTIFUL...
TRUE ELEGANCE...
THEY'RE IN A WHOLE DIFFERENT WORLD...
SO CLASSY...
THE OTHER DORMITORY STUDENTS' MEAL: MAIN DISH, RICE, MISO SOUP, NATTOU, SAUCE, AND SEAWEED
THE 和食!!
TRADITIONAL JAPANESE MEAL!!
FOR ONCE, I'D LIKE TO HAVE A MEAL THAT'S ACTUALLY FILLING...
I'M TIRED OF BREAD.
WHISPER
SIGH
IT'S PART OF OUR JOB. LIVE WITH IT.
JUST EAT BREAD UNTIL YOU'RE FULL.

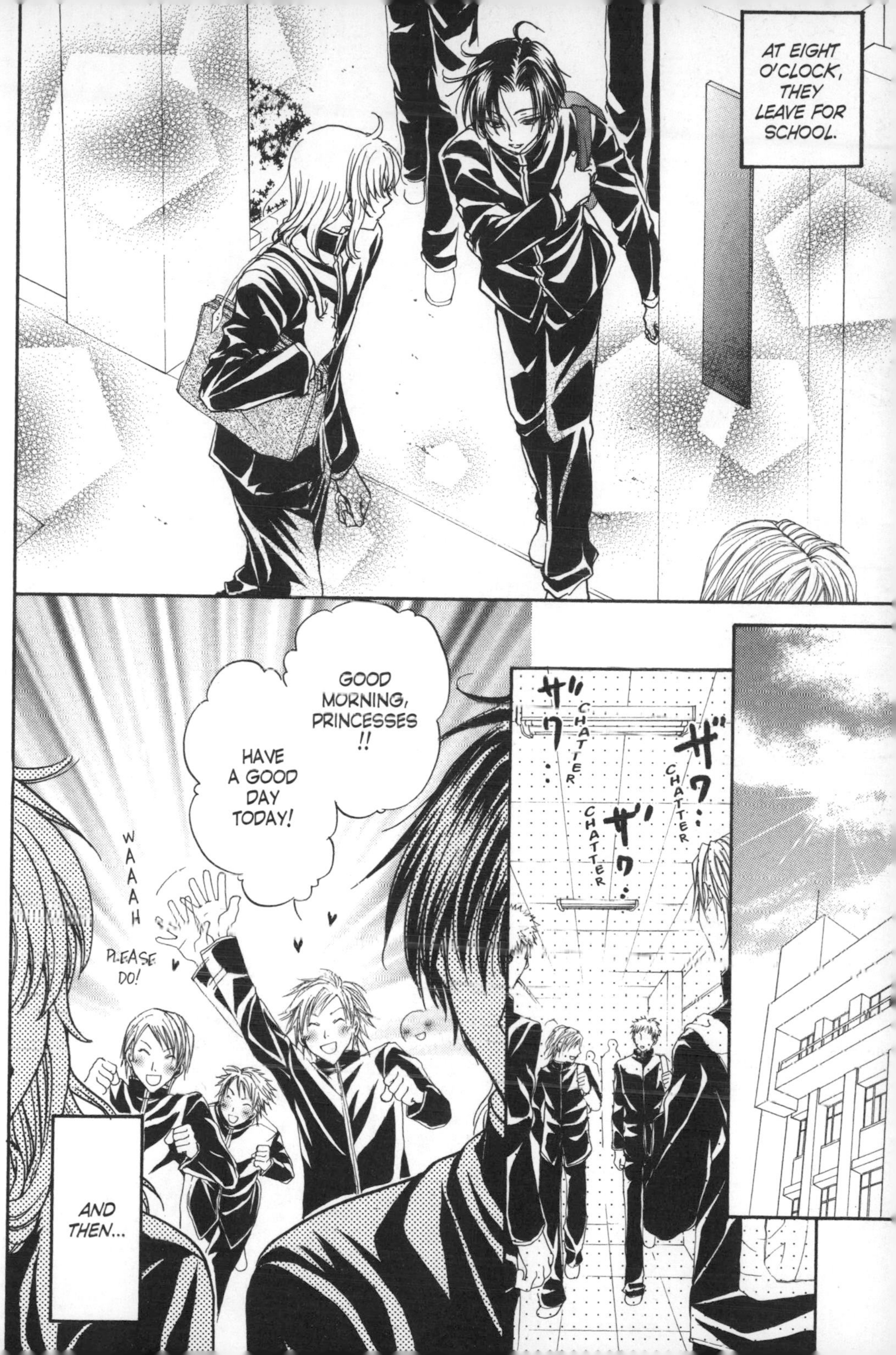
AT EIGHT O'CLOCK, THEY LEAVE FOR SCHOOL.
ザワ..
CHATTER
ザワ..
CHATTER
ザワ..
CHATTER
GOOD MORNING, PRINCESSES!!
HAVE A GOOD DAY TODAY!
WAAAAH
PLEASE DO!
AND THEN...

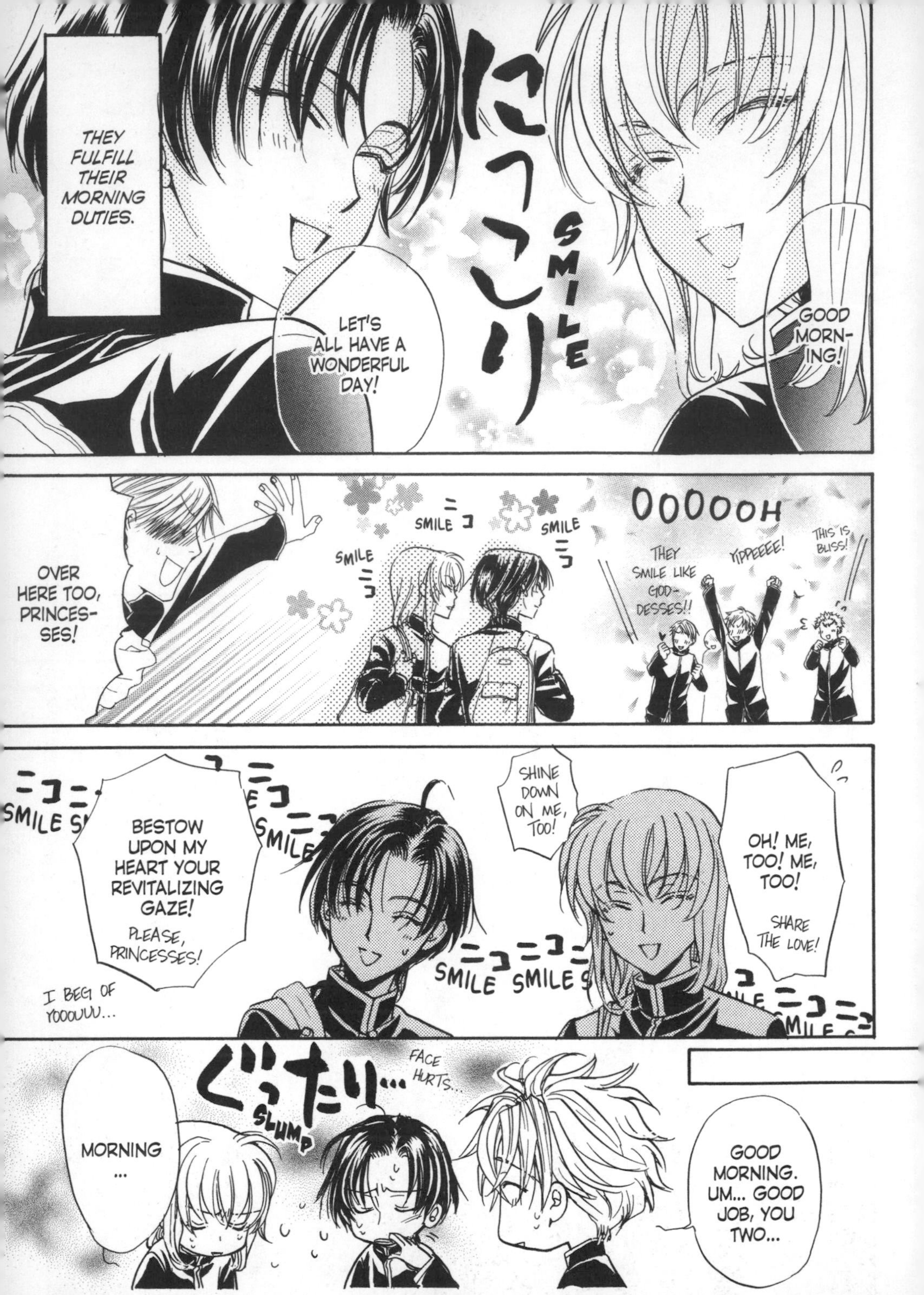
GOOD MORN-ING!
にっこり
SMILE
LET'S ALL HAVE A WONDERFUL DAY!
THEY FULFILL THEIR MORNING DUTIES.
OOOOOOH
THIS IS BLISS!
YIPPEEEE!
THEY SMILE LIKE GOD-DESSES!!
SMILE ニコ
SMILE ニコ
SMILE ニコ
OVER HERE TOO, PRINCESSES!
OH! ME, TOO! ME, TOO!
SHARE THE LOVE!
SHINE DOWN ON ME, TOO!
SMILE SMILE
BESTOW UPON MY HEART YOUR REVITALIZING GAZE!
PLEASE, PRINCESSES!
I BEG OF YOOOUUU...
GOOD MORNING. UM... GOOD JOB, YOU TWO...
FACE HURTS...
ぐったり...
SLUMP
MORNING...

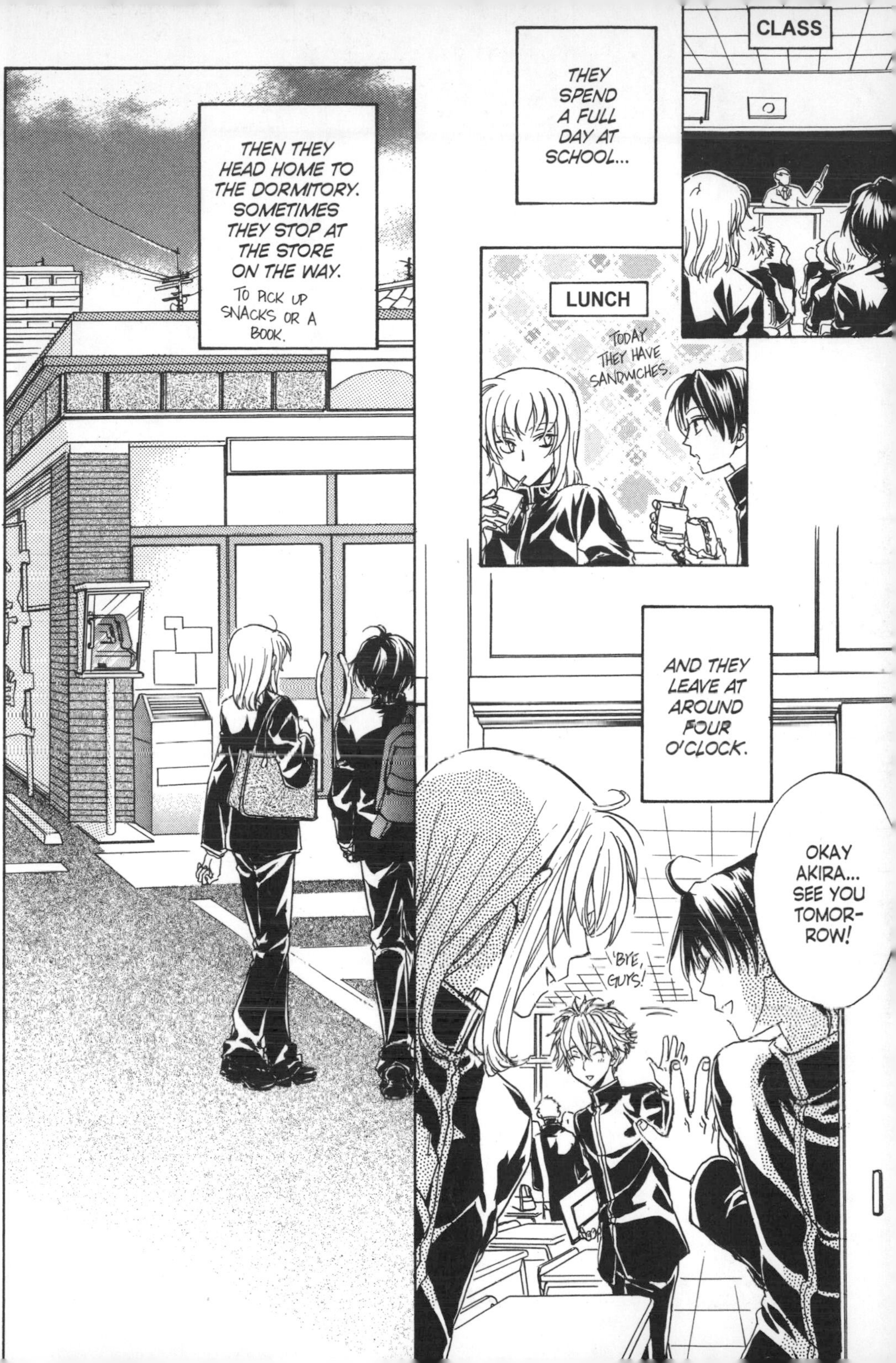
CLASS
THEY SPEND A FULL DAY AT SCHOOL...
LUNCH
TODAY THEY HAVE SANDWICHES.
AND THEY LEAVE AT AROUND FOUR O'CLOCK.
OKAY AKIRA... SEE YOU TOMOR-ROW!
'BYE, GUYS!
THEN THEY HEAD HOME TO THE DORMITORY. SOMETIMES THEY STOP AT THE STORE ON THE WAY.
TO PICK UP SNACKS OR A BOOK.

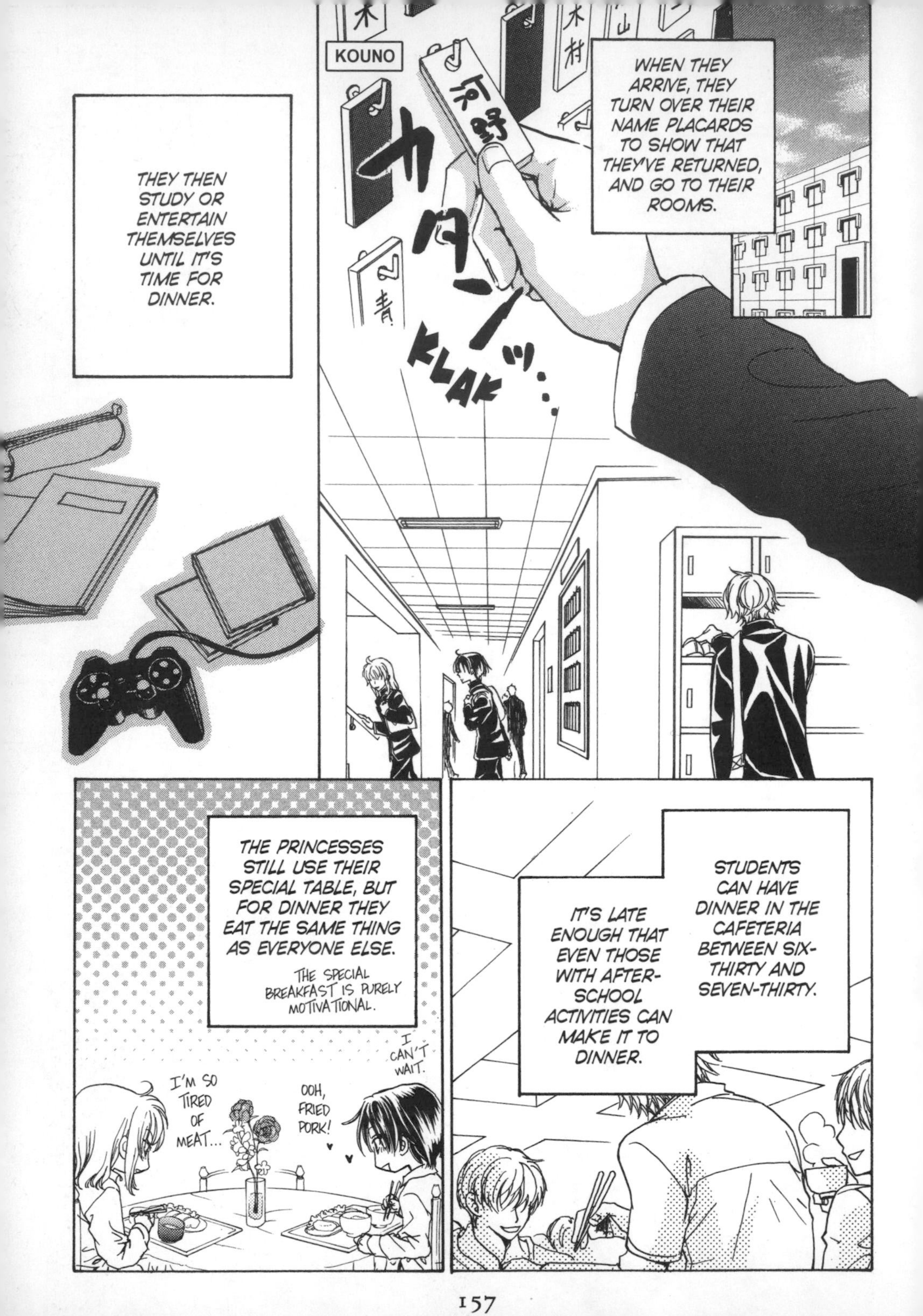

KOUNO
河野
WHEN THEY ARRIVE, THEY TURN OVER THEIR NAME PLACARDS TO SHOW THAT THEY'VE RETURNED, AND GO TO THEIR ROOMS.
KLAK
THEY THEN STUDY OR ENTERTAIN THEMSELVES UNTIL IT'S TIME FOR DINNER.
STUDENTS CAN HAVE DINNER IN THE CAFETERIA BETWEEN SIX-THIRTY AND SEVEN-THIRTY.
IT'S LATE ENOUGH THAT EVEN THOSE WITH AFTER-SCHOOL ACTIVITIES CAN MAKE IT TO DINNER.
THE PRINCESSES STILL USE THEIR SPECIAL TABLE, BUT FOR DINNER THEY EAT THE SAME THING AS EVERYONE ELSE.
THE SPECIAL BREAKFAST IS PURELY MOTIVATIONAL.
I CAN'T WAIT.
OOH, FRIED PORK!
I'M SO TIRED OF MEAT...

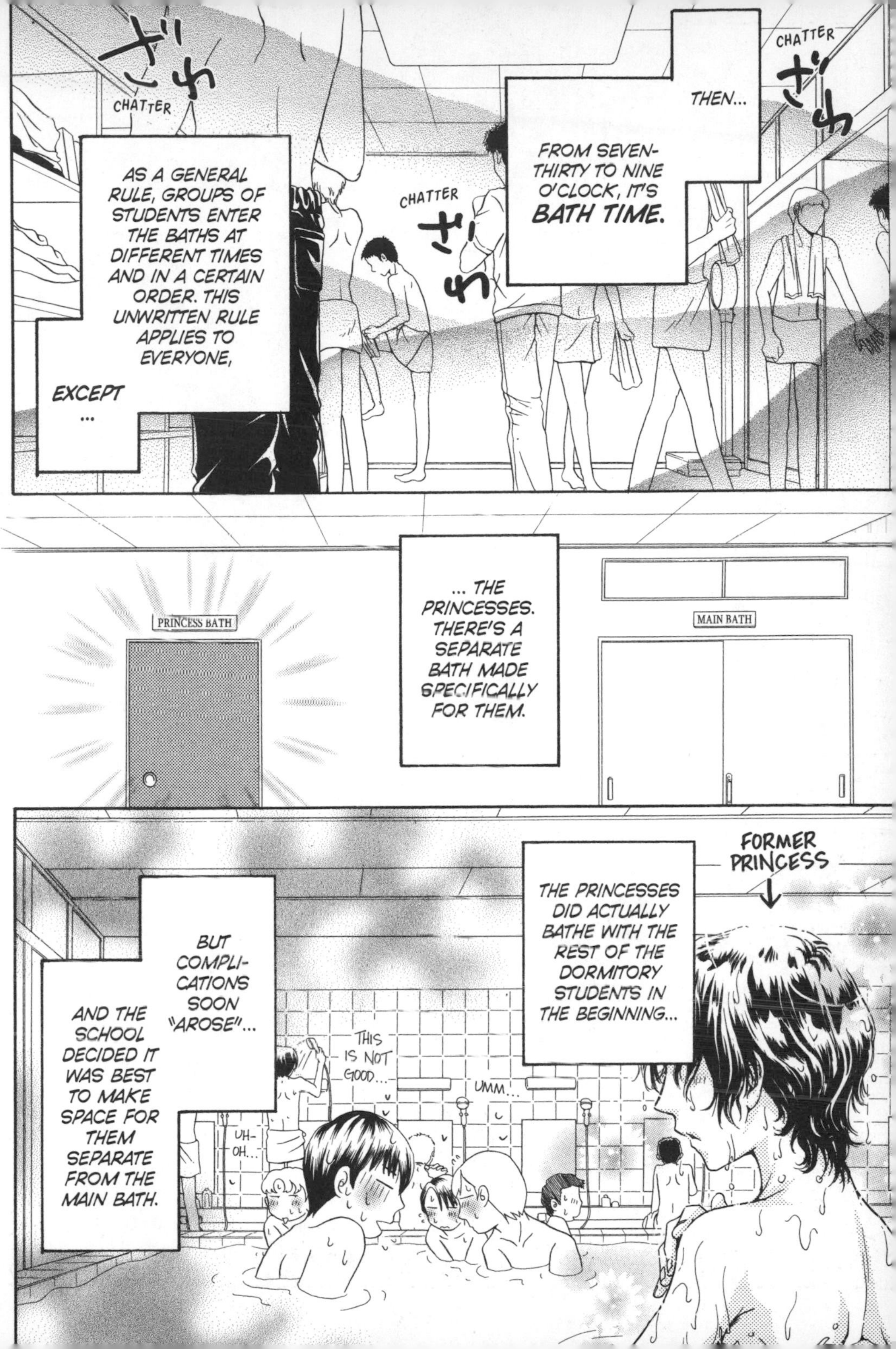
ざわ
CHATTER
THEN...
FROM SEVEN-THIRTY TO NINE O'CLOCK, IT'S BATH TIME.
ざわ
CHATTER
AS A GENERAL RULE, GROUPS OF STUDENTS ENTER THE BATHS AT DIFFERENT TIMES AND IN A CERTAIN ORDER. THIS UNWRITTEN RULE APPLIES TO EVERYONE,
EXCEPT ...
ざわ
CHATTER
MAIN BATH
... THE PRINCESSES. THERE'S A SEPARATE BATH MADE SPECIFICALLY FOR THEM.
PRINCESS BATH
FORMER PRINCESS
THE PRINCESSES DID ACTUALLY BATHE WITH THE REST OF THE DORMITORY STUDENTS IN THE BEGINNING...
UMM...
THIS IS NOT GOOD...
BUT COMPLICATIONS SOON "AROSE"...
AND THE SCHOOL DECIDED IT WAS BEST TO MAKE SPACE FOR THEM SEPARATE FROM THE MAIN BATH.
UH-OH...

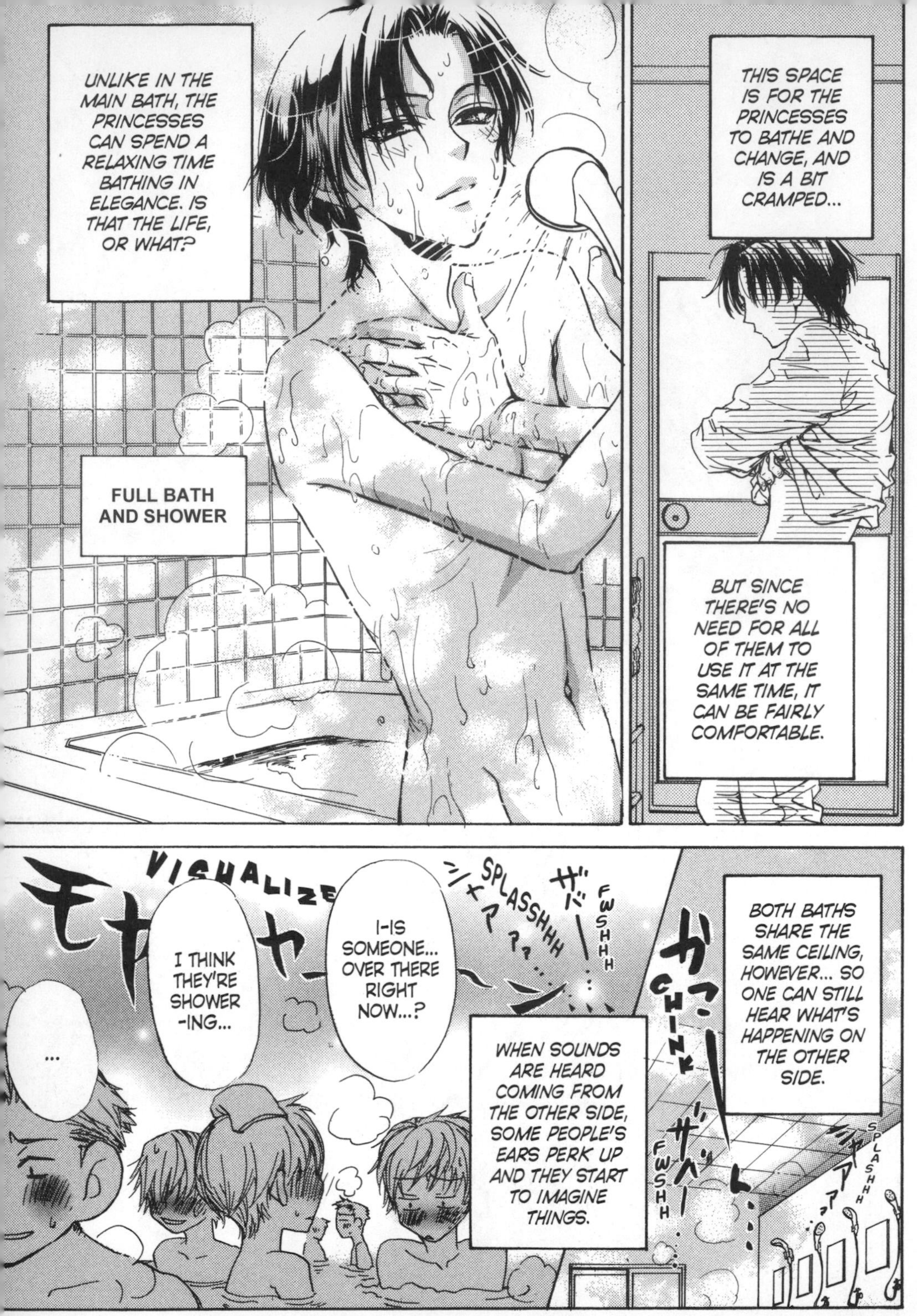
THIS SPACE IS FOR THE PRINCESSES TO BATHE AND CHANGE, AND IS A BIT CRAMPED...
BUT SINCE THERE'S NO NEED FOR ALL OF THEM TO USE IT AT THE SAME TIME, IT CAN BE FAIRLY COMFORTABLE.
UNLIKE IN THE MAIN BATH, THE PRINCESSES CAN SPEND A RELAXING TIME BATHING IN ELEGANCE. IS THAT THE LIFE, OR WHAT?
FULL BATH AND SHOWER
BOTH BATHS SHARE THE SAME CEILING, HOWEVER... SO ONE CAN STILL HEAR WHAT'S HAPPENING ON THE OTHER SIDE.
CHINK
SPLASHH
FWSHH
WHEN SOUNDS ARE HEARD COMING FROM THE OTHER SIDE, SOME PEOPLE'S EARS PERK UP AND THEY START TO IMAGINE THINGS.
FWSHH
SPLASSHHH
I-IS SOMEONE... OVER THERE RIGHT NOW...?
VISUALIZE
I THINK THEY'RE SHOWER -ING...
...

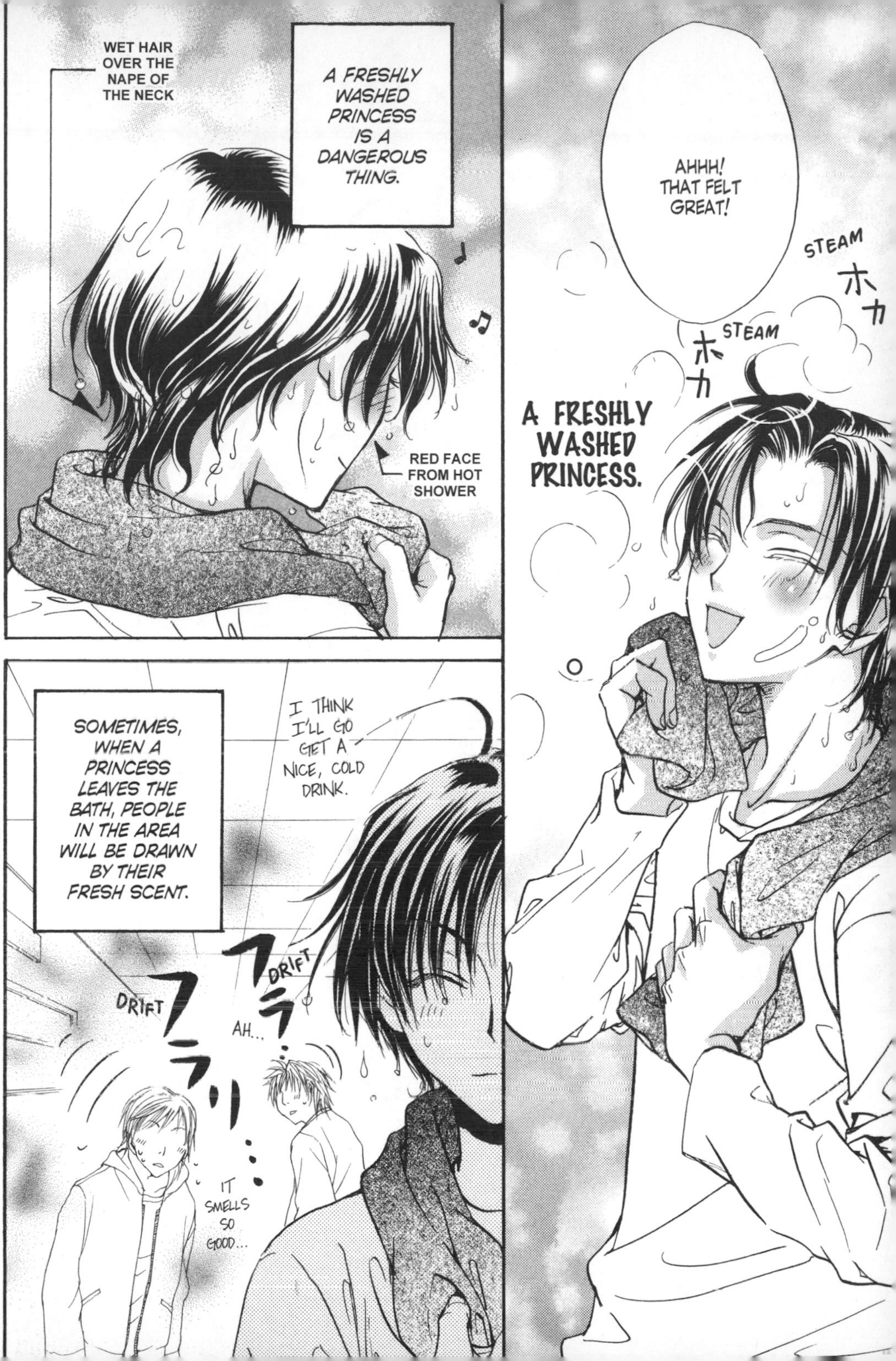
AHHH! THAT FELT GREAT!
STEAM
ホカ
STEAM
ホカ
A FRESHLY WASHED PRINCESS.
A FRESHLY WASHED PRINCESS IS A DANGEROUS THING.
WET HAIR OVER THE NAPE OF THE NECK
RED FACE FROM HOT SHOWER
I THINK I'LL GO GET A NICE, COLD DRINK.
SOMETIMES, WHEN A PRINCESS LEAVES THE BATH, PEOPLE IN THE AREA WILL BE DRAWN BY THEIR FRESH SCENT.
DRIFT
フラ
AH...
DRIFT
フラリ
IT SMELLS SO GOOD...

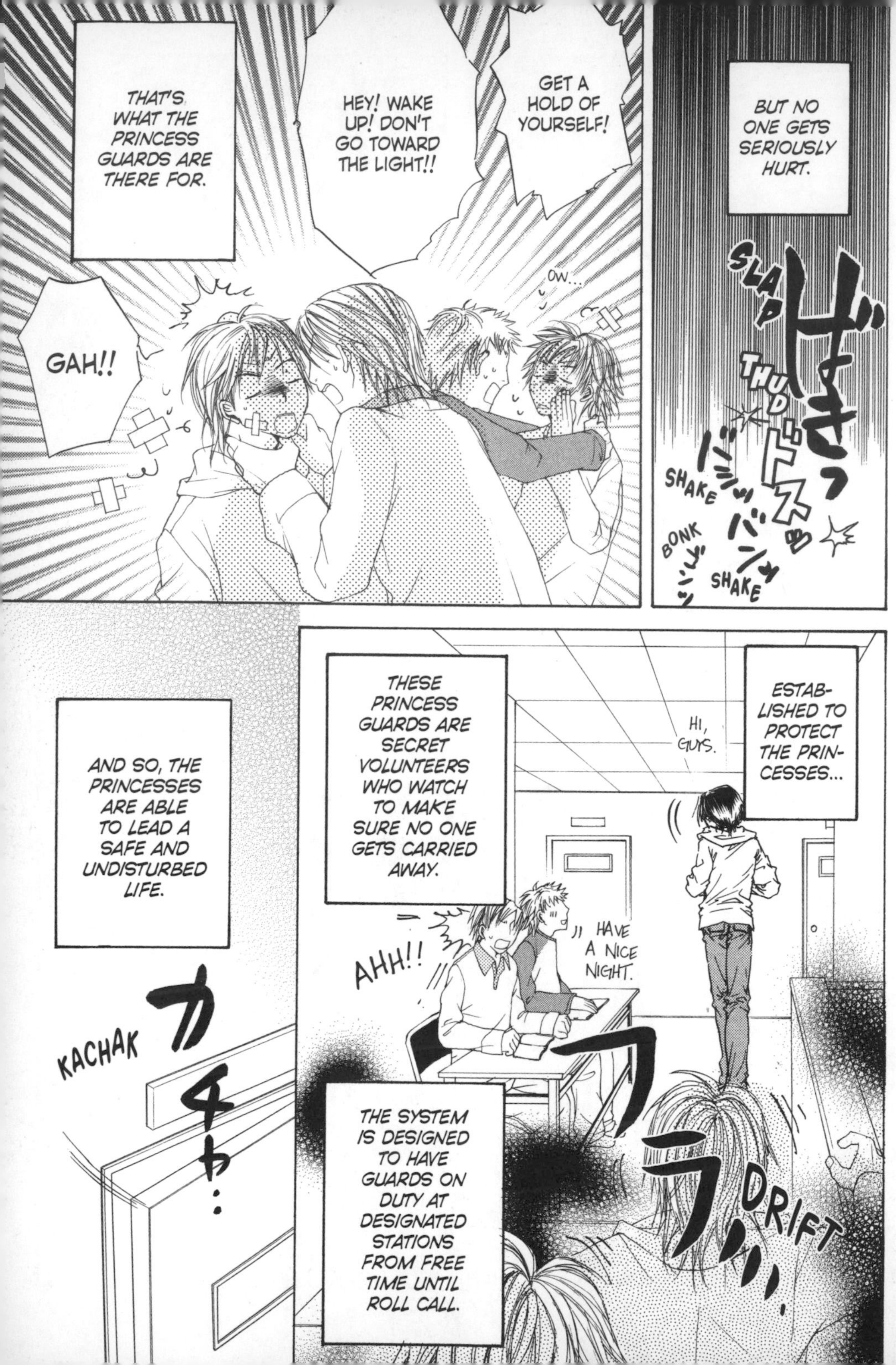
BUT NO ONE GETS SERIOUSLY HURT.
SLAP
THUD
SHAKE
BONK
SHAKE
GET A HOLD OF YOURSELF!
HEY! WAKE UP! DON'T GO TOWARD THE LIGHT!!
THAT'S WHAT THE PRINCESS GUARDS ARE THERE FOR.
OW...
GAH!!
ESTAB-LISHED TO PROTECT THE PRIN-CESSES...
HI, GUYS.
THESE PRINCESS GUARDS ARE SECRET VOLUNTEERS WHO WATCH TO MAKE SURE NO ONE GETS CARRIED AWAY.
HAVE A NICE NIGHT.
AHH!!
THE SYSTEM IS DESIGNED TO HAVE GUARDS ON DUTY AT DESIGNATED STATIONS FROM FREE TIME UNTIL ROLL CALL.
DRIFT
AND SO, THE PRINCESSES ARE ABLE TO LEAD A SAFE AND UNDISTURBED LIFE.
KACHAK

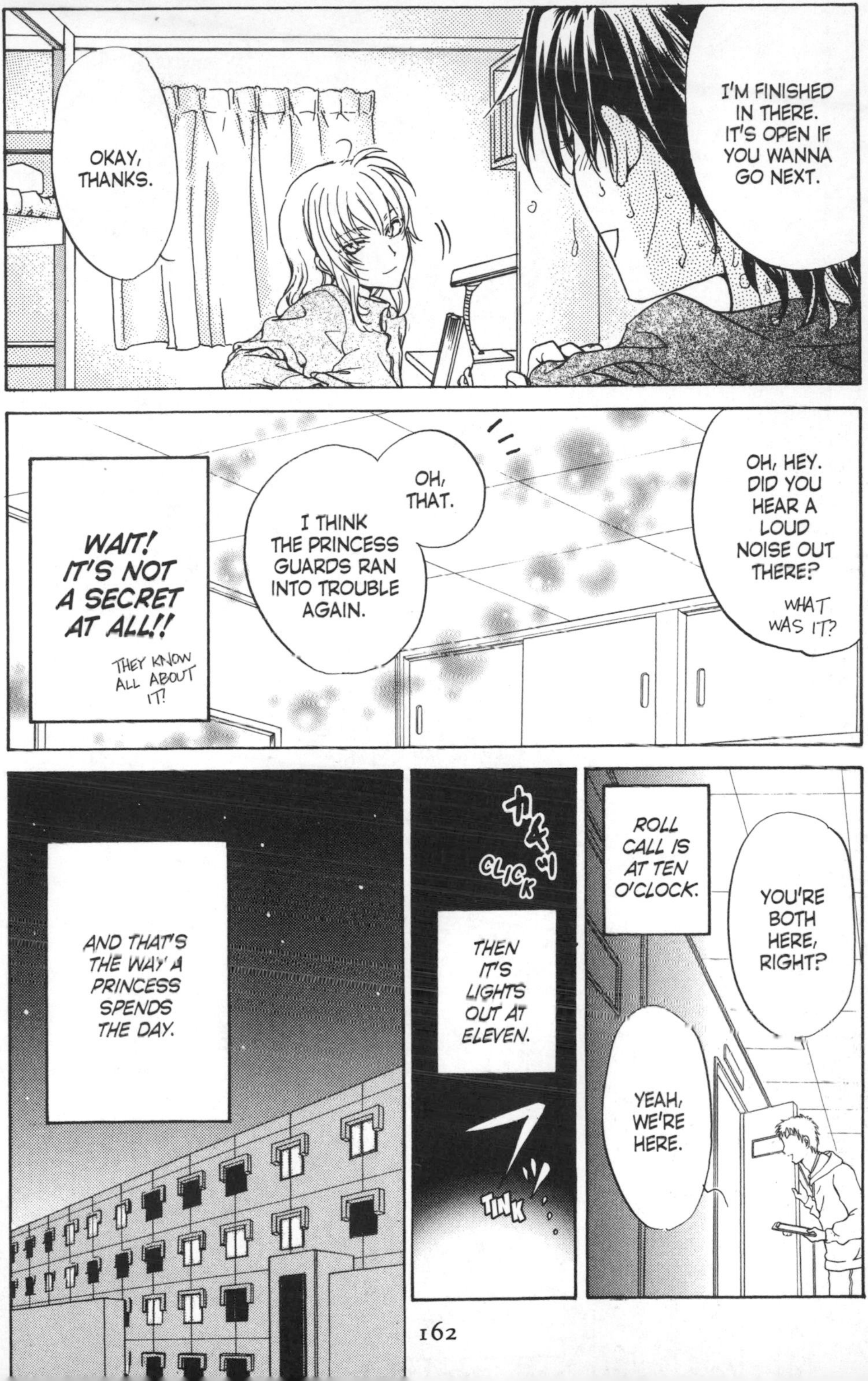
I'M FINISHED IN THERE. IT'S OPEN IF YOU WANNA GO NEXT.
OKAY, THANKS.
OH, HEY. DID YOU HEAR A LOUD NOISE OUT THERE?
WHAT WAS IT?
OH, THAT.
I THINK THE PRINCESS GUARDS RAN INTO TROUBLE AGAIN.
WAIT! IT'S NOT A SECRET AT ALL!!
THEY KNOW ALL ABOUT IT!
ROLL CALL IS AT TEN O'CLOCK.
YOU'RE BOTH HERE, RIGHT?
YEAH, WE'RE HERE.
CLICK
THEN IT'S LIGHTS OUT AT ELEVEN.
TINK
AND THAT'S THE WAY A PRINCESS SPENDS THE DAY.

A DAY IN THE LIFE OF A PRINCESS ✸ END

AFTERWORD

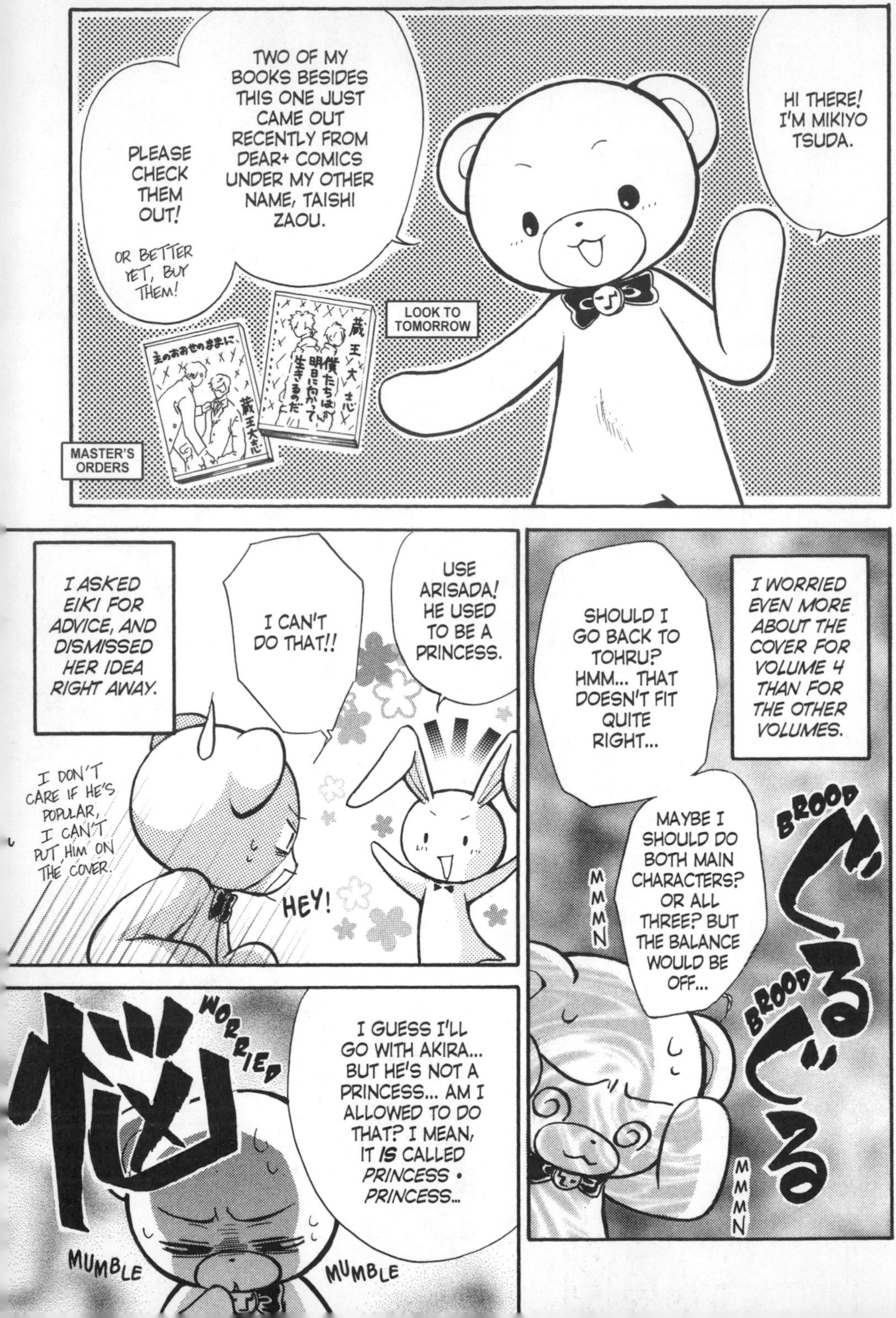
HI THERE! I'M MIKIYO TSUDA.
TWO OF MY BOOKS BESIDES THIS ONE JUST CAME OUT RECENTLY FROM DEAR+ COMICS UNDER MY OTHER NAME, TAISHI ZAOU.
PLEASE CHECK THEM OUT!
OR BETTER YET, BUY THEM!
LOOK TO TOMORROW
蔵王大志
僕たちは明日に向かって生きるのだ
主のおおせのままに。
蔵王大志
MASTER'S ORDERS
I WORRIED EVEN MORE ABOUT THE COVER FOR VOLUME 4 THAN FOR THE OTHER VOLUMES.
SHOULD I GO BACK TO TOHRU? HMM... THAT DOESN'T FIT QUITE RIGHT...
BROOD
MAYBE I SHOULD DO BOTH MAIN CHARACTERS? OR ALL THREE? BUT THE BALANCE WOULD BE OFF...
MMMN
BROOD
ぐるぐる
MMMN
USE ARISADA! HE USED TO BE A PRINCESS.
I CAN'T DO THAT!!
I ASKED EIKI FOR ADVICE, AND DISMISSED HER IDEA RIGHT AWAY.
HEY!
I DON'T CARE IF HE'S POPULAR, I CAN'T PUT HIM ON THE COVER.
I GUESS I'LL GO WITH AKIRA... BUT HE'S NOT A PRINCESS... AM I ALLOWED TO DO THAT? I MEAN, IT *IS* CALLED *PRINCESS • PRINCESS*...
WORRIED
MUMBLE
MUMBLE

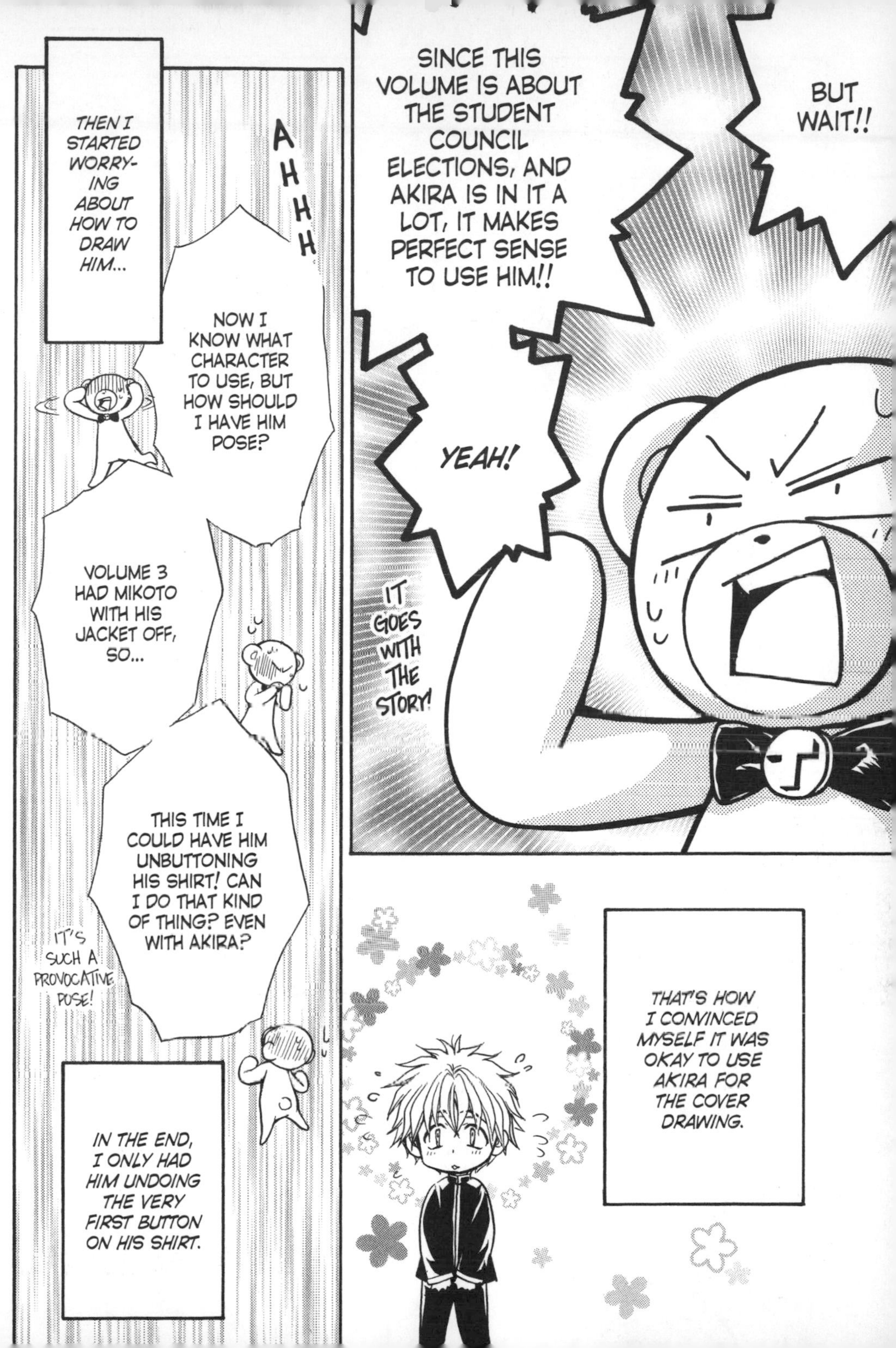

BUT WAIT!!
SINCE THIS VOLUME IS ABOUT THE STUDENT COUNCIL ELECTIONS, AND AKIRA IS IN IT A LOT, IT MAKES PERFECT SENSE TO USE HIM!!
YEAH!
IT GOES WITH THE STORY!
THAT'S HOW I CONVINCED MYSELF IT WAS OKAY TO USE AKIRA FOR THE COVER DRAWING.
THEN I STARTED WORRYING ABOUT HOW TO DRAW HIM...
AHHH
NOW I KNOW WHAT CHARACTER TO USE, BUT HOW SHOULD I HAVE HIM POSE?
VOLUME 3 HAD MIKOTO WITH HIS JACKET OFF, SO...
THIS TIME I COULD HAVE HIM UNBUTTONING HIS SHIRT! CAN I DO THAT KIND OF THING? EVEN WITH AKIRA?
IT'S SUCH A PROVOCATIVE POSE!
IN THE END, I ONLY HAD HIM UNDOING THE VERY FIRST BUTTON ON HIS SHIRT.

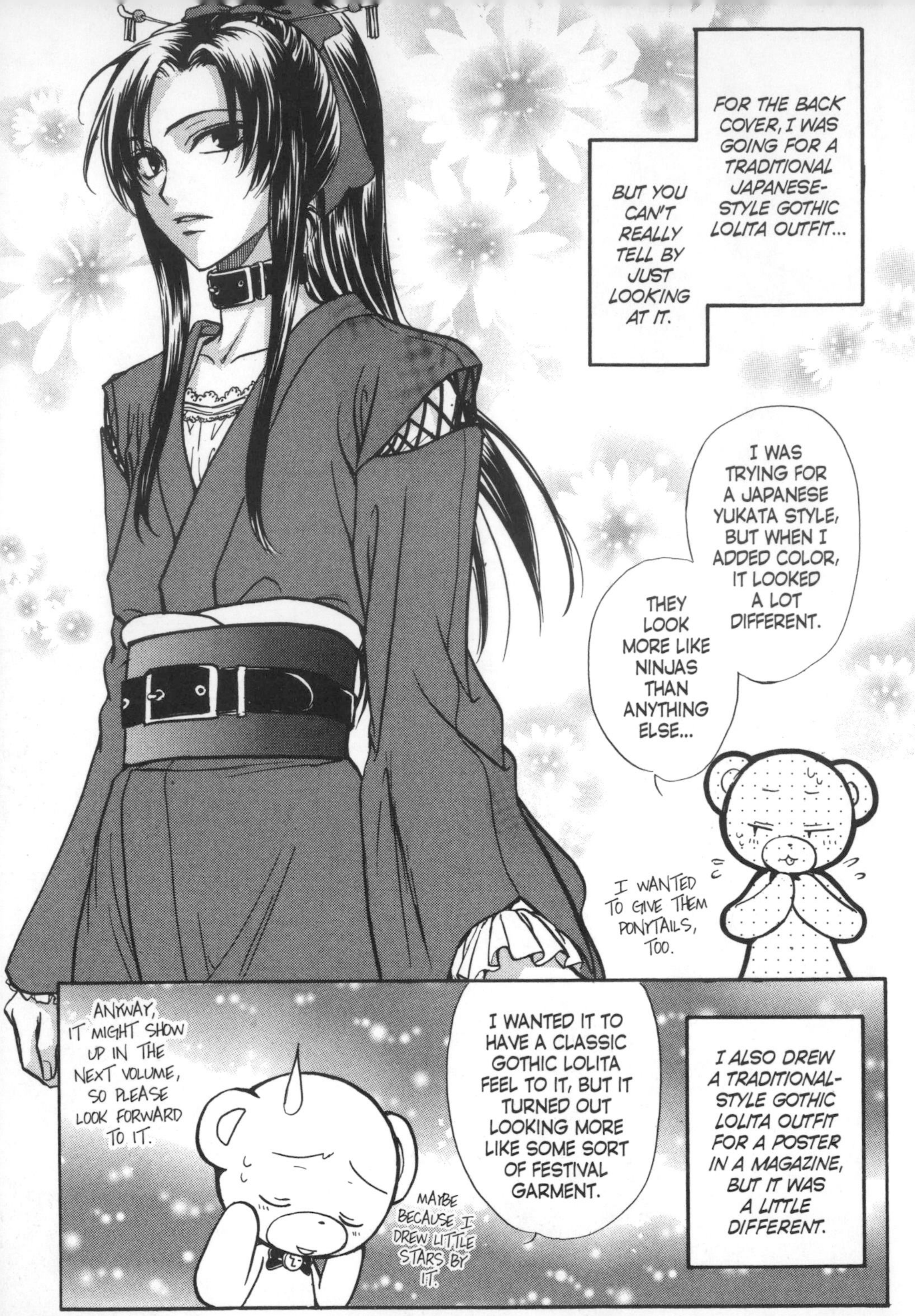
FOR THE BACK COVER, I WAS GOING FOR A TRADITIONAL JAPANESE-STYLE GOTHIC LOLITA OUTFIT...
BUT YOU CAN'T REALLY TELL BY JUST LOOKING AT IT.
I WAS TRYING FOR A JAPANESE YUKATA STYLE, BUT WHEN I ADDED COLOR, IT LOOKED A LOT DIFFERENT.
THEY LOOK MORE LIKE NINJAS THAN ANYTHING ELSE...
I WANTED TO GIVE THEM PONYTAILS, TOO.
I ALSO DREW A TRADITIONAL-STYLE GOTHIC LOLITA OUTFIT FOR A POSTER IN A MAGAZINE, BUT IT WAS A LITTLE DIFFERENT.
I WANTED IT TO HAVE A CLASSIC GOTHIC LOLITA FEEL TO IT, BUT IT TURNED OUT LOOKING MORE LIKE SOME SORT OF FESTIVAL GARMENT.
MAYBE BECAUSE I DREW LITTLE STARS BY IT.
ANYWAY, IT MIGHT SHOW UP IN THE NEXT VOLUME, SO PLEASE LOOK FORWARD TO IT.

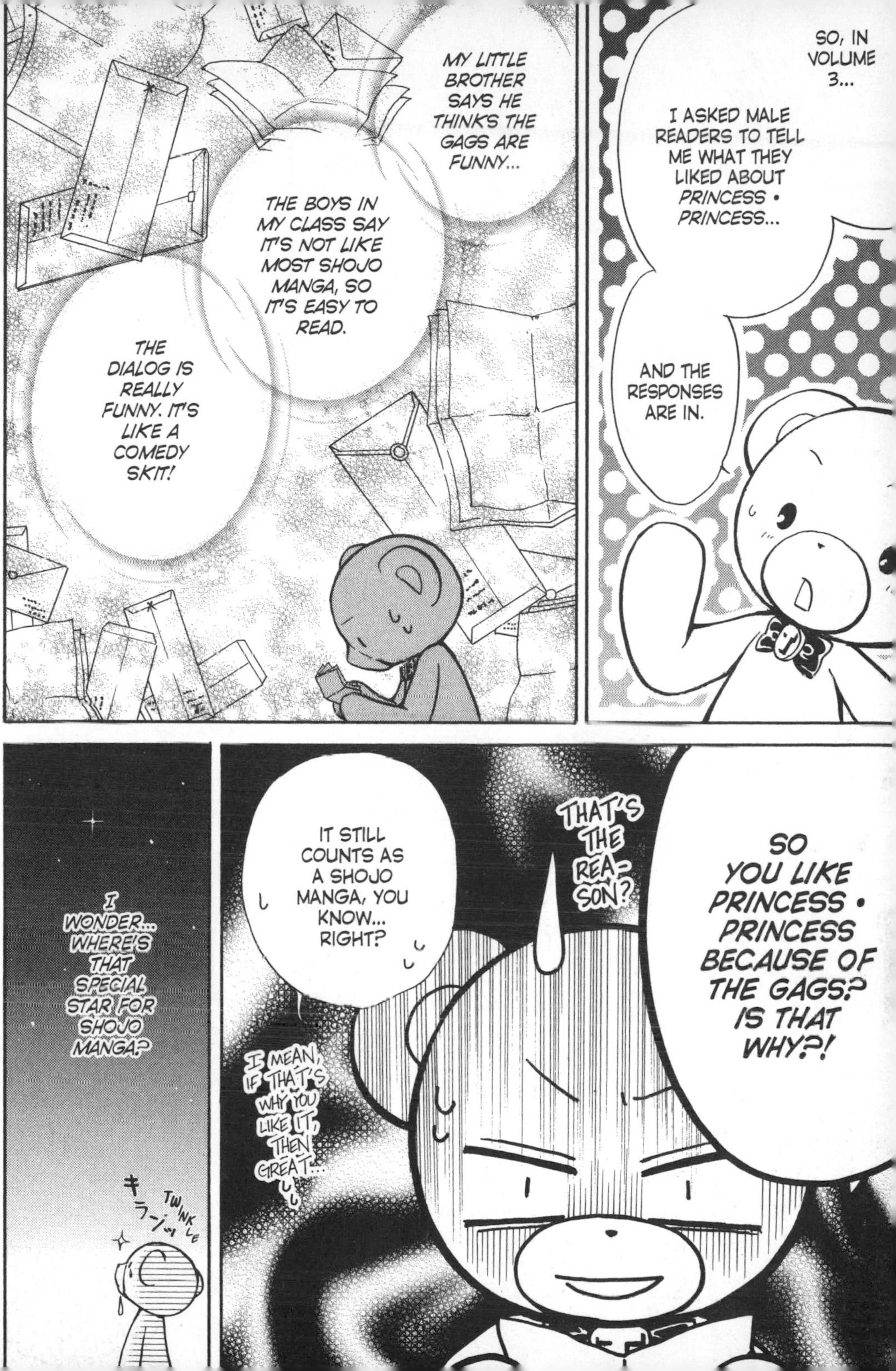
SO, IN VOLUME 3...
I ASKED MALE READERS TO TELL ME WHAT THEY LIKED ABOUT PRINCESS • PRINCESS...
AND THE RESPONSES ARE IN.
MY LITTLE BROTHER SAYS HE THINKS THE GAGS ARE FUNNY...
THE BOYS IN MY CLASS SAY IT'S NOT LIKE MOST SHOJO MANGA, SO IT'S EASY TO READ.
THE DIALOG IS REALLY FUNNY. IT'S LIKE A COMEDY SKIT!
SO YOU LIKE PRINCESS • PRINCESS BECAUSE OF THE GAGS? IS THAT WHY?!
THAT'S THE REA-SON?
IT STILL COUNTS AS A SHOJO MANGA, YOU KNOW... RIGHT?
I MEAN, IF THAT'S WHY YOU LIKE IT, THEN GREAT...
I WONDER... WHERE'S THAT SPECIAL STAR FOR SHOJO MANGA?
キラーンッ
TWINKLE

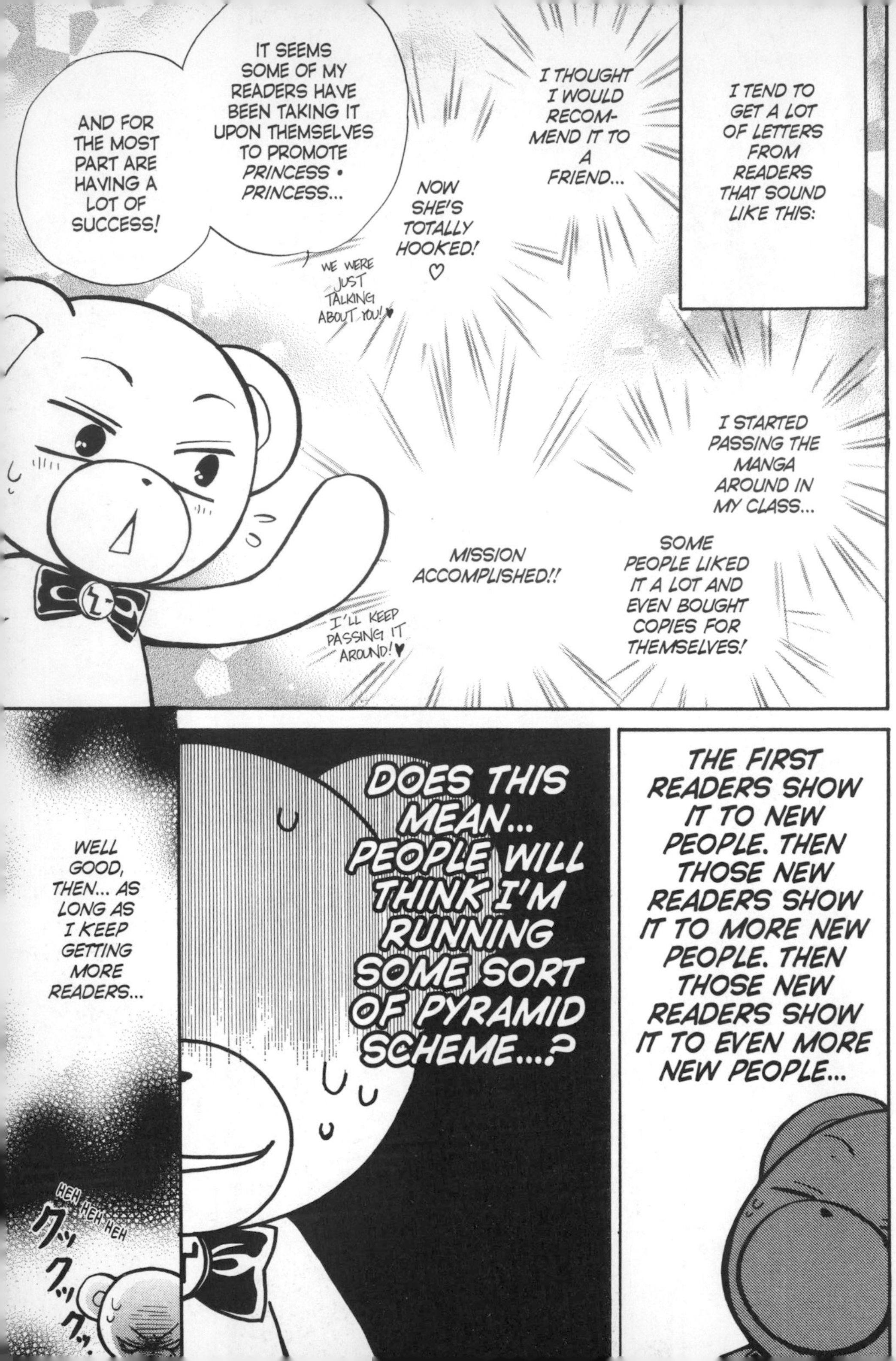
I TEND TO GET A LOT OF LETTERS FROM READERS THAT SOUND LIKE THIS:
I THOUGHT I WOULD RECOMMEND IT TO A FRIEND...
NOW SHE'S TOTALLY HOOKED! ♡
WE WERE JUST TALKING ABOUT YOU! ♥
I STARTED PASSING THE MANGA AROUND IN MY CLASS...
SOME PEOPLE LIKED IT A LOT AND EVEN BOUGHT COPIES FOR THEMSELVES!
MISSION ACCOMPLISHED!!
I'LL KEEP PASSING IT AROUND! ♥
IT SEEMS SOME OF MY READERS HAVE BEEN TAKING IT UPON THEMSELVES TO PROMOTE PRINCESS • PRINCESS...
AND FOR THE MOST PART ARE HAVING A LOT OF SUCCESS!
THE FIRST READERS SHOW IT TO NEW PEOPLE. THEN THOSE NEW READERS SHOW IT TO MORE NEW PEOPLE. THEN THOSE NEW READERS SHOW IT TO EVEN MORE NEW PEOPLE...
DOES THIS MEAN... PEOPLE WILL THINK I'M RUNNING SOME SORT OF PYRAMID SCHEME...?
WELL GOOD, THEN... AS LONG AS I KEEP GETTING MORE READERS...
HEH HEH HEH

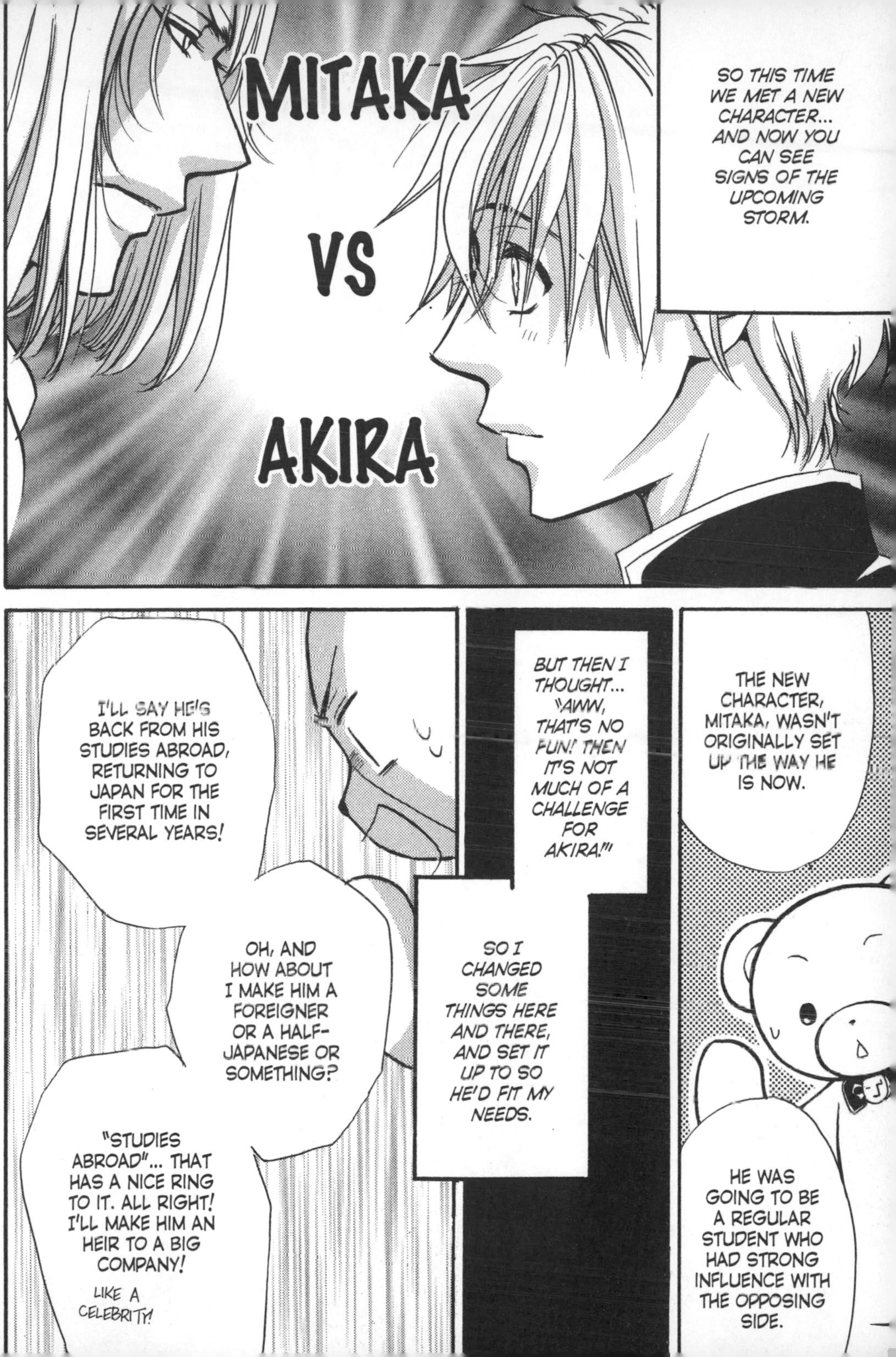
SO THIS TIME WE MET A NEW CHARACTER... AND NOW YOU CAN SEE SIGNS OF THE UPCOMING STORM.
MITAKA
VS
AKIRA
THE NEW CHARACTER, MITAKA, WASN'T ORIGINALLY SET UP THE WAY HE IS NOW.
HE WAS GOING TO BE A REGULAR STUDENT WHO HAD STRONG INFLUENCE WITH THE OPPOSING SIDE.
BUT THEN I THOUGHT... "AWW, THAT'S NO FUN! THEN IT'S NOT MUCH OF A CHALLENGE FOR AKIRA!"
SO I CHANGED SOME THINGS HERE AND THERE, AND SET IT UP TO SO HE'D FIT MY NEEDS.
I'LL SAY HE'S BACK FROM HIS STUDIES ABROAD, RETURNING TO JAPAN FOR THE FIRST TIME IN SEVERAL YEARS!
OH, AND HOW ABOUT I MAKE HIM A FOREIGNER OR A HALF-JAPANESE OR SOMETHING?
"STUDIES ABROAD"... THAT HAS A NICE RING TO IT. ALL RIGHT! I'LL MAKE HIM AN HEIR TO A BIG COMPANY!
LIKE A CELEBRITY!

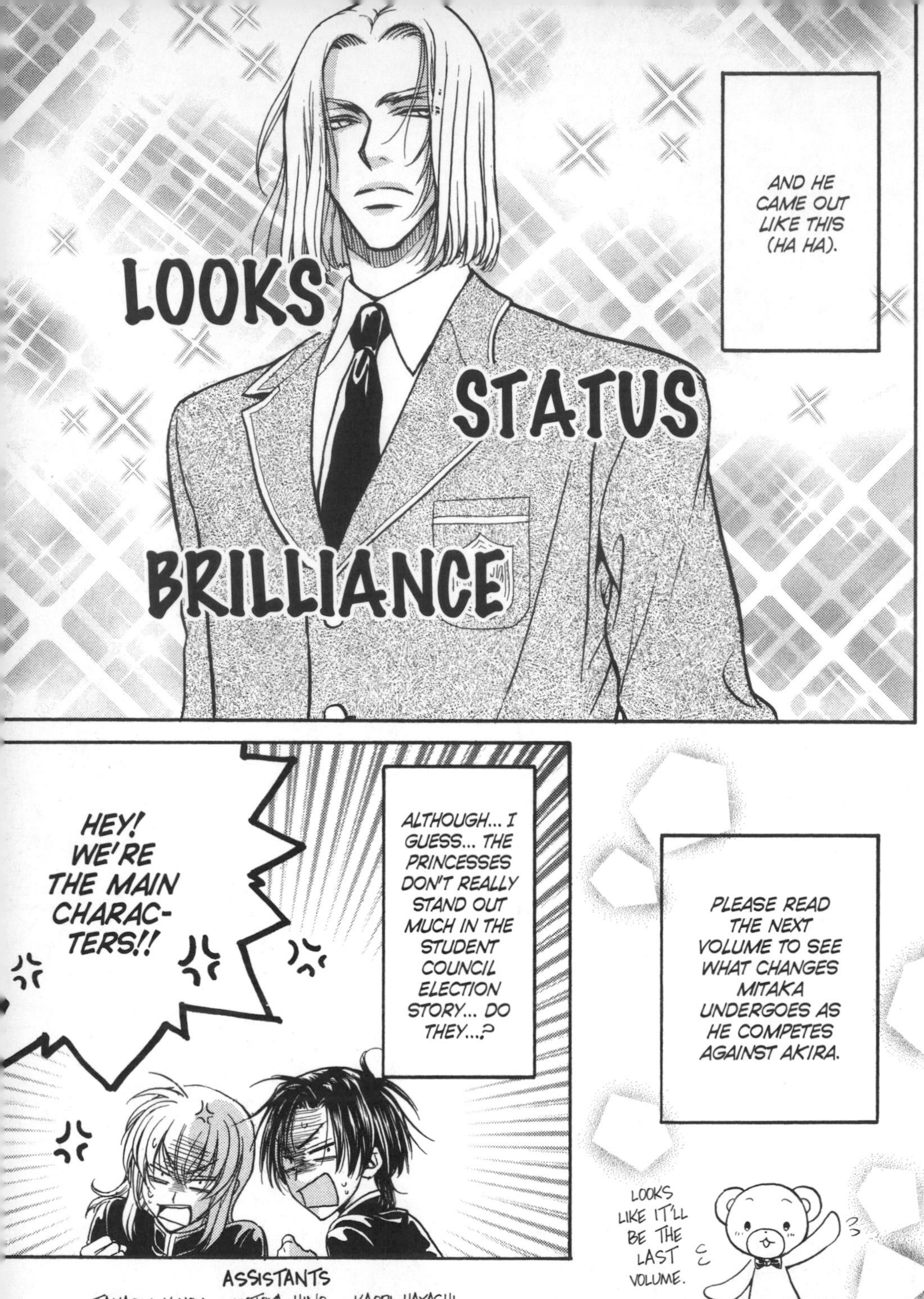
AND HE CAME OUT LIKE THIS (HA HA).
LOOKS
STATUS
BRILLIANCE
PLEASE READ THE NEXT VOLUME TO SEE WHAT CHANGES MITAKA UNDERGOES AS HE COMPETES AGAINST AKIRA.
LOOKS LIKE IT'LL BE THE LAST VOLUME.
ALTHOUGH... I GUESS... THE PRINCESSES DON'T REALLY STAND OUT MUCH IN THE STUDENT COUNCIL ELECTION STORY... DO THEY...?
HEY! WE'RE THE MAIN CHARAC-TERS!!
ASSISTANTS
TAKAOMI KUJOU MOTOYA HINO KAORI HAYASHI
TOHRU HIMUKA AYUMI-SAN YUI-CHAN JUNKO-CHAN
SPECIAL THANKS!
AFTERWORD END

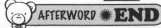

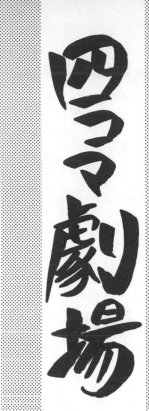

四コマ劇場

4-PANEL COMIC THEATRE

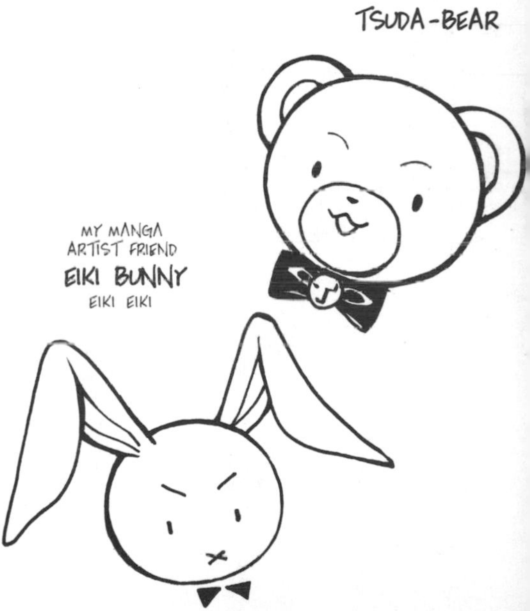
TSUDA-BEAR
MY MANGA ARTIST FRIEND
EIKI BUNNY
EIKI EIKI

OVERWHELMING RESPONSE

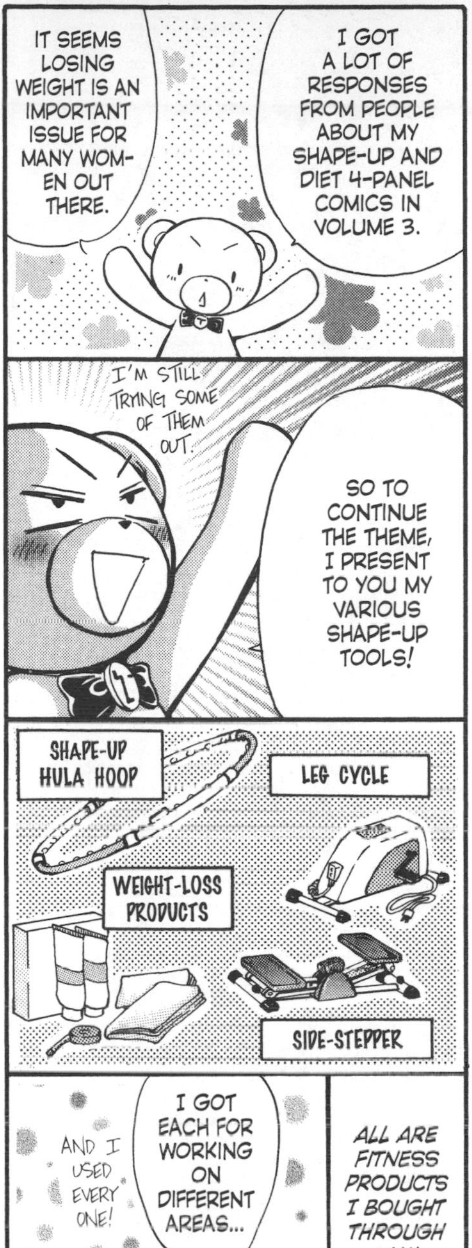
I GOT A LOT OF RESPONSES FROM PEOPLE ABOUT MY SHAPE-UP AND DIET 4-PANEL COMICS IN VOLUME 3.
IT SEEMS LOSING WEIGHT IS AN IMPORTANT ISSUE FOR MANY WOM-EN OUT THERE.
SO TO CONTINUE THE THEME, I PRESENT TO YOU MY VARIOUS SHAPE-UP TOOLS!
I'M STILL TRYING SOME OF THEM OUT.
LEG CYCLE
SHAPE-UP HULA HOOP
WEIGHT-LOSS PRODUCTS
SIDE-STEPPER
ALL ARE FITNESS PRODUCTS I BOUGHT THROUGH MAIL ORDER...
FROM STORES LIKE DINOS, NISSEN, AND HOME GOODS.
I GOT EACH FOR WORKING ON DIFFERENT AREAS...
AND I USED EVERY ONE!

TARGET: BUTT AND UPPER THIGHS

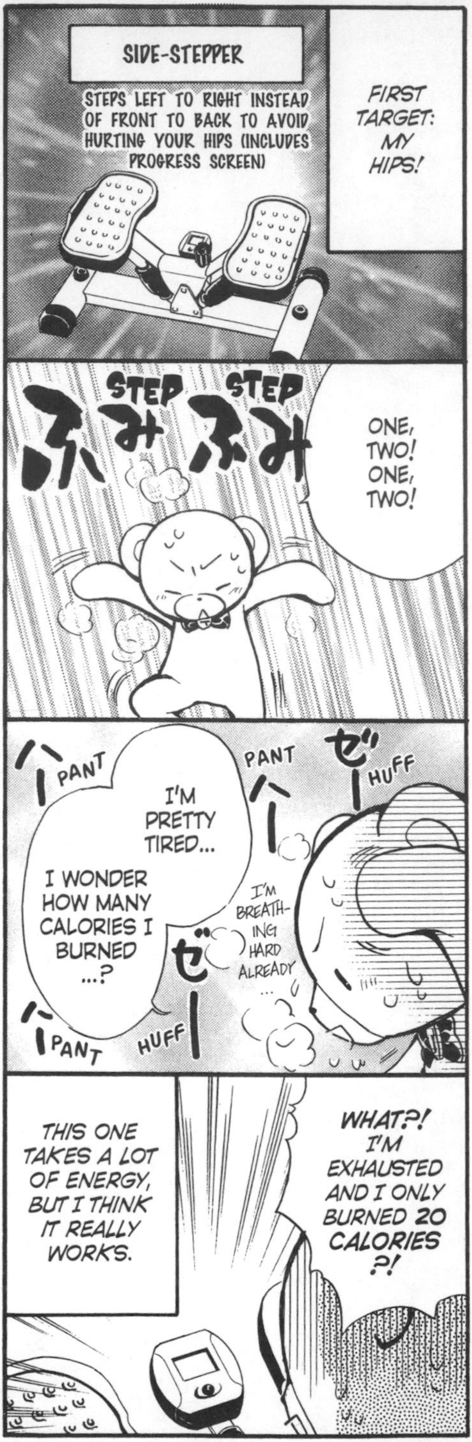
FIRST TARGET: MY HIPS!
SIDE-STEPPER
STEPS LEFT TO RIGHT INSTEAD OF FRONT TO BACK TO AVOID HURTING YOUR HIPS (INCLUDES PROGRESS SCREEN)
ONE, TWO! ONE, TWO!
STEP STEP
ふみ ふみ
HUFF
ゼー
PANT
ハー
I'M BREATHING HARD ALREADY...
I'M PRETTY TIRED...
I WONDER HOW MANY CALORIES I BURNED ...?
PANT
ハー
HUFF
ゼー
PANT
ハー
WHAT?! I'M EXHAUSTED AND I ONLY BURNED 20 CALORIES ?!
THIS ONE TAKES A LOT OF ENERGY, BUT I THINK IT REALLY WORKS.

TARGET: WAIST

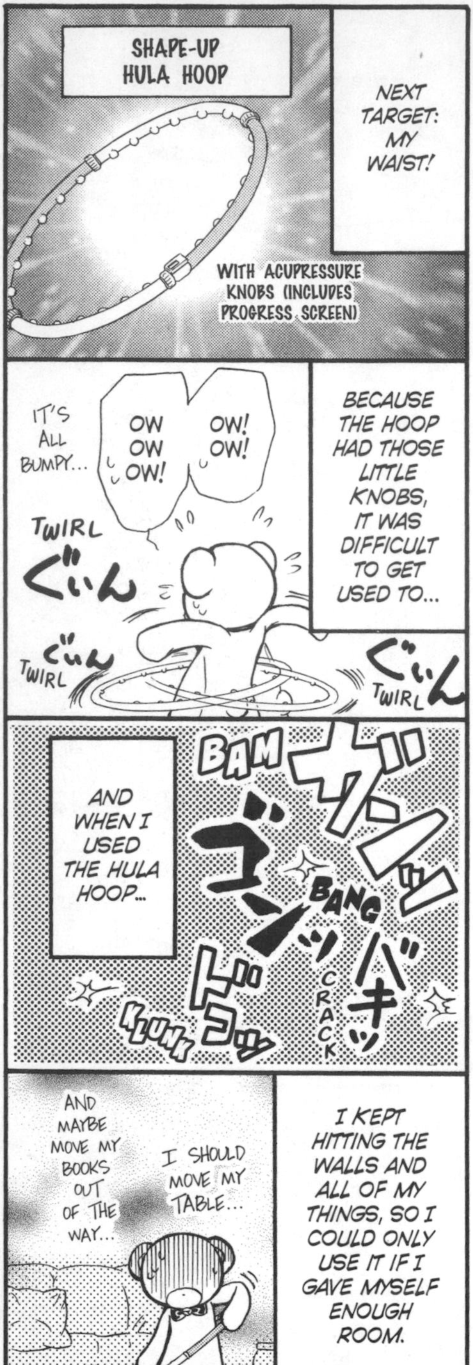
NEXT TARGET: MY WAIST!
SHAPE-UP HULA HOOP
WITH ACUPRESSURE KNOBS (INCLUDES PROGRESS SCREEN)
BECAUSE THE HOOP HAD THOSE LITTLE KNOBS, IT WAS DIFFICULT TO GET USED TO...
OW! OW!
OW OW OW!
IT'S ALL BUMPY...
TWIRL
ぐいん
TWIRL
ぐいん
TWIRL
ぐいん
BAM
BANG
CRACK
KLUNK
AND WHEN I USED THE HULA HOOP...
I KEPT HITTING THE WALLS AND ALL OF MY THINGS, SO I COULD ONLY USE IT IF I GAVE MYSELF ENOUGH ROOM.
I SHOULD MOVE MY TABLE...
AND MAYBE MOVE MY BOOKS OUT OF THE WAY...

ANYTIME

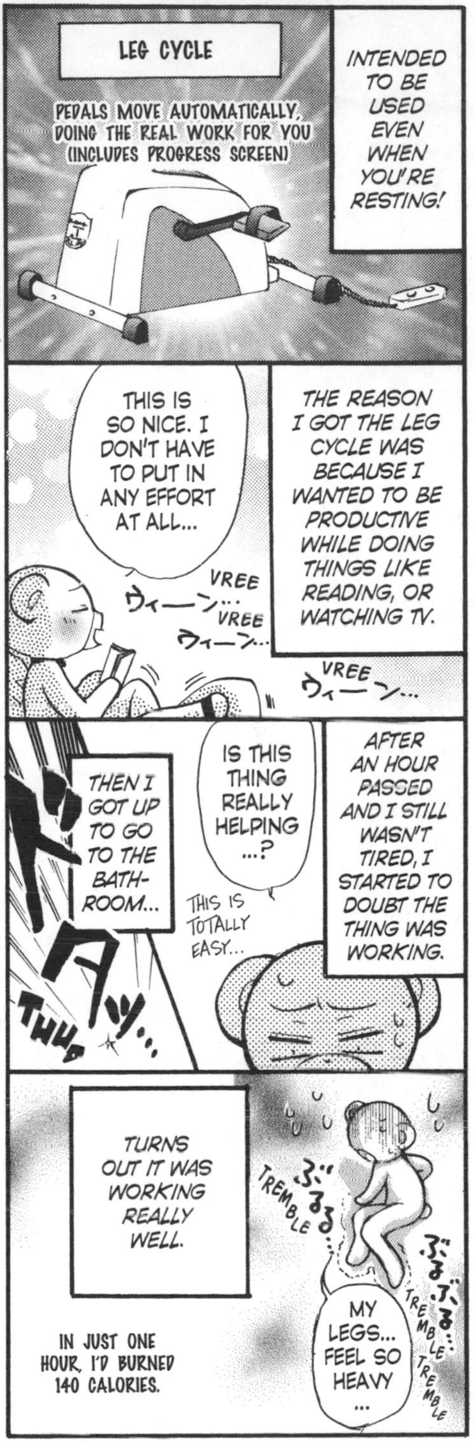
INTENDED TO BE USED EVEN WHEN YOU'RE RESTING!
LEG CYCLE
PEDALS MOVE AUTOMATICALLY, DOING THE REAL WORK FOR YOU (INCLUDES PROGRESS SCREEN)
THE REASON I GOT THE LEG CYCLE WAS BECAUSE I WANTED TO BE PRODUCTIVE WHILE DOING THINGS LIKE READING, OR WATCHING TV.
THIS IS SO NICE. I DON'T HAVE TO PUT IN ANY EFFORT AT ALL...
VREE ウィーン...
VREE ウィーン...
VREE ウィーン...
AFTER AN HOUR PASSED AND I STILL WASN'T TIRED, I STARTED TO DOUBT THE THING WAS WORKING.
IS THIS THING REALLY HELPING ...?
THIS IS TOTALLY EASY...
THEN I GOT UP TO GO TO THE BATH-ROOM...
THUD タッ...
TURNS OUT IT WAS WORKING REALLY WELL.
TREMBLE ぷるる
TREMBLE TREMBLE ぷるぷる...
MY LEGS... FEEL SO HEAVY ...
IN JUST ONE HOUR, I'D BURNED 140 CALORIES.

TARGET: THIGHS!

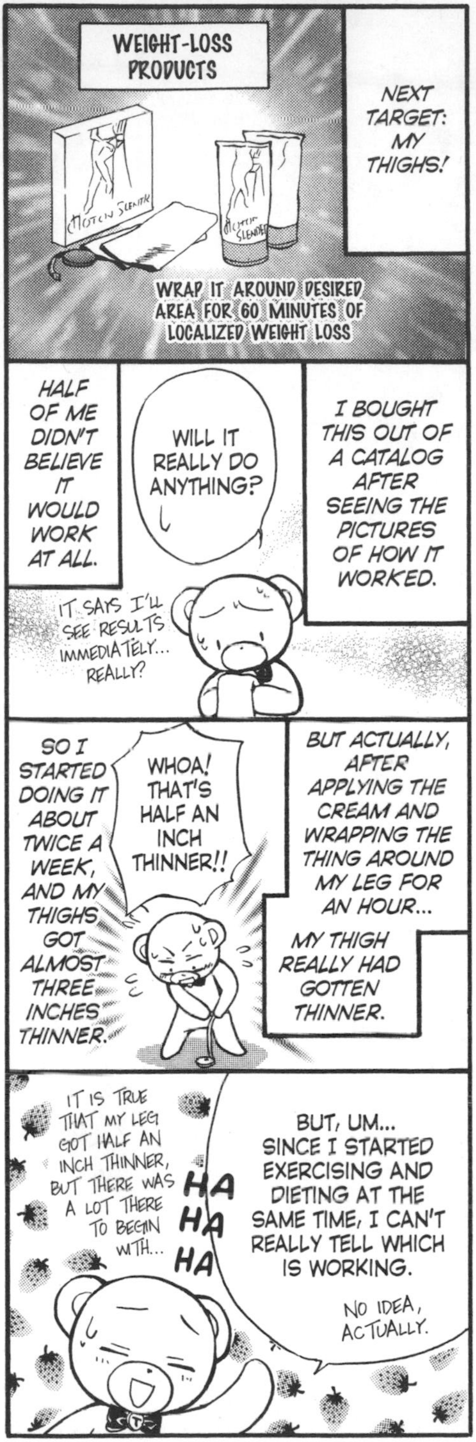
NEXT TARGET: MY THIGHS!
WEIGHT-LOSS PRODUCTS
WRAP IT AROUND DESIRED AREA FOR 60 MINUTES OF LOCALIZED WEIGHT LOSS
I BOUGHT THIS OUT OF A CATALOG AFTER SEEING THE PICTURES OF HOW IT WORKED.
WILL IT REALLY DO ANYTHING?
HALF OF ME DIDN'T BELIEVE IT WOULD WORK AT ALL.
IT SAYS I'LL SEE RESULTS IMMEDIATELY... REALLY?
BUT ACTUALLY, AFTER APPLYING THE CREAM AND WRAPPING THE THING AROUND MY LEG FOR AN HOUR...
WHOA! THAT'S HALF AN INCH THINNER!!
SO I STARTED DOING IT ABOUT TWICE A WEEK, AND MY THIGHS GOT ALMOST THREE INCHES THINNER.
MY THIGH REALLY HAD GOTTEN THINNER.
BUT, UM... SINCE I STARTED EXERCISING AND DIETING AT THE SAME TIME, I CAN'T REALLY TELL WHICH IS WORKING.
NO IDEA, ACTUALLY.
HA HA HA
IT IS TRUE THAT MY LEG GOT HALF AN INCH THINNER, BUT THERE WAS A LOT THERE TO BEGIN WITH...

THERE IT IS AGAIN...

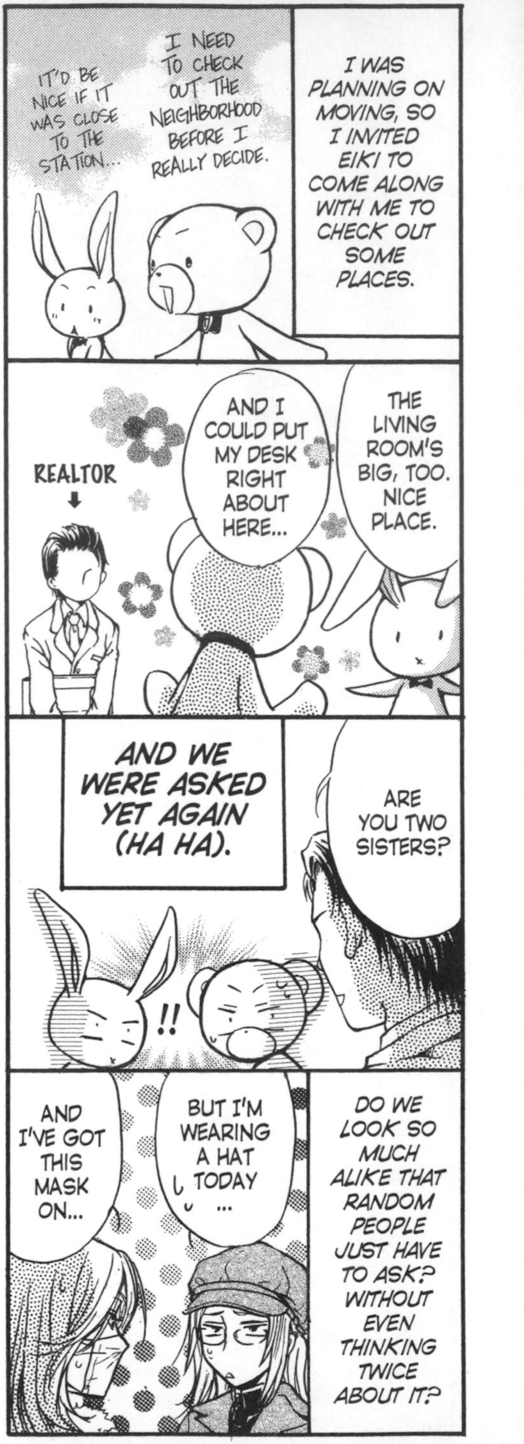
I WAS PLANNING ON MOVING, SO I INVITED EIKI TO COME ALONG WITH ME TO CHECK OUT SOME PLACES.
I NEED TO CHECK OUT THE NEIGHBORHOOD BEFORE I REALLY DECIDE.
IT'D BE NICE IF IT WAS CLOSE TO THE STATION...
THE LIVING ROOM'S BIG, TOO. NICE PLACE.
AND I COULD PUT MY DESK RIGHT ABOUT HERE...
REALTOR
ARE YOU TWO SISTERS?
AND WE WERE ASKED YET AGAIN (HA HA).
!!
DO WE LOOK SO MUCH ALIKE THAT RANDOM PEOPLE JUST HAVE TO ASK? WITHOUT EVEN THINKING TWICE ABOUT IT?
BUT I'M WEARING A HAT TODAY...
AND I'VE GOT THIS MASK ON...

SELF-REVELATION

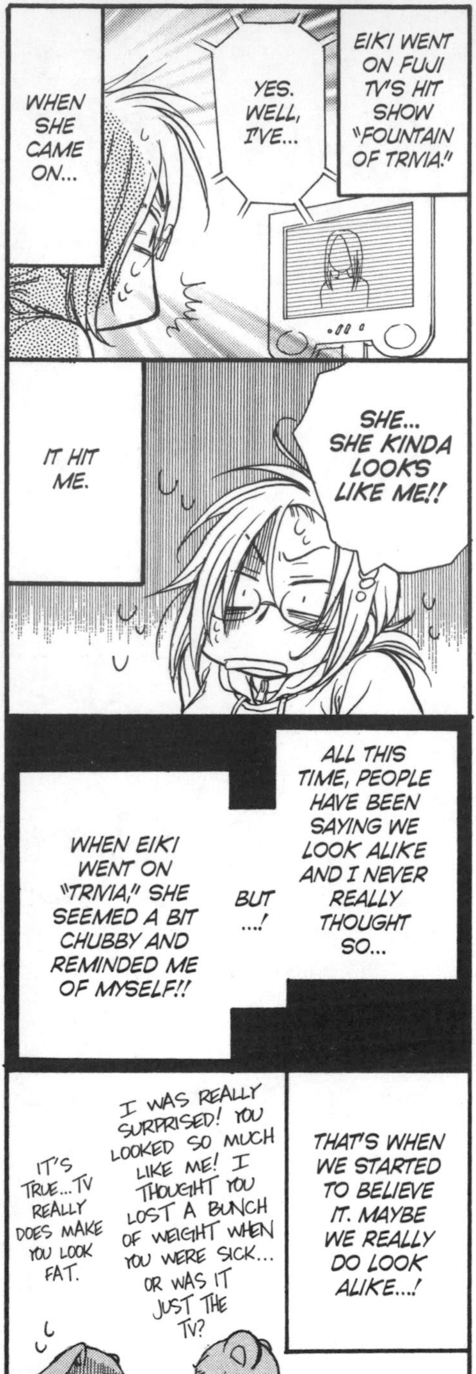
EIKI WENT ON FUJI TV'S HIT SHOW "FOUNTAIN OF TRIVIA."
YES. WELL, I'VE...
WHEN SHE CAME ON...
SHE... SHE KINDA LOOKS LIKE ME!!
IT HIT ME.
ALL THIS TIME, PEOPLE HAVE BEEN SAYING WE LOOK ALIKE AND I NEVER REALLY THOUGHT SO...
BUT ...!
WHEN EIKI WENT ON "TRIVIA," SHE SEEMED A BIT CHUBBY AND REMINDED ME OF MYSELF!!
THAT'S WHEN WE STARTED TO BELIEVE IT. MAYBE WE REALLY DO LOOK ALIKE...!
I WAS REALLY SURPRISED! YOU LOOKED SO MUCH LIKE ME! I THOUGHT YOU LOST A BUNCH OF WEIGHT WHEN YOU WERE SICK... OR WAS IT JUST THE TV?
IT'S TRUE...TV REALLY DOES MAKE YOU LOOK FAT.

4-PANEL COMIC THEATRE ✷ END

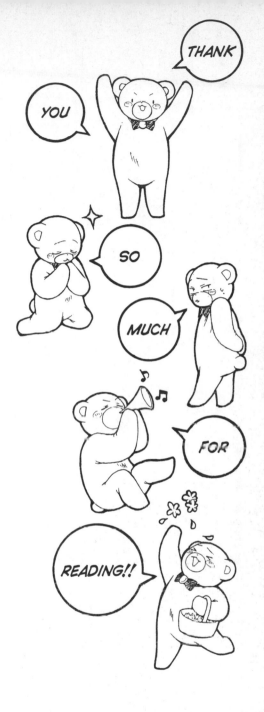

THANK
YOU
SO
MUCH
FOR
READING!!

WE'D LOVE IT IF YOU GIVE US YOUR THOUGHTS AS WELL.

FANS WHO WOULD LIKE TO RECEIVE INFORMATION AND FLIERS ON ACTIVITIES INVOLVING DOUJINSHI SHOULD SEND A SELF-ADDRESSED STAMPED ENVELOPE, ATTENTION: MIKIYO TSUDA. (WITHOUT IT, WE WON'T KNOW WHO IT'S FOR!)

※SELF-ADDRESSED ENVELOPE:

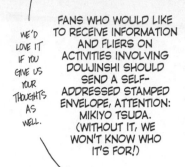

80
YOUR NAME
YOUR ADDRESS
FOLD IT UP SO IT FITS,
IN
TAKE A STAMPED ENVELOPE WITH YOUR FULL NAME AND ADDRESS,
PUT IT INSIDE ANOTHER ENVELOPE AND SEND IT TO US.
YOUR FULL NAME AND ADDRESS

注 WARNING ENVELOPES WITHOUT STAMPS, RETURN ADDRESSES, OR OTHERWISE NOT FOLLOWING THESE GUIDELINES WILL NOT RECEIVE A RESPONSE. (PLEASE DO NOT SEND NON-STANDARD ENVELOPES, AS SOME FLIERS WILL NOT FIT.)

THE INFORMATION YOU WILL RECEIVE IS BASICALLY TAISHI ZAOH RELATED, SO THOSE WHO CAN'T STAND YAOI SHOULD PLEASE REFRAIN FROM SENDING.

WE DO NOT SEND FLIERS TO PEOPLE UNDER THE AGE OF 16.

WE ALSO DO NOT SEND INFORMATION FOR EIKI EIKI. PLEASE DO NOT ASK.

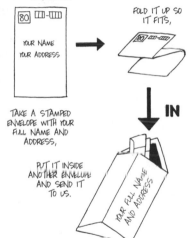

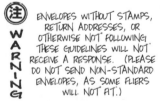

THE DAY OF REVOLUTION

MIKIYO TSUDA

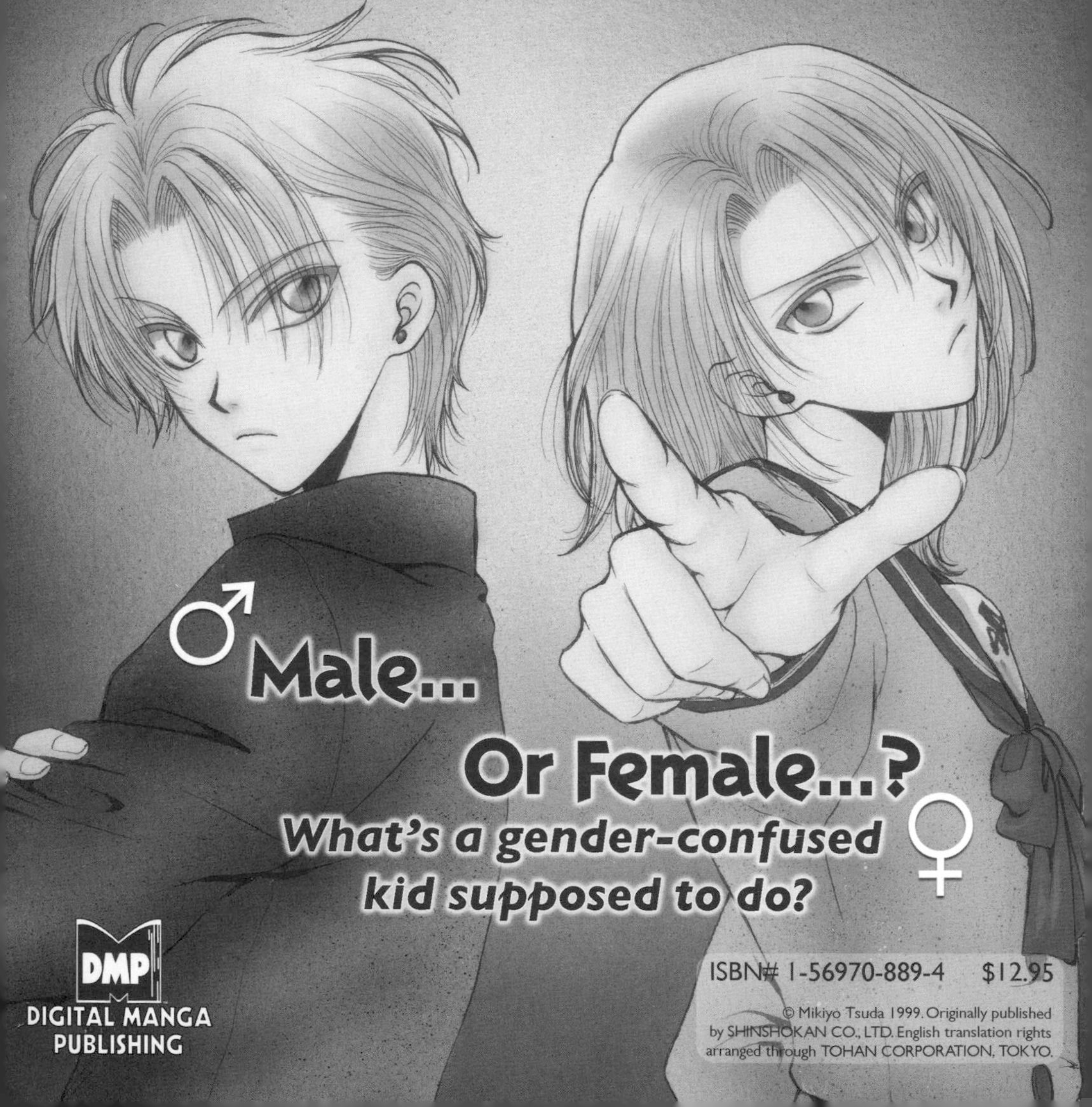

♂ **Male...**

Or Female...? ♀

What's a gender-confused kid supposed to do?

DMP
DIGITAL MANGA PUBLISHING

ISBN# 1-56970-889-4 $12.95

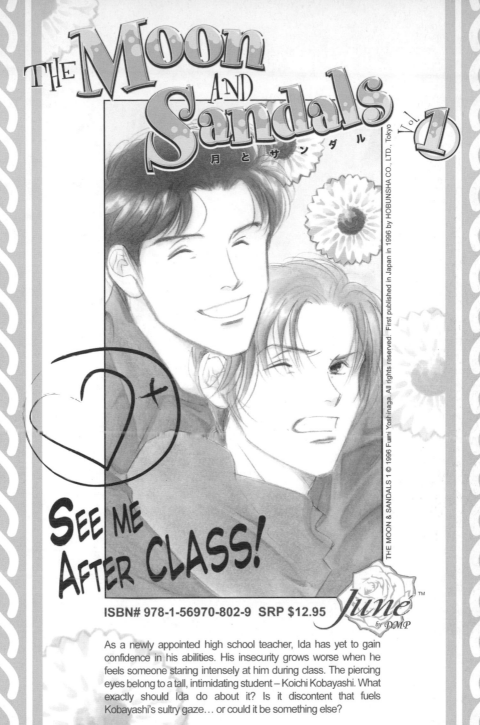

The Moon and Sandals Vol. 1

月とサンダル

See me After Class!

ISBN# 978-1-56970-802-9 SRP $12.95

june
by DMP

As a newly appointed high school teacher, Ida has yet to gain confidence in his abilities. His insecurity grows worse when he feels someone staring intensely at him during class. The piercing eyes belong to a tall, intimidating student – Koichi Kobayashi. What exactly should Ida do about it? Is it discontent that fuels Kobayashi's sultry gaze… or could it be something else?

Written and Illustrated by:
Fumi Yoshinaga

junemanga.com

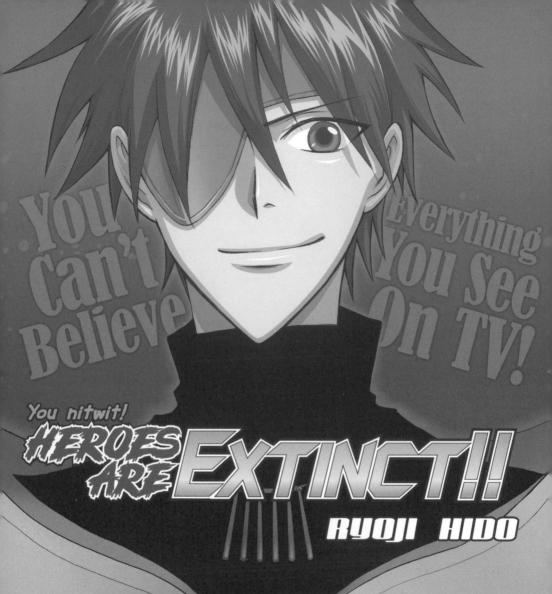

...You Can't Believe

Everything You See On TV!

You nitwit!

HEROES ARE EXTINCT!!

RYOJI HIDO

A conquerer from a distant star lands on Earth to pit his strength against Earth's famous superheroes! Only problem is... Earth doesn't have any real superheroes!

VOLUME 1	ISBN# 978-1-56970-794-4	$12.95
VOLUME 2	ISBN# 978-1-56970-793-7	$12.95
VOLUME 3	ISBN# 978-1-56970-792-0	$12.95

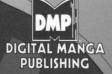

DMP
DIGITAL MANGA
PUBLISHING

HEROES ARE EXTINCT 1 – Tennen! Zetsumetsu Hero Vol. 1 © Ryoji Hido 2003.
Originally published in Japan in 2003 by SHINSHOKAN CO., LTD.

Flower of Life

Welcome to high school life ...in full bloom!

Forced to enroll late after recovering from a serious illness, Harutaro does his best to make friends that last a lifetime!

By

Fumi Yoshinaga

Creator of "Antique Bakery"

VOLUME 1 - ISBN# 978-1-56970-874-3 $12.95
VOLUME 2 - ISBN# 978-1-56970-873-6 $12.95
VOLUME 3 - ISBN# 978-1-56970-829-3 $12.95

FLOWER OF LIFE 1 © 2004 Fumi Yoshinaga.
Originally published in Japan in 2004-2005 by SHINSHOKAN Co., Ltd.

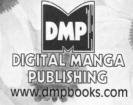

DIGITAL MANGA PUBLISHING
www.dmpbooks.com

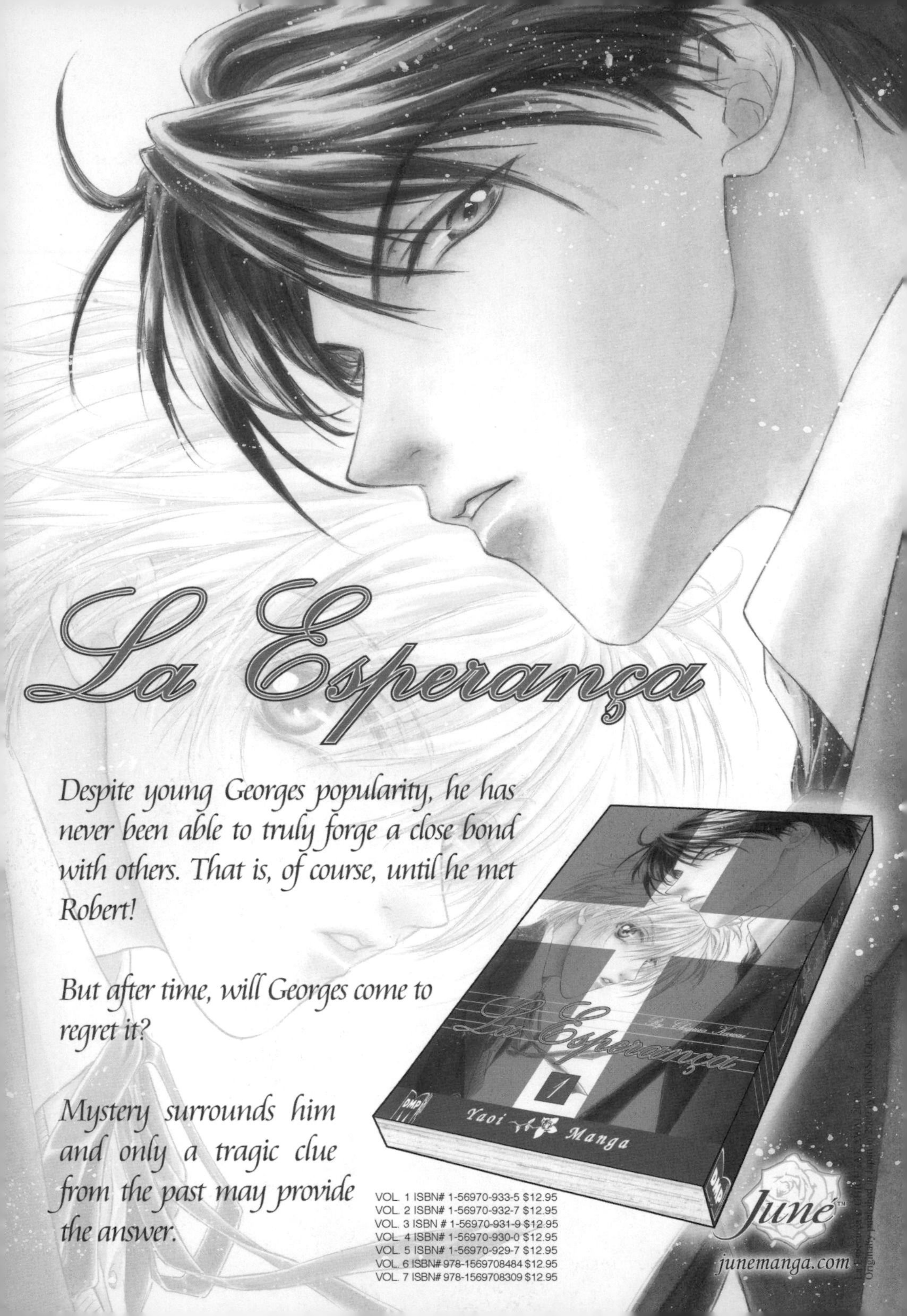
La Esperança
Despite young Georges popularity, he has never been able to truly forge a close bond with others. That is, of course, until he met Robert!
But after time, will Georges come to regret it?
Mystery surrounds him and only a tragic clue from the past may provide the answer.
La Esperança
1
Yaoi Manga
DMP
VOL. 1 ISBN# 1-56970-933-5 $12.95
VOL. 2 ISBN# 1-56970-932-7 $12.95
VOL. 3 ISBN # 1-56970-931-9 $12.95
VOL. 4 ISBN# 1-56970-930-0 $12.95
VOL. 5 ISBN# 1-56970-929-7 $12.95
VOL. 6 ISBN# 978-1569708484 $12.95
VOL. 7 ISBN# 978-1569708309 $12.95
June™
junemanga.com

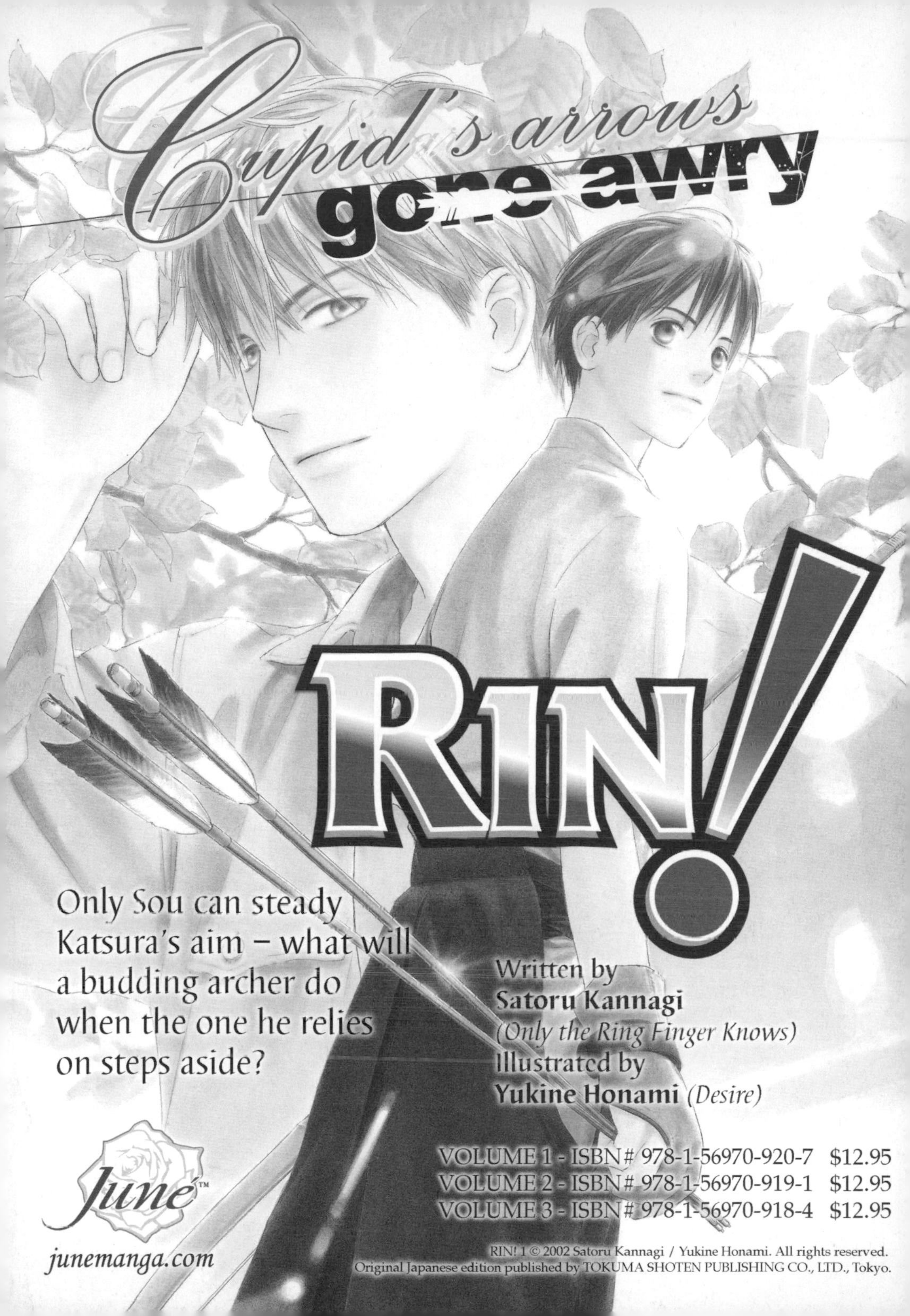
Cupid's arrows gone awry
RIN!
Only Sou can steady Katsura's aim – what will a budding archer do when the one he relies on steps aside?
Written by
Satoru Kannagi
(Only the Ring Finger Knows)
Illustrated by
Yukine Honami (Desire)
VOLUME 1 - ISBN# 978-1-56970-920-7 $12.95
VOLUME 2 - ISBN# 978-1-56970-919-1 $12.95
VOLUME 3 - ISBN# 978-1-56970-918-4 $12.95
June™
junemanga.com
RIN! 1 © 2002 Satoru Kannagi / Yukine Honami. All rights reserved.
Original Japanese edition published by TOKUMA SHOTEN PUBLISHING CO., LTD., Tokyo.

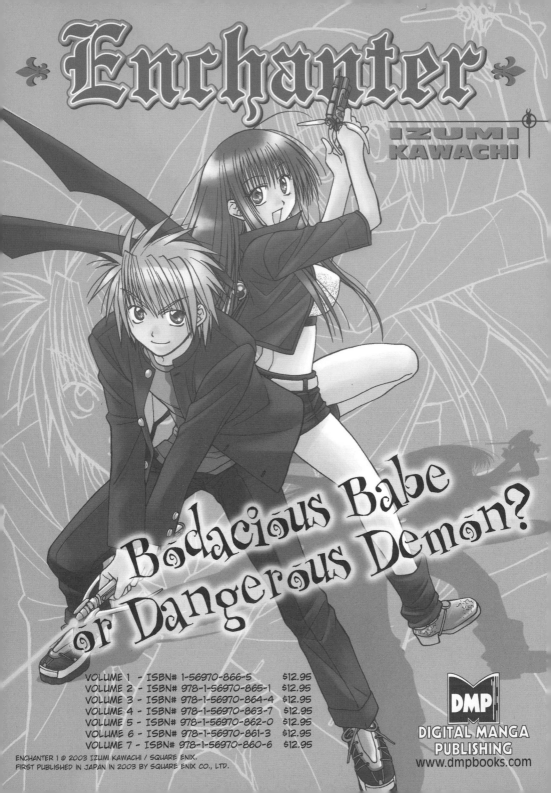

Enchanter

IZUMI KAWACHI

Bodacious Babe or Dangerous Demon?

VOLUME 1 – ISBN# 1-56970-866-5 $12.95
VOLUME 2 – ISBN# 978-1-56970-865-1 $12.95
VOLUME 3 – ISBN# 978-1-56970-864-4 $12.95
VOLUME 4 – ISBN# 978-1-56970-863-7 $12.95
VOLUME 5 – ISBN# 978-1-56970-862-0 $12.95
VOLUME 6 – ISBN# 978-1-56970-861-3 $12.95
VOLUME 7 – ISBN# 978-1-56970-860-6 $12.95

DMP
DIGITAL MANGA
PUBLISHING
www.dmpbooks.com

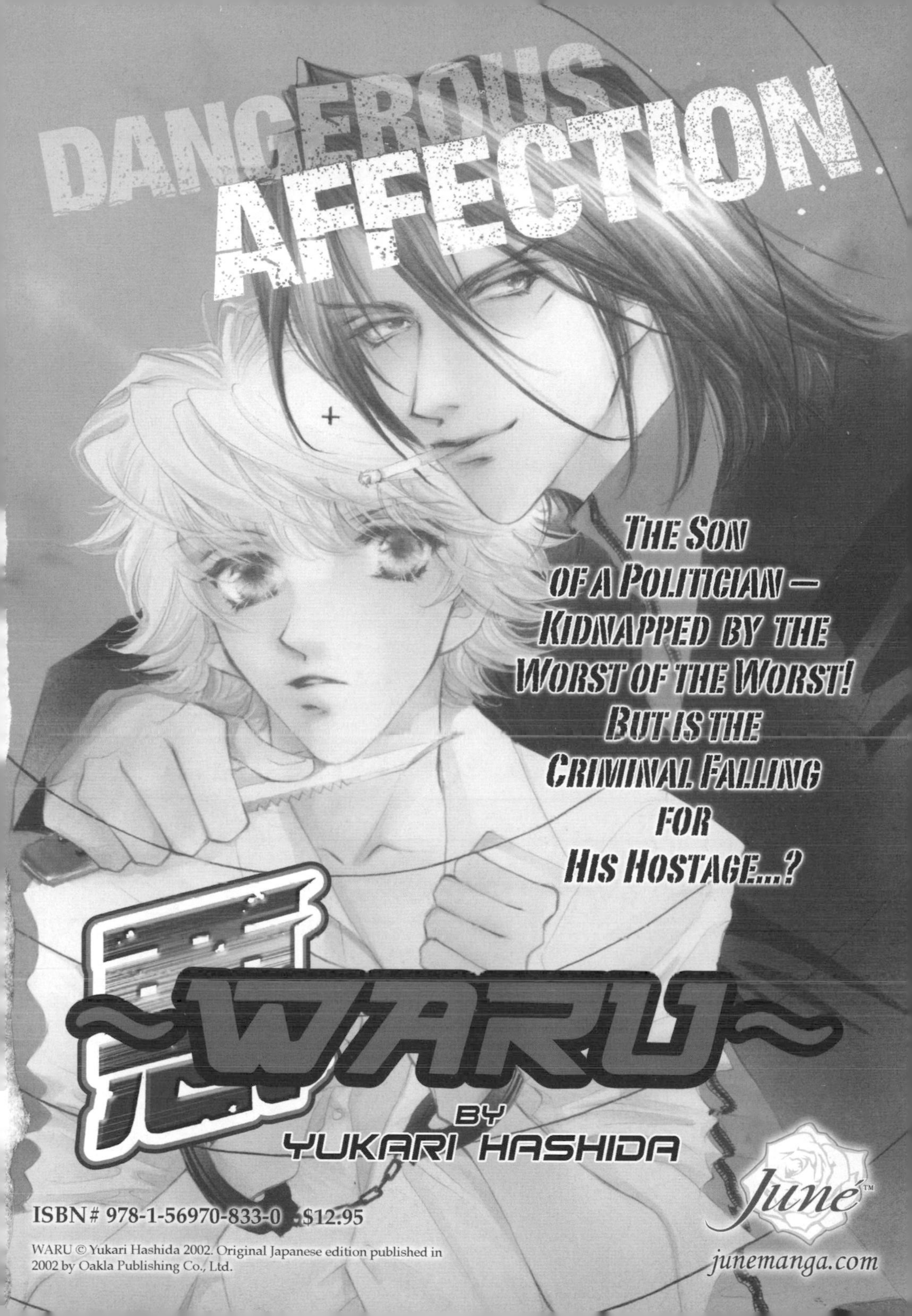
DANGEROUS
AFFECTION
THE SON
OF A POLITICIAN –
KIDNAPPED BY THE
WORST OF THE WORST!
BUT IS THE
CRIMINAL FALLING
FOR
HIS HOSTAGE...?
~WARU~
BY
YUKARI HASHIDA
ISBN# 978-1-56970-833-0 $12.95
WARU © Yukari Hashida 2002. Original Japanese edition published in 2002 by Oakla Publishing Co., Ltd.
Juné™
junemanga.com

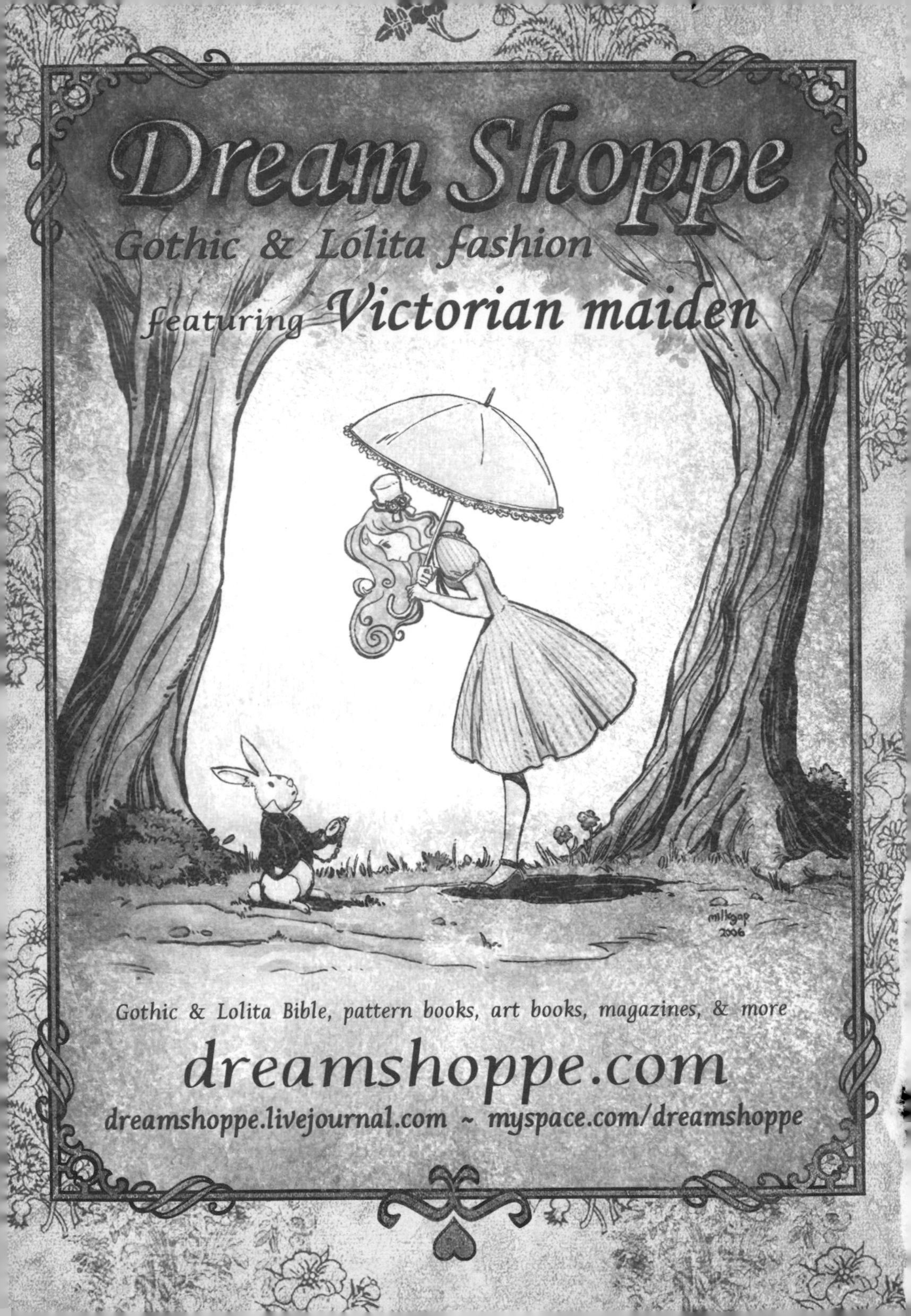

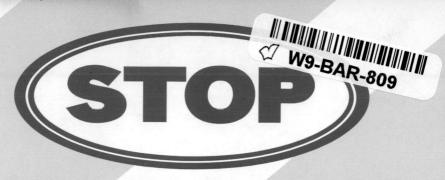

STOP

This is the back of the book! Start from the other side.

NATIVE MANGA readers read manga from *right to left*.

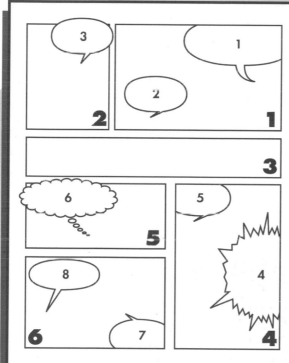

If you run into our *Native Manga* logo on any of our books... you'll know that this manga is published in it's true original native Japanese right to left reading format, as it was intended. Turn to the other side of the book and start reading from right to left, top to bottom.

Follow the diagram to see how its done. *Surf's Up!*

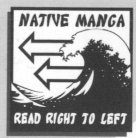

NATIVE MANGA

READ RIGHT TO LEFT